Visions of Modernity

VISIONS

OF

MODERNITY

*American Business and
the Modernization of Germany*

MARY NOLAN

New York   Oxford
OXFORD UNIVERSITY PRESS
1994

Oxford University Press

Oxford   New York   Toronto
Delhi   Bombay   Calcutta   Madras   Karachi
Kuala Lumpur   Singapore   Hong Kong   Tokyo
Nairobi   Dar es Salaam   Cape Town
Melbourne   Auckland   Madrid

and associated companies in
Berlin   Ibadan

Published by Oxford University Press, Inc.,
200 Madison Avenue, New York, New York 10016

Oxford is a registered trademark of Oxford University Press

Library of Congress Cataloging-in-Publication Data
Nolan, Mary, 1944–
Visions of modernity:
American business and the modernization of Germany
Mary Nolan.
p.   cm.   Includes bibliographical references and index.
ISBN 0-19-507021-6 (cloth). — ISBN 0-19-508875-1 (paper)
1. Industrial management—Germany—History—20th century.
2. Industrial management—United States—History—20th century.
3. Industrial relations—Germany—History—20th century.
4. Industrial relations—United States—History—20th century.
5. Germany—Economic policy—1918–1933. 6. Germany—Social policy.
7. United States—Economic policy—To 1933.
8. United States—Social policy.
I. Title.   HD70.G2N64   1994   338.943—dc 20   93-20943

2 4 6 8 9 7 5 3 1

Printed in the United States of America
on acid-free paper

To Jed, Emma, and Rafi

Acknowledgments

I wish to thank the many people and institutions whose support made the completion of this book possible. A fellowship from the Alexander von Humboldt Stiftung enabled me to conduct the research for this book in Germany. There my work was aided by the generous assistance of the staffs of the Bergbau Archiv, the Bosch Firmenarchiv, the Historisches Archiv Krupp, the Thyssen Archiv A.G., the Siemens Archiv, and the Bundes Archiv. I particularly wish to thank Dr. Wessel of the Mannesmann Archiv and Dr. Bodo Herzog, head of the Historisches Archiv des Gutehoffnungshütte for their advice. A sabbatical and a leave-in-residence from New York University freed me from teaching and administrative responsibilities so that I could complete the writing of this book.

Several friends read all or part of the manuscript. Marilyn Young read each chapter along the way, offering both useful criticism and much-needed encouragement. Throughout this project I benefited from repeated conversations with Andy Rabinbach about dilemmas of rationalization as well as the German science of work which informed it; his comments on various chapters and bibliographic suggestions were invaluable. Claudia Koonz read the completed manuscript and helped to focus my arguments and improve my prose. Atina Grossmann read several chapters, especially those on women; our many discussions on rationalization, modernity, and gender inform many parts of this book. Members of the German Women's History Study Group read several chapters and provided insightful criticism and pointed suggestions; my thanks to Bonnie Anderson, Renata Bridenthal, Jane Caplan, Atina Grossmann, Amy Hackett, and Marion Kaplan.

Many parts of this book were originally presented at conferences and seminars, where I benefited from the questions and comments of participants. I would particularly like to thank my former colleagues at the Harvard Center for European Studies, where I presented my first thoughts on this subject. The comments of participants at the conference on Women in Dark Times, held in Bellagio in 1985, were of enormous help in facilitating my work on household rationalization, while ideas presented at a conference on Social Rationalization held in Berlin in 1989 sharpened my thinking on Dinta and company social policy. Finally, the conference on Americanism in Weimar, sponsored by the Goethe Institute in Boston in 1990, gave me an opportunity to present my general argument and receive particularly useful criticism from those working on Weimar culture.

Nancy Lane, my editor, supported the book from an early stage. Her encouragement and admonitions to keep it clear and concise were much appreciated.

My final thanks are to my children, Emma and Rafi, who resolutely resisted my efforts to rationalize housework and child care.

Contents

Contents

Part II   Modernizing Germany

Abbreviations

ADGB
: Allgemeiner Deutscher Gewerkschaftsbund (General Confederation of German Trade Unions)

DATSCH
: Deutscher Ausschuss für Technisches Schulwesen (German Bureau for Technical Education)

Dinta
: Deutsches Institut für Technische Arbeitsschulung (German Institute for Technical Labor Training)

DMV
: Deutscher Metallarbeiter Verband (German Metalworkers' Union)

DNA
: Deutscher Normen Ausschuss (German Standards Committee)

KPD
: Kommunistische Partei Deutschlands (German Communist Party)

RDI
: Reichsverband der Deutschen Industrie (National Association of German Industry)

Refa
: Reichsausschuss für Arbeitszeitermittlung (National Committee for Time Study)

RKW
: Reichskuratorium für Wirtschaftlichkeit (National Productivity Board)

SPD
: Sozialdemokratische Partei Deutschlands (Social Democratic Party of Germany)

VDA
: Vereinigung der Deutschen Arbeitgeberverbände (Association of German Employers' Organizations)

Vestag
: Vereinigte Stahlwerk A.G. (United Steel Company)

VDI
: Verein Deutscher Ingenieure (Association of German Engineers)

VDESI
: Verein Deutscher Eisen- und Stahlindustrieller (Association of German Iron and Steel Industrialists)

Visions of Modernity

1

Introduction

America was very much on the minds of Germans in the mid-1920s. Its advanced technology and unprecedented economic prosperity, its high wages and brisk work pace, its dizzying consumption patterns and emergent mass culture, its "new women" and disturbing family life—all were the subject of intense debate. In closed conferences and public forums, industrialists sought to unravel the secrets of American economic success, while engineers from universities and firms analyzed American technology and probed factory organization. Trade unionists of varying political affiliations debated the reality and significance of American wages, assessed working conditions, and pondered the possibilities of mass consumption in Germany. For industrialists, engineers, and trade unionists alike, the character of American entrepreneurs and the mentality of American workers were a source of constant fascination and disputation. Nothing symbolized the economic performance and promise of America better than Henry Ford and "Fordism," as the technological system and economic ideology embodied in the Ford automobile company was grandiously labeled.

Nor was attention riveted exclusively on "Economic America," to cite the title of one of the most famous books published during this period.[1] In a surprising departure from the usual German discourses about Germany, observers generally divorced American technology and economy from American politics. But they seldom relegated culture and society to a separate and subordinate role. Thus the debate about America was filled with observations, both astute and fanciful, about American class structure and consciousness, about daily life and American high culture, which bore little

3

if any resemblance to German *Kultur*. And the seemingly emancipated American woman was a subject of intense and anxious observation in even some of the most narrowly economic of treatises.

The German preoccupation with America was not restricted to an economic or intellectual elite, nor was it the preserve of any single political party or social class. In the popular press and public lectures, in inexpensive and readable tracts, serious scholarly tomes, and lively travel reports, America was described and criticized, pondered and praised. Over fifty books on American technology, economic prosperity, and mass consumption were published in the 1920s, and many other studies of economic rationalization referred to the American experience extensively.[2] Every serious business and engineering publication ran regular articles on American technology, labor policy and marketing.[3] Company newspapers, delivered free to employees, offered their visions of America.[4] Such academic social science journals as the *Archiv für Sozialwissenschaft und Sozialpolitik* explored the broader implications of Americanism and Fordism, the technological system and economic ideology embodied in the Ford automobile company, while Social Democrats analyzed the American economic model incessantly—and overall quite positively. Regular trade union papers (like that of the Metalworkers' Union), reformist journals (like the *Sozialistische Monatshefte*), and more theoretical and radical publications (such as *Die Gesellschaft* and *Die Arbeit*) regularly printed everything from complex statistical analyses of American wages to speculative essays on mass consumption and firsthand reports of German workers about American factories. Even Communists joined the debate, viewing America with a mixture of admiration and anxiety that was captured in the title of Jakob Walcher's book, *Ford or Marx: The Practical Solution to the Social Question*.[5] And no self-respecting newspaper or journal failed to review regularly the vast outpouring of literature on America, Americanism, and Fordism.

Those preferring the spoken to the written word had ample opportunity to participate in the debate about America. Industrialists' organizations ranging from the National Association of German Industry (RDI) on down to branch and regional associations heard lectures on this theme, often by men who had but recently returned from the requisite pilgrimage to America's industrial heartland. The leadership of the German Metalworkers' Union, a leftist Social Democratic organization, prepared for its members a slide lecture entitled *Ford: His Ideas and Work Methods*.[6] Vocational teachers, women social workers, and leaders of the Housewives Association visited American homes and analyzed American domestic science as they prepared to rationalize the German home and housewife. In 1926 the Social Museum in Frankfurt, a gathering place for entrepreneurs, engineers, and industrial sociologists, psychologists, and physiologists, held a conference with the suggestive title, "Ford and Us."[7] In short, whatever one's class, sex, or political persuasion, it was scarcely possible to avoid America and Americanism, topics at once fascinating and perplexing, appealing and abhorrent.

This debate about America and the elusive essence of Americanism continued a long-standing German interest in America's politics and society, its cities and frontier. But that earlier interest was expressed as much in the Wild West novels of Karl May as in serious or popular analyses of contemporary conditions. America was a vast panorama on which Germans could project fantasies of escape and freedom; it was a colossus of staggering size and diversity,[8] but it was also immature, underdeveloped, and unique. However fascinating, America was seen to have little to teach Germans about their current problems or future development, and discussions of Americanism were not central to German economic and political life in the late nineteenth and early twentieth century.

The Weimar debate about the American economic model, its social and cultural implications, and the possibilities of German emulation was, by contrast, central to understanding Germany in the 1920s. The much-studied preoccupation of the Weimar avant-garde with American jazz and sports, movies and mass culture reveals a great deal about Weimar culture and the attitudes of its leading artists, writers, and intellectuals.[9] So, too, does the more prosaic fascination with Fordism and economic Americanism disclose much about Weimar economic policy and visions of industrial restructuring, as well as the expectations and anxieties, perceptions and prejudices of industrialists and trade unionists, economists and politicians.

Proposals for economic reform, which were proffered in such abundance in the wake of the ravages of World War I, the inflation, and the ensuing disruptive stabilization, were couched in terms of the American model. Or more precisely, the incompatible proposals of industrialists and trade union functionaries, of engineers and housewives, were couched in terms of contradictory understandings of the secrets of American economic success. Each visitor to the United States, each author on Fordism, each self-proclaimed expert on modernity in its most blatant guise, imagined America rather differently. But each of them imagined America as the first step toward reforming or transforming Germany. To be sure there were those who discussed the nitty gritty details of economic rationalization with no reference to the Ford works or Sears, Roebuck and Company. There were those who argued about wage rates and the eight-hour day, with no mention of American mass consumption, production per capita, or industrial competitiveness. And certainly long-standing conflicts between labor and capital, exacerbated by new economic problems and new forms of state intervention, influenced economic debate and policy.[10] But behind even the most narrow analysis, there generally lay a broader vision of what was economically possible and desirable. And that imaginative vision of Germany's future was shaped, in significant ways, by the perception of America's present.

There are many reasons why the debate about German economic reform was conducted in the idiom of Americanism and Fordism. These can perhaps be better understood by analogy with the American debate about Japan in the 1970s and 1980s.[11] America was the economic success story of the 1920s, just as Japan is the economic success story of the late twentieth century. Both pioneered new technologies, developed new products, and expanded demand; both claimed to have revolutionized the organization of production and the management of labor. Understandably, once-powerful economies experiencing severe structural crises turned to the newest leader of the world economy, seeking to unravel its secrets, emulate its accomplishments, and adapt its innovations to a different culture and society. And in both cases, it was not only traditional heavy industries, suffering acutely from technological backwardness and foreign competition, that sought new models, but the labor movement, politicians, economists, and engineers as well.

But German admiration was not for America's attainment of success *per se.* Rather it was for success attained by means of rationalization—to use the German term—or efficiency—to employ the American one. As one perceptive Weimar commentator noted, "It is no accident that the word rationalization is without exception linked to the expression 'Americanization' in the European literature. The United States of North America is without doubt the basic 'ideal' of the rationalization of production, its exemplary embodiment, even if this 'ideal' is unattainable for Europe."[12]

Neither rationalization nor efficiency were clear and concise concepts. Indeed, a large part of their popularity lay in their elasticity, in their ability to encompass so many phenomena achieved or desired. In the popular debates of the 1920s, "rationalization" was not used in the sweeping Weberian sense of those phenomena that characterized the development of the modern economic and social order—instrumental rationality, predictability, calculability, systematic organization, and the elimination of tradition, arbitrariness, and magic. For Weimar Germans, rationalization referred to narrower, specifically twentieth-century visions of industrial restructuring and economic modernity, even though those visions were permeated with the broader attributes and goals that Max Weber posited as the essence of rationalization.[13] At the factory level, rationalization meant increasing productivity by integration and consolidation, technological modernization and labor process reorganization, the assembly line, and the time-and-motion studies of Frederick W. Taylor. It anticipated the emergence of a new worker who would embrace the idea of productivity in the factory and restructure his private life according to the principles of discipline, order, and efficiency. For some, rationalization also meant new consumer products, improved marketing, and possibilities for enhanced consumption. For others, it implied an austere but scientifically regulated society from which conflict would have been eliminated. Although their definitions of rationalization differed on key points, all who favored it regarded rationalization as a panacea for the ills besetting the German economy—and perhaps for those plaguing society and politics as well.[14]

But fascination and fear alone do not fully explain why Germans spoke the language of Americanism and Fordism, or why Americans today obsess about Japan. Appealing to a new and thriving model added legitimacy to one's proposed reforms and goals. They could be presented not only as conceivable or desirable, but as possible—indeed, actually existing. More-over, by referring to a concrete success story, replete with glowing pro-duction statistics, glossy new factories and offices, clever capitalists, and cooperative workers—for these are stock elements in the tales told about both economies—popular reformers could dispense with abstract models and complex theories. In words and pictures, they could capture the power and seductiveness of the new technology, be it the assembly line or the robot. They could speak to the fears and fantasies of a broad popular audience, drawing it into a vivid debate about how the new technologies and eco-nomic strategies might affect their jobs, their homes, their very character as individuals and as a nation. Discussing German economic reform in terms of America (or American reform in terms of Japan) thus gave the debate a scope, an immediacy, and a persuasiveness that it would have lacked had it been conducted solely under the rubric of "rationalization" or of "indus-trial restructuring."

By discussing their own economic problems in terms of a successful society that was both geographically distant and culturally distinct, Ger-mans were able to introduce greater freedom into the debate even as they multiplied its complexities. Far from being a well-known and time-honored competitor, America had risen suddenly and unexpectedly to economic prominence. Germans approached it with ignorance and anxiety, but also with a surprising openness. The longstanding economic and military con-flicts, cultural prejudices, and political rivalries that clouded German under-standing of Britain, for example, were absent in the case of America. The deep-seated racial and cultural stereotypes that dominate contemporary American debates about the Japanese economy were also missing. America was seen as economically creative, not cleverly imitative; as honest and lucky, not treacherous and deceiving. On the one hand, this meant that Germans were ready—perhaps too ready—to take American self-represen-tations at face value. On the other hand, it encouraged them to be more imaginative in the questions they asked and more comprehensive in the answers they offered.

Because the American economic model was embedded in a society that was not European, Germans did not assume that piecemeal borrowing would be simple or sufficient. It was necessary to analyze America's class struc-ture and character, its educational system and consumer culture, its women and families, to understand American prosperity and assess the prospects of German emulation. Was it nature or culture, technology or a new mana-gerial spirit that made modern America what it was? Would German indus-trialists and workers accept Fordism or was it incompatible with the insti-tutional arrangements dear to capital and labor? Was Americanism as a social system and an ideology complex and emancipatory or superficial, repressive, and inimical to traditional German values and mores? Because the debate about economic reform was couched in terms of Americanism, it became a debate about culture, society, and human nature as much as about technol-ogy and economy.

America featured so prominently in Weimar debates about economic reform because it represented one of only two available models for economic and social modernity—the Soviet Union representing the other. As Arthur Holitscher concluded after his travels to both countries in the late 1920s, America and Russia "are the two poles of the contemporary era."[15] America was undoubtedly appealing to many as "the capitalist countermodel to the Russian 'experiment' with Communism."[16] But America did not provide Germans with a simple and straightforward model of anticommunism. For some, America represented traditional, unfettered capitalism and staunch antisocialism; for others, a new social capitalism of high wages and mass consumption. And even for those most critical of capitalism, Americanism offered technological and organizational innovations that were considered compatible with socialism and that were more relevant to the German economy of the 1920s than developments in backward but socialist Russia. Russian communism lurked in the background of all discussions of German economic restructuring, serving as an impetus to examine American capitalism in detail, but bolshevism and Americanism were seldom posited as simple alternatives.

Finally, the debate about German economic rationalization was conducted in terms of Americanism because such debates have a structure and dynamic of their own. Just as in the contemporary United States reformers cannot talk credibly about America's economic problems without reference to Japan, so too in Weimar Germany reference to America was all but mandatory. Once the initial spate of prominent industrial and academic commentators had forcefully inserted their interpretation of the American model into the debate about German economic restructuring in the mid-1920s, others had little choice but to respond in kind, offering their assessment of America to bolster their reform plans. If everyone was making references, both complimentary and critical, to Henry Ford's best-selling autobiography *My Life and Work*, it was all but impossible to ignore.[17] And if so many analyzed America from personal experience, one could only speak with equal authority by embarking for New York as soon as possible.

The debate about America is central to understanding Germany not only because German problems were discussed with reference to America. To a certain extent, of course, the German historian Peter Berg is correct to argue that "the German picture of America really involved an explicitly German problematic. . . . Such a picture is . . . the result of the most diverse interests. One's own presumptions, hope and fears shape it."[18] But not entirely. Germany's acute economic problems provided the impetus for industrialists and engineers, professors and newspaper editors, industrial psychologists and social workers, socialists and intellectuals, trade union functionaries and factory workers to make the pilgrimage to America in the mid-1920s. Certainly their German experiences, social position, political proclivities, and individual aspirations shaped their perceptions of America; but America also changed their understanding of Germany—what it was and what it could become. It raised new questions about mass consump-

tion and the social position of women, and opened new possibilities. Reflect-
ing on her trips to the United States in the 1920s, Alice Salomon, Germany's
pioneer social worker, sweepingly summarized that experience. "Whoever
goes through the world with an open mind dates a new period of his life
from his trip to America. He expands his European experiences to a 'world
view.' He learns to think without the assumptions with which he was
raised. . . . He grasps more sharply the past of his own nation. . . . Simultaneously, he glimpses the future of humanity."[19]

Salomon suggests that Germans were motivated not only by a desire to
solve pressing economic problems, but by something both broader and more
elusive. Envisioning America involved imagining modernity. If, as many
argued, America was not exceptional but rather simply advanced, Germans
could find their future written there—or one possible future—an indubitably modern future, stripped (or liberated) of history and tradition, bereft
of kinship, domestic comfort, and *Kultur*, standardized, simplified and materialistic, yet seductively efficient, functional, and prosperous.

America did not provide a model of modernity to which Germans aspired
in toto. A desire for slavish imitation was as rare among those studying the
American economy as it was among those inspired by American architecture, music, and movies. But America did provide a working version of
modernity from which Germans could pick and choose different elements
as they strove to imagine not an ideal future, but at least an updated and
improved one. America, Americanism, and Fordism provided not only a
model to emulate or modify, but a vivid, colorful, and controversial language
in which to debate modernity. Indeed, for those outside the communist left,
it was the only available language for expressing visions of modernity. One
could strive to speak it with different national, class, and gender accents,
but one could not avoid its use to describe a rationalized, efficient, functional, and untraditional world.

Who, then, were the Weimar Germans who debated economic Americanism and sought to incorporate elements of that model in a German program of rationalization? They included industrialists, engineers, sociologists
and psychologists, and workers who were products of and deeply involved
in modern industrial society and who were distant from, if not hostile to,
more traditional groups who occupied a marginal or precarious position
within it. While some were prominent in economic or political life, many
held mid-level positions in management, political parties, and universities;
some were low-level workers and technicians. Many wrote for the popular
press or for more technical publications. Few produced works of enduring
intellectual or aesthetic merit or gained a lasting reputation, but this did
not lessen their influence on their contemporaries.

Politically, they ranged across the spectrum. There were reactionary
modernists who sought to combine economic and technological modernity
with traditional social institutions and authoritarian politics.[20] There were
innumerable adherents of the German People's Party, some from its more
intransigent antilabor wing, others from its more moderate one. The politi-

cal interests of Catholics were represented by Christian trade unionists, and liberals within the German Democratic Party were represented by an occasional politician or businessman. Social Democrats—intellectuals and functionaries, trade unionists, and simple workers—abounded, while Communists joined in the debates more sporadically.

Despite their many political disagreements and social conflicts, these groups shared certain assumptions, as well as some anxiety, about Americanism and modernity. Unlike many from the ranks of the lower middle class, middle class, and peasantry, they did not harbor romantic longings for a preindustrial past. Nor did they view rationalization and modernity with the same pessimism as Max Weber, Theodor Adorno, and Max Horkheimer, who viewed rationalized modernity as bleak and repressive.[21] But unlike the bold and confident visionaries associated with the Bauhaus movement, they were unsure of the shape of the future.[22] They did not perceive America as the epitomy of modernity and its evils. On the contrary, in the words of one Weimar observer, they believed that "America was a good idea."[23] But it was an idea filled with uncertainties and dangers. They all applauded American forms of production but differed about what forms of consumption and leisure, culture and society, family and gender should or would accompany that new technology and factory organization. Americanism and rationalization were seen as inevitable and economically progressive, but in what ways they were socially emancipatory was a subject of often bitter dispute.

Americanism and Fordism were debated not as an academic exercise but as an aid to reforming the German economy. America was a provocation that demanded a response.[24] But a response of what kind? From their separate vantage points, manufacturers, engineers, and Social Democrats foresaw different benefits and possible dangers in the American economic model, and they prescribed dramatically different cures for the ailing German economy. Industry sought to gain the economic benefits of modern technology and factory organization without any of the leveling effects of Americanism. They wanted higher productivity without mass production; greater exports without mass consumption; and higher profits without higher wages. Efficiency was to be achieved without expensive technology by means of intensified labor and in a context of austerity. Social Democrats, by contrast, insisted that the problem of modern capitalism was consumption, not production, and believed that Fordism suggested the solution. In their view, a modern economy must be based not merely on technological and organizational rationalization, but on high wages to create mass consumption for mass products. Engineers and industrial sociologists envisioned rationalization as a mixture of technological efficiency and social engineering, which would create not only new factories but new workers and new working-class homes.

The economic vision of industrialists and the social aims of engineers and industrial sociologists shaped the contours of the rationalization movement of the mid- and late 1920s more forcefully than the optimistic image of Americanism projected by Social Democrats. German industry was modernized without mass production and mass consumption, and it vastly increased productivity without massive investment in technology. Firms established extensive apprenticeship training programs and offered company welfare to instill a commitment to efficiency, productivity, austerity, and the firm. In short, Fordism, no matter how defined, did not flourish on German soil.

Workers, both organized and unorganized, suffered most from capital-ist rationalization and from Social Democracy's naïve embrace of Ameri-canism and rationalization in a situation where it controlled neither economic restructuring nor state power. But if industry won, it was a Pyrrhic vic-tory; capital got much of what it wanted but not what it needed. It increased productivity but could not expand markets; it improved capacity but did not decrease costs; it reduced the labor force but could not lower wages. Industry was powerful, but it displayed a self-defeating ignorance of mar-kets and mass consumption. Rationalization, far from being a panacea, pro-duced new economic problems and intensified the political and social crisis of late Weimar.

This book explores how the discourses about Americanism and Fordism shaped economic and social transformations in Germany and how the pro-cess of economic restructuring and the political struggles around it subverted the assumptions and expectations of those discourses. It is neither an eco-nomic history of the rationalization movement, a social history of its mul-tiple effects, nor a new cultural history of attitudes toward economic Americanism; rather, it is a partial and eclectic combination of all three.

In part I, the varied ways in which Weimar Germans perceived eco-nomic America and approached Fordism is examined. My discussion is based primarily on the numerous published reports of Weimar travelers to America, the extensive press discussion of Ford's autobiography and of Fordism, the prolific writings of industrial sociologists and psychologists, and the ruminations of cultural critics. In chapter 2, I introduce the numer-ous and socially diverse Germans who journeyed to the United States in the 1920s, reconstruct their itineraries, and explore their motives. Chapter 3 concerns itself with that mecca of German pilgrims, the Ford works in Detroit, Michigan. I examine both the object of fascination and the diverse and conflicting interpretations of Fordism developed by Germans. In chap-ter 4, I explore the lively and far-reaching German debates about the secrets of American economic success and the possibilities for German emulation of the American economic model. Chapters 5 and 6 present an examina-tion of the factious debates about the costs and benefits of economic Ameri-canism in social and economic terms, with chapter 5 focusing on discussions of the future of German quality work, "joy in work," and vocational com-mitment in an Americanized economy, and chapter 6 uncovering pervasive anxieties about mass consumption and the modern American woman.

In part II, I turn to the Weimar rationalization movement, looking not merely at economic restructuring narrowly conceived but at social rationalization as well. In chapter 7, I present case studies of rationalization in Ruhr coal mining, iron and steel production, and machine making, as well as the attempts by the National Productivity Board to promote rationalization. In chapter 8, I assess who won or lost in these limited, contradictory, and—for all concerned—unsatisfactory restructuring efforts. In chapter 9, I investigate the educational programs of right-wing engineers from Dinta, the German Institute for Technical Labor Training, which sought to create a new worker technically, socially, and politically more suited to perform the new rationalized work. In chapter 10, I examine the movement to rationalize and partially Americanize the working-class home by Taylorizing the working-class housewife—a movement supported by industrialists, engineers, trade unionists, and bourgeois feminists. These case studies are based on material from Ruhr company archives; the trade union, industry, and engineering press; and the publications of the National Productivity Board. In an epilogue, I trace the fate of Americanism and rationalization through the Nazi era.

This book not only seeks to contribute a better understanding of how Germany was Americanized in the 1920s but, equally important, it demonstrates how Americanism was Germanized, both conceptually and in practice. It is concerned not with what the American state and American business sought to export or impose but rather with the complex ways in which Germans understood and responded to economic Americanism. This response should be understood in terms of negotiation and contestation by Germans and not the imposition of a hegemonic economic and cultural model by Americans.[25] This book underscores the need for a complex approach to understanding transformations in technology and the labor process, one that examines how work, industrial structures, factories, and homes are shaped by the images and visions that are socially and culturally available and, conversely, how the implementation of those visions is shaped by the realities of class conflict and capitalist crisis. Finally, in this book I seek to show that during the 1920s Americanism and rationalization, as slogans and in practice, were not seen as unambiguously positive or negative. Nor should the historian seek to judge them in such unequivocal terms.[26] Rather, they were simultaneously promising and dangerous, liberating and imprisoning, emancipatory and controlling.

The ambivalence Weimar Germans displayed toward Americanism and economic and social rationalization is not unique; rather, it is a persistent theme in German history since World War I. This study sheds light on the continuities and discontinuities in industrial structure and practice and attempts to clarify the economic theories and rhetoric of Social Democrats, industrialists, and engineers. It illustrates the complex coexistence of modernity and tradition, Americanism and anti-Americanism that has characterized economic discourses and practices in twentieth-century Germany.

The confused analyses of America and Americanism by Weimar Germans and their torturous debates and misguided policies about rationalization suggest just how difficult it was for them to imagine more modern forms of work and leisure, production and consumption, culture and gender. It was not simply a question of accepting modernity or rejecting it; rather, the difficulties lay in understanding precisely what it might entail and whether one could or should implement it. The economic dilemmas of Weimar Germans shed light on a world that tentatively came into being in the period between the wars, and was fully realized after World War II—a world that is now being transformed in as undetermined a direction as was Weimar Germany in the 1920s.

I

IMAGINING
AMERICA

2

Journeys to America

In their search for models of modernity, Weimar Germans of many classes and varied political outlooks traveled to America. They were certainly not the first Germans to venture across the Atlantic to explore the United States, observe the peculiarities of its people and institutions, and record their impressions. In the decades before World War I, for example, Carl Legien, the head of the Social Democratic General Confederation of Ger-man Trade Unions, crisscrossed the land, meeting with socialists and trade unionists.[1] The novelist and world traveler Arthur Holitscher, with less purpose and a distinct taste for the picaresque, wandered across America absorbing nature and culture, politics and architecture, ethnicity and race.[2] Erwin Rosen, the black sheep of a respectable southern German bourgeois family, worked and traveled in America for five years after he was expelled from his academic high school.[3] The sociologist Werner Sombart made the journey before completing *Why Is There No Socialism in the United States?*[4] And Hugo Münsterberg, the German psychologist who taught for years at Harvard, produced a weighty tome on American life and the American psyche in 1904.[5]

The Weimar travelers, however, were a rather different lot. They were much more numerous and every bit as socially diverse yet they shared more homogeneous motives and a distinctly economic agenda of concerns. They traveled to places in America's industrial heartland that their predecessors had ignored, and they viewed places that had previously been visited from a different perspective. They came to learn from America's achievements rather than to be amused by its eccentricities or to expose its immaturity.

They displayed the explorer's zeal to uncover the "real" America and the missionary's passion to preach a newfound "truth" to as wide an audience as possible.

Travelers and Commentators

Weimar industrialists began the pilgrimage to America in 1924, according to Paul Riebensahm, an engineer and professor at the Berlin Technische Hochschule who was himself among that year's travelers. "At first a few leading personalities came individually; then major firms sent employees in groups of twos and threes. . . . Soon the passenger lists of the beautiful ships of the Hamburg–Amerika line and the North German Lloyd looked like a register of the leading industrial firms in Germany." Things quickly reached the point where businessmen no longer asked one another, "were you in America?" for everyone who was anyone had been there. Rather, they compared their favorite hotels or boasted of having met Henry Ford himself.[6]

Carl Köttgen, the general director of Siemens and the vice president of the Reichskuratorium für Wirtschaftlichkeit (RKW), or National Productivity Board, was one of the most prominent and certainly the most well-publicized industrial visitors. But he was hardly the only one. Paul Reusch, the head of the industrial giant Gutehoffnungshütte, whose integrated holdings ranged from coal to machinery, made the journey in 1926. He immediately wrote the head of Krupp, Gustav Krupp von Bohlen and Halbach, "I have gained valuable impressions in America. . . . I can only advise you also to see that country once again."[7] Top managers from metal, machine making, and chemical manufacturing joined the pilgrimage as well.[8] Fritz Tänzler, head of the Association of German Employers' Organisations, traveled widely in 1926, investigating not only the economy but also social policy and labor relations.[9] Those who stayed at home avidly read and reviewed the outpouring of literature. Better still, they sent their technical experts and middle managers to study American machinery, organization, and labor management at first hand.

Engineers were particularly favored emissaries, for they could offer their industrial employers not merely general judgments about American economic success but detailed assessments of particular technologies. Herman Bleibtreu from Saarbrücken, for example, investigated the state-of-the-art technology in American coal mines and railroads, as well as government policies and labor relations.[10] Paul Rieppel, from the Machine Factory Augsburg/Nürnberg (MAN), concentrated exclusively on the Ford works.[11] Mannesmann, Germany's largest pipe producer and a major part of the newly formed United Steel concern, sent Alvermann in 1925.

The following year, the Pipe Association sponsored a trip to America for representatives of member firms.[12] Gutehoffnungshütte sent the engineer Lilge to investigate the American iron and steel industry. After visiting 11 major firms—including Bethlehem Steel, Carnegie, Weirton, and Ford—he produced a 250-page report, for internal company use only, filled with drawings of machines and plant layouts, diagrams of production processes, and numerous photos. According to Lilge, so many others followed a similar itinerary that some American firms, which unlike European ones were generally noted for their willingness to open their factories to outsiders, complained both to individual German visitors and to the Association of German Iron and Steel Industrialists (VDESI).[13] The complaints were probably justified, for when the engineer Otto Moog, manager of an unnamed German machine factory, wrote about his 1926 trip, he noted apologetically that he was one of the last to make this all-important journey.[14]

Behind the businessmen and practicing engineers came the academics. From the Berlin Technische Hochschule there was, in addition to Paul Riebensahm, Georg Schlesinger, a major proponent of rationalization and an expert on American scientific management.[15] Friedrich Aereboe, director of the Institute for Management and the Science of Work at the Berlin Agricultural College, journeyed late in the decade but with as much enthusiasm for American technology and management practices as earlier pilgrims.[16] Other observers occupied research positions in government or private organizations. Julius Hirsch, author of an influential work entitled *The American Economic Miracle* and a former state secretary in the Economics Ministry, was a professor at the Berlin Commercial College.[17] Dr. G. Faldix was a professor and head of the economics office in Düsseldorf.[18]

Between 1924 and 1928, over one hundred German students studied in America as part of a newly established academic exchange program. In 1926 the exchange was expanded to include recent university graduates who were invited to work in American firms for two years. By the end of the decade, 166 German engineers, agriculturalists, and sales personnel had availed themselves of this opportunity.[19]

Although most of the academics who wrote on America had close ties to industry and studied engineering, management, or economics, there were important exceptions. The prolific and original economist Moritz J. Bonn had close connections to government. A member of the German Democratic Party, he advised the government on reparations and was a delegate at conferences held in Spa, Genoa, and Brussels. He had been a visiting professor at Berkeley, Wisconsin, and Cornell before World War I, and returned to the United States in 1924 and 1926 as the guest of the Institute for Politics in Williamstown, Massachusetts.[20]

There were other middle-class travelers who defy neat categorization. Some newspapers sent their own journalists. Arthur Feiler, business editor for the *Frankfurter Zeitung*, for example, spent three months in the United States in 1925.[21] Alice Salomon, Germany's most prominent social worker and one of the few women to write on America, went to attend the National Conference of Social Workers. Irene Witte, an expert on Taylorism, traveled to inspect American homes and household technology.[22] Anton Erkelenz, a member of Parliament from the German Democratic Party, and Gustav Böss, the mayor of Berlin, were among the few politicians to come.[23]

Arthur Holitscher, who had written extensively on his prewar trip, returned to the United States in the late 1920s to reassess the country and his views of it.[24]

Not all travelers were middle class or from the liberal center or nationalist right of the political spectrum. As a measure of Social Democrats' interest in Americanism and Fordism, the General Confederation of German Trade Unions (ADGB) and several individual unions sent a delegation to the United States in 1925. Included were Franz Josef Furtwängler, secretary of the ADGB; Fritz Tarnow, head of the Woodworkers' Union; F. Husemann, head of the Miners' Union; F. Münter, president of the Municipal and State Workers' Union; and B. Meyer, head of the Workers' Bank, as well as the leaders of the clothing, railroad, and food workers' unions. Surprisingly absent were union representatives from the metal, chemical, and textile industries, which were later strongly affected by rationalization.[25]

Toni Sender, a left wing Social Democrat and editor of the *Betriebsräte Zeitschrift* of the German Metalworkers' Union (DMV), spent several months lecturing and observing conditions in the United States in 1926 and returned for brief visits in 1927 and again in 1930. Although she did not write directly about her experiences, her journal published a great deal on American economic and social life.[26] This included, for example, the report of Gustav Dabringhaus, DMV functionary and head of the factory council at Krupp, who worked his way around America in 1927.[27] Finally, Charlotte Lütkens, a socialist intellectual who not only wrote the very perceptive *State and Society in America*, but also reviewed all the major works on America written in German and English, traveled extensively in the United States.[28]

The rank and file of the Social Democratic union movement participated in the debate as well. To be sure, they did not write analytic essays or extensive travelogues; rather, they sent back reports describing their struggles to get jobs, their impressions of American factories—gained from actual work experience—and their evaluation of American mass consumption. The *Metallarbeiter-Zeitung*, for example, regularly published the letters of its former members who had crossed the ocean on temporary or permanent stays. From 1926 to 1929 a tool maker periodically reported on his working and living experiences, as did the auto worker Fritz Kummer, who in 1913 had published a book about his earlier trip to America and the Far East. Others, such as Karl Möller and Oswald Bamberger, sent only single contributions, albeit ones that displayed their knowledge of both America and the debates about Americanism and Fordism within Germany.[29] The *Bergarbeiter-Zeitung* reported less extensively on Americanism and Fordism, but it published occasional letters from miners who had emigrated to the United States.[30]

Workers who held other political views had fewer opportunities to travel to the United States and fewer outlets for their views within Germany. For example, *Bosch-Zünder*, a company newspaper that periodically published letters from America, only printed one by a worker; the rest were submitted by engineers and managers.[31] *Deutsche Arbeit*, an organ of the Christian trade union movement, critically reviewed Social Democratic writings on America but sent only Edmund Kleinschmitt to report at first hand.[32] The principal Communist Party contributions to the debate, Jakob Walcher's *Ford or Marx* and Alexander Friedrich's *Henry Ford, the King of Autos and the Ruler of Souls*, were based solely on secondary sources and Ford's autobiography.[33] Whether Walcher and Friedrich chose not to visit America, or were unable to raise funds or get visas, is not clear.

As the Communist example suggests, not all individual participants in the debate about Americanism and Fordism traveled to the object of their speculation. Friedrich von Gottl-Ottlilienfeld, a professor of economics at Kiel, seems to have dramatically reassessed his initial negative evaluation of Fordism and become an enthusiastic proponent after reading Henry Ford's autobiography.[34] Moreover, some groups who were very concerned with the state of the economy and problems of production are strikingly absent from the list of travelers. Those engaged in trade and commerce, for example, did not go in significant numbers. Perhaps they felt, as did many industrialists, that America's aggressive marketing techniques, mail-order houses, and credit-buying practices were not transferable to Germany.[35] Engineers, such as those involved in Karl Arnhold's German Institute for Technical Labor Training (Dinta), who strove to create a new, conservative worker and a factory community (*Betriebsgemeinschaft*) through factory education programs and company social policy, studied America only from afar.[36] But most of those who did not go felt impelled to apologize. "I myself have never been to America," wrote the economist Lujo Brentano in the opening line of an essay comparing America and Europe, "but if I nonetheless allow myself to write about it, the reason is that four books about the United States of America are lying before me, which put me in a better position to gain a sense of conditions there than only a fleeting visit would."[37]

Germans did not travel exclusively to America in their search for the answers to their economic problems. The Mining Association, for example, sent Doctor Roelen to visit English mines in 1927 and dispatched others to investigate those outside the Ruhr. Not until 1936 and 1937 did they inspect American mines.[38] Gutehoffnungshütte sent engineers and managers to visit other factories within Germany on those occasions when it had orders with a firm or when the Oberhausen-based core of the concern had acquired a factory or, more rarely, when a company was having an open house to display its new machinery.[39] Overall, however, access was more limited than in America. Of greater importance, there was less to learn about technology, organization, and management from those embroiled in the same crisis. The Communist left looked to Russia as a political and social model but could hardly have wished to emulate it technologically. Indeed, even Lenin admired Taylorism and insisted Russia must imitate American technology—but not, of course, American social relations.[40]

Germans did not have a monopoly on visits to America. Several perceptive French observers journeyed to America in the 1920s, among them the economist André Siegfried, who spent six months touring the entire country in 1925 before writing *America Comes of Age*, a wide-ranging analysis of ethnicity, economics, and politics.[41] H. Dubreuil, a skilled metalworker who served as secretary of the General Confederation of Labor, spent 15 months in America, working in factories that ranged from the primitive to the ultramodern. His *Robots or Men?* is a vivid portrait of everyday life in working-class America and a resounding defense of Taylorism and modern technology.[42] But as the historian Richard Kuisel has argued, during the 1920s "progress to most French capitalists was not to be found in America." Trade unionists and Socialists were more receptive to rationalization, but they, like other modernizers, were distinctly on the defensive.[43]

Taylorism and Fordism were debated in other European countries, but less information is available about actual visits made to the United States. Travelers from other countries seem to have come in a trickle, whereas those from Germany formed a steady stream. Elsewhere the discussion of Americanism, Taylorism, and Fordism was conducted on the margins of economic debate, whereas in Germany it stood at the core.[44] André Siegfried or the Italian Communist Antonio Gramsci may have offered the most sophisticated analyses of Americanism and Fordism,[45] but they were isolated individuals; Carl Köttgen, Fritz Tarnow, Julius Hirsch, and Paul Riebensahm, were visible public figures and influential opinion makers, however superficial or wrongheaded their image of America and their recommendations for Germany.

Motives

It is hardly surprising that Germans were the most numerous visitors to America and the most passionate disputants about Americanism and Fordism. Nor is it surprising that visits and debate escalated dramatically in 1924, given Germany's postwar economic situation. War, revolution, inflation, and stabilization had created not merely cyclical crises but structural dislocations. The ways in which war debts, reparations, and currency stabilization were handled politically not only allocated costs unevenly but also contributed to problems concerning productivity, investments, and markets. By 1924 Germany suffered, in the words of one contemporary analyst, from a crisis of competitiveness and a crisis of industrial backwardness.[46] While these problems were hardly unique to Germany, they were particularly acute there.

Germany's industrial sector, which had been Europe's largest and most modern in the prewar era, was by no means prostrate after 1918.[47] Germany did not suffer from postwar depression, as did Britain, and it experienced no serious unemployment, but growth was much slower in the early 1920s than before the war. By mid-decade neither production nor productivity per worker had reached prewar levels. Inflation, which had plagued the economy since the war, encouraged investment; indeed, as currency became

worthless, there was a "flight into real values." But inflation did not promote efficiency; much capital investment went into outmoded plants and
was made with little regard to market conditions. The once-dominant heavy
industry was further hurt by territorial losses imposed by Versailles.[48]
Although Germany's electotechnical and chemical industries remained technologically advanced, they had more competition from abroad and no longer
stimulated the overall economy to the extent that they had at the turn of
the century. Passive resistance to the French occupation of the Ruhr and
the resulting hyperinflation of 1923—less a result of reparations than of
Germany's efforts to resist paying them—brought the economy to the verge
of collapse.[49]

Germany's economic problems in the period between the wars involved
consumption as much as production. Not only was Germany less competitive in world markets, but these markets were also smaller. The dominance
of America, the industrialization of some of Europe's colonies and former
colonies, the exclusion of Russia from the world economy, and the disloca-
tion suffered by all Western European nations produced a dramatic reduction in foreign trade. The German domestic market was also limited, for
war hurt agriculture and small business, while inflation wiped out the savings of much of the middle and lower middle classes and nullified the wage
gains of workers.[50]

Technological backwardness, limited markets, and low productivity
were not the only economic problems Germany faced. Reparations, originally set at 300 billion marks and reduced considerably by the Dawes Plan
in 1924, presented challenges to both industry and labor,[51] as did the costs
of the Weimar Republic's vastly expanded social policy programs.

By 1924 hyperinflation was halted and the worst of the postwar crisis
was over, but monetary stabilization created new problems even as it solved
old ones. Unemployment soared to nearly a million, or over 13 percent of
trade union membership; numerous firms went bankrupt and profit rates
dropped. Far from being a comprehensive solution to Germany's economic
problems, the new Mark and renegotiated reparations merely created a
respite. Many Germans were now eager to define that amorphous term
"rationalization," which kept cropping up in debates on economic reform.
They desperately sought efficient, modern models for individual aspects of
production and management and for the country's economic life as a whole.
America was the logical place to turn.

America was no longer seen, as it had been before World War I, as "the
rapidly developing child who cannot dispense with the guidance of the European mother in economic as well as in cultural affairs."[52] Nor was it viewed
with the fear that is evident in the opening lines of Erwin Rosen's 1920
tract, *The Americans*. He urges his readers to imagine a man with a scale.
If the man tips the scale one way, Europe eats; if he tips it the other, Europe
starves. That man is the American, and Germans must learn to understand
him, admonished Rosen.[53] With the end of Germany's acute postwar
dependency and instability, America came to be seen as an economic model.

In the words of one observer, "One seeks to learn from her, to study her organization, management, and technology."[54] Another noted with a certain embarrassment, "Today we go to America as the Japanese once came to Germany."[55]

Some came to learn quite specific information. Carl Köttgen, for example, had a complex agenda, but one distinct element stemmed from his desire to revitalize the RKW by remodeling it along the lines of American public and private institutions which promoted efficiency.[56] Engineers sent by their industrial employers had quite specific assignments. Mannesmann sent Paul Inden to study whether a particular metalwork procedure could be profitably adopted. Alvermann, sent by the same firm, inspected American pipe production more generally and sent back highly detailed, technical reports. These were necessary, he noted, because "relatively little has been made public about the details of equipment and the like. Such details would explain to the German manager rates of productivity, some of which seem amazingly high, and would enable him to examine his own equipment to see whether changes of one sort or another are possible in order to increase productivity."[57]

Most visitors harbored more sweeping expectations. Industrialists wanted to unravel the secrets of American productivity and competitiveness. According to Paul Reusch, head of Gutehoffnungshütte, "The development which the country has undergone since my last visit two decades ago is impressive. . . . One sees a great deal of what one must do, but also a great deal of what one may not do."[58] Köttgen argued that a close study of "the first power in the world" could instruct Germans "about what was possible and attainable under our economic conditions in relationship to wage levels as well as the introduction of mechanized production processes. . . . "[59] Köttgen, like most industrialists, was optimistic about introducing new technology but insistent that any approximation of American wages was impossible.

Social Democratic trade unionists viewed industry's aspirations considerably more cynically. According to Karl Zwing, what industrialists learned and sought to import from America was, simply put, "rationalization at the expense of the worker."[60] But this might not be the only lesson America had to teach. Hence Social Democrats and trade unionists embarked on a trip to the new world, eager to investigate what industry had overlooked. They would probe the secrets of high wages and mass consumption—the symbols of American economic success, in their eyes—and examine prevailing assumptions about America's arduous work pace and its happy, prosperous, and unpolitical workers. By witnessing America at first hand, they could add a working-class voice to the chorus of middle-class opinions.[61]

Although the Social Democrats initially turned to America in response to industry's well-publicized travels and opinions, their interest was not merely reactive. Weimar Social Democracy lacked the brilliant theoretical disputes, the sharp tactical divisions, and the political tension and drama of the prewar movement. The party and unions remained overwhelmingly working-class, but most radical adherents had left or been jettisoned, and the younger generation never joined. The party's unifying theory was an updated version of Kautskyian orthodoxy, provided by Rudolf Hilferding, and displayed all the economic determinism and political passivity of the original. Long-term economic goals were postponed indefinitely; reformist Socialists did not wish to socialize an economy of austerity and crisis, preferring to await capitalism's full and contradictory development. The short-term democratization of the "improvised Republic" was pursued half-heartedly and ineffectually, and for a leadership scarred by memories of the 1918–1919 revolution, keeping the rank and file unmobilized remained a pressing concern. But despite—or because of—all this, Weimar Social Democracy was committed to a vigorous defense of the social and economic interests of workers in the short run.[62]

In this context, one suspects, America was appealing, as well as thought provoking. It suggested that coming to terms with capitalism in the short run might be done on terms considerably more beneficial to the working class than those currently existing in Germany. It offered means to hasten the development of capitalism, and hence the advent of socialism, in ways that required only appeals to industry and the state rather than militant action by the membership. The American model appealed to social democratic productivism and technological determinism on the one hand, while enabling reformist Social Democrats to rethink their traditional views about work and consumption on the other. Exploring America both reenforced reformism and allowed for innovation within that tradition.

Whereas industrialists and trade unionists looked to America for answers to the riddles of production and consumption, wages and profits, others thought it could or would provide solutions to still broader problems. Franz Westermann, an engineer who traveled on his own to the United States, insisted Germans must master not only the facts of American technology but the principles of American economic life. Only then could they reorganize their own economy and end class struggle.[63] Theodor Lüddecke, in his introduction to essays by such Americans as Peter Filene, argued that Germans needed new concepts, a new language, to address economic reorganization and the larger societal crisis of which it was but one symptom. America could serve as a model not only for technology and production, but also for consumption and new social relationships, including a new factory community (*Werksgemeinschaft*) built on personality and leadership (*Führung*).[64] In the words of Moritz J. Bonn, who was usually more prone to nuanced analyses than sweeping claims, "The fate of modern capitalism will be decided in America. There it must show what it can accomplish."[65]

Implicitly, and often explicitly, America came to be seen as a model of modernity—Russia serving as the alternative. This transformation in the perceptions among Germans is evident from the tone of Arthur Holitscher's reflections on New York City. In 1912, he described New York as "an abnormally and inconsolably nasty city and, with all that, not even efficiently constructed." He complained that traffic was chaotic, housing unaesthetic, and the skyscraper "not only the problem of New York and America but also a problem of our era more generally."[66] In 1930 he no longer found the New York City skyline to be horrible. Rather, it was a symbol of power that immediately made Holitscher think of Russian cities, for Russia and America were "the two poles of the contemporary era . . . two worlds and, at the same time, two aspects of power, which sprang from the same source—service to humanity—arising from the same instinct, the same unfolding of will, the secret, unknown, eternally active energy of human thinking and feeling." If skyscrapers inspired such murky reflections on the emergent meaning of America and Russia, they also called up memories of "old, sinking Europe."[67] Paul Wengraf adopted tough and provocative language to make the same point: America and Russia were "the two most modern states in the world." The former tackled the problems of the twentieth century from the side of production, the latter from that of distribution. He argued that "Americanism and bolshevism—however opposite they are in their conscious will—represent the two forms of expression of the only living movement from which the twentieth century will be carried."[68]

To be sure, there were dissenting voices who argued that America was not a model of modernity. Arthur Feiler insisted that Europe was not becoming Americanized; rather America was being transformed into a unique, non-European entity. He labeled America a "colonial country" in order to capture the raw and unfinished quality he sensed there.[69] If the label seems at first glance inappropriate, it is, upon reflection, perhaps the only one available that could suggest social and cultural backwardness while leaving open the possibility of economic achievement. Charlotte Lütkens offered a similar assessment. America, she argued, had "an unsaturated and speculative colonial economy with a strong will to technology and an essentially dynamic and socially undifferentiated society." Far from being in the forefront of modernity, it represented only "pseudo late capitalism."[70] But these were the insightful assessments of a distinct minority. Even those, such as Adolf Halfeld, who rejected Americanism because of its crass materialism and soulless culture, viewed America as the quintessentially rationalized and modern civilization. Halfeld simply considered traditional values and European *Kultur* superior.[71] Jakob Walcher wanted to harness Fordist ideas to the Marxist cause.[72]

Itineraries

In their desire to unravel the secrets of American economic prosperity and understand the implications of modernity, German travelers sought out what was most rationalized and modernized, what was—or was thought to be—quintessentially American. Their itineraries, which display a remarkable sameness, reflected these shared concerns and simultaneously limited, even distorted, their understanding of America.

While no two travelers followed exactly the same itinerary, there was a classic route that included essential stops that even the most hurried journey had to make. Engineer Franz Westermann took such a trip, beginning in New York and continuing on to Detroit, with a brief stop at Niagara Falls. Next came Chicago (others visited the Pittsburgh region) and then back to New York.[73] To be sure, some were more adventurous. Anton Erkelenz added Washington, D.C., and Philadelphia. Alice Salomon, Arthur Feiler, and Gustav Böss all ventured to the West Coast. The trade union delegation dispersed its members in small groups to study both general conditions and specific issues in a variety of settings, all itineraries carefully planned in advance down to the smallest detail. Their only shared experience was the 1925 American Federation of Labor convention in Atlantic City.[74] Despite such variations, the essential experiences, judged by their centrality in the America literature, remained New York, Detroit, Chicago, and Pittsburgh.

Several aspects of this itinerary merit comment. It was urban, industrial and midwestern. Every trip began and ended in New York City, for that was where the ships docked, and everyone wanted to see the fabled skyline, stand on Broadway amid the flashing lights and speeding traffic, and experience the extraordinary mixture of cultures, languages and lifestyles. But, as several authors took pains to explain, wonderful or horrible as New York was, it was emphatically not America. According to Moritz Bonn, the size, speed, and noise of New York were American, but the European ghettos made it something apart.[75] Its inhabitants remained ethnically distinct and unintegrated; its industries were older and often technologically backward. For Arthur Feiler the real America lay far to the west, in such new planned cities as Longview (Washington) or, at the very least, in Chicago and Los Angeles.[76]

It was America's industrial heartland that fascinated Germans, or rather the heartland of the second industrial revolution of iron, steel and machine making. This was "the technology of girders and gears," a world of continuous production and component parts, staggering productivity, and a minutely subdivided labor process.[77] Its most visible symbols were Ford's Highland Park and River Rouge factories and the Model T, but it also included the vast iron and steel works that stretched from western Pennsylvania, through Ohio and Indiana, and into Chicago. This was the successful American counterpart of Germany's large, labor-intensive and crisis-ridden heavy industry sector, which was at the center of the Weimar rationalization movement. It seemed the most likely place to look for answers to the riddle of technological and organizational rationalization. But it also was an area of major innovation in labor management, wage policy, and the marketing of new consumer goods. The object of investigation for German visitors was the primary manufacturing sector, noted for modern production methods, regular employment, high wages, and a labor force dominated by white men, whether immigrant or native.

Other industrial sectors were all but ignored. The textile mills of New England, then rapidly migrating to the South, and the garment trade and machine shops of New York held no interest, for the German textile sector had always been of secondary importance and Germans could study out-moded small shop technology in abundance at home. Nor did the emerging electrotechnical, chemical, and oil industries attract many visitors, prob-ably because the German chemical and electrotechnical firms enjoyed a prosperity and competitiveness their counterparts in the metal sector dis-tinctly did not. Those who visited Chicago seldom went to the famous slaughterhouses that were models for the assembly lines of the 1920s. As Arthur Holitscher remarked even before the war, there was little point in seeing them at first hand, for Upton Sinclair had provided "the outstand-ing and definitive description."[78]

This focus on factories was peculiar to the 1920s. On his prewar trip, Holitscher inspected some, but his descriptions of slaughterhouses and power stations were minor themes in a narrative dominated by observations of nature and culture, interesting individuals, and new life-styles. Erwin Rosen discussed his own work experiences in detail, but not industrial activity more generally. Even Carl Legien, the trade union leader, visited only two or three factories and commented exclusively on safety features.[79] Only when Germans went to America in search of economic answers did factory visits become the raison d'être of their journey.

As the factory gained primacy, much else receded or was seen in a new light. Germans were fascinated by Ford's marketing techniques, for example, and a visit to Sears, Roebuck and Co., with its assembly line organization of mail-order sales, was mandatory if one went to Chicago. But there was little curiosity about credit buying or advertising or new consumer durables, in short, about anything beyond these forms of marketing that were tied so closely to production and a new division of labor. Agriculture was discussed but usually on the basis of readily available statistics rather than first-hand observation.

If whole sectors of economic life were ignored, so too were entire regions of the country. New England received few visitors, and almost everyone avoided the South, thereby, as Charlotte Lütkens noted, ignoring the area of greatest industrial and agricultural backwardness.[80] This severely lim-ited Germans' understanding of the position of blacks in American life, and even the importance of that question. Few went to the West, because of time constraints and the region's lack of industry. Most seem to have anti-cipated that, with the frontier closed, it would simply replicate what they saw in the Midwest.

Nature was all but overlooked. No longer were Germans fascinated with the vast expanses of a continental state; no longer did they admire America's mountains and rivers and extraordinary natural diversity. Almost the only natural wonder visited was Niagara Falls, for it was on the route from New York City to Detroit, but most expressed "disappointment and pain at the caged-in Niagara."[81] For those in search of technological wonders, nature seemed static, dull, and insignificant.

A central focus on the factory did not mean that society was ignored. But, as will be discussed in later chapters, it did mean that only those elements of family life, culture, education, and social life deemed most relevant to understanding America's economic success were included, while others were passed over. Prohibition and its effects on the work pace, the work ethic, and mass consumption were endlessly debated, but politics were otherwise generally neglected. The implications of immigration restrictions for labor markets and the American character and culture were discussed, but the position of blacks and the changing sexual division of labor were not. Education, high culture, and women's visibility in both areas were analyzed, or more often criticized, but primarily as a manifestation of the male preoccupation with economic affairs, that is, as the unwanted price of economic modernity.

Most visitors to America spent only a few weeks or, at best, a few months there. Gone were the leisurely prewar trips that mixed work and leisure and allowed an intimate acquaintance with American life. Edmund Kleinschmitt was one of the few who stayed several months, living in one or two cities and working at a few firms. He took pride in the depth of his knowledge as compared to those who stayed in first-class hotels, elegant clubs, and Pullman cars and who saw only the facade of society.[82] Most travelers were like the engineer Dr. Valentine Litz, who visited over 80 firms in the summer of 1924,[83] or like Carl Hollweg, who said everything on his visit was "hurried, as American life will have it." He lamented that he hardly had time "to organize and work through what he had seen and heard." His very prose has the breathless and disjointed quality of the world he was describing.[84]

Despite the shortness of the stay, many who visited America felt impelled to record their observations and share their experiences. They generally did so in the form of the travel report, which set down immediate impressions, captured the pace of travel and life in the United States, and highlighted the contrast between Germany and America.[85] Such efforts to understand America were important, Moritz Bonn argued, not because the American example was to be imitated or avoided, but simply "because America is."[86] In fact, Bonn himself was never such a disinterested reporter, and neither were most others. Their travel reports were often one-sided and tendentious, even inaccurate, but they provided the raw materials for Germans to envision American-style economic modernity and debate a course for reform at home. Let us explore what they saw, beginning with Detroit, for as Paul Riebensahm pointed out, "The Henry Ford Works were generally the goal of the trip."[87]

3

The Infatuation with Fordism

> I have long gone through life with perceptive eyes, a thinking soul, and an open heart, enthusiastic about everything beautiful, be it nature, art, sport, or productivity. Nonetheless, my most powerful experience was a visit to the Ford works, that gigantic production facility created in a short time by human hands, which not only impresses the eyes by its size and the manner of its technical construction but whose living spirit is palpably present to such a degree that it simply draws people into its orbit.[1]

Few observers spoke quite as rhapsodically about Ford's Highland Park and River Rouge factories as the engineer Franz Westermann, but most shared his sense of awe, regardless of whether it inspired approval, anxiety, or repulsion.

In Detroit Germans found something startlingly new. The size and speed of production, the degree of mechanization and division of labor could scarcely be grasped by even the most technologically experienced observer. Nature's most impressive wonders, such as Niagara Falls, which most Germans visited on the way to Detroit, paled in comparison to such a mechanical creation.[2] Production alone did not exhaust the allure and enigma of Fordism. There was the product and the marketing strategy that lay behind it, the Model T and mass consumption; there was the surprising coexistence of high wages and low prices; and there was the man and his philosophy, that spirit of "service" that ostensibly animated every aspect of Fordism, explained its success, and distinguished it—ideologically and practically—from previous forms of capitalism.

Henry Ford and Fordism were very much on the public agenda in Germany in the mid-1920s. As Wilhelm Vershofen, a professor of economics at the Handelshochschule Nürnberg, soberly put it, seldom had issues of production and sales "found such general interest as the accomplishments of Ford."[3] Every element of production, distribution, financing, and labor policy at the Ford works was analyzed and evaluated in newspapers and journals of all political persuasions. The German translation of Ford's auto-biography *My Life and Work* "caused a sensation."[4] At least a dozen books were devoted to the man and his economic accomplishments. Irene Witte, a leading proponent of scientific management, exclaimed, "we are being overfed with Ford literature."[5]

A quick survey of titles suggests the diversity of concerns and ap-proaches. Several works, including Emil Honermeier's *The Ford Motor Company*, the German Metalworkers' Unions's *Ford, His Ideas and Work Methods*, and Paul Rieppel's *The Ford Firm and Ford Methods*, explained technical and economic details about the factory itself in a relatively objec-tive manner, reserving judgment until the end. Others, such as Friedrich von Gottl-Ottlilienfeld, the impassioned champion of Fordism, were most interested in its ideological content, while yet a third approach, represented by G. Faldix's *Henry Ford as Economic Politician*, focused on Ford himself. Virtually no author was indifferent toward the man and his accomplish-ments, and many revealed suspicion and hostility in such titles as *The False Messiah, Henry Ford: An Alarm Signal for the Entire German People*, and *Anti-Ford, or About the Value of Humanity*. All were convinced that Ford and Fordism spoke directly to the German condition, even if they disagreed bitterly on what the message was. *Ford and Us*, the title chosen by the Frankfurt Social Museum for its collection of essays, could have served as the title for countless books, articles, and reviews.[6] Germany did indeed seem to suffer from a "Ford psychosis."[7]

What was the source of the fear of some, the infatuation of others, and the fascination among all? There are no simple answers. All participants in the debate on Fordism believed that it represented something quintessentially American. The Social Democratic trade union leader, Franz Josef Furtwängler, for example, insisted that the Ford works—its size, tempo, standardization, and philosophy of production as service—was the most American thing he saw in the United States.[8] According to the engineer Paul Riebensahm, "Henry Ford was not identical with America, but a great deal of what one found at Ford was to be found elsewhere in America."[9] Both supporters and critics of Fordism insisted that it epitomized the current stage of American capitalist development and that the car industry was "the key to understand-ing economic and social relations in the United States."[10] Or, to borrow Arthur Feiler's more colorful formulation, "Automobiles have so completely changed the American's mode of life that today one can hardly imagine being with-out a car. It is difficult to remember what life was like before Mr. Ford began preaching his doctrine of salvation. . . . [11] For many, the man, like the company, embodied the elusive essence of Americanism. And all observers shared the conviction of the *Frankfurter Zeitung*, that Fordism had much to teach about modern economic life.[12]

There was little agreement, however, about precisely what it taught, for multiple readings could be given of both the man and the system. Fordism could be seen as a technologically and economically unmatched system of production, that was either diametrically opposed to Taylorism or had incorporated and transcended it. Alternatively, the essence of Fordism could be seen in the way it generated mass consumption for an entirely new kind of mass produced product, the automobile, by a policy of high wages and low prices. Or the emphasis could be placed on Fordism as an ideology of service, an ethic of capitalism, or a style of entrepreneurial leadership. These interpretations were not so much incompatible as overlapping; it was less a question of exclusive focus than of emphasis, often with a corresponding wish to emulate or avoid.[13] To complicate matters, the productivist, consumptionist, and ideological readings could each be associated with quite different political agendas, and each could serve as the basis for sober short-run recommendations or utopian projections.

In short, Americanism was understood through Fordism. Both *My Life and Work* and the Detroit shaped by Henry Ford provided Germans with common objects of study, a shared language in which to discuss them, and a shared symbolism on which to project hopes and fears. But there was no shared understanding of Fordism itself. The first step in analyzing Weimar Germans' complex quest to untangle the mysteries of modernity in its American guise must center on the debate about Fordism. We will look first at the fascination with Ford himself, who became something of a hero of German popular culture in the mid 1920s. Then we will reconstruct the various understandings of Fordism and explore how they both expanded and limited Germans' understanding of what was economically possible and desirable. Finally, we will suggest not only the promise of Fordism, but the problems it raised for Germans who sought to construct a vision of modernity and reconstruct their own economy accordingly.

The Man and the Book

In 1922 Henry Ford was at the pinnacle of his success. The sole owner of the Ford Motor Company, he was the richest man in the United States. He had revolutionized the production of cars at his vast Highland Park and River Rouge plants, transforming the labor process, the product, the laborer, and American culture alike. In 1922 he sold nearly a million cars—the famous and inexpensive Model T—and that number would double within two years. The Ford Motor Company's expansion abroad to Canada, Europe, Latin America, and Asia, which had begun before World War I, was continuing apace. And Ford had already begun the series of forays into politics that were to bring him notoriety.[14] Nearing sixty and as arrogant and outspoken as ever, Ford seems to have felt the time was ripe to retell his accomplishments, summarize his business strategy, and detail his philosophy of service and his vision of the future.

The result was *My Life and Work*, a rambling book that is part auto-biography, part company history, and part effort to systematize his opinions and practices into a coherent whole. In it Ford presents himself in several lights—the born technician and passionate inventor, the insightful and innovative manager, and the creator of useful products that could be widely sold. With pride he depicts himself as that quintessential American figure, the self-made man, who rose to success via hard work and without the aid of finance capital. In all his personae, Ford claimed to be a man who placed service above profit, or rather, who understood how to make profit by providing service.

In chapters with such catchy titles as "The Secret of Manufacturing and Serving," "The Terror of the Machine," and "How Cheaply Can Things Be Made?" Ford explicated the principles underlying his sprawling automobile empire. His self-proclaimed aim was "to emphasize that the ordinary way of doing business is not the best way" and to show how his radical break with custom led to "the extraordinary success of the company."[15] Production was integrated, from raw materials through to the finished Model T. At Highland Park and River Rouge the machinery, the labor process, and the product were constantly critiqued and improved so as to maximize output and minimize cost. Mechanization, the assembly line, and an extreme division of labor, rather than direct personal supervision, were the key to increased productivity. Moreover, the resulting repetitive, unskilled assembly line jobs found favor with workers, or so Ford claimed, because all men were not equal and most did not desire jobs demanding skill, intelligence, or physical exertion.[16]

Ford's approach to sales is described with equal clarity. First, useful, standardized products must be produced, prices must be low, while wages should be high. Low prices would spur the search to cut costs, while high wages would sustain demand. And if demand slackened, prices could be cut still more, thereby creating new demand and spurring the search for further cost-cutting mechanisms. This virtuous circle would increase productivity per worker, expand the overall number of jobs, and steadily widen the market. A happier scenario of rationalization could hardly be imagined.

Finally, the book is filled with attacks on the ideas and institutions which were anathema to Ford and which, he claimed, stood in the way of economic well-being for all. These were many and varied. Quite predictably, he attacked bolshevism, was suspicious of democracy, criticized trade unionism, and rejected the right to strike. But he also attacked incompetent, exploitative owners. In place of corrupt union leaders and "blind bosses" he advocated "the only true labour leader . . . who leads labour to work and to wages." A true labor leader—and Ford unquestionably saw himself as one—could create "the union of all whose interests are interdependent, whose interests are altogether dependent on the usefulness and efficiency of the service they render."[17] If Ford was an outspoken capitalist, he was nonetheless an advocate of capitalism of a particular sort.

Although he expanded his operations worldwide, he warned of the "delu-sions" of foreign trade and favored developing America rather than other countries. He participated profitably in the war economy but preached paci-fism. Much more consistent were his insistence on self-financing and his attacks on finance capitalism—both accompanied by explicit anti-Semitism.

My Life and Work, which sold respectably in the United States, soon found a diverse and enthusiastic international audience as well. By 1924 the work had been translated into the major western European languages, and four Russian editions were published.[18] The German edition, published in November 1923, quickly became "a bestseller and the canonical work of the period of stabilization."[19] Within one year it went through 13 printings, and by the end of the decade more than 200,000 copies had been sold.[20] Readers included such Communists as Jakob Walcher; such Social Demo-crats as Fritz Tarnow; industrialists such as Carl Köttgen and Carl Hollweg; engineers such as Paul Riebensahm; government economists such as Dr. Ernst Berger; and right-wing commentators such as Theodor Lüddecke. Hitler read Ford's book while in Landsberg Prison after the failed 1923 Beerhall Putsch and developed a lifelong admiration for the man and his automobiles.[21] The autobiography was widely and seriously reviewed in the daily press, political journals, scientific and technical magazines, and government labor publications.[22]

To be sure, some German commentators dismissed the work as blatant self-advertisement, claiming that Americans saw it for what it was.[23] Others insisted it was "a book that should really not be taken seriously," for it was full of naïve views and contradictory assertions.[24] Richard Seidel, a left-wing leader of the German Metalworkers' Union, acknowledged that Ford's book was immensely popular but dismissed it as ephemeral and inconsequential. He argued that any refutation of Ford's ideas was "superfluous," and con-sidered Walcher's comparison of Marx and "this comical eccentric and his social-science confusion" to be "rather painful."[25]

Most commentators, however, felt that the book could not and should not be dismissed. Those especially impressed by Ford's ideology of service, such as Hollweg, claimed to have been "deeply moved" by the autobiog-raphy, but most couched their defense of the book's significance in economic rather than emotional terms.[26] In however confused a fashion, it did present the outlines of Ford's system, Irene Witte insisted, and would stimulate discussion about what Germany needed most, namely, efficient produc-tion.[27] To the editors of the *Frankfurter Zeitung und Handelsblatt* "it appears unquestionably necessary that German trade and industry concern them-selves seriously and thoroughly with the technical and economic content of Fordism. *There is much to learn there.*"[28] According to the trade unionist Tarnow, who was admittedly the most enthusiastic Social Democratic pro-ponent of Fordism, My Life and Work was "the most revolutionary work in the entire field of economics."[29] Others agreed with Tarnow that Ford's book was much more than a detailed case study of brilliant economic suc-cess. Waldemar Zimmermann, professor of economic theory, argued that

tures and laudatory text, the DMV slide lecture about Ford presented all
major machines used, from the smelting of the iron to the final assembly of
the Model T. According to its authors, "scientists, construction workers,
plant personnel, and workers cooperate to organize the [plant] design and
materials in the best way imaginable."[43]

Ford was never content to rest on his accomplishments, as observers
from the left and the right recognized. Friedrich von Gottl-Ottlilienfeld
praised Ford for constantly improving all aspects of production not only in
the auto plant proper, but also in all ancillary factories.[44] Noting the same
phenomenon, Jakob Walcher saw it as a "brilliant confirmation" of Marx's
claim that capitalism never regards any production process as permanent.[45]

All German observers commented on how thoroughly Ford had integrated and concentrated production, both vertically and horizontally. But the
same phenomenon was evident at home, albeit to a lesser degree. More original and captivating was Ford's method for moving materials through his vast
production complex. Constant motion was the essence of Fordist production,
according to more than one author. It was achieved not just by the assembly
line, but by a vast system of railroads and conveyors. As one observer exclaimed, "in regard to transportation, the entire factory is a work of art."[46]
Raw materials streamed into Highland Park and River Rouge, and once they
entered the iron and steel mills, the cotton factory, or the sawmill they never
stopped moving. At each stage until the Model T or the Fordson tractor rolled
off the assembly line, the product came to the worker, rather than the reverse,
and all transport was done mechanically. Energy, materials, and time were
thereby saved, and costs were cut accordingly.[47]

If much of America struck observers as hectic, disorderly, even chaotic,
the Ford works seemed the ultimate in order and planning. However German
visitors judged the pace of production—and opinions differed markedly—
all agreed that the production process was planned, predictable, and rationally integrated.[48] According to one commentator "each individual worker
and each feature of the plant is fitted into the factory whole with planned
expediency. . . . [T]he whole is something organic." It was seen as the result
"of a unified and directed will, a will that affects even the smallest details.
The whole is not schematic, not a paper plan."[49] In the words of another
observer, "The entire factory is an interconnected construction. The human
as a means [of production] is built into the system in the most efficient
possible way."[50] It was, noted a third, "altogether a symphony, a baccha-
nal of work, an entirely closed whole, a single other-worldly machine. . . ."[51]
The first statement was made by a Social Democratic trade unionist; the
second, by a right-wing professor of political economy; and the third, by
an engineer. This suggests how pervasive the infatuation with Fordist production methods was and how difficult it is to read social position or politics from statements expressing productivist enthusiasm.

The appeal of Fordist production methods had complex roots. In part
it stemmed from the dismal contrast between the American automobile
industry and its German counterpart. In 1925 the United States produced

approximately 3.5 million cars, while Germany manufactured fewer than 40,000.[52] Whereas the United States had over 17 million cars and trucks on the road, Germany had only 255,000—less than half as many as France and only a quarter as many as England.[53] Of equal importance, German produc' tion methods were antiquated and excruciatingly slow; models proliferated and prices were very high. The Fordist model thus appealed to those con' cerned about the troubled German automobile industry. Or, to be more precise, it appealed to the minority of observers who believed that Germany could mass produce cars if the automobile industry and economy as a whole were radically restructured.[54]

Industrialists, however much they admired Ford's productivist accom' plishments, did not view them as a cure for the problems of the German automobile industry. They did not believe that Germany had the markets or the wage structure to sustain car production on anything approaching the American scale.[55] Indeed, most shared Carl Köttgen's pessimistic assess' ment that "the Fordist development will not be repeated anywhere in the world, not even in the United States. It is unparalleled." Nonetheless, they also shared Köttgen's belief that Ford's "principles, which are so tenaciously implemented, are economically healthy and are the solution for much." It was argued that one could isolate Ford's production innovations from the radically new product, marketing, and wage strategies with which they were associated in the United States and apply them to anything for which there was already a mass market in Germany, such as typewriters, watches, and kitchen utensils.[56]

For industrialists, as well as for many trade union leaders, Fordist productivism offered a possible solution to the economic problems of low productivity, inefficient technology, lack of standardization, and the result' ing high costs that plagued the economy as a whole. However much they disagreed about wages and hours, workers' rights, and market strategies, labor and capital concurred that the first step in reforming the German economy entailed rationalizing production. Rationalization, at least in the first instance, was defined by all in technological and productivist terms.[57] A shared perception of the problems of German production led to a shared belief that there was no better place to start learning alternative produc' tion methods than from Ford, the embodiment of American technological leadership, efficiency, and cost cutting.

Fordist productivism addressed the perceived crisis of the German economy as well as the most basic assumptions of industrialists, engineers, and trade unionists. It not only promised solutions to concrete problems, but also promoted the contradictory utopian visions of different groups.

Industrialists were not attracted by technological progress per se. As Eric Hobsbawm so succinctly noted, "it is often assumed that an economy of private enterprise has an automatic bias towards innovation, but this is not so. It has a bias only towards profit."[58] Industrialists were less capti' vated by the modernist industrial aesthetic of River Rouge and Highland Park than were the engineers. What seems to have appealed to industrial' ists—in addition, of course, to Ford's stunning profitability—was the role assigned to the capitalist in achieving it.

Fordism, unlike Taylorism, based its claims not on science but on practical economic success achieved through the farsighted vision and painstaking efforts of the entrepreneur. According to Charles Maier, this refurbishment of the industrialist at the expense of the technocrat to whom Taylor gave primacy was comforting to business circles. Fordist productivism was rooted in unbridled capitalism, not in a technocracy that might undermine it. But if Fordism eliminated one "potential for subversion,"[59] it added another. Like Taylorism, Fordism promised to depoliticize production, but instead of applying ostensibly scientific principles of work organization, it would do so by altering what was produced and how it was distributed. It replaced the dangers of technocracy with those of mass consumption built on high wages and low prices.

Fordism did not validate the position of the engineer or promote visions of a society dominated by technology or technocrats, yet there was much in Ford's productive methods that appealed to engineers. Ford factories were built on principles of efficiency, simplicity, and the integration of multiple parts. In all areas, Ford's machines represented the best that modern engineering could design. Engineers could scarcely find enough laudatory adjectives to describe Fordist production and the energy (*Schwung*) that animated it. Many supplemented their prose with photos of Highland Park and River Rouge, as though fearing that words alone would not convey how impressive, how terribly modern, the works were.[60] On a more practical level, Fordist rationalization promised to provide work aplenty for German engineers, whose profession was overcrowded during those years.[61]

Social Democrats were equally susceptible to the allure of Fordist productivism. Their enthusiastic and uncritical acceptance of the new technology and methods of work organization was a product of their understanding of economic development. Party and trade union officials hailed Ford's productive accomplishments as a reformed version of capitalism that promoted socialism. For example, Heinrich Ströbel, a left-wing Social Democrat and former *Vorwärts* editor, admitted that Ford might be correct in claiming that his economic methods could solve the social question within a capitalist framework, "if only all capitalists were economic organizers of the calibre of Henry Ford."[62] While most Social Democrats would not go that far, they did see the Ford works as a telling example of how economic organization and social hygiene in America far surpassed that of Germany. Ford showed what was possible even without a fundamental transformation of the economy. According to Ströbel, Ford was, without suspecting it, "the most powerful and welcome ally of socialism."[63] In the view of many Social Democrats, "Ford is the one who, even within a capitalist economic order shows the way that must be traveled in order that a socialist economy can first be built."[64]

This "technological optimism" was deeply embedded in both Marxist theory and the popular Marxism of German Social Democracy.[65] Social

Democrats prided themselves on being scientific socialists who admired the accomplishments of natural science, rather than utopian dreamers who fantasized alternative but impossible labor processes, or Luddites who futilely sought to block innovations. They viewed technology in abstraction from the economic system in which it was embedded and considered it to be progressive by definition. Advances in technology, they believed, would lead inexorably toward greater mechanization, automation, concentration, specialization, and division of labor. Although technology could be used to extract more value from workers and create repressive working conditions under capitalism, it was not by nature an instrument of exploitation. While the social relations of production would need to be fundamentally restructured under socialism, the technical character of production would not.[66]

Social Democrats believed that the further technology and productivity developed, the greater the contradictions between the social character of production and its ownership in private hands; the greater the productive capacity of capitalism, the easier it would be to build socialism. Economic development was thus leading inexorably—if rather too slowly—toward socialism, regardless of what capitalists intended or whether workers actively sought that goal. The working class had to struggle for the "blessings of technology," to use a favorite trade union phrase, that is, over wages, hours, and the intensity of work—but they should not contest the form of technology. To oppose technological progress and the accompanying increases in productivity would be unscientific. It would go against the inevitable direction of historical development, against the realization of socialism itself.

Sometimes the purported link between technology and socialism was expressed in rather simplistic terms, as when Ludwig Preller argued that the assembly line and flow production tended to promote a planned economy.[67] More often it was argued that socialists should use Fordism's powerful ability to increase productivity for their own ends.[68] In all cases, optimism about technology and an obsession with productivism informed the socialists' understanding of the direction in which history was moving and their vision of where it would end.

Despite its fascination with technology, Social Democracy failed to produce any serious or even fanciful proposals for the use of alternative technologies.[69] It did not advocate innovative reorganization of the labor process; it questioned neither the work ethic nor the notion of limitless economic growth. Its understanding of the nature of technology and the primacy of productivism was not so different from that of engineers and industrialists. Social Democrats spoke the same productivist language as their opponents, despite fundamental disagreements about distribution and ownership. August Bebel, the founder of German Social Democracy and author of the enormously popular book, *Women and Socialism*, imagined socialism as a world filled with technological wonders. As Heinz Marr noted, Bebel "drew a picture of the future state as an immense factory, ordered according to the principles of Fordization. . . . Mr. Ford would certainly have been thoroughly in agreement with this 'Bebelreich,' insofar as he himself could have been director."[70]

Technological determinism and productivism were not the exclusive preserve of Social Democratic trade unionists and politicians, even though they received the most criticism from contemporaries and later scholars for their often naïve faith in the positive benefits of technological rationaliza-tion.[71] The German Communist Party (KPD) was consistently critical of the effects of rationalization in America and in Weimar Germany. It viewed Fordism not as a reformed version of capitalism but as more intensively exploitative. The KPD was attentive to every example of how new tech-nology and reorganized labor processes worsened working conditions, decreased workers' share in productivity, and increased the already exces-sive profits of capital.[72] Yet, like their rivals, the Social Democrats, the Communists were equally convinced that the same technology that served capitalism could also serve socialism. Hilda Weiss's insistence that "the machine in the hands of capital is one of the most powerful instruments of oppression and impoverishment" marked her as a Communist critic of ration-alization. But her assertion that "industrial progress, the development of machinery, is *the necessary prerequisite for the establishment of a truly socialist system of production*" could just as well have been stated by a Social Demo-crat.[73] Weiss's views were widely shared not only among German Com-munists, but among their Russian counterparts as well, with Lenin leading the way.

Although information concerning the attitudes among rank and file workers in Weimar Germany is impressionistic, it does suggest that they were deeply interested in technological progress, regarded more mechanized forms of work positively, and shared productivist values. Elisabeth Schalldach in her investigation of the attitude among Weimar free trade unions toward rationalization, notes that metal workers were particularly interested in economic and technological developments in the United States.[74] The elaborate slide lecture on the Ford works that the DMV pro-duced supports that view. To be sure, managers at Krupp were more skep-tical, pointing to the workers' "inadequate recognition of the importance of intensive productivity and the elimination of all unproductive work and dead time." The Workers' Council, however, which was controlled by free and Christian trade union members, requested that a film about Ford be shown, and the Krupp management eagerly complied.[75]

In a 1930 dissertation on "*Technical Progress and Workers*," Liselotte Imhof analyzed both Hendrik de Man's interviews with 78 workers and a Christian Metalworkers' Union questionnaire about reactions to mecha-nized, monotonous work that was administered to 150 of its members. Although admitting that it was extremely difficult to generalize from such a small sample, she nonetheless concluded that workers fell into three broad categories: those who opposed mechanized work, those who disliked it but found compensations elsewhere, and those who actively sought mechanized work. Overall, she argued, "One does not find among workers a directly hostile attitude toward technical rationalization that would limit technical progress in its development. If workers turn against rationalized and intensive work methods, then many factors play a role." These included the failure of wages to rise as much as productivity, the loss of skills, and more general opposition to the socioeconomic system.[76] At issue was not technology per se, but the context in which it was used.

Fordism also achieved widespread acclaim because it held the promise of extraordinary gains in productivity either by finding alternatives to Taylorism or by incorporating some of its elements in ways that nullified the ill effects of that system in its pure form. The appeal of Fordism flowed out of the negative reception of Taylorism in Imperial and Weimar Germany. It is to that history that we must turn, if we are to understand the often naïve assessment of the beneficent character of Fordist production.

Taylorism and Fordism

From the mid-1890s on, the American engineer Frederick Taylor tirelessly publicized his program for the scientific management of labor. He proposed to divide jobs, analyze them by time-and-motion studies, and establish planning departments to prescribe new tasks and teach workers how to execute them properly. Workers were to be paid by an elaborate premium bonus system and be supervised by scientifically trained functional foremen. Both knowledge and control on the shop floor would thus be removed from workers and traditional supervisors and placed firmly in the hands of engineers. In theory these new methods were applicable to all kinds of work and would eliminate wasted movements and materials, thereby vastly increasing productivity per worker without the need of expensive technological innovations. Moreover, according to Taylor and his supporters, these methods would eliminate conflict on the shop floor by organizing the labor process according to ostensibly objective scientific principles and by providing workers with the opportunity to increase earnings as they increased productivity.[77]

The gospel of scientific management, with its emphasis on the centrality of the bourgeois expert, was advanced not only by Taylor in numerous books, articles and speeches, but by such disciples as Henry Laurence Gantt, Frank and Lillien Gilbreth, and, after 1910, by the Society to Promote the Study of Scientific Management, later known as the Taylor Society. Taylorism as ideology found many converts in American business, government, and engineering circles, for it addressed pervasive concerns about economic efficiency and workers' unrest, as well as middle-class anxieties about social status in an advanced industrial society.[78] Taylorism in practice was less pervasive, but scholars disagree on just how widely adopted full-scale Taylorism or isolated Taylorist practices such as time-and-motion studies were in the United States before World War I.[79]

Taylorism was introduced later in Imperial Germany and to a more limited audience whose attitude was highly equivocal. Some Germans perceived an "American danger" that stemmed from its innovations and organizational techniques.[80] American proponents of Taylorism traveled to Germany and Taylor's writings began to be translated as early as 1907.[81] But the emerging "America syndrome"[82] and the ensuing debate on Taylorism occurred primarily in engineering circles. American visitors met with vocational educators and the membership of the Association of German Engineers (VDI). Academic engineers, such as Georg Schlesinger and Adolf Walliches, a professor of machine building in Aachen, were particularly active in spreading Taylorist ideas. In 1913 the prewar discussion reached its high point when the VDI devoted its annual meeting to a discussion of Taylorism, with Schlesinger as the featured speaker. He endorsed both the political and economic goals of Taylorism, stressing that it would create peace on the shop floor, enhance the social and technical role of the engineer, and increase productivity and profits. On a practical plane, he advocated the adoption of time-and-motion studies, the division of tasks, the adoption of norms, and the implementation of planning departments and functional foremanship. He hesitated to recommend the complicated premium bonus systems that were an integral part of American Taylorism, and emphasized matching the aptitudes of the worker with the demands of the job.[83]

Other prewar commentators were more critical, including those who contributed to the 1914 issue of the *Archiv für Sozialwissenschaft und Sozialpolitik*, the journal of the influential Verein für Sozialpolitik.[84] Some found Taylorist methods unsuitable for German conditions, citing the cost of implementing job analyses, planning departments and functional foremanship, the unpredictability of the results, and the possibility of significant working-class oppostion.[85] Others worried that Taylorism challenged the academically based European science of work, which claimed to be more scientific, more politically neutral, and more concerned with both the needs of workers and the issue of social reform than American scientific management.[86]

The debates among engineers found little resonance elsewhere, and there was no effort to establish an organization comparable to the Taylor Society. Industrialists did not yet feel the pressing need to enhance productivity and competitiveness that they would in the mid-1920s, and only a few firms, such as Siemens, Borsig and Osram in Berlin, and Bosch in Stuttgart, experimented with Taylorist measures. In the case of Bosch, the attempt was met with significant working-class opposition.[87] The trade unions did not seriously concern themselves with the issue, for most were occupied with confronting traditional employer tactics for eroding wages, skills, and union power rather than time-and-motion studies, premium bonus systems, and planning bureaus.[88] Only the DMV, whose organizing efforts were concentrated in the industries most affected by Taylorism, analyzed the new American methods. The reaction was predominently negative, but some union functionaries, such as the engineer Richard Woldt, looked more favorably on Taylorist methods for increasing productivity—provided that workers could help determine piece rates and production norms.[89]

The outbreak of war in 1914 abruptly interrupted the emerging debate on Taylorism.[90] It resumed only at the war's end, and then in a quite different form. The renewed interest in Taylorism was not a result of the changes in production brought about by the needs of war, for although rationalization, deskilled labor, and mass production were introduced, German industry did not adopt Taylorism proper.[91] Moreover, wartime changes in the labor process were viewed by capital and labor alike as temporary expedients. The renewed discussion of Taylorism formed part of the debate about postwar economic recovery and reform.

In the first phase of the postwar debate, men of such varied occupational and political backgrounds as the industrialist Walther Rathenau, the aristocrat and engineer Wichard von Moellendorf, and the Social Democratic Minister of Economics Rudolf Wissel advocated Taylorism as part of a new rational, planned *Gemeinwirtschaft*. Building on the prewar critique of the limits and biases of American scientific management, they insisted that Taylorism must be but one element in a comprehensive economic restructuring that would be used to benefit all elements of society rather than profit-seeking capitalists alone. The technocratic and productivist elements of this vision of a reformed and more collective society made it appealing to engineers and some state officials, but its association with revolution and economic planning discredited both the sweeping vision and Taylorism in the eyes of industry and the military. Social Democrats were ambivalent, for although they found the technological and productivist character of *Gemeinwirtschaft* attractive, they had doubts about the primacy accorded to technocrats rather than workers, and the focus on planning rather than politics. They were unsure whether a Taylorized *Gemeinwirtschaft* would be a step toward socialism or away from it.[92]

This utopian phase of the Taylorism debate in Germany was a short-lived product of the immediate postwar revolutionary conjuncture. With the establishment of republican government, the repression of workers' unrest, and the demise of all plans for comprehensive economic reform, the discussion of Taylorism settled into much more prosaic forms, reminiscent of the prewar debates.

In the early 1920s, engineers and industrial sociologists and physiologists were divided on the merits of Taylorism's various organizational techniques and its explicitly procapitalist orientation.[93] Most no longer saw it as the best means to position the engineer as a key social mediator and leader. Those who retained such aspirations—and they were numerous—found other justifications in home-grown theories of the factory community, human economy, and *Menschenführung*.[94] Those, such as Friedrich Meyenberg, who enthusiastically defended Taylorism, admitted that it had sometimes been misapplied but insisted that it was both efficient and humane if correctly implemented. Moreover, it did not dispense with skilled labor or apprenticeship, as many German commentators feared.[95] Such critics as Gustav Frenz argued that Taylorism produced excessive centralization and deskilling. Instead of trying to raise productivity by promoting job satisfaction, Taylorism resorted to bonus systems and aptitude testing that evaluated only physical fitness and not workers' interests.[96] Many engineers and industrial sociologists and psychologists may have shared the more complex assessment of Dr. Fritz Söllheim, who introduced his detailed survey of the use of Taylorist methods in Germany with a stern warning: "remain competitive or starve . . . increased productivity or impoverishment." He offered a mixed evaluation of various Taylorist techniques and concluded that "Taylorism, as a correctly understood idea for the practical rationalization of life, will not decline, even if it appears under other names. . . ." But he offered a critique shared by many Germans: "After Taylor has taught us how to think economically, we must learn to economize humanely. Our goal must not be a one-sided increase in production but more occupational satisfaction and vocational happiness."[97]

In the wake of inflation, the hyperinflation of 1923, and the stabilization crisis of 1924–1925, the discussion of Taylorism became part of the larger debate on rationalization. At issue was not whether Germany would restructure its economy, for from 1924 on, industry was committed to technical modernization and efficiency, and it was on the offensive against a labor movement that was excluded from the national government, divided politically, and weakened by high unemployment.[98] The question was what form rationalization would take. Because of their overriding concern with economic recovery, industrialists, engineers, and Social Democrats were less hostile to individual Taylorist techniques than before the war. But they remained unconvinced that Taylorism as an ideology and a practical organizational system provided the best solution. The publication of the German edition of Ford's autobiography in late 1923, as well as the reports from German travelers to Detroit from 1924 on and the resulting deluge of reviews, reports, lectures, and conferences, provided those committed to restructuring with an alternative vision of rationalization—one that claimed to be far superior to Taylorism. For Social Democrats above all, Fordism reenforced longstanding doubts about Taylorism and provided a concrete program around which to rally. This emerges clearly from an exploration of post-1920 trade union debates about Taylorism.

Following World War I, the trade union movement in Germany, like its counterparts elsewhere, reassessed its overwhelmingly negative attitude toward Taylorism. In each country motives differed, but in Britain, France, and the United States, as well as in Germany, the trade unions tried to work with Taylorism, or more precisely, tried to make Taylorism work for workers.[99] To be sure, workers on the shop floor continued to mistrust Taylorism, seeing premium bonus systems as a way to cut wages and time-and-motion studies as a means of intensifying work and endangering workers' health. They resented patronizing engineers who imposed detailed job instructions, even if work thereby became physically easier. "People don't want such 'American methods,'" concluded one report.[100]

Union functionaries and theorists were less dismissive. Some were confident that greater working-class economic and political power would mitigate the ill effects of Taylorism, and most saw increased productivity as a prerequisite for short-term reform, as well as for eventual socialization.[101] All had to grapple with the "profound dilemma" that Taylorism created for Marxism, "because it combined a welcome method of rationalizing and modernizing production while increasing and accelerating exploitation."[102] Most did so by breaking down Taylorism into its component parts in order to see which ones might benefit workers. Workers who served on factory councils would thereby be able to evaluate the new technologies and labor processes that management proposed.

The Social Democrats' critical appropriation of Taylorism echoed that of engineers and industrial sociologists.[103] Some, like Kurt Lewin in his pamphlet on *The Socialization of the Taylor System*, laid great emphasis on increasing productivity by aptitude testing, vocational counseling, and industrial psychology.[104] Many other authors, including several who wrote for the DMV's *Betriebsräte Zeitschrift*, a publication aimed at factory council delegates, insisted that minutely divided, mechanized, and monotonous work was inevitable, but argued that it would be bearable if the work pace was not intensified and if hours were shortened.[105]

Those who were yet more enthusiastic praised the productivist benefits of Taylorism, with little or no concrete attention to its exploitative aspects. Hermann Jäckel, a featured speaker at the 1925 conference of the General Federation of German Trade Unions, insisted that "the worker in his union is obligated to cooperate with employers in order to find those forms of rationalization, of standardization, of Taylorism, etc., that are necessary for the economy." But he added that unions must oppose crude Taylorism, for workers needed to experience "joy in work."[106] In his defense of Taylorism, Engelbert Graf invoked the socialist belief in progress: "[I]n comparison to earlier anarchic and arbitrary work methods, the Taylor system represents progress, a higher stage of technical development, which leads to increased production and a better use of raw materials and energy."[107] Max Fiehn, writing in the theoretical journal *Neue Zeit*, was even more extravagant in his claims for the beneficial aspects of scientific management: Work might be divided and dull, but more was produced with equal or less effort. Work might be monotonous and mindless, but it did not absorb all the "spiritual energy" of the worker. Employing his best dialectical reasoning, Fiehn concluded, "The enslavement of humans to machinery creates revolutionizing technical liberation through the machine."[108]

Those who raised more critical objection did not so much reject Taylorism as condemn the context in which it was used. This was certainly the recurring theme of Communist analyses. A minute division of labor, careful planning of tasks, or extensive mechanization were not in and of themselves detrimental to workers. What created exploitation, impoverishment, and inhuman working conditions was capitalist misuse of these techniques.[109] The economism and technological fetishism of Second International Marxism, as well as bolshevism's sympathy with Taylorism undoubtedly shaped the KPD's views. So too did the fact that its members were predominantly unskilled or semiskilled and hence were not threatened by Taylorism's attack on the craft worker. But the appeal of productivist ideology was probably more influential than the sociology of the movement.

That was certainly the case for left-wing Social Democrats, whose base was overwhelmingly among skilled and white-collar workers; yet they made precisely the same arguments about Taylorism as their Communist rivals. Richard Seidel, for example, who wrote for the *Betriebsräte Zeitschrift* and *Die Gesellschaft*, initially attacked all Socialist efforts to appropriate Taylorism within a capitalist economy. In 1920 he argued that capitalists used Taylorism only to exploit workers and would permit aptitude testing and psychotechnical analyses of the labor process only if capital benefited. Under socialism, however, the tools of capitalism would have the opposite effect.[110] By mid-decade, however, Seidel and others were arguing that more than ownership would have to change if scientific management techniques were to benefit workers. At the same time, they suggested that certain kinds of capitalist reorganizations of production were significantly better for workers than others. Seidel, for example, dismissed Taylorism as outmoded science because its overriding aim was to force the maximum productivity out of the individual worker. He nonetheless approved of particular Taylorist practices, such as time-and-motion studies and carefully planned and divided tasks, as useful under two conditions: First, they had to be combined with and modified by the research of the German science of work, which paid attention to psychological and sociological issues. Of greater importance, the aim of any reorganization should be to optimize all factors of production.[111]

The concept of optimization was popular in many circles in the mid-1920s, but Social Democrats seem to have borrowed it from J. Ermanski, a Russian scientist noted for his study of work and energy expenditure. His major study of scientific work organization was translated into German in 1925 and widely and approvingly read among trade unionists. Ermanski insisted that optimizing output, that is, getting the maximum output for the least input of materials and energy, was fundamentally different from maximizing output by intensifying work and thereby increasing the energy expenditure of the worker.[112] The optimum was to be achieved by Taylorist techniques for dividing tasks and eliminating wasted motion, but equally important, by rationalizing and mechanizing the flow of materials, reorganizing repair work, mechanizing production, and introducing standardization. In short, all aspects of the production process were to be transformed, not just the worker's performance of his or her task. Only under socialism, however, could optimization be fully realized.[113]

The popularity of the concept of optimization provides an indication of why Fordism was so much more appealing than Taylorism. Like Ermanski's concept, Fordist production promised a way out of the vicious Taylorist cycle that linked productivity and exploitation. It claimed to increase productivity without intensifying work; it insisted on analyzing and improving all factors of production rather than extracting more from the worker alone. It dispensed with those aspects of Taylorism that work- ers found most onerous—time-and-motion studies, premium bonus systems, and functional foremen supervising the worker's every move. Fordism as a system of production, a set of labor processes, and a style of management enabled Social Democrats to embrace unequivocally both productivism and the most modern productive methods. And it offered Communists a vision of how they would organize the work process once they owned the means of production.

Economists, industrial sociologists and physiologists, and functionaries from the Christian trade union movement, who disagreed with the left about much else, used similar arguments about the optimization of all factors of production and the humanization of work to defend Ford over Taylor. Most insisted that Taylorism and Fordism represented fundamentally different systems of production and methods of organizing work. Friedrich von Gottl- Ottlilienfeld, author of the widely read pamphlet, *Fordism*, was the most noted exponent of this view. While he was most enamoured of Ford's per- sonality and his ideology of service, he had nothing but praise for Ford's production methods. He measured Fordism and Taylorism according to the criterion of "technical reason," that is, how to attain the maximum output for the minimum input, and found Taylorism wanting, indeed positively dangerous. He believed that Taylorism had an inherent tendency to degen- erate into what he called irrational "Taylorei," because it focused only on attaining the maximum from the individual worker; it decided what was possible by highly artificial time-and-motion studies of ideal workers; and it dictated every move to the worker, isolated him, and made him depen- dent on the planning bureau. A truely Taylorized firm achieved, at best, artificial and temporary social peace and failed to combine economic and technical rationality. Ford, in contrast, mechanized and rationalized all aspects of production to an unheard of degree and gave the worker greater freedom to perform his individual task. To be sure, such tasks were minutely divided, but "within the ever-so-narrow limits that the hard style of large- scale technology prescribes, the Ford worker can live freely as a creative personality."[114] In short, Ford realized a happy "dictatorship of technical reason."[115]

Many others from the political center and right elaborated on Gottl- Ottlilienfeld's themes.[116] The engineer Emil Honermeier argued that High- land Park and River Rouge were not "giant Taylorized factories," for Ford was concerned with the technical efficiency of the firm while Taylor focused only on the efficiency of the worker.[117] Goetz Briefs, an industrial sociolo- gist at the Technische Hochschule of Berlin, shared this view but also stressed the rhythmic and therefore positive character of work at the Ford plant.[118] Christian Metalworkers' Union functionary Edmund Kleinschmitt, who had actually worked at Ford, also praised the rhythm of the assembly line but laid greater emphasis on what he saw as the distinguishing charac- teristic of Fordized work, namely, that "each worker performs the assigned task as it suits him individually"; because "technology accomplished so much," Ford did not need to force workers to artificially high levels of production by minutely prescribing how a job was to be performed. The average productivity of the average worker was the norm.[119]

To be sure, there were some dissenting voices. Dr. Heidebroek, professor of engineering at the Technical University in Darmstadt, insisted that Taylorism and Fordism represented complementary systems. Taylor taught the proper method of analyzing and regulating each task, while Ford put those tasks together on the assembly line, which set the pace of work, and let management dispense with piece rates and bonus systems.[120] Waldemar Zimmermann also criticized Gottl-Ottlilienfeld for sharply contrasting Taylor and Ford, as well as for insisting that the Ford worker was "Herr im Haus" (master) of his task. Ford certainly used Taylor's organizational techniques, and work at Ford was even more mechanized and regulated than in a Taylorized firm. Zimmermann did acknowledge, however, that the work pace was geared to the average Ford worker rather than the exceptional one, and that Ford understood the worker, whereas Taylor did not. Or to use Zimmermann's colorful formulation, Taylor was "a physiological mechanic," whereas Ford was "a psychological engineer."[121]

Those who saw Fordism as a negation of Taylorism and those who saw it as incorporating and improving on it, did not dispute the facts, for they all described work at Ford in remarkably similar terms. They did disagree about how to label it. Was an extreme division of labor Taylorist in and of itself or only if a planning bureau prescribed how to carry out each task? Was work on the assembly line satisfying and freer because it was rhythmic, as Taylorism was not, or was it equally regimented because the line determined the work pace? One's answer depended on whether or not one was willing to invoke the controversial name of Taylor for productive innovations of which one approved.

In whatever manner academics, trade unionists, and engineers judged the relationship between Taylorism and Fordism, they all expressed a distinct preference for the latter. It was viewed as a higher stage in the organization of production, an improved means of structuring work, and a laudable way of optimizing all factors of production rather than simply exploiting labor. Whether or not this was so in the United States or in Germany will be explored in subsequent chapters. For our present purposes, the accuracy of these arguments is less important than the similarity of their underlying structure. By embracing Fordism as a system of production, groups which otherwise often bitterly disagreed found themselves in agreement about what constituted the newest American methods and what it meant to be economically modern. Fordism expressed their shared commitment to productivity and to the concerns of the German science of work.

Productivism was only one aspect of Fordism, albeit a central one. It could be and was combined with other elements—such as Ford's wage policy, his promotion of mass consumption, his marketing strategy, his service ideology—to produce quite different visions of how a modern economy

and society would look. The consensus created by the productivist reading
of Fordism was shattered by controversies surrounding the relationship of
mass consumption and high wages to the ultrarationalized Fordist organization of production.

Fordism as Consumption

Ford was as famous for what he produced and how he sold it as for how he
organized production. He was certainly not the first industrialist to mass
produce complex goods—munitions manufacturers accomplished that in the
nineteenth century. Nor was he the first to mass produce a consumer
durable, for sewing machines and bicycles predated the car. But Ford did
pioneer the mass production of a very complex and new consumer durable,
the automobile, which revolutionized American transportation, its culture,
and its expectations about consumption. Of equal importance, Ford pioneered new wage and pricing policies, symbolized by the five-dollar-a-day
wage and the low-priced Model T. According to Ford, high wages and low
prices were not extraneous to his economic success; they were not fringe
benefits made possible by the exceptionalism of American prosperity.
Rather, high wages and low prices were an integral part of Fordist mass
production, for they created effective demand for cars as well as the permanent pressure to revolutionize production methods.

There was scarcely a commentator on Fordism who did not at least mention mass consumption, but the views among Social Democrats concerning
the relative importance and relationship of wages, prices, consumption, and
production differed significantly from those of non-Socialists. Many of the
latter were open to the idea of Fordist mass consumption, even if they
doubted that it was possible in Germany, but what they singled out as integral to its success varied. Some, such as Waldemar Zimmermann, praised
the creation of a single consumer durable, whose quality was constantly
improved while its price was steadily lowered.[122] Others, such as Irene
Witte and Theodor Lüddecke admired Ford's sales techniques, which
included franchising, advertising, and credit buying as well as low pricing.[123]
They occasionally mentioned high wages but paid less attention to this
controversial issue than to low prices, and few saw Ford's wage-and-price
policy as the motor that drove Fordist production and profitability.[124] One
who did, Günther Stein, attributed Ford's wage-and-price policy to his
concept of service, rather than to his astute understanding of the essential
conditions for successful rationalized mass production under advanced capitalism.[125]

Although non-Social Democrats did not see high wages and low prices
as the key to Ford's success, they nonetheless took them seriously. Ford's
product, his pricing policy, and his sales strategy represented both a threat
to European production and a potential model for Germany to imitate at
least partially.[126] As the psychologist Fritz Giese insisted, the notion of
influencing the market through the mass production of inexpensive goods

had a most promising future.[127] In addition, some observers claimed that Ford's wage-and-price policy created a happy three-way relationship among workers, employers, and consumers. In Friedrich von Gottl-Ottlilienfeld's phrase, "The opposition between consumers and producers is ended."[128] In this argument, consumption is the key to reforming capitalism. A third analysis, advanced by Moritz J. Bonn, held that consumption does not so much reform capitalism as co-opt workers and legitimate the growing concentration of capital.[129]

Social Democrats saw high wages and low prices as the prerequisite for successful Fordism. To be sure, the Fordist wage-and-price policy was in workers' self-interest, as no movement leader would deny. Ford seemed able to combine the incompatible by increasing productivity without increasing exploitation, and by paying workers more for producing goods which cost less. According to a German worker who had been employed in both the Ruhr and Detroit, "In the current situation it is more pleasant to allow oneself to be exploited by Ford than by Krupp."[130] Ford's wage-and-price policy was especially appealing to German labor after 1924, when industry attacked both the eight-hour day and existing wage levels, claiming that the former needed to be lengthened and the latter significantly lowered if the German economy was to recover and be rationalized. As Witte noted, trade unionists enjoyed using this side of Ford—the quintessential American capitalist—as a weapon against German industrialists.[131]

Social Democrats advocated high wages so that workers could not only live better but live differently. They viewed mass consumption as positive in principle, even if, as we will see in later chapters, they were unsure precisely what forms of mass consumption and mass culture were possible and desirable in Germany. Just as the good economy was defined in terms of constantly expanding production, so too was the good society defined in terms of constantly expanding consumption. Social Democratic theorists also viewed material abundance as a compensation for workers' loss of skills and control on the shop floor and as their reward for accepting, indeed supporting, rationalized production.

But Weimar Social Democrats did not argue on the basis of class interest alone. As was their wont, they insisted that promoting the interests of workers would also promote the interests of society as a whole. Social Democrats believed that Germany could expand its markets at home but not abroad. As they correctly noted, Germany exported less in the mid-1920s than it had before the war. Even if exports increased, it was unlikely that they could ever keep up with the vastly expanded productive capacity of rationalized industry.[132] Thus they argued that domestic demand must be stimulated by high wages and low prices.

Examples of this reasoning abound. In a 1926 lecture to the Berlin Factory Council Conference (which was subsequently published as a pamphlet entitled *Rationalization and the Working Class*), Wilhelm Eggert, a member of the ADGB Executive Council, insisted that Germany's current economic crisis stemmed from problems with the domestic market. Productivity had increased markedly, but cartels committed an "economic crime" by keeping prices high and thereby limiting demand. The solution was not to halt rationalization "because it lay in the march of economic development." Rather, the solution was to reintroduce the eight-hour day so that workers could recover from monotonous assembly line work and to raise wages so that the domestic market would expand. The factory council conference at which Eggert first presented these ideas, officially endorsed them.[133] In the same year the *Metallarbeiter-Zeitung*, reporting on the introduction of the five-day work week at the Ford works, praised Ford for recognizing that "in the end, a higher wage and shorter work time benefit business more than the workers themselves, because it is only thanks to a higher income and shorter hours that workers are able to buy more and use what they buy."[134] In short, the lesson the Social Democrats learned from Ford was that demand takes primacy over supply. If people cannot buy, industry will not produce.

Whereas Ford advocated expanding domestic consumption by restructuring prices and wages simultaneously, and non-Socialists favored starting with prices, Social Democrats insisted that wages must be raised first. Their preference did not reflect elaborate theory but rather the needs of their constituency and the practical difficulties of influencing prices. The efforts of the Luther government to lower price levels in 1925 had been ineffective, and German prices remained high in the mid- and late-1920s. According to trade unionists, high general costs, excess profits at many levels, unproductive methods, and inefficient business organization all contributed to the price problem.[135] The highly developed cartel structure of German industry on the one hand and the influence of the world economy on the other further limited the prospects of lowering German prices.[136]

Without an expansion of domestic demand, rationalization would create high and persistent unemployment. Indeed, this was precisely the case in Germany in 1926, when the first wave of rationalization pushed unemployment over the two million mark.[137] In its memorandum entitled "The Present Tasks of German Economic Policy," the General Federation of German Trade Unions (ADGB) addressed this issue directly: "Rationalization is necessary. . . . Its goal must be a decrease in production costs and prices and a simultaneous increase in wages. Only by means of this increase in mass purchasing power can the unemployed worker find a new job."[138] As rationalization restructured a particular industry and enabled fewer workers to produce more and cheaper goods, workers in that plant or sector would be dismissed. But if prices were lowered and wages were raised, increased demand would stimulate an expansion of production, enabling the unemployed to find new jobs, either in their old sectors or in new ones.[139] This model of rationalization, based on the Social Democrats' reading of Fordism, goes far toward explaining why they viewed the cost of rationalization so complacently. They were convinced that unemployment would only be temporary, for any other outcome would harm capital even more than labor.

No one argued this with more passion than Fritz Tarnow, head of the Woodworkers' Union, who was a member of the 1925 trade union delegation to the United States and a member of the National Economic Council. A champion of rationalization par excellence, Tarnow's most comprehensive argument was presented in a book published in 1928 by the ADGB entitled *Why Be Poor?* Its title, taken from a chapter in Ford's autobiography, suggests how deeply Ford influenced Tarnow. Tarnow's book is filled with admiration for the American model, praise for Ford, and quotations from innumerable American authors. But Tarnow's greatest enthusiasm was for the Fordist model of mass consumption.

The Malthusian world of scarcity, overpopulation, and low wages had come to an end, Tarnow argued with naïve optimism, for science, technology, and work organization had conquered nature and solved the problem of production. The problem of consumption was now on the agenda. Germany could only utilize its productive capacity by expanding the domestic market, for the world market was limited and highly competitive, and domestic consumption could only be expanded by increasing wages. Wage earners were the most promising source of demand, for most other groups had lost their money in the inflation. Moreover, if firms rationalized in the American way, they would cut their overall wage bill as well as other costs and thus could afford higher wages. According to Tarnow, industry's adherence to "the economic recipe of working more and consuming less is just as sensible as ordering a fever patient to take aspirin tablets and then lie naked in the snow."[140] German poverty was not an economic necessity but rather a social illness that could be cured even under capitalism. In his view, industry needed to recognize that "increasing consumption is the key to developing production and thereby increasing wealth. . . . As paradoxical as it may sound, saving makes you poor and spending makes you rich."[141]

Emphasizing the centrality of consumption to Fordism made economic sense to Social Democratic leaders and promised tangible material benefits to workers. It was also an appealing political strategy. The prospect of high wages and low prices enabled politicians and trade union functionaries to accept rationalization and anticipate a significantly reformed capitalism. Such reform would ostensibly come not as a result of victory in a zero-sum game, but as the outcome of cooperation between capital and labor in a mutually beneficial restructuring of production and consumption.

Significant segments of the party and trade union leadership had been committed to such cooperation since World War I.[142] Moreover, such collaboration would require workers' passive toleration but not their active participation. The wartime radicalization of the rank and file, the 1918–1919 revolution, and the permanent split in the labor movement had left leading Social Democrats with an ineradicable fear of rank and file militancy and a determination to limit all grass roots movements. The prospect of high wages, low prices, and mass consumption led many Social Democrats to believe Fordist rationalization could bring about the best of all possible worlds—productivism and mass consumption, militant reformism, and a demobilized rank and file. Most of these hopes proved illusory, but the allure of the vision was extraordinarily powerful in the mid-1920s.

There were voices within the labor movement that were considerably less enthusiastic about Fordist mass consumption than were Tarnow and the majority of Social Democratic leaders. Eduard Weckerle, writing in the *Gewerkschafts-Archiv*, said trade unionists were wrong to focus narrowly on the wage increases of some workers in rationalized industries. Overall, wages did not increase nearly as fast as productivity, either in America or in Germany, and what improvements there were came only with greatly intensified work.[143] Christian Schmitz, author of a very negative essay on Ford in the *Betriebsräte Zeitschrift*, said Ford paid high wages only because they aided productivity.[144] Such criticism of Ford's motives suggests how difficult it was for left-wing trade unionists to attack Ford's wage-and-price policy. No Social Democrat denied that Ford's first concern was productivity and profitability. What was important for such observers as Tarnow and Eggert was the outcome for workers, not the intention of capitalists. A few Communists, such as Alexander Friedrich, dismissed mass consumption completely. Just as Mephisto tempted Faust, Friedrich argued, so did Ford seduce his workers with glittering promises of material goods. But they had to pay with their bodies and souls. Ford's workers were slaves, he insisted, and it was only a difference of form, not substance, whether a slave was impoverished and beaten or drove a car and owned a radio.[145] Such arguments were hardly persuasive and squared poorly with the KPD's materialism and productivism.

More realistic Communists, such as Jakob Walcher, admired Ford's strategies for increasing consumption but wondered when he would run up against the laws of limited markets under capitalism.[146] Hilda Weiss insisted that increased productivity could not be transformed into increased consumption in Germany because capitalism could not reform itself in the direction of Fordist mass consumption.[147] As we will see in the next chapter, capitalists, such as Carl Köttgen, came to the same conclusion as these Communists yet they used very different arguments for why high wages, low prices, and mass consumption were impossible in Weimar Germany. Fordism understood as mass consumption thus proved much more divisive than Fordism defined as productivism.

Fordism as Ideology

Fordism, understood as productivism or as mass consumption, found adherents on the left and the right as well as among those claiming to occupy a neutral, scientific position outside of politics. The ideological readings of Fordism were, however, the exclusive property of those who were antisocialist but committed to modernizing and revitalizing the German economy. Socialists dismissed Ford's talk of service to the community as ideological window dressing. He was as determined to maximize profits as any capitalist, they argued; he simply understood how to do so better than most.[148] Ford's ideology appealed to industrialists, engineers, industrial sociologists, and economists who believed that technology or pricing policy alone would not cure Germany's pervasive economic ills. They insisted that a new spirit of capitalism, and a new form of entrepreneurship, were necessary. Ford claimed to offer these.

Those Germans who sought to reconstruct Ford's ideology from his writings and his business practices agreed with Theodor Lüddecke that Fordism and Americanism were above all a new "mentality," a "new economic spirit."[149] Yet they disagreed about what constituted its essential elements.[150] Some commentators singled out Ford's claim that he structured his business around the principle of service to all. Others focused on his style of leadership in the firm and in the economy at large. For a third group, the values animating Ford's practice were less important than the goal to which he ostensibly aspired, namely social peace. Some viewed Ford's ideology as separate from his production and marketing practices, while others viewed it as a consequence.

For those who linked Ford's philosophy to the shop floor, service was the essence of Ford's ideology. Service was equated with low prices, high wages, and the resulting satisfaction that mass consumption achieved. Waldemar Zimmermann praised Ford for serving the masses by enabling them to buy what only the wealthy had previously enjoyed and concluded that "mass work organized for the common good in the service of mass provisioning for the common good—this is the higher social meaning of the Fordist entrepreneurial idea."[151] Ernest Berger, ministerial adviser in the National Labor Office, agreed that increased production, greater consumption, and the notion of service were inseparable for Ford.[152] Although some commentators whose definition of Ford's service ethic was very materialist stressed consumer satisfaction as an end in itself, others believed that low prices and high wages were only the first service Ford provided to society. Carl Hollweg, for example, praised mass consumption as service but argued that Ford also gave workers "joy in work and meaning in their lives, and in addition security in old age"—And all this was achieved without concessions to socialist programs![153]

Some of those who were enamored with Ford's service ethic saw it as a manifestation of some unique aspect of American culture, such as Protestantism or Emersonian individualism.[154] Others found parallels between Ford's ideology and the Prussian concept of service to the nation.[155] All saw adoption of Ford's service ethic as a way of smoothing the rough edges of capitalism while retaining its essential structural features. And everyone who defined service in terms of consumption insisted that this new ethic enhanced profits and benefited not only the capitalist but also his workers, and consumers in general.

This argument, which was favored by academics and engineers but not by industrialists, was remarkably similar to that of such Social Democrats as Fritz Tarnow. To be sure, Social Democrats dismissed the language of service as ideological camouflage for the naked pursuit of profit, whereas economists and engineers, such as Zimmermann and Hollweg, regarded it as an indication of the genuinely new values that animated the Fordist version of capitalism. The concrete practices they espoused, however, were identical, as was their insistance that all elements of society would benefit from them.

Whereas service was the essence of Fordist entrepreneurship for some, others focused on his leadership abilities. Fritz Bredow, a South German visitor to the Ford works, painted an extravagantly enthusiastic picture of Ford's leadership: Ford was neither a revolutionary nor a reactionary but a keenly practical man who had broad experience in many different occupations. He understood that poverty would be eliminated only by producing and distributing more and set about doing so with his admirable leadership skills. In Bredow's view, Ford was "a true leader [Führer]" who provided a model for Germans that would enable them to recover economically and realize their best national characteristics.[156] Paul Rieppel was one of several commentators who regarded peaceful labor relations as the clearest manifestation of Ford's leadership qualitites.[157] Theodor Lüddecke made the most far-reaching and amorphous claims. Ford's personality, he argued, represented a "symbolic transcendence of money-grubbing private capitalism." It was the symbolic expression "of a grandiose system of organic economic leadership of the most excellent sort that had developed in America."[158]

Ford's role as führer was not central to the mid-1920s debate on Fordism; rather, the dominant issues were production and consumption. German businessmen were unsure just how much of Ford's ideosyncratic style and philosophy they wanted to emulate. Many of Ford's leadership methods appealed to them: Ford gave pride of place to owners rather than managers and technocrats; he dispensed with trade unions and dismissed the welfare state as unnecessary, indeed detrimental to all. Yet Ford also insisted that high wages, low prices, and mass consumption were essential to his successful leadership within the firm and within the economy at large. It was all but impossible to separate service and consumption, leadership and high wages, in the Fordist ideology. German businessmen preferred to limit discussion to concrete production techniques and output norms, and to admire Ford's profit rates without delving into the details of his leadership philosophy. For their part, Social Democrats admired the way Ford and other American businessmen ran their affairs, but they did not consider Ford to be a model economic führer; such a notion of leadership was the preserve of the political right. It connoted hierarchy, authoritarianism, and murky ideas about the organic factory community. Thus Social Democrats praised the system rather than the man. They stressed the mutual benefits of profitability and mass consumption, rather than the qualities of will, vision, and an ability to inspire followers that Ford ostensibly displayed.

Within certain circles Ford's leadership ideology, divorced from his wage-and-price policy, resonated. In some right-wing political circles and among some academics, engineers, and economic commentators close to them, the concept of leaders and followers and of organic factory communities animated by a strong will, was pervasive. The engineers who founded Dinta, such Ruhr industrialists as Alfred Vögler, such philosophers as Oswald Spengler, and such commentators as Theodor Lüddecke, who popularized the ideas of American businessmen, were among those who believed that underlying all other problems, the German economy suffered from a crisis in leadership.[159] Leadership was seen as the key to successful rationalization. Both were defined using elements drawn from Fordism, from German industrial sociology, and from theories, or more aptly, slogans, of the factory community.

"Ford and Us," a conference sponsored by the Frankfurt Social Museum, provided one example of how these seemingly incompatible ideas were mixed. The engineer H. Benkert gave a lecture suggestively titled "Work Leadership and Work Pedagogy in a Rationalized Firm." According to Benkert, "The leader [*Führer*] must stand at the top, unencumbered by any limiting and false capitalist profit mania, free from every individual spirit of domination. He should become the leader of a factory community that creates with him, that recognizes as the purpose of its activity only dutiful performance and for whom it is a question of bringing this performance—and thus itself—to perfection."[160]

Friedrich von Gottl-Ottlilienfeld's famous essay on Fordism brought together all the various strands of ideological intrepretation, painting a picture of Fordism as a veritable utopia. Material prosperity, harmonious labor relations, joy in work and pride in productivity, a spirit of service, a new style of leadership—all these, he claimed, were realized in Fordism. The result was a new kind of community, a "white socialism of pure, active conviction."[161]

Fordism as "white socialism" was an arresting slogan. Some commentators have used it to capture the enthusiastic reception of Fordism in Weimar Germany.[162] But it is wrong to project the sweeping sociopolitical aspirations of someone like Gottl-Ottlilienfeld onto the innumerable businessmen, engineers, and trade unionists who endorsed Fordism. Gottl-Ottlilienfeld's utopia contained many elements objectionable to capital and many others offensive to Social Democracy. Both groups preferred, albeit for different reasons, to praise Fordist productivism and ignore Fordist ideology. They were the main protagonists in the struggle to appropriate and implement Fordism in Weimar Germany. This struggle was fought less over issues of ethics and ideology than over the nuts and bolts of machines and assembly lines, wages and skill levels, products and pricing. Fordism promised quite different things to capital and to labor, but both aspired toward a reformed capitalism, not a quasi-utopian transcendence of it.

4

American Economic Success and German Emulation

It was one thing for German visitors to Detroit to be infatuated with Fordism; it was quite another for industrialists, trade unionists, engineers, and economists to restructure the troubled German economy along American lines. From 1924 on, few disputed the need for dramatic economic restructuring—or rationalization, to use the term preferred by Germans—but controversy did surround what form rationalization should take. Which American economic principles and practices could be adopted and which were valid only in the circumstances of the New World? Did Fordism have to be implemented in toto or could one pick and choose among its elements and still attain the desired levels of profitability and prosperity? Would economic modernization along American lines automatically bring about an Americanization of society and culture? German proponents of Fordism and Americanism quickly found themselves embroiled in a far-ranging and often acrimonious debate about America's past and present and Germany's future.

The secrets of American economic success such as Fordism, were interpreted in contradictory ways. German commentators disagreed about the relative importance of natural endowments, technological achievements, and innovative products. Some identified mass markets as a cause of prosperity; others, as a consequence. Many Social Democrats insisted that farsighted, resourceful, and daring entrepreneurs created the American economic miracle, whereas industrialists singled out America's ostensibly enthusiastic, hardworking, and apolitical workers as the critical factor.

German proposals for imitating the American economic model were equally diverse and contradictory. They ran the gamut from specific rec-ommendations for the adoption of particular machines and labor processes to sweeping advocacy (or rejection) of assembly line production, high wages, and mass consumption. Those on the political right proposed rationaliza-tion controlled by capital; those on the left suggested reform implemented through corporatist cooperation between capital and labor. Some advocated a prominent role for the state, either in promoting economic restructuring or mitigating its detrimental consequences; others viewed any state action as counterproductive. Finally, capital and labor developed utterly differ-ent scenarios for when and to what degree prices, wages, and profits would change in the process of rationalization, and who would benefit and who would bear the costs.

America—real and imagined in multiple ways—thus shaped the Ger-man understandings of available economic options. But German class con-flicts and political ideologies also influenced which alternatives were pre-ferred by businessmen, Social Democrats, and engineers. Divergent analyses of America both intensified and altered long-standing disagreements be-tween capital and labor about wage levels and state arbitration, and about the eight-hour day and state social policy. To give primacy to one or the other misses the complex ways in which Germans defined and redefined their visions of economic reform and social modernity according to their inter-pretation of economy and society, both at home and in America.

This chapter explores the debates on the American economic model and the possibilities of importing it. Its central concern is with the question that was of foremost importance to economic modernizers in Weimar—*could* Ger-many imitate America?. The two subsequent chapters will examine the equally troubling question—*should* Germany do so? These far-reaching debates reveal the different ways in which Germans tried to appropriate Americanism for their own economic and political ends.

The Secrets of American Economic Success

In 1925 Carl Köttgen published *Economic America*. This widely read work discussed the roots of American prosperity and modernity and offered an endorsement of the ideology of rationalization, along with a proposal for a particular and limited form of economic restructuring in Germany. Articu-lating the understandings and aspirations of German industry, Köttgen believed that natural resources and work intensity were central to America's economic superiority and emphasized America's incommensurability with Germany. While industrial circles applauded his work, Social Democrats, economic liberals, and engineers insisted that the similarities between Ger-many and America outweighed the differences. They offered varied expla-nations for American preeminence. This debate was conducted in the daily press, political and technical journals, company magazines, and popular books and pamphlets, as well as in the meeting rooms of major firms and economic organizations.

Everyone acknowledged that World War I and the ensuing economic disruption of Germany and Europe as a whole had been an enormous boon to America. Disagreement set in, however, about whether American superiority was temporary or permanent, and whether it was built on fortuitous contingencies or structural advantages. Everyone recognized that America was abundantly endowed with natural resources but disagreed about how much weight to give to nature as opposed to technology or markets, wages or prices. There were also such intangibles to consider as culture and national psyche. Should the secrets of American economic success—and hence the possibilities of German emulation—be discussed in terms of iron ore deposits and population density, wage rates and market size, machine output and the division of labor? Or did "the great problem of American technology and economy lie," as the engineer Paul Riebensahm maintained, "not in the 'big number,' or in numbers at all, but rather in many other things that lie between numbers and facts."[1] Our investigation of these issues must of necessity begin with *Economic America*, the opening salvo in the war of words about the American economic miracle.

When Köttgen traveled to America in 1925, he was at the pinnacle of his success and public visibility. He was the general director of the vast Siemens electrotechnical concern, the acting head of the RKW, and an activist in the VDI and in such organizations as the German Standards Committee and the Committee for Efficient Production. Köttgen combined expertise in technology and economics in a way that was unusual but greatly admired in Weimar engineering and industrial circles.[2]

Köttgen was born in 1871, the year the German Empire was founded, and his fortunes blossomed with those of the new state. An engineer by training, Köttgen studied both machine building and electrical engineering at the Technische Hochschule in Berlin, graduating in 1894. He began working immediately at Siemens and Halske, becoming a departmental director in 1897 and head clerk a year later. Siemens was one of Germany's two giant electrotechnical firms and was noted for its advanced technology, modern labor processes, and—at least in comparison to Ruhr heavy industry—less repressive and anti-Social Democratic labor policies.[3] Köttgen was most influential in developing technologies for applying electricity to heavy industry and making them profitable. He joined the board of directors of the new Siemens-Schukert work in 1905, and in 1907 became director of Siemens in England, a position he held until 1914, when he was interned for the duration of the war by the British government. In 1919 he returned to Berlin to lead the central administration of Siemens-Schuckert and became head of the board in 1921.[4] That same year, the RKW was established. Carl von Siemens, Köttgen's boss, was its honorary head, while Köttgen himself became acting director.[5] Köttgen thus represented the most technologically and organizationally advanced forces in German economic life. He was singularly open to receiving the American gospel of efficiency and profitability. He translated it into a German version of rationalization and preached it to all who would listen.

During his stay in America, Köttgen pursued many projects. He attended to the interests of the firm to which he devoted his life, concluding an agreement between Siemens and Westinghouse for the exchange of patents and information about production processes, and he toured all major Westinghouse plants. He shared these experiences only with Siemens' top management.[6]

The official purpose of his trip and the subject of his book was to explain why America had become the world's dominant economic power. Once an objective picture of the American economy was presented and certain basic and immutable laws of economic life were explained, he asserted, it would be possible "to carry into the widest circles of our population enlightenment about what is possible and achievable in our economic circumstances not only in terms of wage rates, but also in terms of the introduction of purely mechanical procedures."[7] Köttgen was equally interested in exploring the U.S. government's role in encouraging productivity, standardization, and the elimination of waste. Köttgen hoped that the American example would help the RKW and its industrial and engineering supporters to win greater political and financial support from the government.[8]

In discussing these issues, Köttgen avoided all anecdotal and personal comments; instead he bolstered his arguments with innumerable statistics, graphs, charts, economic equations, and photographs of factory interiors—all of which lent his book the desired aura of scientific seriousness, even if they did little to enhance its readability. Köttgen was careful not to appear to be the spokesman for Siemens or the electrotechnical sector; rather, he presented himself as the selfless champion of a universally benefical rationalization and as the disinterested representative of "the economy"—as German industrialists, with characteristic immodesty, thought of themselves.

The secrets of America's economic success, Köttgen argued, were its greater absolute production and greater productivity as well as its recognition that production determined consumption and wages. These, in turn, resulted from the beneficial interaction of natural advantages, extensive rationalization, and more intensive work. According to Köttgen, the average American man earned a real income that was 70 percent greater than his German counterpart.[9] Half of that was due to America's natural resources, above all its fertile soil for agriculture. Climate, soil, sheer size, and, to a lesser degree, mechanization and state-sponsored research had so increased agricultural productivity that only 29 percent of the American labor force worked in agriculture, as opposed to 43 percent in Germany. As a result, not only was food cheaper but more workers were available to produce other goods.[10] Coal and iron were also abundant and easily accessible, thereby lowering the costs of fuel and raw materials.[11]

For Köttgen these unique natural endowments gave the United States some permanent and inimitable advantages, but its prosperity was also due to rationalization in the forms of standardization, simplification, mass production, and mechanization. Köttgen detailed American innovation in appendixes devoted to the general principles of efficiency and to the specifics of production at Ford.[12] He was particularly impressed by how much more rationalized the American machine industry was than its German counterpart, attributing this difference to the war and postwar booms, combined with a larger market and "the natural preference of Americans for that which is uniform, standardized, the same model."[13]

Last, but certainly not least in Köttgen's eyes, America's economic superiority and greater per capita productivity derived from its more intense work pace and its longer workday. There was no "schematic" and state-imposed eight-hour day, no limitations on overtime, and no restrictions on firings. Of equal importance, he claimed that "it is second nature to everyone, even the humblest, that 'production per person' is decisive for the economy, that an increase in production per person benefits everyone."[14]

Although Köttgen's primary concern was production, he expressed admiration for the cafeteria, the chain store, and, above all, the 5-and-10-cent store. These he viewed as a product of rationalized manufacturing, rather than as a means of promoting domestic consumption and thereby encouraging industrial restructuring.[15] He was even more impressed by the government's "especially strong initiatives" to orchestrate the voluntary cooperation of industry, commerce, and consumers in the setting and implementing of norms and standards.[16] Not only did the U.S. Department of Commerce have a Bureau of Standards, but Herbert Hoover, when he was secretary of commerce, had established a Division of Simplified Practice and a Bureau of Specifications. Here was a clear cause of American superiority that was separable from its unique history and natural endowments.

Like most German industrialists, Köttgen did not first discover Germany's lagging productivity when he went to the United States. He had obsessed about it in a 1923 pamphlet entitled *Work* (a more appropriate title would have been *More Work*).[17] He blamed Germany's low postwar productivity on the Social Democrats, who had inspired government policies which regulated hours and dismissals, expanded the number of unproductive workers, and narrowed wage differentials so that the industrious were not adequately rewarded. Köttgen's solution was straightforward and simple: "more production through more intensive work." In a scathing attack on the Social Democrat Frieda Wünderlich, published in *Soziale Praxis*, Köttgen claimed that Germany was not technologically backward and that high wages would neither increase consumption nor enhance German competitiveness.[18]

After visiting America, Köttgen could not deny the painful shortcomings of German technology and factory organization or assert that work intensity alone would enhance productivity and profitability. He had to invent more complex arguments to justify denying or postponing wage increases in Germany. He sketched out the basic position from which industrialists were to argue for the remainder of the decade: per capita productivity was greater in America due to mass production, which, in turn, was made possible by large markets that resulted from the fortuitous conjuncture of size, low food costs—hence more disposable income—and a cultural preference for uniform goods. High wages were theoretically possible in Germany, but their practical realization in the foreseeable future was dismissed. The American experience showed the necessity of increasing productivity by intensified work, better organization, or perhaps even more mechanization, before wages and domestic consumption were raised.[19]

Köttgen envisioned a new economic role for the state. He combined continued attacks on the interventionist Social Democratic welfare state with pleas for state intervention to promote standardization and rationalization. Quite predictably, the former was described as imposing coercive policies, the latter, as encouraging voluntary "cooperative work." The former was class-based and economically counterproductive; the latter, universally beneficial and economically essential. For Köttgen, America both reenforced industry's traditional opposition to the emerging welfare state and suggested new forms of state activism that would aid industry but provide neither immediate benefits nor an active role for workers and their representatives.

When Köttgen returned from America, he became a tireless propagandist for these ideas. In addition to writing *Economic America*, which the VDI published, he spoke about his experiences before the RKW, the annual meeting of the National Association of German Industry (RDI), and the German World Economy Society. These lectures, as well as other articles, appeared in publications of the RDI and the German World Economy Society; in *Die Arbeitgeber*, journal of the Association of German Employers' Organisations (VDA); in the VDI's *Technik und Wirtschaft*; and in such daily papers as the *Deutsche Allgemeine Zeitung*.[20]

Given Köttgen's prominence, his promotional activities, as well as the support he was given by both Carl von Siemens and the Siemens firm, his book was widely reviewed.[21] Business circles received his message enthusiastically. At the 1925 meeting of the RDI, the association's business manager, Ludwig Kastl, echoed many of Köttgen's arguments about America. "In all areas and with all factors of production there is an effort to speed up and intensify the production process," he noted with unconcealed admiration. "There is happy cooperation in the completion and improvement of individual products."[22] An unnamed reviewer in the *Deutsche volkswirtschaftliche Correspondenz* endorsed Köttgen's views uncritically and used them to attack both Christian and Social Democratic trade unionists with a viciousness unparalled in Köttgen's own writings. He blamed Social Democrats for Germany's inflation, lack of capital, and uncompetitiveness. He stated that they "were not able to think economically and thus not able to act economically." They utterly failed to grasp the most important lesson of Köttgen's book, namely, that American wages were built upon greater productivity per worker, which in turn enabled America to rationalize so extensively.[23] Köttgen would no doubt have agreed with the substance of this argument, even if he preferred to speak from the high ground of science and leave the political thrust of his argument implicit.

Those in or close to the trade union movements—Christian and liberal as well as Social Democratic—found Köttgen's statistics questionable, his economic theory weak, his conclusions wrong, and his pessimism mis-placed. Several authors attacked Köttgen's arguments about American ag-riculture. If it was not the key to prosperity, productivity, and high wages, then Germany's less efficient agricultural production did not pose a per-manent obstacle to these goals, as Köttgen had implied. Dr. Hermann Lufft disputed Köttgen's statistics and accused him of using "methods over which he had insufficient command and which he applied purely mechanically and formally to reach conclusions that had eminently political meaning."[24] The liberal trade unionist and member of parliament Anton Erkelenz denied that American food was significantly cheaper, while the Catholic trade unionist Edmund Kleinschmitt dismissed the significance of agriculture in particular and natural resources in general in advanced industrial societies. The secret of American economic success, both insisted, was its superior technology, extensive mechanization, and superb factory organization, that is, factors that could be emulated.[25]

Social Democratic commentators marshaled a variety of arguments against Köttgen. The *Gewerkschafts-Zeitung* praised him for giving an accu-rate picture of the land, people, and economy in America and for detailing advances in mechanization and scientific management. But it criticized Köttgen for failing to grasp that American productivity and high wages were achieved through superior technology and factory organization, not through exploitation of the individual worker. Quoting Ford against Köttgen, the review concluded, "Everything can be made better than it previously was."[26] The SPD national daily, *Vorwärts*, stressed markets rather than tech-nological arguments: "The highest wages and the lowest prices strengthen buying power in America and expand consumption so that with the help of mass sales only in the domestic market, that mass production is devel-oped which enables America to be enormously competitive in the world market."[27]

Kurt Heinig, a functionary of the Foreman's Union, a radical turned revisionist, and a member of the 1925 trade union delegation to America, focused his scathing critique of Köttgen's book on the lamentable inferior-ity of German entrepreneurship vis-a-vis its American counterpart. He described *Economic America* as a hodgepodge of "business platitudes, . . . work maxims—for others—so-called economic principles, and illogical con-clusions." According to Heinig, Köttgen had seen America but had not understood how production was organized and management was chosen. He was living proof that "our entrepreneurs have declined markedly in quality over the last decade." Like other industrialists, Köttgen grasped only Taylorism and interpreted even that in the narrowest way. American entre-preneurs, Heinig argued, were a different breed entirely.

Heinig knew full well that American industrialists ranged from back-ward to modern, but he could not resist the temptation to develop an ideal type, based on Henry Ford, to use as a cudgel against German capitalists. Thus in Heinig's adulatory view, American industrialists across the board understood that economic success derived from Fordist mass production and consumption, and that the secret of Fordism, in turn, was the careful organization of production, with a minute division of labor and the mechanization of all transport within the factory. Fordism did not alter the fundamentals of capitalism, Heinig concluded, "but we would be content if our . . . entrepreneurs at least grasped Fordism, understood the domestic market and their responsibility toward it."[28]

Not surprisingly Köttgen brusquely rejected these criticisms; his assessment might be pessimistic, but so were the "economic facts."[29] He conceded only that his analysis paid too little attention to the high rate of capital formation in the United States. Germany could only accumulate comparable investment capital through "more intensive work."

Social Democratic trade unionists were not content to interpret America based only on the suspect analyses of conservative industrialists, liberal journalists, and apolitical engineers. America could only be understood if seen at first hand. Therefore in September of 1925 the General Confederation of German Trade Unions (ADGB) sent 14 leading functionaries to America. After attending the American Federation of Labor congress in Atlantic City, New Jersey, paying their respects at the grave of Samuel Gompers, the founder of the American trade union movement, and meeting with the U.S. secretary of labor, the trade unionists fanned out across the land. Displaying the organizational fetishism that was at once the strength and weakness of German Social Democracy, the delegation carefully divided research responsibilities. William Eggert and Franz Josef Furtwängler from the national executive traveled in the Northeast and Midwest, inspecting farms, factories, and oil fields in order to evaluate social conditions. Kurt Heinig was responsible for determining how the economy as a whole functioned. The representatives of the miners', garment workers', transport workers' and woodworkers' unions investigated their particular industries, while trade unionists from the food and beverage workers' organization explored the puzzling phenomenon of Prohibition. Finally, Fritz Tarnow studied the trade union movement and B. Meyer examined workers' banks. After two months of inspecting and interviewing, counting and categorizing, the delegation returned to Germany, where four of its members produced *The American Journey of German Trade Union Leaders*, a weighty tome on economy and society in America.[30]

Unlike such prewar trade unionists as Carl Legien, who visited America to learn about a less developed workers' movement, the 1925 delegates came to learn about a more successful form of capitalism. The trip and the book it engendered sought to elaborate a Social Democratic explanation for American economic success and to determine which practices the labor movement believed could and should be imitated. Of equal importance, the delegation promised to uncover the dark side of the American economic miracle.[31] Given that bourgeois observers either ignored the social and economic conditions in which the majority of workers lived or treated workers as the abstract embodiment of virtues deemed desirable by industry, one can readily understand this desire to expose the seamy side of American capitalism. Finally, responding to Köttgen, the trade unionists explored the relationship between work intensity and prosperity.[32]

Like those who had preceded them, the trade unionists were concerned first and foremost with American production and productivity. With admirable thoroughness, Heinig and Furtwängler weighed the evidence gathered about work intensity, factory organization, mechanization, standardization, sales, and wages. Industry by industry, Heinig made his case: the work pace was least intense in the most modern and productive sectors; the eight-hour day, even if far from universal, was more widespread than in Germany; and American machines did not, on the whole, run faster. American factories, especially the most modern ones, were guided by the "principle of the optimum—an attempt to get the greatest result from the least possible use of energy and material"—not by the Taylorist precept of maximum effort by the individual worker. Optimization was achieved through mechanization, but even better results were possible when the factory was organized to bring work, parts, and tools to the worker.[33] Instead of lowering their wage bill, American firms sought to cut costs in all other areas. They paid attention to Hoover's investigation of waste in industry, which pointed out deficiences and layed the blame on employers. The German trade unionists were astonished and envious that government would initiate such a study and that industry would cooperate. Perhaps, Heinig suggested, America might best be described of as a form of "state socialist private capitalism."[34]

According to the ADGB delegation, norms and standardization played an important role in American productivity, even if it was a different process from what most German observers claimed. According to the ADGB delegation, high output and low prices were not attained by manufacturing standardized goods, but rather by producing interchangable parts that could be used in many different models. American mass production was further aided by the size and volume of its markets as well as by the tastes of its immigrant populations. But these advantages were created rather than naturally given, for American industrialists operated according to the maxim, "sell a lot and sell quickly." Hence, they were able to lower prices.[35] More important, they paid high wages.

American wage rates, not only for skilled workers but for many unskilled ones as well, were roughly four times greater than German ones. Americans could buy more for their wages, since food and clothing were scarcely more expensive in absolute terms in America than in Germany and at times they were even cheaper.[36] To be sure, the trade unionists noted the existence of child labor and exploited women's work; they acknowledged the underclass of black and new immigrant workers; they admitted that one-third of American workers lived in poverty. But even the most impoverished workers seemed substantially better off than their German counterparts. The American poverty line was set well above the German one, and those below it spent only 40 percent of their income on food, as opposed to 55 percent in Germany.[37] Workers occupying the bottom rungs of the proletariat seldom remained there permanently, at least if they were of British or German origin, noted Furtwängler, ignoring the situation of blacks, immigrants from southern and eastern Europe, and women.[38]

According to the *The American Journey*, U.S. entrepreneurs viewed wage rates not just as "an object of social power struggles" but as a question of importance for the whole economy because they determined its prosperity. This attitude was "a revelation" to German trade unionists, leading them to conclude that "if the compulsion to pay high wages is there, this compulsion proves to be an irresistible force for rationalization and increasing productivity."[39]

In early chapters of *The American Journey*, the trade unionists stressed the enormous differences between Germany and America in size, population, raw materials, and productive capacity. Above all their economic histories differed. Germany was an "old cultural land," which had developed modern capitalism over hundreds of years, and many residues of previous economic systems survived intact. America, by contrast, "had no economic past, no centuries-old and fossilized forms that needed to be circumnavigated, blown up, pushed aside, and reformed. . . ." It had vast unsettled territories that could be developed by enterprising immigrants.[40] Both the material aspects of the American economy and the spirit animating it were "organic parts of a particular social formation," the trade unionists insisted, warning that "our domestic economy cannot be altered by mindless copying, by imitation of individual gears of the American productive machinery, or by innoculation with the American spirit."[41]

By the book's conclusion all such caution had been thrown to the wind. America was held up not only as a model for Germany's economic future, but as a textbook from which one could read the revised laws of capitalist development. America did not provide the impetus to criticize orthodox Marxism, for reformist Social Democrats had long questioned the theory that capitalist development would inevitably bring economic crisis, social polarization, and increased unemployment. But America did offer much more convincing proof than Germany's own history that Marx's theory of immiserization was wrong, that it was possible for workers to share in the benefits of increased productivity, even under capitalism, and that capitalism itself could be restructured.[42] If America was the quintessential late capitalist country, as Britain had been the paradigm of early capitalism, then depressing domestic developments were less important than encouraging American ones.

The most astonishing American accomplishment, concluded the report, lay not in technology or work organization but in consumption. Like every other industrialized country, America was experiencing rapidly expanding productive capacity, but only America understood how to expand domestic buying power. High wages, low prices, fast turnover, and low profit per piece combined to create a vast internal market, which in turn promoted "the wonders of technology and work organization."[43] Without pausing to assess whether Germany could follow suit, the trade unionists insisted that

"the central problem of the European economy is and will remain increasing mass purchasing power. . . . Thus it is completely clear that the trade
union struggle to increase wages is not only a social necessity but also a task
upon whose accomplishment the further development of the whole economy
depends."[44] Demand, and hence wages, were more important than supply,
and rationalization was a product of expanded consumption, not its pre-
cursor. The logic of successful capitalism was quite different from what
narrow-minded and self-defeating German entrepreneurs, such as Köttgen,
imagined. According to the trade union delegation, the farsighted and open-
minded American entrepreneur and not the industrious and selfless worker,
bore prime responsibility for American achievements.

A cautious and nuanced analysis of American society and economy had
given way to an uncritical endorsement of the American model of production and consumption. Both the productivism of Social Democratic theory
and the self-interest of the trade union membership encouraged this embrace
of the American model. But why were there so few reservations about the
extent of American accomplishments or the possibilities of German emulation? The answer probably lies in the timing of the trip. It was easy to pin-
point the failings of the American model but harder to convince a German
audience, for, as Toni Sender noted, "What a different life the American
scene presented in those years of prosperity, as compared with battletorn
and suffering Germany!"[45] Moreover, the trip was undertaken not only to
refute alternative analyses, but to shape concrete reform plans at a time when
all sides endorsed the necessity of rationalization. It would have been rhetorically ineffective and politically self-defeating for Social Democrats
to hedge their admiration with too many qualifications and conditions.
Better to translate their praise for America into a simple prescription for
Germany's economic ills.

The naïve optimism of the book's conclusion may well reflect more than
just a belief that America offered hope for an improved version of capitalism. According to Sender, if American capitalism could develop such productivity and prosperity, who knew what was possible under socialism. Far
from making socialism a superfluous idea, America "offers socialist hopes
the strongest confirmation."[46]

Needless to say, *The American Journey* was not well received by industrialists. Communists were also highly critical, claiming that it not only
glossed over poverty, exploitation, and inequitable wage rates, but also
denied the applicability of the laws of capitalist crises to America.[47] Some
liberal economic commentators, however, supported the Social Democratic
analysis of American economic success, even if they saw Americanism as a
way to eliminate the danger of socialism, rather than to hasten its arrival.[48]
Arthur Feiler denied that either natural resources or low wages explained
American productivity and competitiveness; rather, it was the size of the
domestic market, the prevalence of mass production, the extensive division
of labor, and the health of the workers.[49] Julius Hirsch developed similar
arguments in his widely read book, *The American Economic Miracle.* Al-

though abundant natural resources and vast size gave America some economic advantages, the real key to its prosperity was "a special organization of work in production and transportation that is built on a great shortage of workers, enormously high real wages, and buying power that is thereby strengthened."[50] The hallmarks of that organization of work, Hirsch concluded, included rationalization, standardization, and "the assembly line, which means simultaneously lower prices, higher wages, shorter hours, and increased production." It did not entail more intensive work.[51] No wonder his critics mistakenly labeled him a Social Democrat.[52]

Moritz J. Bonn, who traveled and taught extensively in the United States, was the most prolific liberal analyst, comparing Germany and America in numerous books and articles. He lambasted German entrepreneurs for clinging to medieval ideas of a just price and a fair return and for avoiding risk and competition. They needed to learn from capitalism in America, which "is not ethically better than in Germany," he wrote, "but is economically much smarter."[53] Capitalism could legitimate itself either through high wages or social welfare; America had chosen the former.[54] "American industry has understood that it can only produce if it can sell," Bonn argued, and therefore it promoted buying power and cultivated consumer loyalty. German heavy industry, in contrast, would prefer "an economy without customers."[55]

While Bonn's analysis was practically identical to that of the Social Democrats, he saw Americanism as an end in itself, as liberal capitalism at its best, with rationalized production, mass consumption, and no cartels. For Bonn, this represented an alternative not only to welfare state capitalism and socialism, but also to Köttgen's vision of an efficient but austere German economy.

Engineers, who were so central to the theory and practice of economic rationalization, traveled to America in great numbers and carved out a position in this complex debate that reflected their professional culture and concerns. While they produced few popular books, they did flood technical and economic journals, as well as the offices of their employers, with assessments of machines, factory organization, job structures, and management practices. They were unquestionably the most serious students and ardent admirers of American factories and were correspondingly critical of German deficiencies. Such engineers as Georg Schlesinger and Franz Westermann emphasized that in America the preparation of materials, the machines, and the transportation system within factories were all significantly better than in Germany.[56] Paul Riebensahm noted that Americans used machine tools in "new, practical, and inventive ways."[57]

In unpublished reports to their firms, engineers were equally unrestrained in their praise. Lilge, from Gutehoffnungshütte, attributed the "fabulous and enviable" American productivity not to more intensive work but to thoroughgoing mechanization.[58] After visiting 23 American factories, Maschinenfabrik Augsburg-Nürnberg Director Lauster confessed that "automated production gives a really high degree of quality and accuracy, which I had not imagined before seeing it." American firms had eliminated all unproductive work and unnecessary transport within the factory. Their machine tools and products were simply designed. Americans found German models "too complicated, too scientific, and in many cases too difficult to produce."[59] A study of American blast furnaces, commissioned by the Phoenix division of Vestag, praised the standardized preparation of materials, the simplicity and efficiency of the machinery and the high quality and uniformity of the product. Germans had everything to learn from the American example, the report concluded.[60]

Engineers offered divergent judgements of the American work pace, but even those who believed it was significantly greater than in Germany did not attribute American productivity and competitiveness to the work pace any more than they did to America's admittedly rich natural resources. For all their admiration of American mass production, engineers were singularly silent about its economic, as opposed to technological, aspects. They recognized that mass production lowered costs and increased sales, and unlike many Germans, they admired the uniformity and quality of standardized products. But they never explored whether high wages were essential for this modern form of capitalism.

The arguments of engineers began and ended with technology and factory organization, for this was what they knew best. The American factory offered concrete proof of what engineers could accomplish if they were properly valued, as German engineers felt their American counterparts were. Thus, while workers attributed American economic success to farsighted and daring entrepreneurs, and industrialists assigned responsibility to diligent and unpolitical workers, engineers credited their own profession.

These differing visions of the American economic model informed the quite different proposals for economic reform that were introduced in Germany in 1925 and 1926.

Americanizing Germany/Germanizing Americanism

Nearly every observer of the American scene, from the most enthusiastic to the most critical, warned against "wanting to make Europe into America," by a wholesale adoption of the American methods of production and consumption and a mindless cultivation of American values.[61] Slavish imitation was "not worthy of a great cultural people," admonished Siegfried Hartmann.[62] Fordism required certain economic prerequisites as well as a preference for mass production over quality work, warned Wilhelm Vershofen.[63] Germany needed to develop its men rather than its machines, for which it, in any case, lacked the necessary capital, insisted Karl Arnhold.[64] It must learn from America but avoid "the schematic transfer of externals, which have their roots in the different circumstances of the new world," wrote Bruno Birnbaum.[65] The ADGB delegation agreed and in a revealingly classless twist on a famous Marxist slogan, argued that "the liberation of the European economy from the chains of its backwardness can only be the work of Europe itself."[66]

Some German observers even predicted that America would become Europeanized, or at least face European problems. Moritz J. Bonn noted that America could no longer find markets by extending its frontier or allowing mass immigration.[67] Charlotte Lütkens was already convinced that America represented an early form of capitalism with immature social relations. Its prosperity derived from its extraordinary natural wealth, not from successful rationalization; late capitalist Europe had nothing to learn from across the sea.[68]

Most Germans, however, were convinced that America represented the future toward which Europe must of necessity aspire, at least in part. As Hirsch put it, "[T]he inner, immutable laws of development will lead inevitably to phenomena that are very similar to those which have led to such astonishing economic productivity in America." But they did not necessarily agree with him that the only question for Europe was "who will adapt most quickly."[69]

It was not only the long-term logic of capitalism, but also the immediate capitalist crisis in Germany that seemed to promote Americanism. Although industrialists, engineers, and trade unionists analyzed the crisis differently, they agreed that dramatic reforms were required to solve it. The American example could be used or abused; it could not be ignored. As A. Braunthal wrote in the *Gewerkschafts-Archiv*, "In view of the current economic situation, there can only be one opinion about the necessity of rationalization. The only question is what one means by rationalization."[70]

In the mid-1920s arguments about imitating America led to calls for rationalizing Germany. The shift in terminology from Americanism to rationalization is revealing and provides a starting point for exploring the varied reform plans of different groups.

"Rationalization is a new word, made in Germany," noted the German correspondent for the *Manchester Guardian*. "Nobody has yet succeeded in saying shortly what it means, but that it means something of importance is not open to doubt."[71] Therein lay the extraordinary appeal of this elusive term. Rationalization was a singularly capacious and elastic concept. It sounded appealingly modern, yet unlike "efficiency" or "Fordism," it was distinctly German. It offered the possibility of selecting individual aspects of American production, management, and sales without adopting Americanism or Fordism— however defined—in toto. It enabled Germans to speak a common language about some aspects of economic reform, while accommodating their incompatible ideas about others. In short, the term "rationalization" could at one and the same time incorporate, transcend, and Germanize various versions of Americanism. For example, Herbert Hinnenthal, who became business manager of the RKW in the late 1920s, argued that rationalization encompassed "everything that could serve to

restore equilibrium, regardless of whether it involves imitation of American models, adaption of American methods to German conditions, or independent German endeavors."[72]

To insist that rationalization should only mean technological and organizational change, for example, or only refer to the attainment of greater
output with the same or smaller input, might produce a succinct and elegant
argument, but it would gravely distort the contemporary discourse about
the term. It would miss the complex movement and the bitter conflicts that
developed around it and would fail to reveal why the sober term "rationalization" came to capture the imagination and encapsulate the hopes of so
many Weimar Germans.[73]

Central to the German idea of rationalization was the American idea
of efficiency, but efficiency, or *Wirtschaftlichkeit*, captured only the narrowest understanding of rationalization. A survey of definitions reveals a
consensus about economic means but not about the social and political ends
they should serve. The RKW defined rationalization as "the employment
of all means of technique and ordered plans which serve to elevate the whole
of industry and to increase production, lower its costs and improve its quality."[74] In a 1925 document entitled *German Economic and Financial Policy*,
the Association of German Industrialists stated, "By rationalization we
understand the reasonable employment of all technical and organizational
means in order to increase the productivity of human work as much as possible. All those employed in the production of goods must strive to improve,
increase, and cheapen production through the use of these means."[75] The
ADGB fired back a position paper on *The Present Tasks of the German
Economy*, which attacked most of industry's arguments but accepted much
of this definition of rationalization.[76]

There also was agreement about how to categorize the bewildering array
of rationalization strategies, advocated or employed. Technical and organizational rationalization encompassed changes most directly affecting production and the labor process on the shop floor. Commercial rationalization
covered both new methods of cost accounting and firm management and
new techniques of sales and service. Finally, human or social rationalization referred to personnel management, vocational testing and training, and
company social policy. Rationalization methods employed within the firm
and in the economy as a whole, it was acknowledged, were related and
interdependent yet different.[77]

Consensus about general definitions was achieved by circumventing
the economically central and politically divisive questions about precisely
which rationalization measures should be implemented, at whose expense,
and at which point in the processes of restructuring. Just how little the
shared commitment to efficiency and productivism meant in the face of
disagreement over such issues emerges clearly in the debates surrounding
technical and organizational rationalization, that is, about the Americanization of the production process itself.

A variety of disparate phenomena fell under the rubric of technical and organizational rationalization. There was the restructuring of firms and industrial sectors by the elimination of inefficient and backward factories and the concentration and integration of those that survived. There was the transformation of individual factories by mechanization or by the reorganization of the labor process with or without new technology. Such restructuring could take the form of flow production—that is, moving the raw materials or work pieces to the worker, who performed complex tasks—or it could take the form of the Fordist assembly line, staffed by semiskilled detail workers. Either innovation could affect an entire plant or selected parts. Finally, there was the standardization of work and product through time-and-motion studies and through industry-wide norms and interchangeable parts.

German industry evinced suprisingly little enthusiasm for technical and organizational rationalization in any of its forms. Far from wanting to modernize production and deskill workers, industrialist after industrialist insisted on the impossibility of introducing any but the most minimal innovations. To be sure, there was widespread approval, within industry and beyond, for concentration and integration, vertical and especially horizonal.[78] Industrial circles as well as engineering and trade union ones recognized that inflation had preserved innumerable inefficient and technologically backward production facilities which must be closed down.[79] This negative rationalization, as it was euphemistically labeled, had detrimental short-term consequences for capital and labor alike, but was regarded as unavoidable. Even the Miners' Union, which saw tens of thousands of its members laid off in the "closure mania" of 1925, insisted that the process was "in its fundamentals correct and necessary." In practice, however, it was unbearable because it was done solely for profit and without state aid to protect workers.[80]

Industry, however, viewed mechanization, flow production, the assembly line and standardization much more negatively, and considered full-scale Fordism to be utterly unrealizable. The RDI's *German Economic and Financial Policy*, written at a crucial early stage in the rationalization debate, summarized the views of leading industrialists. First, the source of Germany's current economic crisis, which purportedly threatened the very livelihood of the nation, was not its technological backwardness; rather, industry placed the blame squarely on the policies of left-leaning politicians and allegedly spendthrift bureaucrats. In tones of outrage, the RDI claimed that taxes and social welfare payments had increased from 14 percent of national income in 1913 to 25–30 percent in 1925—a burden it considered unacceptable. The cure for the economic crisis was not mechanization or reorganization but dramatic cuts in social welfare payments and taxes. The RDI policy statement mentioned rationalization only after every aspect of the state's tax, tariff, welfare, monetary, and credit policies had been criticized at length. The principal means recommended were concentration of production and cartels, with standardization and worker education mentioned in passing.[81]

Technical rationalization was not only of secondary importance; it was also prohibitively expensive. "The question of rationalization is first and foremost a question of money," insisted the RDI—a fact those who constantly referred to the American model failed to realize.[82] Germany had become an impoverished country, living austerely on the margin, noted many industrialists as well as some engineers. War, inflation, and reparations had destroyed the savings and profits that might otherwise have funded technological rationalization.[83]

Industrialists disagreed about whether rationalization by other means would eventually produce the capital necessary for extensive mechanization and reorganization. Köttgen, for example, left open the possibility that, at some unspecified point in the future, capital might be available for investment if—and this was central to industry's vision—in the present work was intensified, hours were lengthened, and wages were held down. In Köttgen's rationalization scenario—which groups such as the Employers' Association and the German Brown Coal Association in Halle, shared— more intensive work and stable or lower wages would increase productivity and lead to greater exports and higher profits, which in turn would provide capital for gradual investment in technological and organizational improvements. This would further enhance productivity, cut costs, increase profits, and lead, step by step, to further technical and organizational rationalization that eventually would lower prices and raise wages.[84]

Others regarded rationalized mass production as a threat to the essence of German economic success, which they defined as specialized quality products made by skilled workers. They argued that German quality work, especially German special-order finished goods, had an international reputation that should not be sacrificed in a futile attempt to compete with American mass production.[85] As C. F. von Siemens put it, "In the German economy there is a strong streak of individualism that has carried us forward and that must be maintained under all circumstances."[86] Germany's vast and prestigious machine tool industry was especially anxious to maintain its reputation for flexibility and excellence.[87] Moreover, according to a favorite right-wing slogan of the day, Germany was poor in capital and rich in men. Since labor was neither scarce nor as expensive as in America, it made no sense to replace men with machines.[88] On the contrary, industry should pay special attention to the "education of the next generation."[89] This plea to value men over machines was for some industrialists an excuse to avoid rationalization; for others it was a cover for intensified exploitation, or a key element in a program to create a new, more productive and politically conservative working class. In all cases it was used to explain why rationalization would look distinctly different in Germany.

Various engineers tried to persuade industry that quality and quantity are compatible, that the assembly line and mechanization produced cheap goods but not necessarily shoddy ones. Of equal importance, flexible, specialized production could be maintained while the advantages of standardization and mechanization were gained, if firms adhered to industry-wide norms, used interchangeable parts, and introduced flow production or the assembly line at certain stages of their production process.[90] Finally, Germans could significantly lower costs, even without American-scale, production runs, by adopting Fordist methods for keeping raw materials and work pieces steadily in motion, thereby eliminating unproductive time and work.[91]

These arguments fell on deaf ears. Some industrialists, such as Carl Köttgen, Robert Bosch, and Felix Deutsch of A.E.G., argued that the Fordist assembly line was applicable only to a limited number of products, such as bicycles, lamps, sewing machines, and watches.[92] Many argued that factories could introduce individual elements of Fordist production but would not attain anything like Ford's economic success unless they adopted his total system.[93] Few believed that was possible. Gutehoffnungshütte engineer Lilge summarized the prevailing view when he insisted that without a vastly expanded domestic market and the nearly universal adoption of norms and standardized parts, American technology would be costly and inefficient and mass production utterly unrealistic.[94]

Never was pessimism greater than when the automobile industry was discussed. While some trade unionists and economic analysts cited the Opel assembly line as proof of what was possible, such industrialists as Köttgen and Bosch, and engineering professors, such as Vershofen, insisted that Germany could not sustain a Fordized automobile industry.[95] Ernst Neuberg, director of the Deutsche Automobil-Construktionsgesellschaft, had nothing but praise for Henry Ford's successful battles on the economic field, comparing their importance to Waterloo and Sedan. Nonetheless, he argued that Germany lacked the markets and capital to imitate Ford and that German consumers and workers would reject Fordist innovations. The most German auto makers could learn from Ford was how to reduce inventories and speed materials through the plant.[96]

Industrialists supported Köttgen's proposal of an independent but state-funded agency to promote rationalization and produce norms and standards for industry and trade. Or, to be more precise, industry allowed itself to be mobilized behind this project by Köttgen and Siemens.[97] Industry viewed the proposed RKW much more favorably than other rationalization strategies first and foremost because it was cheap and easy. The cost would be borne primarily by the state, rather than the individual firm, and in the initial stages business was only asked to share information and endorse the principle of norms, not to restructure products and production processes. Moreover, norms were compatible with specialized products and limited markets; they did not necessarily entail standardized mass production. Finally, Köttgen's revamped RKW was built on the principle of voluntary collaboration among businessmen and engineers—"cooperative work" was the code word—and not on the practice of bureaucratic decision making and governmental compulsion.[98] The state would pay but not supervise; politicians and officials would participate, but in a distinctly subordinate role.

Some improvements in internal factory transportation and the adoption of certain norms—these were the meager recommendations for technical and organizational rationalization that German capitalists distilled from the glowing vision of speeding assembly lines, marvelous specialized machine tools, and stunning standardization in American factories. The representatives of industry blamed the poverty of their imagination and practice on forces beyond their control, such as "the extraordinary diversity of our production, the desperate lack of capital, and state imposed burdens."[99] They rebuffed the charge that industry itself was to blame for Germany's backwardness because it hid behind cartels, shunned technical innovation, clung to outmoded market strategies, and refused to take risks.[100] Industry thus quietly endorsed the theoretical desirability of technical and organizational rationalization, while loudly denying its practical feasibility.

This left the Social Democratic trade unions, and to a lesser extent their Christian and liberal counterparts, as the principal proponents of technical and organizational rationalization.[101] The DMV vigorously debated how far one could imitate American methods, but not whether one had to move in that direction.[102] The Miners' Union complained about the difficulties created by rationalization, given shrinking world markets and high unemployment in single-industry mining towns, but they directed their attack against the unregulated capitalist context in which rationalization was occurring, not against mechanization and reorganization per se.[103]

The situation was ironic indeed. Those least able to modernize the shop floor were most in favor of doing so. Those who risked the short-term loss of jobs and skills due to mechanization, flow production, and the assembly line insisted that it would bring tremendous benefits in the long run. Those most opposed to the power and prerogatives of capital claimed to understand both the laws of capitalism and the self-interest of capitalists better than the capitalists themselves.

The Social Democratic endorsement of rationalization, like the industialists' rejection of it, had complex roots. Trade union functionaries, party politicians, and large numbers of workers shared a fascination with technology, a commitment to productivism, and a belief that the dialectic of capitalist development would ultimately benefit workers most.[104] They prided themselves on not being Luddites.[105] Economic and technological developments were unfolding in only one direction, they insisted, and to oppose rationalization would be to "tilt at windmills."[106] Social Democrats could imagine rationalized capitalism as the basis of a reformist welfare state or as a building block of a socialist society; they could not imagining a better future that did not entail extensive rationalization.

The politics of productivity pushed Social Democrats in the same direction as these fundamental and often weakly articulated values. Social Democrats embraced rationalization in part because after 1923 capital had successfully abrogated the eight-hour day in several industries and was demanding still longer hours and more intensive work as the first step toward economic recovery.[107] Labor agreed that Germany needed to produce more at less cost if it was to become competitive abroad and prosperous at home, but, according to Richard Woldt, "the employers' demand for more productivity from human labor power was answered with the trade unions' counterdemand for more productivity from the material factors of production."[108] If industrialists modernized their factories, labor leaders argued, productivity would increase without Taylorist exploitation of the worker or elimination of the eight-hour day.

Labor and capital had struggled over the eight-hour day since its introduction by the government immediately after World War I. Industrialists produced innumerable statistics to prove that shorter hours decimated productivity, and labor predictably dismissed both the specific figures and the proposed correlation.[109] As with so many of the Weimar battles over productivity and profitability, the numbers were of questionable value and of secondary importance to the issues of principle that divided both sides. Industry regarded the eight-hour-day law as a violation of the prerogatives of manufacturers and the fundamental principles of capitalism, while labor considered it the prerequisite for a humane existence.[110] The introduction of the American model into the debate about hours neither lessened its intensity nor altered its basic parameters, but it enabled labor to circumvent tedious statistical battles and hold up a concrete example of the positive results of technical and organizational rationalization. Work was neither longer nor more intense, trade unionists stressed, even if the eight-hour day was not the officially mandated norm. Industry emphasized precisely the last point, depicting America as a land where the absence of state regulation of hours provided industry with the necessary flexibility to increase productivity. The American model thus failed to provide a resolution to the political debate on productivity, for industrialists and trade unionists understood both Americanism and Germany's crisis differently.

While trade union leaders acknowledged that the economic crisis of 1925–26 was the most severe in recent history, they did not believe it endangered the very basis of Germany's industrial economy, as the RDI claimed. Nor did they see it primarily as a crisis of production and investment; rather, according to the ADGB's *The Present Tasks of the German Economy*, Germany was experiencing "a serious disruption of the production process as a result of a disruption of circulation owing to the lack of buying power of the great mass of the population."[111] For Friedrich Olk the principal obstacle to recovery was not the multitude of politicians and bureaucrats who taxed and spent with abandon; it was the "intellectual attitude of German industrialists."[112] Manufacturers clung to particularism and family tradition; their mentality was almost guildlike, complained the Social Democrat Fritz König.[113] His Christian trade union counterpart, Joseph Jahn, concurred, lamenting that entrepreneurs had lost all sense of "developmental tendencies." Even firms with new buildings and machines did not "live up to modern criteria for technology, factory organization, and marketing."[114] In a speech to factory council delegates, G. Graf, head of the DMV economics school, dramatically proclaimed that "Entrepreneurs have failed. The proletariat must step in. On the basis of a careful analysis of the crisis, it must attempt to solve or moderate it."[115]

"Careful analysis" persuaded Social Democratic, Christian, and liberal trade unionists that the main manifestations of crisis were high prices and soaring unemployment, not high wages and shrinking export markets as industry claimed.[116] "Trade unions of all political persuasions have repeat-edly emphasized the importance of the domestic market," noted the ADGB. "Using the example of the United States, they have laid out the importance of high wages and the urgency of enlarging mass buying power."[117] Industry's program of austerity, exports, and intensified work would harm not only labor but capital as well, whereas a simultaneous restructuring of production and consumption would be mutually beneficial.[118]

High wages were central to this strategy. During Weimar, wage levels were a hotly contested issue, and they remain so among scholars of the period. There is little disagreement about nominal and real wage levels. Money wages reached their pre–World War I level in 1925; real wages only passed the 1913 mark in 1928.[119] Wages as a percentage of costs were much lower in Germany than in America. Otto Moog cited 18 and 32 percent, respectively.[120] Controversy, then and now, involves whether wage levels were objectively too high in relation to productivity, thereby crippling economic growth and restructuring.[121]

Trade unionists never questioned the feasibility and desirability of high wages. Raising wages, they insisted, was an act of economic policy and not just social policy.[122] Although they sometimes justified high wages as com-pensation for the rigors of rationalized work, they generally downplayed the detrimental aspects of rationalization.[123] They appealed, instead, to the laws of advanced capitalism and the interests of society as a whole—which happily coincided with those of the working class. Modern industrial econo-mies were driven by demand, not supply. Germany was experiencing a cri-sis of underconsumption, not underproduction, because high costs, high prices, low wages, and the destruction of middle-class savings during the inflation limited the domestic market and made industry uncompetitive in world trade. American capitalists, like Ford and Filene, had shown the cure for this distinctly modern economic illness. By raising the wages of blue- and white-collar workers, they increased buying power to correspond to expanded productive capacity. Only adequate consumption could restore profitability and full employment and raise the standard of living.[124] There-fore, argued the Christian trade union journal *Deutsche Arbeit*, it was "the duty" of trade unionists to pursue "an active wage policy."[125]

Germany was indeed uncompetitive, acknowledged Social Democrats like Eugen Prager, but this was due to technological and organizational back-wardness, not high wages.[126] As the American model showed, high wages would cure, not compound, that problem. According to Edmund Klein-schmitt, labor shortages in America led to high wages, which in turn forced industrialists to increase productivity by rationalization. In Germany, trade unions must create the same impetus toward rationalization by demanding high wages.[127] Social Democrats endorsed the view that high wages would translate into high demand and high profits, from which the necessary capital for technical and organizational restructuring would be derived. The newly rationalized factories would produce at lower costs, sell at lower prices, and thereby increase real wages still further, fueling another round of modernization and enhanced prosperity.[128]

While these views found support from liberal economists like Julius Hirsch and Bruno Rauecker, and from idiosyncratic conservatives, such as Theodor Lüddecke, they were flatly rejected by industry.[129] Until 1924 industry claimed that wage hikes fueled inflation; thereafter, that they hurt productivity and competitiveness.[130] Although the RDI acknowledged that real wages were lower than before the war, it fought attempts to raise them to that level, let alone to that of the United States. Although industry constantly compared Weimar productivity, taxes, and welfare costs to their prewar levels, it insisted that prewar wages could not be taken as a norm, for "today we have a different economic basis, that cannot be compared to the living and production conditions of the year 1913."[131] It was necessary to increase productivity, lower costs, and cut prices first, argued Ludwig Kastl, before real wages could be raised.[132]

Although it was theoretically feasible to increase consumption by lowering prices, trade unionists doubted the efficacy of this strategy, for it was based on too many improbable assumptions. First, industry would have to cut costs by technical and organizational rationalization—which unions doubted would happen without the prod of higher wages. Then industry would have to translate lower costs into lower prices—which it showed little desire to do, and which the government could encourage but not enforce.[133] Finally, industry would have to keep wages stable or raise them, instead of lowering nominal wages and perpetuating underconsumption.[134]

For leftists and liberal economists alike, the highly cartelized nature of German industry was the principal obstacle to lower prices. In all sectors of German manufacturing, individual firms banded together in organizations that allocated production quotas, set prices, and in some cases actually marketed products. Although the RDI claimed that such cartels stabilized prices without blocking modernization, economists like Moritz J. Bonn maintained that "by their essential nature cartels are hostile to rationalization."[135] According to the DMV, cartels protected inefficient firms, discouraged rationalization, and caused high prices that both limited exports and restricted the domestic market.[136] Lacking the economic and political power to weaken cartels, trade unions saw little choice but to fight underconsumption from the wage side rather than the price side.

The trade unions' advocacy of high wages was tied to their assessment of the world market in the 1920s. Labor and capital both recognized that German foreign trade was suffering, not only from high German production costs but also from shrinking world trade. This decline, in turn, resulted from the increased capacity of industrialized countries—especially the United States, the industrialization of new countries during and after

World War I, and the more limited ability of other European countries to absorb imports.[137] But a shared diagnosis of the ailment did not lead to a common prescription for a cure. For Social Democratic, Christian, and liberal trade unionists, expanding the domestic market, both absolutely and in relation to exports, was not only desirable but essential, for even if exports could be increased substantially, they would not utilize all of the expanded productive capacity of Germany's rationalized industries. German manufacturers did not need to abandon exports, but they had to realize the potential of domestic markets, as American capitalists had done.[138]

Trade union leaders downplayed the obstacles to mass consumption. Germany was not America, Edmund Kleinschmitt admitted, but it had a relatively large and dense population.[139] Germany was facing labor shortages and double-income families, Julius Hirsch pointed out, and this would increase income for mass consumption.[140] It was unlikely that Germany would develop a mass market for cars, predicted Otto Meibes, a contemporary analyst of the automobile industry, but if costs and prices were lowered it could develop one for motorcycles.[141] The metalworker Fritz Kummer, who had worked in the United States, offered an even more optimistic prognosis: If a single large auto firm was created from the multiplicity of existing ones, and if it consolidated, specialized, standardized, and rationalized production, costs would drop dramatically. If wages were raised, a mass market for cars would develop.[142] In short, future prosperity could be achieved not by competing in the shrinking and increasingly competitive European or world markets, but at home.

Industry remained unconvinced. According to Siemens, the economic and cultural obstacles to mass domestic markets of the American type were enormous.[143] The Association of German Employers' Organisations paid lip service to the necessity of raising domestic buying power, claiming that the home market was central to the future "of the German people, German culture, yes, even the German state." But it quickly added that the domestic market could only be developed if exports were increased, capital was accumulated,and factories were rationalized.[144]

These debates had a frustratingly abstract quality. Trade unionists rarely discussed what should be produced and consumed in a reoriented German economy. They understood the necessity for mass consumption in a rationalized economy, but not the necessity for a new type of mass produced good, namely consumer durables. Even Fritz Kummer, who painted a rosy picture of a Fordized German automobile industry, was extremely vague about who would be able to afford one. Social Democrats concentrated on countering industry's continued emphasis on exports rather then detailing the economic order they desired. Industry recognized the new problems of world trade but sought to solve them with old production and marketing strategies. Observers one step removed from the political fray were no more successful at discussing Germany's market crisis concretely. Birnbaum anguished that "for Germany the problem lies in reconciling the unconditional necessity of stimulating the domestic market . . . and the need for exports to be more competitive."[145] Minister of Economics Neuhaus merely made a general plea for more domestic consumption and more exports.[146]

Leading Social Democrats denied that their commitment to rationaliza-tion meant they had abandoned the class struggle. Rudolf Hilferding, Fritz Naphtali, and other movement theorists insisted that a primary task of Social Democracy was to bring a modernized, integrated, and rationalized economy under the control of a democratic state. Political democracy must be aug-mented by economic democracy.[147] At the same time, stated the ADGB leadership, "we also believe that, for the solution of various economic, finan-cial, and political problems, a joint effort by all parties is worthwhile, with the object of overcoming the present crisis and developing the productive capacity of German industry."[148] For Social Democrats, rationalization thus provided another possible arena for the kind of collaboration with industry and the state that had been tried—admittedly with little success—during World War I and with the Arbeitsgemeinschaften after the war.[149] Ratio-nalization had the additional advantage of being compatible with the re-formist program of welfare state capitalism as well as with the aspirations of those who advocated economic democracy and eventual socialism.

Communists attacked both the Social Democratic leadership's commit-ment to rationalization and its advocacy of cooperation with industry. Sounding rather like their capitalist enemies, Hilda Weiss and Alexander Friedrich accused the Social Democrats of failing to understand just how serious the current crisis was.[150] Rationalization represented a futile attempt to compensate for the decline of German capitalism and imperialism.[151] While few of the technical and organizational measures employed were new, they were being introduced at an intensified pace, creating long-term structural unemployment.[152] The reformist trade unionists failed to realize that capi-talist industry desired such unemployment and, in any case, was powerless to eliminate it, as shown by the English experience—which Communists considered more relevant than the American one.[153] Capital would, indeed must, implement its program of longer hours, lower wages, plant closings, and exports. Social Democratic wage theory was based on illusions that were belied by the laws of capitalism and the interests of capitalists.[154]

Whether the KPD had a more accurate analysis of the economic crisis than did the SPD is open to debate. Certainly it better understood the multiple reasons why capital did not want to—and in the short run did not have to—follow the Social Democratic program for consumption-oriented rationalization. But the well-founded pessimism of its analysis did nothing to compensate for the powerlessness of the movement or the poverty of its program. In the era of rationalization and relative stabilization that began in 1924, the Communists were on the margins not only of mainstream poli-tics but of working-class life as well. Party membership dropped, union strength declined, and unemployment, due in part to rationalization, took a devastating toll.[155] Both theory and personal experience led Communists to insist that trade unions should not promote rationalization, for that was the responsibility of industry alone. But they were equally convinced that

the class struggle should not be directed to oppose it, because the modernization of production was inevitable and would promote the interests of labor
in the long run. The shared productivism and technological determinism of
the Second and Third Internationals led to a shared inability to imagine any
forms of production other than highly rationalized ones.

The KPD's neither-endorse-nor-oppose stance was necessary but weak,
acknowledged August Enderle, a Communist trade union expert and member of the DMV.[156] The Social Democratic trade union program of Fordism,
mass consumption, and economic democracy was sowing confusion not only
in its own ranks but among Communists and the unorganized as well. Communists might deny that all was well for American workers, but they had
developed no serious Marxist analysis of that nation's economy.[157] In the
short run, all Enderle could prescribe was a struggle for higher wages and
shorter hours, while waiting for the capitalist crisis to intensify.[158] But this
was identical to the strategy of Social Democratic and Christian trade unionists. They did not differ in their short-term demands but in their views on
whether capitalist recovery was possible and whether workers might gain
anything from it.

The Communists' attitude toward rationalization, like that of reformist trade unionists, engineers, and industrialists, was shaped by their analyses
of Germany's failures and America's successes, by prior theories, and by
the ability or inability of Fordism to modify or refute them. After 1926 all
parties would debate rationalization primarily in terms of practices within
Germany rather than the promise of the American model, however construed. Before turning to those practices, however, we need to explore the
debates on the possible social and cultural consequences of Americanism
on and off the shopfloor, for the forms of rationalization that were implemented were shaped not only by what was considered possible, but by what
was considered desirable in political, social, and cultural as well as in purely
economic terms.

5

Work, Workers, and
the Workplace
in America

Fordism claimed to have transformed the nature of work as well as workers' reactions to it, and Germans took that claim seriously. They saw mechanization, flow production, the assembly line, and Taylorism not merely as technological improvements with economic consequences, but also as social innovations with psychological and political implications. This restructured system of work raised old questions about exploitation, job satisfaction, and occupational identities and cultures but expressed in new ways. It cast doubts on the future of German quality work and the German skilled worker, and it raised the problematic issue of whether work shaped the worker or had to be shaped to the cultural and political peculiarities of a given nation.

German concern with the Americanization of work focused on a set of interrelated themes. The links between rationalization and deskilling, between mechanization and quality—of both the product and the producer—were of key importance in a country that industry and labor alike defined in terms of German quality work. The issues of work intensity, monotony, and job satisfaction—or "joy in work," to borrow the elusive but ubiquitous concept—were central to German debates on the crisis of work which many believed afflicted Weimar Germany. Did most workers want mindless detail work, as Ford repeatedly asserted?[1] Or were their desires for meaningful tasks and work-centered identities thwarted by technology and flow production?

Germans were fascinated by industrial relations on the American shop floor. And well they should be, according to Paul Riebensahm, for Americans had "a good nose for what lies beyond material, machines, and accounting."[2] Whether or not Germans approved of the seeming harmony of the shop floor and impotence of American trade unions, they were puzzled by their very existence in advanced capitalism. Did Fordism inevitably depoliticize workers or were American industrial relations a product of that country's peculiar history? Would the rationalized semiskilled worker retain any commitment to the firm? Could class conflict be subdued inside the factory without mass consumption outside?

The debates within Weimar Germany on work, workers, and industrial relations were shaped not only by the political and social position of different observers and the situations they encountered in America, but also by the German science of work. *Arbeitswissenschaft* was a multifaceted interdisciplinary field devoted to analyzing and improving all aspects of work. Its principal branches—psychotechnics and industrial sociology—helped create a common discourse about work among Weimar engineers, industrialists, academics, and even trade unionists.[3] They set the agenda of topics to be investigated: fatigue and job satisfaction, aptitude testing and vocational education, and company social policy for workers and their families. They contributed the terms that informed the debates and gave them their distinctly German quality: *entgeistete* or *entseelte Arbeit* (despiritualized work); *Betriebsgemeinschaft* or *Werksgemeinschaft* (the factory community); *Menschenwirtschaft* (human economy); and *menschliche Rationalisierung* (human rationalization).

Although first established in the late nineteenth century, the science of work gained significant influence in industry and universities only in the 1920s.[4] It both promoted and benefited from the pervasive belief that attention to "humans as a factor of production" was a prerequisite for economic success.[5] For some, the science of work offered a solution to the "crisis of work," which was attributed to the meaninglessness of work and the alienation of workers, and had predictably detrimental effects on productivity and industrial relations.[6] While conservatives hoped that psychotechnics and industrial sociology would promote their political and economic goals, those on the left sought to mobilize the science of work for the protection of workers and the promotion of social reform. America featured prominently in both visions.

Quality Work and the Quality Worker

For Germans, Fordism conjured up images not only of mass production but also of untrained, unskilled workers, endlessly repeating the same minute motion on an assembly line.[7] However privileged the Ford worker was in terms of pay, he was seen as no different from most American workers in terms of training and skill or the lack thereof. As many observers noted, America suffered from a chronic shortage of workers, especially skilled ones, which made it necessary and profitable for industry to substitute machines for men. Most Germans overemphasized the extent to which technology had replaced both skilled and crude manual labor, for they read primarily about Detroit and traveled only to the most technologically advanced American factories. Despite this, many questioned whether ruthless deskilling was an inevitable component of economic modernization. They sought to defend the quality worker, so necessary for the production of "German quality work," even as they strove to increase his efficiency.[8]

Far from championing efforts to replace skilled workers with a few engineers and large numbers of semi-skilled workers, industrialists disputed any necessary correlation between rationalization and deskilling. They associated deskilling specifically with the assembly line, and as we saw, such prominent business leaders as Carl Köttgen, Robert Bosch, and Felix Deutsch insisted that the assembly line had very limited applicability in Germany.[9] German industrialists were reluctant to attack the power and prerogatives of skilled workers because many firms produced specialized goods for export markets, rather than mass products for domestic consumption. Moreover, they claimed to lack the investment capital for massive retooling, and they were in any case convinced that workers, not technology, held the key to productivity. They argued that mechanization would affect primarily the unskilled workers who had hauled and lifted what was now to be mechanically transported. It might displace some skills, but it would create new, perhaps even more challenging ones.[10] Skilled workers would have to work in a more intensive and specialized way; they would be subject to more control and expected to be more disciplined. Although their proud craft traditions would likely be undermined, they would not be pushed into the ranks of the semiskilled or unskilled.

Industrial sociologists, engineers, and vocational educators made similar arguments. At a 1924 meeting of the RKW, for example, Professor E. Toussaint asserted that, in the machine industry, skilled workers were being shifted to new jobs rather than eliminated, for many new machines were so complicated that they could only be effectively operated by skilled workers, whereas simpler machines had been manned by the semiskilled. While Ford strove to train the unskilled as quickly as possible to fill repetitive assembly line jobs, claimed Professor Conrad Matschoss, head of VDI, Germany must focus on the education of "quality workers."[11] In her study of apprenticeship, Hella Schmedes asserted that the German iron and steel industry would never use as few skilled workers as its American counterpart (which actually used more skilled workers than the Germans realized), because it produced for more specialized sectors of the market. Such industries as machine tools relied very heavily on skilled workers. Some workers were the traditional type who manipulated a tool, while others served a complex machine or coordinated the work of machines and that of less skilled workers, but all categories were on the increase in a rationalizing economy.[12] Vocational educator Erna Barschak insisted that skill would remain central "for the quality branches on which the economic prestige of Germany rests."[13]

Displaying a surprising complacency about the future of their largely skilled membership, free trade union leaders did not dissent from these views. The rank and file of such unions as the metalworkers feared that the dequalification and feminization of work would accompany rationalization.[14] Some analysts argued that industry was hiring women for rationalized work not only because "women were without doubt very suited for mass production," while men were not, but also to cut wage costs.[15] In general, however, spokespersons for blue-collar trade unions played down the danger of feminization.[16] The labor economist Wladimir Woytinsky, for example, saw it as primarily a white-collar phenomenon, noting that female employment in industry had declined from 24.1 percent in the 1907 occupational census to 23.7 percent in the 1925 census, while among white-collar workers (*Angestellten*) it had increased from 16.2 to 26.8 percent.[17] Deskilling, without feminization, received equally little trade union attention. Otto Richter attributed America's far-reaching mechanization and deskilling of labor to its lack of skilled workers rather than the immutable laws of capitalist development.[18] The engineer Max Hedel admitted that unskilled men and even women could operate new machines, but he assured metalworkers that

> he who is diligent in the trade which he has laboriously learned need not feel uneasy because of this. There are still so infinitely many opportunities in machine building for the "skilled worker" to prove his occupational abilities that he should really welcome the fact that he is freed from the production of "mass goods," and can shift the responsibility for this work onto the "semiskilled worker."[19]

While such facile optimism was rare, few trade union analysts saw deskilling as the major threat posed by rationalization. There were several reasons for this. It was extraordinarily difficult to determine at any stage of the rationalization process which craft workers were losing or gaining skills and whether the losses of the skilled were balanced by gains for the semiskilled and unskilled.[20] Of equal importance, such dangers as work intensity, monotony, and lack of employment for all skill levels seemed more pressing. Finally, trade unionists and industrialists alike shared a commitment to "German quality work," that seemed to form a bulwark against massive deskilling.

"German quality work" was one of the most deceptively straightforward slogans bandied about in the rationalization debate of the 1920s. The criteria for quality were clear cut and widely shared. At the 1927 annual meeting of the RDI, devoted to the theme of "German quality work," the association's business manager Ludwig Kastl defined quality work as "the production of a good or the performance of a service which satisfies the highest demands of consumers of all sorts and especially fulfills all requirements in regard to suitability, reliability, utility, and cost as well as taste and form."[21] Far from disagreeing with this definition, the *Gewerkschafts-Zeitung* claimed that free trade union leader Theodor Leipart had originated it years before. "By quality work," Leipart wrote in a 1916 article, "should be understood good, respectable, functional work. The materials employed and the technical execution should be good as well as the form and color. The form must correspond to the purpose and materials."[22] In fact, the term similarly defined was widely used by the architects, educators and politicians of the Werkbund in the prewar debates concerning functionalism, economics, and aesthetics in manufacturing.[23]

There was agreement that no single group or factor could claim sole credit for quality work. Hans Kraemer, business executive and member of the National Economic Council, explained that it resulted from "the excellence of factory installations, the intelligence and knowledge of firm leaders, and the skill, training, and diligence of workers, [which] are not surpassed by any people in the world."[24] Most industrialists were reluctant to celebrate the quality worker—that is, one who possessed thorough training, manual dexterity, technical knowledge, judgment, and experience— even if they were unwilling to mechanize skilled workers out of existence.[25] In his 1927 speech to the RDI, for example, Ludwig Kastl detailed all possible fiscal, monetary, trade, and social policy prerequisites for the success of German quality work, but scarcely mentioned the training and character of the workforce.[26] Industrial sociologists and psychologists and Social Democratic and Christian trade union leaders, however, sang the praises of the German quality worker. The left-wing journalist Toni Sender opposed importing American methods of mass production, arguing that Germany's wealth was its "well-educated, highly qualified workforce," whose products would win markets.[27] The right-wing engineer and vocational educator Karl Arnold took the same position.[28]

Quality work was a most appealing slogan. It distinguished Germany— and Europe more generally—from America.[29] It seemed to provide a way to speak the modern language of rationalization with German accents, to promise economic recovery by a special German path.[30] Quality work was viewed as central to the success of large, integrated firms and to the survival of small and medium-sized ones.[31] The concept of quality work honored manual labor, appealed to the desire for an aestheticization of industrial production—and implied an ill-defined but uplifting national project built on interclass cooperation.[32]

As was often the case, unanimity at the level of general definitions masked deep disagreements. These concerned the prerequisites for quality work, the forms of production and marketing with which it was compatible, and the broader sociopolitical order to which it would lead. For the RDI, the prerequisites for the success of German quality work were identical to those it had outlined for economic recovery in 1925—lower taxes, decreased government spending, reduced social insurance and social welfare programs, flexible and longer hours, and defense of cartels.[33] For the unions, the worker was key to producing quality work, and the way to produce quality workers was through extensive social welfare programs, improved vocational training, and active worker participation in shaping the production process and economic policy.[34] Labor and capital, in short, insisted that the specific shared goal of quality work could only be realized in the context of macroeconomic and political programs that contradicted one another on every point.

Despite agreement that quality did not mean luxury, there was much dissention about the specific relationship of quality to quantity. Academic commentators, such as Wilhelm Vershofen, argued that quality work and mass production were antithetical, but most engineers agreed with Paul Riebensahm that standards, norms, interchangeable parts, reduced types and even the assembly line were compatible with high quality.[35] While most industrialists rejected full-scale Fordist production, many acknowledged that the challenge was to combine quality and quantity. Hans Kraemer predicted that "with rationalization, norms, and standardization the price of good products will be scarcely higher than for bad ones. . . ."[36]

Social Democrats rarely tried to reconcile their desire for mass production and their defense of quality work, tending instead to discuss the former in relation to higher wages and increased consumption, and the latter in connection with workers' rights and vocational education. Occasionally they argued that the increasingly cultivated tastes of the broad mass of consumers would lead to a growing demand for quality goods.[37] Overall, their discussions about quality work, like those about mass consumption, were conducted in a frustratingly abstract manner. The producers emerged clearly, but not the specific goods that were to be produced and consumed. Labor was adamant, however, that quality work should be for domestic consumption as well as export, whereas industry saw it almost exclusively as a vehicle for winning foreign markets.

The concept of "quality work" was compatible not only with different short-run economic strategies but also with diverse long-term reform visions. Right-wing engineers and industrial sociologists made quality work a central element in their efforts to transform society by restructuring the firm and the labor force. After 1933, the Nazis used quality work as a slogan in their efforts to win labor support and integrate workers rhetorically into the _Volksgemeinschaft_.[38] On the left, such Social Democrats as Karl Zwing argued that German industry required ever more qualified workers, and thus would have to grant them greater rights. "Economic democracy is a necessary result of the increased demand for quality work," he concluded.[39] For Zwing and other Social Democrats, economic democracy was both a restructured form of capitalism and a significant step toward socialism, and it was expected to flow inevitably from economic developments. Such deterministic thinking and naïve confidence in the beneficial effects of transformations in the labor process go far toward explaining the casual and confident way in which Social Democrats regarded work in a rationalized economy.

Many advocates of quality work worried less about the elimination of skilled workers than whether there would be enough of them.[40] In the mid-1920s the RKW, industry, and officials of the state labor offices all fretted about an impending "lack of skilled workers." At first glance this preoccupation seems puzzling, for in the early and mid-1920s there were consistently more adolescents seeking apprenticeships than there were positions available.[41] In light of the high unemployment that accompanied the stabilization crisis of 1924, the rationalization crisis of 1925–26, and the depression that began in 1929, their fears seem to have been wildly misplaced. On closer inspection, however, they reflected concrete problems and legitimate worries.

Some fears were based on demographic changes. World War I had taken a toll on skilled workers, although those in essential war-related industries had often secured exemption from military service. Of greater importance, the birth rate had dropped significantly during the war, limiting the number of adolescents who would be entering the labor market from 1929 to 1935.[42] Other concerns were economic. Industrialists, who ascribed only the narrowest monetary motives to workers' career choices, worried that declining wage differentials between skilled and semiskilled workers would discourage youth from serving apprenticeships.[43] Trade unionists insisted that job insecurity and mistreatment by employers discouraged skilled workers from moving to available jobs.[44] Another area of concern was the quantity and quality of training programs. Despite the demand for skills training, apprenticeships were in short supply, complained Hildegard Böhme in 1924, and industry was responsible.[45] Rationalization would only compound the problem, for workers would need to have factory-specific skills and an understanding of their technological basis on the one hand and be able to adjust to rapidly changing production processes on the other.[46] "Adaptability and intensive occupational knowledge" was Hella Schmedes' succinct summary of the new requirements.[47]

The preferred means for defending quality work and assuring an adequate supply of skilled workers were aptitude testing, vocational advising, and apprenticeship training. Aptitude testing had been part of psychotechnics before 1914, but it was not practiced on a large scale until World War I, when the Kaiser Wilhelm Institute for Labor Physiology tested draftees for their suitability as drivers, pilots, and railroad engineers.[48] In the 1920s aptitude testing and psychotechnics gained broader legitimacy.[49] The Berlin Institute for Psychotechnics, founded by Georg Schlesinger and directed by Walter Moede, and William Stern and Otto Lipmann's Institute for Applied Psychology, as well as individual firms, refined aptitude tests. State labor offices and factories, especially in the machine making and metalworking branches, regularly administered them to job seekers.[50]

Many Germans had high expectations of aptitude testing.[51] Industry hoped to increase quality work and productivity by selecting the "proper" workers. Industrial psychologists, sociologists, and physiologists anticipated an improvement in job satisfaction and industrial relations as well as a decline in fatigue and injuries.[52] For Christian trade union spokesperson Clara Mleinek, testing and advising were important because "the occupation is the basis for the economic existence of men. . . . A failed occupation usually also means a failed life."[53] SPD Reichstag member Heinrich Jäcker saw testing and advising as necessary to prevent unemployment and produce the quality workers Germany needed to compete in the world economy.[54]

More critical trade unionists objected that most aptitude tests were run by and for private industry, while most public and private vocational counselors were poorly trained. Nonetheless, they believed that psycho-technics was an inevitable part of the current stage of capitalist develop-ment. Citing Kurt Lewin's 1920 book on *The Socialization of the Taylor System*, they urged trade unions and factory councils to become involved in shaping testing and advising, instead of rejecting them.[55] Many were convinced that genuinely scientific tests could determine physical and mental aptitudes as well as interests and deep drives.[56] Social Democrats and industrial sociologists and psychologists shared a broad vision of an ordered world in which workers would be rationally slotted into positions for which they were mentally and physically suited, even though they dis-agreed over the rights and responsibilities such workers should have.

It was not enough to test and advise; one had to train as well. Here America, with its multitudes of unskilled and semiskilled workers who learned their jobs quickly on the shop floor, offered little guidance.[57] If Germany was to combine rationalization and quality work, it would have to pioneer its own forms of training, as industrialists, trade unionists, engi-neers, and vocational educators recognized. Before World War I, the vast majority of skilled workers had served apprenticeships in *Handwerk*, that is, in small, technologically backward shops and firms, while the remainder were trained in loosely structured factory apprenticeships.[58] By the mid-1920s most engineers, vocational educators, and industrialists no longer considered this system adequate to impart skills and broad technical knowl-edge.[59] Some carried their critique further, claiming that apprenticeships failed to inculcate joy in work or loyalty to the firm.[60] Unions anticipated that improved skills training would "make the worker not only more pro-ductive but also more self-confident and more demanding."[61]

Industry, labor, and those involved in vocational education wanted apprenticeships to be moved into the factory and technical training to be upgraded. But there agreement ended, for vocational training raised divi-sive political questions. Was apprenticeship primarily a wage relationship or a pedagogical one? Should mandatory, part-time, adolescent education be controlled by the state or the firm? Should programs focus only on tech-nical training or also, offer general moral and political education?[62] When Americanism, Fordism, and economic reform were first debated, however, these disagreements were overshadowed by the pervasive belief that voca-tional testing, advising, and education would be central to a rationalized German economy.[63]

Intensity and Monotony

Although Germans of the most varied social and political backgrounds were remarkably optimistic about the future of quality work and the skilled worker, they recognized that rationalization would demand more special-ized, factory-specific skills, while also creating a growing number of semiskilled and unskilled positions. Worried that monotony and fatigue would result, trade unionists and industrial sociologists and psychologists scrutinized American factories, queried American workers, and studied the reports of American technical experts and personnel managers. Some German workers sent back reports from American assembly lines, and a few engineers and academics even took factory jobs in the United States. Neither theoretical analysis nor participant observations, however, could settle disputes about whether Americanized forms of work were more intensive, physically fatiguing, and psychologically deadening than previous methods.

The issue of work intensity in America was inextricably intertwined with conflicting assessments of the secrets of American economic success. As we saw, industrialists, such as Carl Köttgen, insisted that the more intensive American work pace was a principal cause of America's higher productivity, and the only one which Germany could readily copy. Communist economic analysts, such as Modest Rubinstein, also argued that Taylorism, Fordism, and flow production speeded up work, eliminated pauses, and demanded greater effort from workers.[64] They, like academic opponents of Fordism, emphasized not the positive correlation between intensity and productivity, but the negative one between the pace of work and workers' health. The frenetic American work pace put enormous strain on the nervous system, argued Wilhelm Vershofen, and "labor power which should last a normal lifetime is used up in a much shorter period. . . ."[65]

Social Democratic trade unionists, such economists as Julius Hirsch, and some engineers disagreed. According to the 1925 trade union delegation, "the work pace was not higher than with us in Germany; many times one could determine that work was calmer. . . . "[66] Bourgeois experts wrongly generalized from Upton Sinclair's *The Jungle* and other pessimistic accounts. Moreover, they were in no position to make comparisons, for they had never worked in—indeed, may never even have seen the inside of—a German factory. Greater American productivity came from optimizing all factors of production, not maximizing the output of the individual worker.[67] Social Democrats defended the work pace in America so unequivocally because of their disagreements with industrialists in Germany and because they saw no alternative. As Friedrich Olk argued in the deterministic manner so common among Social Democrats, "Flow production is inevitably coming. . . ." It would alter the relations of men and machines and of worker to worker; it would open new possibilities for exploitation. Nonetheless, he believed "it would be foolish to [oppose it] because one would be limiting new forces of production."[68]

Occasionally a Social Democrat, like Toni Sender, who visited the Ford works in 1927, was more critical. "I have seldom seen men in a factory with such tense facial features," she wrote. "[O]ne is shocked by the apathetic expression, the furrowed brow and cheeks, the bad skin color of most, and the expression of unspeakable tiredness." Nonetheless she too dismissed opposition to the assembly line as Luddism and expressed confidence that

rationalized work would not be too intense if the necessary "social protec-
tions" were implemented.[69]

Germans employed in America generally sided with the optimists in
the work pace debate. We know most about the reactions of organized
workers, for their occasional letters to former comrades or the union local
were published in the trade union press. A German worker in Detroit
reported, "At first glance the work pace in the Ford factories seems to be
surprisingly fast. . . . In fact, the Ford worker does not work more and
especially not more intensively than his German colleague. If one is not
deceived by first impressions, one quickly recognizes that the worker is, of
course, always at his workplace, but that his movements and work energy
are not somehow greater than over there by us."[70] Edmund Kleinschmitt,
who worked briefly at Ford, claimed that the work pace was geared to the
abilities of the "normal" worker, not the exceptionally efficient one.[71] A
toolmaker and longtime DMV member, who emigrated to Detroit in 1926,
reported back regularly and favorably about work—and life—in the United
States. In his first letter he maintained, "In so far as toolmaking is concerned,
people work much more comfortably here than in Germany. . . . The main
thing is that the work done must be good." A year later he still maintained
that foremen never harassed skilled workers and, unlike in Germany,
university-trained engineers with little practical experience never set the
work pace.[72] While a skilled toolmaker in Detroit undoubtedly enjoyed some
of the most privileged working conditions, others less well situated were
no more critical. A recent emigrant to Chicago, who had worked first in
"greenhorn factories," insisted that

> in regard to the infamous pace of work, I can only say that it is in no way as bad
> as people in Germany led us to believe, usually with the words: "Because the
> American works harder, he earns more." I personally can only emphasize that
> the work pace is not faster than in Germany, and that applies not only to firms
> in the metal industry. It is clear that larger amounts [of goods produced] are
> always due to better organization and better machines.[73]

By contrast the voices of dissent were few and far between.[74] In the
Bosch company newspaper, the turner Robert Schönhaar stated emphatically that nothing about the work pace at Ford was worth imitating, and
Otto Fischer claimed to know "more than one German worker" who quit
jobs in America because work was too hard.[75] A Bosch technician, employed
in a large New York auto parts firm, wrote, "There is no loafing here, as
there is in Germany."[76] Writing in 1930, the metalworker Karl Möller complained about the speed-up on the Detroit assembly lines but admitted that
he, like his American colleagues, was powerless to stop the hated practice
because trade unions were weak and unemployment high.[77]

It is all but impossible to determine who was right in the acrimonious
debate about the American work pace, for intensity, like exploitation or
job satisfaction, is a subjective as much as an objective category. It was not
only a matter of how fast the line moved, or how many machines a worker

controlled or was controlled by. It was also a question of how the worker performed his particular tasks and perceived that performance. The context in which a particular work pace was embedded—such as managerial practice, wages, and consumption possibilities—was also a factor. Möller, for example, might have worked more intensively in Detroit than his more optimistic German comrades had earlier in the decade, but it is also possible that a situation of economic crisis, job insecurity, and lower wages made the same work pace seem much more onerous. Finally, the political and economic implications of arguing for or against greater work intensity in America were widely known, not only to industrialists and labor movement functionaries, but to the union rank and file as well. Each side had an enormous investment in finding confirmation in America for its vision of economic rationalization in Germany.

Whether or not Americans worked more intensively than Germans, they certainly worked differently, as every German visitor to Detroit noted. The Ford assembly line worker who performed one detailed task that used only certain muscles and required little or no training represented the extreme on a continuum of rationalized forms of work, all of which were more or less repetitive, one-dimensional, and monotonous. It is hardly surprising that Fordized work attracted such attention, for it seemed the antithesis of German quality work, which, at least in theory, was varied, intellectually demanding, physically multidimensional, and emotionally satisfying. (Fordized work was also a marked alternative to, and improvement on, older forms of unskilled labor, but few paid attention to that.)

Rationalized work created what the economist and social policy expert Bruno Rauecker called "the monotony problem."[78] For most observers monotony posed two potential dangers: physical and/or psychological fatigue and the destruction of all positive intellectual and emotional elements of work.[79] Yet monotony provoked much less controversy than intensity, for labor, capital, and industrial psychologists and sociologists all chose to minimize its negative implications.

There were some exceptions. Writing in the *Gewerkschafts-Archiv*, Eduard Weckerle delivered a scathing indictment of mechanized labor processes, detailing their innumerable deleterious physical, intellectual, and cultural effects.[80] In his critical survey of American flow production, Arthur Feiler argued, "The conveyor is the master. . . . The workers are bound to the conveyor the way the galley slaves were bound to their vessel. This— if I may be permitted to say so—is the idea of the conveyor system." Even though the work pace was not always extreme, it was never orderly or rhythmic.[81] Willy Hellpach of the Institute for Social Psychology of the Technical University in Karlsruhe and his collaborators, the engineer Richard Lang and the lawyer and sociologist Eugen Rosenstock, not only condemned rationalized work, but also sought alternatives. In the early 1920s Hellpach and Lang developed various proposals for group work within factories, while Rosenstock proposed to decentralize production by subcontracting it to small workshops.[82] But these views found little resonance among trade unionists, engineers, or scientists of work, for their analysis of monotony was considered extreme; their rejection of rationalized work in large factories, utopian.[83]

Those who downplayed the monotonous character of modern work employed a variety of arguments. Bosch manager Hugo Borst lamented that artisan work was being replaced by mass production, where work was "one-dimensionally uniform, unchangingly repetitive, and inexorably geared to the speed of the machine." Such jobs endangered both people and culture, he warned, yet the future belonged to them for they provided the only means to secure a decent standard of living.[84] The engineer Otto Moog enthusiastically described a German worker he met in Detroit who had performed the same task for 11 years and now owned not only a house, but also a Nash car rather than a simple Model T.[85] For Social Democrats, such as Fritz Tarnow and Ludwig Preller, such visions of quantitatively and qualitatively new consumption made the acceptance of rationalized work—which, in any case, was seen as inevitable—very palatable.[86]

While some viewed monotonous work as an oppressive means to a desired end, others claimed that flow production created an orderly and clean factory, with none of the unsightly and dangerous piles of raw materials and half-finished products that cluttered the unrationalized factory. Workers could gain an overview of the production process, and in many cases they controlled machines rather than being dependent on them.[87] Franz Westermann, admittedly a Ford enthusiast of the most uncritical sort, waxed poetic about "the work rhythm that sweeps everything along with it, just as a band carries along the legs of the marching troops and even the specta-tors. . . ."[88] Hellmut Hultzsch, a student of Friedrich von Gottl-Ottlilienfeld, who briefly was worker #42922 at the River Rouge Ford plant, also praised the rhythmic character of the assembly line. He claimed that each worker could perform his task as he chose, rather than in a prescribed manner. At the Social Museum's conference on "Ford and Us," Hultzsch delivered the following glowing description: "The line moves itself slowly forward; each worker on the line, however, is constantly [engaged] in his *own movement* back and forth on the line. He is really not 'chained to the line,' but only in the *tempo* of the moving line does he feel the sustaining power of all human body movement! Rhythm! He '*sways in rhythm!*'"[89]

A veritable science of rhythm developed.[90] Based on his work in American factories and observations of German ones, Heinrich Wirtz, a student, former manager at the Concordia mine, and mine director's son, developed an elaborate typology of work based on normal work rhythm, opposing rhythm, and the absence of any rhythm. He assessed the degree to which each was "exhausting," "mindless," and "deadening."[91] Ewalt Sachsenberg, a professor of engineering with close ties to industrial circles, insisted that "The rhythm [of the assembly line] holds all workers together like a spiritual tie . . . and compels them . . . to the same swaying of their limbs." If industry selected assembly line workers properly and described the new work carefully, worker resistance would be minimized. Indeed, productiv-

ity would increase without physical harm to workers, and the subordination of the worker to technology and his incorporation into the firm would
be furthered.[92] No wonder industrialists and right-wing industrial physiologists and psychologists found the idea of rhythm appealing.

They were not alone. The widely read Russian fatigue expert
J. Ermanski, the Social Democrat Ludwig Preller, the liberal reformer Bruno
Rauecker, as well as the editors of the Christian Metalworkers' Union journal and other labor leaders argued that rhythmic work was neither physically exhausting nor psychologically deadening. While labor spokesmen
admitted that flow production was not, in fact, always so structured, they
were confident that if management sought the advice of scientists of work
and workers in the plant, it could be.[93] Although workers on the shop floor
seldom commented on rhythm, one German employed at Ford lent support
to the views of labor leaders: "Everything rolls, pushes, and glides by you
in a particular rhythm. The rhythm seizes you, so that you yourself sway
with it. Just like the rhythm of the smith's hammer on the anvil, this way
of working compels you to an unconscious labor productivity. . . . *Work on
the assembly line is not boring.*" By contrast, he continued, in the foundry
and stamping plant work was "truly mechanical, grueling, and intellectually deadening."[94]

Nonproletarians might find rationalized work abhorrent, argued innumerable industrial, academic, and labor movement commentators, but
workers themselves did not. "One must above all guard against academic
sentimentality," claimed Preller, for "male workers, and especially female
ones, who do such monotonous activity constantly affirm that such work
is pleasant, for their thoughts have free play because their hands quickly
perform the work in a purely mechanical way."[95] A company director,
writing in a Christian trade union journal, argued that "every work, even
the simplist, has a certain intelligence peculiar to it. One must simply understand how to pick it out."[96] Even German students who were used to intellectual work did not find jobs at Ford unpleasant, asserted Adolf Wallichs
in his major study of flow production. Surely this meant that those less
endowed mentally and emotionally would not find the work oppressive.[97]
After seeing the Ford works and automated parts plants in Milwaukee, the
Social Democrat Franz Josef Furtwängler went so far as to argue that "the
mechanization process itself is diminishing the [monotony] problem. Ever
more of these mechanical tasks are being taken over by the machines, and
the duties of 'the machine men' (or at least a great number of them) are again
being made more multifaceted and technically sovereign."[98]

Such arguments assumed that most workers, or at least clearly defin-
able groups of workers, demanded little intellectual stimulation from their
jobs; they only required decent wages and treatment.[99] The economist Bruno
Rauecker, the businessman Carl Hollweg, and the psychotechnician Fritz
Giese insisted that Ford was absolutely correct to claim that only 5 percent of workers wanted challenging jobs.[100] Although worker turnover at
Ford was high and troubling to management, Germans seldom commented

on it. Those who did stay at Ford, performing the same jobs year in and year out, were seen as proof that work was satisfying, even though their job stability may have reflected a belief that all jobs were equally mindless.[101] Others assumed that skilled men had high demands and should be spared repetitive work for which they were unsuited by temperment and training. Why even in Detroit, it was noted with a certain ethnic arrogance, German quality workers were not found on the assembly line; rather they did set-up and repair work.[102]

Those workers who were considered suitable for repetitive, monotonous tasks fell into predictable gender and ethnic categories. Some German commentators regarded American male workers to be generally less intelligent and demanding than their German counterparts, and singularly willing to put up with mindless work in return for high wages, increased consumption, and greater leisure.[103] Others singled out recent immigrants, especially those from eastern and southern Europe.[104] Nearly every commentator believed that in Germany, where there were few immigrants, it was "the apparently unintelligent, female, and young workers who were especially suited for flow and assembly line work."[105] Whether women's perceived special aptitude for rationalized work stemmed from nature or education, from an ability to find repetition challenging or a desire to work mechanically, or, as was usually the case, from a lack of options, was not explored in depth.[106] The prospect that women's work might become widespread if rationalization was extensively implemented was not examined, for this raised male fears of deskilling or unemployment and family disintegration.[107] Thus the compatibility of women and monotonous work was quietly assumed and quickly passed over.

Such ethnic and gender stereotyping was nearly as prevalent in the labor movement as among industrialists and industrial sociologists and psychologists.[108] It sprang from beliefs in the inherent differences between women and men and among ethnic groups; for many, especially on the right, difference implied ineradicable inequality. Gender and ethnic stereotyping both reinforced and gained support from the prevalent belief that there was a right person for every job, no matter how monotonous and oppressive it might appear to be, and that the science of work could determine who that right person was.

Only Communists, such as Modest Rubinstein, insisted "that the unbelievable monotony of the labor processes in rationalized production is extraordinarily oppressive for the majority of workers." But even this oppression had its silver lining, he argued, for the new work would create greater homogeneity among workers and undermine the social basis of reformism which was skilled workers. "Despite powerful exhaustion, it awakens the progressive strata of the workers to social activity and, under suitable circumstances, allows the masses to follow them."[109] It is hard to decide which was more shortsighted and simplistic—the Social Democratic conviction that workers would adjust relatively happily to monotonous work or the Communists' confidence that bad work would automatically produce good politics. Both positions shared the technological determinism and economic reductionism that characterized Second and Third International Marxism. Both dismissed alternative labor processes as neither possible nor desirable.

Those who discussed fatigue and monotony were convinced that any problems stemmed from capitalist exploitation or the "unscientific" selection of workers and organization of the labor process; they were not inherent in rationalized work. Industrial psychologists such as Otto Lipmann and Edgar Atzler discussed in glowing detail how science could match workers and jobs, create a healthy workplace, and minimize fatigue.[110] Hugo Borst and W. Vogt insisted that industry wanted clean, safe, well-lit and ventilated factories, whose work speed would not exhaust employees.[111] Such Social Democrats as Theodor Leipart, Kurt Lewin, Toni Sender, and Richard Seidel shared Ludwig Preller's view that "the application of the objective-scientific findings of the science of work to the labor and production processes is in the interest of the workers."[112] They insisted that factory councils and trade unions should play an active role in implementing these findings, lest capitalists distort the neutral science of work. Only the Communist Party dismissed *Arbeitswissenschaft* itself as a tool of capitalist industry.[113]

Psychotechnics and work physiology, which were practiced in state-funded institutes and private firms, promised to analyze both the job and the workers. These "sciences" sought to match the physical and psychological aptitudes of the worker to the requirements of the job by matching the results of aptitude tests with a detailed classification of occupations (*Berufskunde*). Germany distinguished itself from America by this emphasis on aptitude testing and vocational advising, as many noted at the time.[114] Psychotechnicians and work physiologists also analyzed the work place in an effort to determine the best organization of tools and materials, the best lighting, colors, music, and ventilation. They measured how much energy workers expended in performing a task and how much their output varied in the course of the workday. Finally, they offered to train the semiskilled worker, whom they had selected, to perform a task in the prescribed manner and in an appropriately designed workplace.[115]

Industrialists were least prone to praise psychotechnics and work physiology, because they believed that the laws of capitalism, and not those of science, should determine the workplace and work pace. Nonetheless, they were willing to adopt simple aptitude testing, which determined a worker's suitability for a particular job rather than his or her general abilities and interests, and follow some of the recommendations suggested by studies on fatigue, workplace design, and safety. Psychotechnics proved compatible with different levels of rationalization; its findings could be implemented piecemeal, and some were relatively cheap.[116] For engineers, psychologists, and physiologists, psychotechnics and work physiology represented a continuation of the prewar German science of work, rather than an imitation of American models. Of equal importance, they created a central role for bourgeois experts not only in factories but in technical universities and state labor offices as well.

Many Social Democrats saw psychotechnics and work physiology as genuine sciences that not only refuted Taylorism but moved beyond it by taking workers as well as work seriously. The trade union press printed numerous articles, largely by non-Socialist scientists of work, on aptitude testing and fatigue studies, workplace redesign and training programs. Every major book in the field was reviewed in such journals as *Die Gesellschaft*, *Die Arbeit*, and the *Gewerkschafts-Zeitung*.[117] This reflected the labor movement's continued fascination with science, a fascination that had been so strong a component of Social Democratic culture in the Imperial period. It was not just psychotechnics that found a welcome reception, but eugenics as well.[118] Common to both was a vision of a scientifically structured and rationally ordered society. Social Democrats did not object to the social engineering that was integral to psychotechnics and eugenics; they wanted to combine it with progressive politics. Finally, because psychotechnics and work physiology shared the Fordist emphasis on optimization rather than the Taylorist stress on maximization,[119] they helped Social Democrats to develop an emancipatory version of rationalization.

Psychotechnics promised to solve the problem of physical and psychological exhaustion, but it did not address the issue of whether rationalized work would have sufficient intellectual and emotional content to serve as the basis for a work-centered identity. Yet many Germans wanted the science of work to create job satisfaction and not merely eliminate the most negative aspects of rationalization and encourage quiet resignation.

Joy in Work

"Joy in work was the myth of men of the 1920s, its loss their trauma."[120] This rather enigmatic statement by the historian Carola Sachse captures the centrality of the theme of joy in work in debates about technical and human rationalization, even if it does little to specify what the term meant. The concept of joy in work—job satisfaction is too flat a translation to do justice to *Arbeitsfreude*—originated in pre-World War I Werkbund discussions, where it was usually linked to a preference for artisan work and the conservative politics of the traditional lower middle class.[121] In the 1920s joy in work became a standard theme among such proponents of economic modernity as engineers, vocational educators, psychotechnicians, and industrial sociologists. The RKW urged *Arbeitswissenschaft* to make "the attainment of the greatest possible *joy in work* its goal."[122]

For many Weimar Germans a preoccupation with joy in work was directly related to fears about its absence in rationalized factories. According to the vocational educator Hella Schmedes, "industrial work has developed into a psychological and sociological problem. Today the 'crisis of work' concerns not only those affected by it but also wide circles of intellectuals."[123] Right-wing discussions of "joy in work" and "the crisis of work" reflected anxieties about the effects of rationalization on productivity and politics, workers' identities, and lifestyles. The idea of "joy in work" was central to a discourse that sought psychological and sociological solutions to worker disaffection that was rooted in economics and technology.

According to many engineers, industrial sociologists, and other commentators, the majority of whom were on the political right, workers neither understood the meaning of their jobs nor felt any connection to the product or the firm. In the face of modern technology, argued Heinz Potthoff, editor of the labor law journal *Arbeitsrecht*, workers felt "powerless" and "disarmed," experienced no "connection to the firm" (*Betriebsverbundenheit*), and viewed their jobs as "isolated" and "without purpose."[124] Flow production, the assembly line, and above all Taylorized tasks demanded little initiative from workers and decreased their intelligence.[125] In a much-quoted speech, Ruhr industrialist Albert Vögler asserted that "the majority of blue-collar workers, and I must admit, even white-collar ones, are alienated from and actually hostile to their firm and its labor processes."[126] Rather than realizing themselves in and through work, they only felt human outside of work.[127]

Workers had once had a different relationship to work according to these right-wing analysts, and could develop one again in the future. Instead of working to live, argued Christoph Schrempf, who described himself as "by chance working with his head and not his hands," the worker should want to work because it makes him happy and because he cannot live without joy in work.[128] The religious philosopher Ernst Horneffer echoed these sentiments in pamphlets with such titles as *The Path to Joy in Work* and *The Spiritualization of Economic Work*. He lamented that the worker was no longer "so completely involved in his work that he scarcely thinks about the question of material rewards."[129] Far from being considered an eccentric, Horneffer had his works published by the RDI and the VDA.[130] Industrialists sometimes spoke the same language. At the 1926 annual meeting of the RDI, of which he was the head, Carl Duisberg, a founder of the chemical trust I.G. Farben, argued, "In work and in joy in work lies the true meaning of life."[131]

Mindless and soulless work not only threatened joy in work but the very concept of *Beruf*. In its most concrete meaning of occupation or that economic activity for which one was paid, *Beruf* was not an object of anxious concern. When Bosch director Hugo Borst claimed that rationalized work did not "deserve the honorable name of *Beruf*," he had something much more value-laden and politicized in mind.[132] By the 1920s, the idea of *Beruf* had lost most of the religious connotations given it by Luther, but it was far from being simply a neutral and descriptive economic term. It continued to conjure up a host of amorphous ideas about individual ethics, "natural" aptitudes, and service to society.[133] To merit the designation *Beruf* a blue-collar occupation was supposed to require and encourage manual skills, intellectual abilities, and moral character. It was to elicit and demand a *Berufsethos*, a vocational ethic or commitment. In its idealized form, *Beruf* was ostensibly based on real conditions in a vaguely defined preindustrial past. A man would develop himself and define his identity in terms of his

Beruf, and his relationship to the larger society would be mediated through it.[134] *Beruf* was tied to a specifically German concept of work, according to which, in the words of one Weimar author, "work should lead to the unfolding and development of one's own personality and should be seen as service (*Dienst*) for the great tasks of the people's community to which we belong."[135] It was frequently associated with a conservative vision of an organic society of estates rather than classes, of hierarchy rather than equality.[136]

The preoccupation with *Beruf*, like that with joy in work, was very much an affair of men and about men, for the natural *Beruf* of a woman was considered to be housewifery and motherhood, regardless of whether or not she did waged work. Her relationship to society was mediated through the family, and her identity was determined by her role in reproduction.[137] Only for men, whose work-centered identities and work ethic were ostensibly being destroyed by rationalization, could it be said "there is no longer anything that one can call '*Beruf*' with its own inner meaning."[138]

In addition to endangering spiritual satisfaction, intellectual development, and social cohesion, the crisis of work also harmed the economy. In the absence of joy in work and a *Berufsethos*, discipline and productivity allegedly declined because workers lacked a sense of responsibility and wasted time and materials. They were assumed to change jobs frequently and have little interest in learning a trade. And dissatisfaction with work might well lead to dissatisfaction with society and politics.[139] Heinz Potthoff asserted, "This meaninglessness, this complete lack of spiritual content in the activity of the detail worker in the large factory, has contributed as much as the feeling of being 'exploited' to allowing Marxism to become the religion of millions."[140]

Although some Christian trade unionists were sympathetic to the concepts of *Beruf* and joy in work, their Social Democratic counterparts had little patience for them.[141] Some claimed that joy in work was impossible under capitalism; others insisted that workers were satisfied with rationalized work.[142] Most argued that the discourse of joy in work disguised the real problems presented by rationalization. According to the *Bergarbeiter-Zeitung*, bourgeois economists "discovered their social heart" only when they looked at mechanization and the ostensible "despiritualiztion of work." They raised "heart-wrenching complaints" and then were "very offended and finally even a little angry, when . . . workers perceived very different facts to be the true problems of proletarian people."[143] The "protection of labor power," and not some respiritualization of work, was of central importance.[144] Social Democrats prided themselves on their unsentimental acceptance of rationalized work, an acceptance that was mirrored and reinforced by the sober embrace of modern technology and functionalist aesthetics among left-wing artists and writers of the *Neue Sachlichkeit* movement.[145] The left thus not only rejected the right's construction of the problem of modern work, but also abandoned any possible discourse about alternative technologies and job satisfaction.[146] Work as reality belonged to the proletariat; work as ideology became the distinct preserve of the right.

Both those who obsessed about the crisis of joy in work and those who dismissed it looked to America for insight on how workers coped with work in its most rationalized form. What they found was puzzling and contradictory. In the writings on America—but not necessarily on the American shop floor—joy in work was said to exist in abundance. Numerous observers noted that "workers seem to regard their work as sport."[147] The term is important, for sport, as opposed to play, implies not only enjoyment but achievement, not only cooperation but competition. Workers were invariably described in cheery terms. According to Otto Moog, their faces were "mostly bright and lively."[148] Theodor Lüddecke claimed that they displayed "a robust life energy," while Erwin Rosen maintained that they "distilled joy from compulsion" and "loved their work with a fanatical enthusiasm."[149] The left and the right disagreed on why there was such enthusiasm, and some questioned whether the more intelligent German worker would experience joy under similar circumstances,[150] but only a few like Toni Sender disputed the myth of the happy worker.

In the eyes of industrialists and engineers, joy in work was integrally related to American workers' much discussed "will to production."[151] Because workers understood the centrality of productivity, they found work more enjoyable, and the joyful character of work increased productivity. Whether joy in work and a commitment to productivity produced loyalty to the firm was more difficult to ascertain. Theodor Lüddecke described American workers as "little capitalists."[152] According to the Gutehoffnungshütte's company newspaper, American workers devoted themselves to the firm wholeheartedly because they saw it as theirs.[153] Even the Communist Jakob Walcher argued that Ford had convinced "a large portion of the workers exploited by him" that the fate of the firm was "their own very personal affair." Ford was, however, considered exceptional in this regard.[154]

Most Germans noted that the much admired American devotion to production coexisted with disturbingly high job mobility. At the drop of a hat, workers would quit one firm and sign on with another. They would shift occupations just as readily, for they had "no feeling for a *Beruf*, only a consciousness about earning money."[155] According to the economist Lujo Brentano, the "homo oeconomius of classical economics," who moves according to the dictates of the market and whose existence Brentano had always doubted, was a reality in America.[156] There was no *Berufsethos* among American workers and no work-centered identity. Although Americans worked with incredible energy, they did not live to work; they worked to earn and earned to enjoy themselves. They did not ask about the purpose of work, only its dollar value.[157]

Social Democrats had a simple explanation for American joy in work— high wages.[158] The very same high wages that promoted consumption and prosperity benefited the individual psyche as well. Good pay called forth joy in work, claimed Oswald Bamberger, a metalworker who had emigrated to the States.[159] It created job security, without which happiness on the job was impossible, argued Josef Voigtländer in a critique of Ernst

Horneffer.[160] German employers should learn that if job satisfaction was the goal, decent wages were the best means to attain it. Liberal analysts, such as Moritz J. Bonn, dismissed the possibility of meaningful work but insisted that monetary compensation for its demise would limit worker discontent.[161] Social Democrats, eager to bolster their wage theories, never asked whether high wages and job satisfaction would spell the end of class politics.

While Social Democrats recognized that rationalization threatened the craft tradition from which the workers' movement had drawn much of its strength, they did not mourn its decline to the same degree that the right decried the destruction of *Beruf.* Richard Woldt, the principal rationalization expert of the ADGB, even maintained, "The human factor of production is no longer decisive; material forces are."[162] Although most Social Democrats were unwilling to discount the value of workers so radically, they did not believe that modern work, even skilled work, would or should provide the meaning of life. Some movement spokesmen attempted to imbue meaningless individual work with abstract meaning. Workers should think of "work on the line" as "work for the *Volk*," suggested a particularly apolitical writer in the *Gewerkschafts-Zeitung.*[163] Those more cognizant of the realities of class and power hoped that worker education and an expansion of economic democracy would help workers to understand the economy of which they were a part and to feel solidarity with workers elsewhere, even if they did not experience greater joy in their own work.[164] Still others anticipated that such a general grasp of the economy and one's place in it could be achieved only under socialism.[165] Most, however, looked for satisfaction outside the realm of work entirely. Some stressed leisure, others politics, but all shared Fritz Tarnow's confidence that workers would willingly trade off joy in work for "joy in life."[166]

Industrialists, industrial sociologists, and right-wing engineers were much more ambivalent about American attitudes toward work. The commitment to productivity, the sporting spirit, and the unrestrained optimism that ostensibly reigned were enthusiastically applauded, but the absence of work-centered identities, the lack of job stability, and the earn-more-and-enjoy-now attitude of so many were most definitely not. Workers' attitudes toward work exposed the full contradictions of the American model. The industrialist Carl Köttgen approved of workers' passion for productivity that he saw as the key to American economic success. The educator, Protestant cleric, and scholar of proletarian youth Günter Dehn was struck by the obsession with money, consumption, and leisure and claimed "that it is not socialism but Americanism that will be the end of everything as we have known it."[167] Even more troubling than the fact that both sets of attitudes coexisted was the possibility that they were inextricably connected. If Social Democrats were correct, one could only have joy in work in advanced capitalism by abandoning ideas like *Beruf* and loyalty to the firm and by paying the literal price of high wages as well as the figurative one of a new leisure-oriented society. For many on the right, that option seemed too expensive, too crassly materialistic, and too potentially empowering to workers.

In an effort to gain the advantages of the American model of work without its drawbacks, many industrialists, engineers, and industrial sociologists
sought to revamp shop floor relations. Psychotechnics and vocational education were the prerequisites for this, but many felt it was necessary to go
beyond their narrow focus on adjusting men to machines.[168] As part of this
larger project of reshaping the relationships among workers, between workers and managers, and between the shop floor and the proletarian home,
Germans studied informal and formal shop floor relations, welfare capitalism, and trade unions in America.

The Shop Floor and the Firm

Engineers, industrialists, and academic industrial sociologists displayed the
strongest interest in shop floor labor relations and company welfare measures. Social Democrats focused on the ownership of economic resources
rather than the control of the shop floor, on national collective bargaining
rather than local factory councils, on state social policy rather than company social policy.[169] It was not travels to America but rather wartime and
postwar transformations in Germany that spurred this initial interest of the
right. Goetz Briefs, the father of Weimar industrial sociology noted that
since the war, the factory had become a source of conflict and unrest, but
it was also the potential locus for solving both the problems generated within
it and those of the larger society.[170]

The first to analyze the German factory in new ways was Josef
Winschuh, an academically trained businessman whose 1923 book, *Practical Company Policy*, was widely recognized as heralding a new era in
employer politics.[171] Winschuh insisted that a pragmatic activism was possible inside the firm, even without changes in Weimar social policy or
political arrangements. Smart employers should recognize the new power
structures of the postwar era, deal with trade unions and factory councils,
and avoid petty harassment and losing battles on issues of secondary
importance. They should outmaneuver workers, not ignore or repress
them.[172] Winschuh's goals were traditional ones: "labor peace, discipline,
increased production, healthy authority, and binding the worker to the
firm."[173] But in the face of new circumstances, he recommended new methods to assure that "the industrialist continue as *leader* [*Führer*] since he is
no longer *lord* [*Herr*]."[174]

When German observers looked to America for ideas about how this
might be done, they were struck by three aspects of shop floor relations
and managerial practice. First was the informality and joviality of interactions between workers, on the one hand, and foremen, engineers, and managers, on the other. Second were the peculiar institutional arrangements for
social policy in America—the proliferation of company-based economic and
social measures that went under the label welfare capitalism, combined with
the complete lack of state social policy. Third was the weakness, if not total
absence, of trade unions. As was so often the case, Germans agreed on what

was uniquely American much more readily than on why it existed or whether it could be emulated.

The atmosphere in American factories seemed far removed from any-thing encountered or imagined in Germany. According to engineers and industrialists there was an openness, an aura of friendliness, and a spirit of cooperation.[175] Observers differed about whether this resulted from a national spirit of egalitarianism and camaraderie, a shared respect for achieve-ment and mobility, or the remarkable cultural homogeneity of the popula-tion, but they agreed on the range of gestures and behavior that created a seemingly different world inside factories and offices.[176] Franz Westermann told of foremen who, instead of complaining and swearing, patted workers on the back, asked how they were doing and gave a friendly word of en-couragement.[177] Otto Moog described white-collar workers who greeted their employers with a wave and a "hello boss."[178] According to Theodor Lüddecke, "In place of the passion of managers for commanding and the resentment among workers that dominates German factories, there is unqualified tact on both sides."[179] Lauster of MAN insisted that "there was no noticable difference" in the treatment of skilled and unskilled, white-collar and blue-collar workers.[180] This was a highly romanticized view of American shop floor relations, and some observers admitted that the infor-mality seen there might be superficial.[181] The English language, for example, has only one form of the pronoun "you," rather than the formal *Sie* and informal *du* of German. Workers and bosses, of necessity, addressed one another in the same way, rather than in forms that inevitably express authority and subordination.[182] Adolf Halfeld concluded that "openness and mutual trust were probably not very deep," but they were nonetheless real enough to put German managers to shame.[183]

Free and Christian trade union observers reached similar conclusions.[184] According to Paul Otto, who had held both manual and white-collar jobs in Germany before becoming a factory worker in America, "The treatment of the worker is extraordinarily polite."[185] Foremen were friendly and respectful to subordinates, several German workers reported, and each addressed the other by their first name.[186] The 1925 trade union delegation agreed that "relations were in general better, freer, less autocratic." Neither workers on the shop floor nor trade union functionaries had any illusions about why American managers adopted such methods—it paid, economi-cally and politically.[187] American businessmen recognized that "the best treatment of workers is also the best business," argued Otto. Moreover, it also warded off unrest and rebellion.[188] Only one observer credited the osten-sibly better treatment of workers to the "long and hard struggles" of trade unions.[189]

The Social Democrats' analysis of shop floor relations followed a familiar pattern. Labor attributed favorable aspects to the farsightedness of busi-nessmen not the achievements of workers. The prevalence of good work-ing conditions was assumed uncritically, and ambiguities were not explored. Instead the American example, presented in a simplistic and rosy way, was used as a cudgel to beat German industry. In the rhetoric of labor, German bosses were not only mean but stupid, for they did not even know how to make money.

From the perspective of industrialists and engineers, the American shop floor had little to teach. The most striking difference between German and American shop floor relations was the behavior of managers, not the out-look of workers, and few capitalists recommended emulating that aspect of the American model. Even those industrialists and industrial sociologists of work who felt that German managerial practice had to change did not want to imitate the substance of egalitarianism they discerned in Ameri-can labor relations. They were only willing to adopt the style of informal-ity and respect.[190]

America had an extensive system of company-based social programs, commonly called "welfare capitalism." According to a 1926 survey of the 1,500 largest firms, 80 percent had at least one form of welfare program, and roughly half had comprehensive programs, such as those at Ford and U.S. Steel.[191] These were the firms Germans studied. Some welfare mea-sures focused on health and housing, others on education or recreation, and still others on worker participation through employee stock options, profit sharing, and plant assemblies or shop councils. Different programs targeted different audiences (men only or women but not children, for example, or immigrants only) and served such varied purposes as Americanization or health and safety. All programs were designed to restructure interpersonal relationships in the firm and reward workers differentially for performance, loyalty, and apolitical deference. The overarching aim was to increase pro-ductivity and limit, if not fully exclude, unions from the firm.[192] American welfare capitalism was in the position—enviable to some and appalling to others—of being neither an adjunct to nor a substitute for state welfare institutions, which were remarkable only for their absence.

Welfare capitalism embodied the major developments in American management in the 1920s. As the historian David Montgomery notes, American managers "enjoyed an international reputation for organizing efficient production by faithful employees comparable to that of their Japa-nese counterparts in the 1980s."[193] German industrialists and right-wing engineers and industrial sociologists were understandably impressed. The absence of state social policy freed American industry from burdensome taxes and "schematic" labor regulations. Business could reward individual achievement and enhance differentials among workers, rather than lump-ing them into a few large wage and social welfare categories, over which the individual firm had little control.[194] The firm was autonomous from the state—perhaps even more powerful.[195] In German capital's rosy picture, American workers accepted the lack of state social policy, either because they were staunchly individualistic or because high wages and welfare capi-talism obviated the need.[196] Finally, welfare capitalism seemed far removed from nineteenth-century patriarchal welfare policy; it addressed the par-ticular social, psychological, and physical problems created by rationalized

work and focused on enhancing productivity and profitability.[197] This mixture of industrial psychology and cost accounting was most appealing to
German business.

Yet Weimar industrialists and industrial sociologists conducted no
investigations of welfare capitalism that paralleled their detailed studies of
particular technologies and factories. Even visitors to Detroit sketched
Ford's schools, hospitals, housing, and recreation programs in only a few
sentences or paragraphs, after devoting chapters to descriptions of machines
and assembly lines. For the right, American welfare capitalism was more a
source of political inspiration than concrete information, owing probably
to both Germany's arrogance and America's irrelevance. Since the nineteenth century German firms had prided themselves on being the leaders
in company welfare. If America had surpassed them by the 1920s, they were
nonetheless a close second and, in such areas as vocational education, were
well ahead.[198] For all its innovativeness, welfare capitalism was geared to
semiskilled workers in mass production industries; it did not explicitly
address the object of concern in German business and education circles—
the skilled worker who would produce German quality work. For German
industrialists, engineers, and industrial sociologists welfare capitalism was
interesting but incidental to the essence of Americanism.

Of equal importance, American welfare capitalism was embedded in a
completely different set of institutional arrangements and power relationships. Labor law, collective bargaining, the state, and trade unions bore so
little resemblance to their German counterparts that the American model
seemed inapplicable. Employee representation plans, for example, which
were a staple item in the American managerial repertoire of the 1920s, were
a means of excluding trade unions, whereas German employers had to bar-
gain not only with unions, but also with state-sanctioned factory councils.[199]
Americans could spend freely on welfare capitalism, it was argued, while
German industrialists were forced to foot the bill for extravagant state social-
policy programs. (Whether American welfare capitalists actually spent more
or less than did their German counterparts for state and company social
policy was never investigated.)

Some aspects of welfare capitalism, such as profit sharing and stock ownership, were explicitly rejected by German businessmen, even though their
avowed aim was to contain radicalism.[200] German industrialists and engineers wanted to create efficient employees and loyal followers, not to turn
workers into capitalists on however insignificant a scale. "Industrial democracy"—the slogan for a variety of employee representation plans—was even
more objectionable, for it sounded suspiciously close to the Social Democratic slogan of "economic democracy." The proponents of company social
policy in Germany needed different programs and different ideological pack-
aging as well.

Social Democrats paid surprisingly little attention to American social
policy.[201] Toni Sender, Charlotte Lütkens, and members of the trade union
delegation all deplored, albeit in a rather perfunctory manner, the lack of

state social policy; they displayed characteristic skepticism toward the democratic character of "industrial democracy" and the economic benefits of stock plans and profit sharing. They realized that welfare capitalists were deeply antiunion, often combining social welfare policy and the use of company spies, black lists, strikebreakers, and company towns. Yet Social Democrats were convinced that welfare capitalism did bring some concrete benefits.[202] These attitudes reflected the Social Democrats' reluctance to dwell on the dark side of American capitalism as well as their tendency to dismiss welfare capitalism as economically nonessential and politically unsophisticated. Perhaps Social Democrats doubted that German employers would or could launch a similar offensive. If so, they seriously underestimated their enemy.

Left and right, workers and employers, engineers and educators agreed that American trade unions, which had never rivaled their German counterparts in size, radicalism, and effectiveness in the prewar era, were at their nadir in the 1920s. The small size, relative powerlessness and deep conservatism of the American workers' movement was attributed to American exceptionalism. The lack of class consciousness and class politics were products of past history and contemporary prosperity; the absence of feudalism and the colonial character of America, the fluidity of class boundaries and the prospects for upward mobility, high wages and mass consumption were all cited.[203] Some bourgeois observers added a cultural argument: individualism, pragmatism, and optimism were central to the American value system.[204] Many Social Democrats accused capital of explicitly obstructing trade unionism through welfare capitalism, spies, blacklists, Pinkertons, and police, as well as through the cultivation of ethnic and racial divisions.[205]

Exceptional historical and material factors thus made class politics all but impossible in America. Its labor movement was neither a warning nor an inspiration; it was simply an oddity. Informal shop floor relations and company welfare policies were of much more interest to Germans. So too were American patterns of consumption, family life, and culture.

6

The Cultural Consequences
of Americanism

For many Weimar observers, Americanism and Fordism symbolized much more than a stunningly efficient, modern system of production; they represented a world view, a way of life, and a set of gender relations organized around the primacy of economics and consumption and the devaluation of high culture.[1] They embodied a spirit of pragmatism and materialism, an acceptance of—indeed, a desire for—uniformity, and a thoroughly rational, unromantic attitude toward production, work, and the factory as well as reproduction, leisure, and the home. The majority of Americans seemed to approach their lives in the same way that a minority of German artists and intellectuals in the *Neue Sachlichkeit* movement analyzed modern society. They soberly accepted industrialization, urbanization and mass culture, eschewing angry protest or utopian fantasies. To most German commentators, the American political system was irrelevant to American economic success and thus was not discussed at length; however, American culture, gender, and everyday life were not ignored. Economists, journalists, engineers, and social workers debated whether economic modernity in its American guise inherently required or inevitably produced not only new products and styles of consumption but also new men and women.

German travelers to America asked this question in two different ways. Charlotte Lütkens and Adolf Halfeld were interested in the links between rationalized American capitalism and those phenomena invariably described as characteristic of American society in the 1920s: movies, sports, jazz, the emancipation of youth, the displacement of traditional cultural leaders, the democratization of consumption, the rise in divorce, and the altered position of women. They explored whether these were the product of such peculiar American institutions as the frontier or Puritanism and the revolt against it. If not, were they inevitable manifestations of advanced capitalism?[2] Did "the Fordization of all aspects of American culture condemn the healthy instincts of a young race to intellectual indifference and drill the life expression of millions and millions of people into a regimented existence," as Adolf Halfeld, a German newspaper correspondent living in America, argued?[3] Were the efficient but cold American women and the functional but soulless American homes (as Germans viewed them) the unavoidable products of economic modernity?

Other commentators were less concerned about the consequences of capitalist development than about the consciousness it bred. Did American men's single-minded pursuit of productivity, efficiency, and the almighty dollar—so admired when economics was discussed—have alarming consequences for culture and gender? Did the demands that Fordism placed on men—whether owners or managers, technicians or workers—lead to a fundamental redefinition of masculinity and femininity, a fundamental shift in domestic responsibilities and social roles? Was the peculiar superficiality and striking feminization of American culture the necessary flip side of male devotion to technology and profits?

Culture and gender were inextricably intertwined in these ruminations about the consequences of economic Americanism, for Americanism and Fordism called into question traditional assumptions about culture and gender and the gendered nature of culture. America not only lacked *Kultur* in the German sense of both high culture and a high value placed on intellectual and artistic matters; American culture was ostensibly controlled by women. Americans not only consumed standardized, mass produced goods, but such consumption also transformed both public culture and private life. While men embraced the ideology of rationalization in the public sphere, women did so in the home. In the Weimar debates on rationalization, mass consumption and the American woman were considered emblematic of the social and cultural consequences of economic Americanism and of the hopes and fears they engendered.[4] It is to them that we must turn.

Mass Consumption

"The almighty dollar and its use are the meaning and goal of American life," wrote Moritz J. Bonn. "A civilization has emerged whose essential feature lies exclusively in the satisfaction of more or less material needs with the technically most perfect, most comfortable, labor-saving machines." Puritanism had once provided sense and structure to life and directed economic activity toward savings and investment; now "enjoying pleasure though immediate consumption" and winning consumers for new products shaped the mentality and culture of Americans.[5] Bonn's equation of Americanism with consumption was widely shared by his contemporaries as well as by historians.[6]

When defining Fordism or analyzing the secrets of American economic success, Germans of all classes and political persuasions debated whether consumption was a prerequisite for economic modernization or a consequence; whether it was the cause of American economic success or a fortuituous but secondary feature? But when they examined American society and culture, the primacy of consumption was indisputable. Germans had come to America to study new technology and labor processes; once there, they were overwhelmed by the way the products of the new technology affected all aspects of society.[7] Every visitor to America was struck by the abundance of consumer goods—cars, radios, every imaginable household appliance, and the thousands of products sold by Sears and Roebuck. Enormous inequalities in consumption seemed less important than the existence of mass consumption on a scale unparalleled in Germany. American prosperity was symbolized by American mass consumption as much as by mass production.

Despite the fascination with American consumption, remarkably little attention was paid to precisely what was consumed, by whom, and in what amounts. To be sure, German observers commented on the spread of the automobile, above all the Model T, to town and country, and among all classes. And no wonder, for whereas the United States had 183 cars per thousand inhabitants in 1932, Germany had only 8.[8] Moreover, the car transformed rural and urban areas and the relationship between them; it introduced new forms of work and play, sociability, and family life.[9] But Germans paid little attention to the proliferation of such goods as radios, telephones, refrigerators, vacuum cleaners, and washing machines.[10] Bourgeois and working-class observers alike seemed more interested in the high wages that fueled consumption, than in exploring how they were spent. They noted the prevalence of home ownership but did not investigate what kinds of goods were purchased for those homes or how their occupants lived. The major exceptions were Irene Witte, whose study, *Home and Technology in America*, detailed the mass consumption of appliances, and Moritz J. Bonn, whose books were filled with details of daily life gleaned from his many years in the United States.[11] Perhaps because so much of American mass consumption involved women and the home, most German men preferred to discuss it in abstract cultural terms, rather than concrete material ones.

Those discussions centered in part on the relationship of mass consumption to the creation of an American society that, in comparison to Europe, seemed uniform, homogeneous and monotonous. When describing American conventions—whether clothing or food, housing or transportation, tastes or needs—Germans saw only far-reaching standardization.[12] Walking the streets of Chicago, Arthur Feiler was overwhelmed by "the monstrous uniformity of these passing individuals," all dressed and coiffed alike.[13] Surveying housing, Alfred Rühl complained that "just as the outside of the house, which is often purchased finished from the factory, conforms to a conventional style, so too the inside reveals nothing of the personality of the builder or owner. Everywhere one encounters the same objects; everything is a mass product."[14] With a mixture of admiration and disdain, Bonn noted that Sears and Roebuck "twice a year determines what men and women and children should wear. It clothes them, despite all variations, in one style. . . . It creates the same form of life for a large part of the American population."[15] Admirers of America stressed uniformity as much as did its critics. According to Julius Hirsch, everything from underwear to automobiles was standardized, and people purchased not just similar goods but brand names, such as the Arrow shirt collar or Wrigley's chewing gum.[16]

No one doubted that standardized mass consumption was efficient, in terms of productivity and price, but they questioned the value of uniformity and its effects on society and culture. Adolf Halfeld raised aesthetic objections, claiming that mass goods lacked the beauty and good taste of items produced in cultures with a strong artisan tradition.[17] Many feared that "the dazzling colorfulness of European individuals, religions, and nationalities will be replaced by the gray, monotone, mechanistic uniformity of the American norm."[18] Nearly all recognized that there was a democratization of consumption in America, in contrast to Europe, where needs were class-specific.[19] As some reported with approval and others with dismay, workers dressed, ate, and drove cars just like middle-class Americans.[20]

If more uniform and egalitarian mass consumption seemed emancipatory to German trade unionists and workers, it raised the frightening spectre of mass man to many middle-class observers.[21] According to Bonn, America pioneered the "normal individual, a mass individual," who considered himself free but lived just as others did.[22] Standardized production and consumption produced standardized people, argued Paul Wengraf. Indeed, in their thoughts and feelings Americans were more uniform and more closely patterned on the average person than people in any other society, including Russians.[23] Agreeing wholeheartedly, Arthur Holitscher tried to specify the mechanisms of mass consumption that were responsible. "Mail order catalogs standardized goods and people," he argued, while "newspapers and the radio standardized needs and opinions."[24]

Social Democrats countered by asserting that standardization did not produce oppressive uniformity, that mass production did not mean monotony. The 1925 trade union delegation investigated the anxious German rumor that there were only three kinds of bedsteads and four types of alarm clocks in all of America. As they crisscrossed the land, they carefully counted the different bedframes encountered in hotels and homes, read bed ads in newspapers and magazines, and discussed this issue with trade unionists, store owners, and manufacturers alike. Diversity abounded, the delegates happily reported, and not only in beds. Despite the prevalence of the Model T, there were at least 54 different types of cars produced. Moreover, goods of the same style came in every possible price and quality. It was thus a serious mistake to equate American norms and interchangeable parts with a uniform, universally manufactured model.[25]

As he puzzled out the contradictions of Americanism, Wengraf argued that people there might be homogeneous, but America had created the highest standard of living for the greatest number. The average middle-class

European might be more cultivated and educated, but compared to the average American worker with a home and car, his life was "highly primitive, uncomfortable, unhygenic, and often downright unworthy." However Germans judged the value of material abundance versus cultural achievement, or uniformity versus diversity, there was no denying that in America "the outlines of a future type of human, a future human society, is visible."[26]

While Germans disagreed on whether the standardization of consumer goods in America had been carried to extremes, they were convinced that standardization, as a cultural and social value, was held in high esteem by Americans. Many found this validation of uniformity more troubling than the still diverse reality they encountered in the streets and stores of the United States. Americans simply did not understand the importance of multiplicity and differentiation, lamented Paul Rohrbach.[27] According to Arthur Feiler, they actually tried to be inconspicuous, to be like everyone else.[28] Alice Salomon concurred, claiming that individualism was not an ideal for Americans.[29] Rather than clinging to particularism as Germans did, Americans, including immigrants, wanted to eliminate all differences in lifestyle, speech and thought as well, argued Julius Hirsch. "Standardization wants to be the essence of the nation."[30]

Uniformity was one lens through which the reality of American mass consumption was viewed and frequently found wanting; culture was the other. When Germans anguished over whether America had or would develop *Kultur*, they employed a term laden with meanings to express multiple concerns. Both their general argument and the specific tropes they employed borrowed heavily from German critiques of modernity, couched in terms of culture versus civilization, *Gemeinschaft* versus *Gesellschaft*, and also from a Europe-wide discourse on America's mediocrity, superficiality, and inadequacy.[31] Commentators on economic Americanism assumed, perpetuated and popularized available images of America that had emerged in Germany since the turn of the century. These images no longer centered around the nineteenth-century themes of Indians, wilderness and freedom, but rather around industry, modernity and *Kultur*.[32]

Some of the cultural stereotypes and concerns that shaped the perceptions of travelers were quite straightforward and self-evident. Most Germans felt that America had not produced great artists, musicians, and authors; it lacked first-rate museums, operas, and concert halls. Its universities were, at best, pale replicas of European ones, while its colleges, with their emphasis on practical training, sports, and sociability, did nothing to promote science or culture.[33] In short, the institutions and representatives of high culture were lacking. Even those, like Julius Hirsch, who insisted that America had a great deal of high culture in the European sense, admitted that it was embedded in a very different context.[34]

In part, the context singled out was American mass culture—movies, radio, jazz, and spectator sports—but only in very small part. While many Weimar Germans debated the new mass culture, most commentators on American economic life discussed very little about new leisure activities.

They were more concerned about the values expressed in and encouraged by mass consumption than about the concrete forms in which they were expressed.[35] Mass culture, like mass consumption, was a reflection of a deeper problem. America not only lacked high culture; most Americans did not hold cultural institutions and achievements in high esteem. Their most basic values seemed antithetical to *Kultur*.

Germans of varied political outlooks, such as Arthur Feiler, Charlotte Lütkens, Adolf Halfeld, Moritz J. Bonn and Alfred Rühl, elaborated on these charges by describing a series of dichotomies that allegedly charac-terized the societies and mentalities of Germany and America. In their view, Germany endorsed the disinterested pursuit of intellectual and aesthetic matters and the inner development of the individual, whereas America legi-timated the production of material goods and the attainment of visible success. German culture appreciated the complex, the ambiguous, and the unique; America valorized the straightforward, the functional, and the attainable. Germans and other Europeans favored disinterested, free-flowing contemplation; Americans preferred instrumental rationality. German cul-ture was built on the creative use of leisure; America emphasized action, speed, and functionalism, whether at work or play. Germany appreciated quality; America sought to reduce everything to quantitative terms.[36] Europe understood the fundamental distinction between culture and civi-lization, whereas America merged the two, regarding technological achieve-ments as cultural accomplishments.[37]

Each author presented these dichotomies in slightly different terms, yet each came to a similar conclusion. Germany had spirit or intellect (*Geist*); America had materialism. Germany had *Kultur*; America had consumption. According to one disgruntled observer from the Ruhr, America was less the land of unlimited possibilities than "the land of absolute materialism."[38] Yet Theodor Lüddecke praised Americanism as "the most marked manifes-tation of the economic instinct in all facts of private and public life."[39] Neither condemning nor praising, Arthur Feiler wondered "what might have become the great aim of the masses of the population . . . if this eco-nomic system itself had not been able to offer them material aims which are near at hand and so relatively easy to reach?"[40] That was idle speculation, according to Paul Wengraf, for in America one was seeing the full implica-tions of a thoroughgoing materialism: "The ideal, the dream" was of a humanity, well fed, well housed and healthy, whose intellectual and social level was average, and whose enjoyments were simple and unproblematic.[41]

If American civilization was not German *Kultur*, just what was it? In trying to specify the values and activities that structured American life, Germans referred again and again to work, achievement, and pragmatism. America was a society that made a religion out of work, argued Irene Witte.[42] Economic activity was valued above all else, according to Alfred Rühl; work filled people's lives and fulfilled their spiritual and intellectual needs.[43] "Work, productivity, and a sense of responsibility are valued more than literary education," claimed an approving article in a major Ruhr business journal.[44] Taking a slightly different tack, the social worker Alice Salomon saw the distinguishing characteristic of America as the practical application of knowledge and science to conquer nature and solve concrete problems. Attentive to the situation of women, as few male travelers were, she cited the electrification of the home as a prime example of this. [45]America had, in the words of the engineer Franz Westermann, "a culture of the here and now, a culture of reality."[46] Every aspect of it was imbued with a robustness and energy that some Germans saw as the secret of America's strength and others as a sign of restlessness and emptiness.[47]

Instead of enumerating abstract values, many Germans simply described the American man. They shared the view, expressed in its most extreme form by Erwin Rosen, that "the American nation was born at the moment when the American ideal of manhood was fully articulated."[48] By German standards, the American man and the American ideal of masculinity were effective but limited, arousing admiration and anxiety in equal measure. The American man was regarded as naïve and overly optimistic, or, in harsher formulations, uncomplicated, almost childlike. He was in Rosen's words, "a very simply constructed person, very natural."[49] The language was similar to the way Europeans described their colonial subjects; but Americans could not be dismissed as unsophisticated and immature. Their naïveté was combined with incredible determination and energy, noted Westermann.[50] American optimism was built on the conscious denial of the inadequacies and evils of the world, but it instilled enormous self-assurance and an empowering sense of superiority.[51] The American man might well be a philistine, admitted his defenders, like Anton Erkelenz, but most Germans were not different.[52]

Others dissented. Adolf Halfeld condemned Americans as narrow economic men who "in their noneconomic activities are probably less demanding and more indifferent . . . than any of their contemporaries."[53] Peter Mennicken, another harsh critic of the United States, contrasted the American *homo faber*, who promoted progress and civilization, unfavorably with the European homo sapiens, who created *Kultur* and embodied *Geist*. In the discourse of which Mennicken was a part, both civilization and progress were negative terms, connoting materialism, pragmatism, fragmentation, superficiality, and conformity. Mennicken regarded Ford, that quintessential representative of America, as the perfect "*Zivilisationsmensch*." He was an organizer, not a leader (*Führer*); an inventor, not a genius. He had achievements (*Leistungen*) but no personality.[54] Like the "Ford-man" he had created, Ford had "drugged himself with work and accumulation," which had become ends in themselves instead of means to a higher end. Ford, a businessman who could talk only business, was markedly inferior to Walter Rathenau, head of German General Electric, a diplomat and politician who, in Mennicken's eyes, was "a philosopher" who could also discuss business and economics.[55]

While admitting that Americans devoted themselves exclusively to work, many Germans admired the creative and confident way in which they did so. The American man was practical, cooperative, and proud of his economic accomplishments, noted Theodor Lüddecke, Carl Köttgen, and Erwin Rosen.[56] He might lack *Kultur*, but he both understood and accepted the principles of capitalism.[57] He had a "healthy egoism," according to both Franz Westermann and Paul Wengraf. Both admired his fresh spirit and commitment to practical progress.[58] Rosen described in detail an average day in the life of Mr. Thompson, a department store sales manager in New York City. He rushed and bounced from one activity to the next, enthusiastic about everything. He personified the key characteristic of the American man, the source at once of his strength and his limitations: "the compulsion to act" (*Drang zur Tat*).[59] According to Wengraf, the American man was a "man of deeds," a "man of facts." He represented "a new bourgeois type, the Babbit . . . a mass man." Although he lacked individuality, he enabled America to fulfill its "mission" of creating a high level of civilization for mass humanity.[60]

Most Germans characterized America in similar terms, but they disagreed on whether this world of materialism, pragmatism, and instrumental rationality was the antithesis of *Kultur*, as Adolf Halfeld feared, or the harbinger of a distinctly new, as yet ill-defined kind of culture, as Julius Hirsch and Paul Wengraf maintained.[61] Some insisted it was both. Arthur Holitscher, for example, regretted the demise of European *Kultur* and he applauded the rise of Americanism and bolshevism as alternatives.[62] Germans also differed on whether "the hunt for the dollar" was predominant in American society to the exclusion of all else, as Alfred Rühl and Martin Wagner claimed, or whether materialism and idealism coexisted in surprising and new combinations, as Arthur Holitscher and Mortiz J. Bonn insisted.[63] Finally, they disagreed about whether mass consumption was an inevitable stage of capitalist development—an attribute of modernized production that Europe could embrace or reject as it chose—or an impossibility anywhere but in America.

In an effort to resolve this last question, German observers explored the prerequisites for the new American culture of consumption. Those who worried about the relationship of consumption to *Kultur* were not concerned with what kinds of technology, wages, and markets led to mass consumption—issues that preoccupied and bitterly divided industrialists and trade unionists; rather, they were interested in what kind of individual, history, and society produced that result.

American consumption was built on American consumers, who had a reputation among Germans for being unsophisticated and easily satisfied. Whereas Germans—or at any rate, those in the middle and upper classes who could afford it—insisted that goods, whether for business or personal use, be made to their specifications, Americans were content with standardized products. German needs were purportedly defined by tradition; American needs, by the market. German tastes changed slowly; Americans were swept up by one fad after another. These stereotypes, which both reflected and exaggerated American consumption patterns, had existed prior to World

War I.[64] Weimar Germans did not question their validity, choosing instead to explore how Americans developed these tastes and habits of consumption.

American mass consumption went hand in hand with a uniformity of lifestyles and attitudes, as many observers noted. Public opinion, personal appearance, and behavior were so standardized that German visitors often had trouble knowing whether they were dealing with a businessman, a professional, or a worker. Every aspect of American society, from the relative absence of class conflict to the imposition of prohibition and the one-class transportation system, reflected this homogeneity.[65] But what was cause and what was effect? Some sought an answer in the specific dynamics of mass production and consumption. Wilhelm Vershofen maintained that highly rationalized, Fordist production methods so exhausted and exploited workers that they sought relief in stimulating, sensual, and irrational consumption, symbolized by the automobile.[66] Viewing the relationship more positively, Theodor Lüddecke stated that standardized production shaped people's character, accustoming them to standardized goods.[67] According to Moritz J. Bonn, there was "a democratization of need satisfaction" in America that contrasted sharply with the class-specific consumption patterns of Europe. As demand became generalized, prices were lowered, and lower prices enabled demand to become yet more general, with the ironic result that manufacturers became rich while the poor ceased to envy them because they, too, participated in consumption. "This democratization of need satisfaction is simultaneously a prerequisite for and a result of standardization," Bonn concluded.[68] This was an accurate description but nonetheless unsatisfying, for it failed to explain whether the supply of uniform goods automatically created its own demand, or whether the peculiarities of American history produced the desire for mass products.[69]

Several authors pointed out the multiple ways in which American business sought to create demand instead of waiting passively for it to arise. High wages and standardized mass production were the principal but not the only means. Advertising and credit buying, the chain store, and the mail order catalog were also singled out. They expanded markets geographically and socially; of equal importance, they suggested new needs and created new demands.[70] Whereas these measures were not completely unknown in Europe, they originated in America and were much more developed there. Many Germans seem to have viewed them warily, as products of the American character and value system and hence antithetical to German culture.

Many sought the roots of uniform consumption in American history, singling out two distinctly American phenomena. One was the frontier experience, which forced pioneers to focus on basic needs and generated a desire for equality; the other was Puritanism, which stressed conformity in belief and lifestyle and condemned individuality as arrogance.[71] Heinz Marr viewed Fordism as an expression of radical Puritanism, and standardization in production and consumption as an effort to subject people to the "ideal monotony and uniformity of the Puritan regementation of life."[72]

German observers did not explore the emergence in the late nineteenth and early twentieth century of a new consumer culture with its ethos of self-realization through consumption.[73]

Most Weimar Germans were less concerned with American tradition than with the lack of traditional thought and behavior that characterized American society. They saw immigration as the key to explaining the mutability and uniformity of needs and demands. Immigrants to America were regarded as creatures very different from the Germans or Englishmen or Russians they had once been. Far from being burdened with the customs and values of the old world, the millions of Europeans who immigrated to America were eager and able to assimilate. The typical lower-class immigrant brought little from his homeland, argued Moritz J. Bonn, because "he is not only socially disenfranchised but also intellectually and spiritually disinherited."[74] According to Alfred Rühl, "he wanted to leave behind and forget his tradition, he wished to become a different person."[75] In this interpretation, the experience of crossing the Atlantic erased the immigrant's previous culture. The immigrant mind was a kind of tabula rasa on which American culture—or, more aptly, American consumption—could write what it chose. Immigrants were preoccupied with "the creation of an existence, the hope for savings and possessions," according to the trade union delegation.[76] Immigrants let business define needs and determine what type and style of goods would satisfy them. Even those wishing to preserve some tradition or some individualism were unlikely to succeed, for, once in America, "greenhorns" were subject to extraordinary pressures to conform. What they chose to think or buy was influenced by their workplace, school or church, and by the media. As a result, diverse immigrants quickly became Americanized and were willing, indeed eager, to consume whatever mass goods were available.[77]

This view of immigrants and immigration was superficial and schematic, ignoring the different experiences and opportunities of women and men and among different generations and ethnic groups. It exaggerated the extent of mass consumption in America while downplaying the spread of standardized, although not necessarily mass produced, goods in Germany. From the perspective of the late twentieth century, when mass consumption is so widespread not only in Europe but elsewhere, the effort to link American mass consumption to the frontier or Puritanism seems farfetched. Nonetheless, American consumption, especially in the industrial Midwest to which so many Germans traveled, did differ qualitatively and quantitatively from that in Weimar Germany. Germans were genuinely puzzled by the dynamics of mass consumption. They sought to understand which goods were candidates for such consumption; whether people of any or all classes would purchase them; and whether desirable or detrimental social and cultural consequences would come in their wake. Their contorted theories about the heritage of Puritanism, the effects of immigration, and the fate of *Kultur* are a testament to just how difficult it was to imagine mass consumption in all its complexity.

Middle-class commentators were divided about the future of mass consumption in Germany. As we saw, most industrialists argued that mass production and mass consumption were impossible, at least in the foreseeable future, because Germany lacked markets, capital, and the ability to pay high wages. The automobile would never be widely purchased, mail-order houses were impossible, and the chain store was a threat to traditional businesses. Some cultural critics of mass consumption worried that it might come— either because Germans foolishly desired it or because it was essential to economic recovery and successful competition with America.[78] Only a few, like the engineer F. Warlimont, thought that Germany could and should consciously imitate Ford's sales strategies and consumption model.[79] Fewer still agreed with Paul Wengraf that, even though American mass consumption represented the triumph of civilization over *Kultur*, "the Americanization of Europe is an irresistible fact."[80] Thus, whether they argued in terms of hard economic facts or took a romantic view of German traditions, most bourgeois visitors did not believe that the culture of consumption would soon transform the fatherland.

As we discussed earlier, party and trade union leaders, functionaries, and intellectuals believed that mass consumption, and the high wages and standardized mass production on which it had to be built, would serve the interests not only of workers but also of capitalists. Mass consumption was the essence of Fordism and the secret of American economic successs. It represented the logic of the next stage of capitalist development—which had already been realized in America—and it transformed production in ways that would promote socialism. Those trade union members who immigrated to America wrote back glowing reports of the goods they could acquire and the more satisfying life they led as a result.[81]

Social Democrats and trade unionists viewed mass consumption as necessary but were not convinced that it was inevitable. They encountered staunch capitalist resistance to their proposals for mass-consumption in the earliest stages of the debate about Fordism and rationalization, and would continue to encounter it throughout the late 1920s. Even though Social Democrats asserted that capitalism must develop, sooner or later, in the direction of technological rationalization, mass production and mass consumption, they worried that industrialists would distort capitalist development, to their own detriment and that of workers.

Although Social Democrats preached the gospel of mass consumption, they were uncertain how such an economy would function in Germany. Some assumed there was a ready market for more mass-produced goods; others argued that Germans would have to be educated to purchase the standardized products of rationalized industry.[82] Most ignored advertising and viewed credit buying with suspicion.[83] The left was as vague about what values would structure a culture of consumption as they were about its economic mechanisms. Social Democrats naïvely assumed that Germany could have mass consumption without oppressive uniformity, just as they had insisted that it could have mass production without undermining quality work.[84] They wanted the virtues of Americanism without the perceived vices.

Social Democrats defined the content of mass consumption largely in negative terms. Most were convinced that the automobile would not be the center of production and consumption in Germany as it was in America. According to Kurt Heinig, those who desired an American-style car culture suffered from "autoism."[85] Nor could Germany, given its size and diversity, sustain mail-order houses like Sears and Roebuck.[86] Efforts to develop a more positive picture of German mass consumption proved singularly unsuccessful. Tarnow's famous slogan, his advice to German capitalists to produce, "not baking ovens but bread,"[87] was symptomatic of the movement's difficulties in imagining mass consumption. It emphasized the satisfaction of basic subsistence needs, by a most basic good, rather than the creation of new needs, or the satisfaction of existing ones by new means. Tarnow's slogan missed the whole point of the American economic model, and it failed to offer a concrete cure for the German economy. Yes, Tarnow did recognize the importance of domestic demand and the need to stimulate it; he valued spending not saving. But he seemed to have little idea of what should be produced for domestic consumption. He and his fellow Social Democrats may have been right that it couldn't be cars, but it certainly wasn't bread. "Not machine tools but motorcycles." "Not exports but appliances" would have been better slogans. Yet Social Democrats did not explore the wealth of goods between the extremes of bread and cars. Their vision of a consumer society remained devoid of consumer goods.

The difficulties in imagining mass consumption sprang in part from the constricted material circumstances of the mid- and late 1920s. Real wages did not reach their prewar level until 1928, and roughly 75 percent of workers' income went for food, rent, and clothing. Food alone accounted for 45 percent of a working-class family's wages, as against only a third of that of white-collar workers and civil servants. The majority of workers lived in housing built before World War I; half of the apartments lacked toilets, and an even greater number lacked electricity. The housing built during Weimar—often as a result of state programs initiated by the SPD—was much better, but only the best-paid workers could afford it.[88] Given the limited disposable income of the average worker, it was hard to imagine precisely what could be produced and consumed on a mass scale to have the desired macroeconomic effects on productivity and employment. It was easier for Social Democrats to begin with wage demands and worry later about what increased wages might purchase. Given the inadequacy of the housing stock, it seemed sensible to concentrate on building new housing rather than focus on what kinds of appliances and furniture would be needed. Social Democrats were more at ease inventing strategies to increase aggregate wages and social consumption than those to satisfy individual needs.

The Social Democrats' vision of "the new person" and an "ennobled" mass culture further shaped, and limited, their vision of mass consumption. As Adelheid von Saldern argues, Social Democrats were very concerned

with reforming, rationalizing, and disciplining working-class life. They
sought to eliminate the perceived evils of older proletarian lifestyles, such
as taking in roomers and boarders, frequenting pubs, and having numerous
children, and the new distractions and temptations of mass culture, such as
movies, radio, and spectator sports. As a feature of the new lifestyle, only
carefully chosen and functional products would be acquired in rational and
efficient ways.[89] The product was less important than how it was consumed.
Consumption was seen neither as an end in itself nor as a means to self-
realization or as a positive source of pleasure.[90] The "new person" was to
have modern consumer preferences but not be defined by what he or she
consumed. The Social Democrats wanted mass consumption but not a culture of consumption.

The American Woman

Many of the deepest fears and reservations Weimar Germans expressed about
the culture of consumption and the consequences of economic modernity centered around the American woman and American gender relations. At first
glance, this seems puzzling. After all, it was Henry Ford and his engineers
and auto workers—that is, men, individually and collectively—who were
the icons of the new economic order. Detroit, that mecca of German travelers to America, had an overwhelmingly male workforce.[91] And it was German men who debated the economic aspects of Fordism in terms first and
foremost of their impact on men's wages, work, and profits.

The prominence of women and gender in this debate can be understood
more as a product of German anxieties than of American realities. War and
revolution, economic crisis and new attitudes toward sexuality, political
instability and emergent mass culture had altered German women's position—sometimes in ways that were emancipatory, often not—and created
enormous anxieties about male power and privilege as well as about women's
roles and responsibilities. German economic and political debates were
haunted by the figures of the "new woman"—young, stylish, liberated—
who rejected marriage or combined it with work and motherhood; of the
woman voter, unpredictable but presumably conservative; and of the older
woman, single or married, who worked from necessity, not choice, at jobs
many men felt should be theirs.[92] Already preoccupied with gender at home,
Germans confronted not only the realities of women and gender in America
but the representations of women in American mass culture in Germany.
For many, women came to symbolize all the contradictions and ambiguities,
as well as the opportunities, of modernity. Debates about the German economic crisis and the possibilities of a Fordist solution thus slid easily, almost
inevitably, into discussions of American culture, high and low, and of the
erotic crisis that purportedly loomed large in both societies.[93]

The amorphous anxiety expressed about women and gender relations
in America coalesced around three principal concerns. Those preoccupied
with the American culture of consumption questioned whether women and

an elusive but powerful feminine sensibility bore the primary responsibility—or blame—for promoting standardized mass consumption. Others, concerned more with *Kultur* than consumption, scrutinized the relationship between women's powerful position in American society and the ostensible feminization of American high culture. Nearly all bemoaned the transformation of home, family, and sexuality in America in ways that might well be modern and rationalized but which seemed soulless, disturbing, and distinctly unEuropean. Whereas the American man, whether worker or capitalist, aroused admiration even as his limitations were acknowledged, the American woman engendered anxiety or hostility in the majority of German commentators. Her achievements and virtues were considered to be as problematic as her failings. Before we explore the pervasive and pernicious influence attributed to women, we must examine the image of the American woman constructed by Weimar Germans.

Discussions of "the American woman" were conducted almost exclusively about middle-class women. To be sure, "middle class" was broadly construed, for the image of the American woman was a composite picture, drawn from the experiences of shopgirls and secretaries, professional women and college students, middle-class social reformers and church women, and the nonemployed wives of businessmen. But certain groups were virtually omitted and invisible—factory girls, domestic servants, married homeworkers, recent immigrants, and black women from the North and South.[94]

The commentators, like the objects of their analysis, were overwhelmingly bourgeois. Now and again Social Democrats, trade unionists, or workers who had immigrated made a passing and usually derogatory reference to women and gender.[95] Social Democrats tried to redefine the American bourgeois "new woman" in ways compatible with the movement's vision of politics and motherhood, while Communists dismissed her as one more perversion of capitalist culture. The American working-class woman was seen as yet another example of suffering and exploited proletarian womanhood, such as existed in abundance in Germany.[96] In general, however, the left remained resolutely focused on male workers and male capitalists, on the world of work and technology. Not so bourgeois observers, whose gaze wandered nervously from the factory floor to both the home and the public sphere of politics and culture.

In America middle-class Germans encountered what prewar Germans, such as the Harvard psychology professor Hugo Münsterberg, had already discovered, namely that women seemed to enjoy much greater equality and power than their European counterparts.[97] Germans claimed that American women were held in high regard and were able to make their influence felt at home and at work, in culture and society.[98] Women had much greater legal equality and public visibility.[99] They had the same educational opportunities as men; indeed, they often received more education, for men frequently abandoned their studies for lucrative jobs. The education might well be superficial by European standards, but women had access not merely to the same kinds of schooling, but the very same institutions, as men.[100]

According to German observers, American women viewed paid employment as positive and natural, yet they did not pursue the almighty dollar
with the single-minded devotion of American men.[101] They were believed
to work in greater numbers than their European counterparts (a false
assumption) and have a greater chance to compete with men for desirable
jobs.[102] According to Arthur Holitscher, in both business and the professions, "the American woman has established herself much more securely
and has achieved much higher paying positions than the European woman."[103]
Both before and after the war, she had a better chance of marrying.[104] Due
to both the general level of prosperity and to household technology, she
had an easier home life and more time for a career, cultural activity, or "serious social work."[105] And if she chose to remain single, claimed Alice
Salomon, she could own a car, have a country house, and be accepted as a
success.[106] There were those who viewed the American woman's economic
role and public presence much more negatively, seeing her as leading a life
of decadent leisure and frivolous consumption. But even they acknowledged
her greater equality and influence.[107]

This was undoubtedly an exaggerated and one-sided view, as some of
those who were most enthusiastic about the position of American women
eventually discovered. In the 1920s, for example, Salomon said she wanted
to be born in America in her next reincarnation; in the 1930s she found
herself there as a refugee from Hitler and was bitterly disappointed at the
lack of opportunities, recognition, and support America offered.[108] Nonetheless, when viewed quickly or from afar, the American woman in the
decade after World War I did seem to enjoy an enviable kind of equality
and freedom, whether or not she worked, and whether or not she married
and had children. Though she may not have shattered traditional gender
definitions, she had loosened their grip.

In an effort to discover the source of the American woman's power and
influence—which some found admirable and others "exorbitant"[109]—German
commentators traced their roots to the country's early history. They believed
that, as in many colonial societies, there had been a relative lack of women
that persisted through the settling of the frontier in the nineteenth century.
Because the women were essential to building a new country and guarding
morality, they were highly prized by men.[110] Women took advantage of the
situation to enhance their influence in both the public and private spheres,
transforming a "state with men's rights" into a "woman's state."[111] But how
was women's advantageous position perpetuated long after the frontier was
closed? Some argued that American women had secured legal rights and positions of economic and cultural power from which they could not be dislodged.
Coeducation, a phenomenon that fascinated many Germans, further expanded
women's opportunities and influence.[112]

Thus, by the twentieth century the American woman's exceptional
status no longer depended on imbalanced sex ratios or male consent. But
male recognition she did have, as many noted. In distraught tones, Adolf
Halfeld condemned American men not only for tolerating women's promi-

nence, but also for believing that woman actually were morally, intellectually, and aesthetically superior.[113] Others saw the key to women's pervasive influence in men's preoccupation with economic affairs and lack of
interest in culture.

If the American woman was viewed as "a creature especially favored
by fate," she was also seen as the embodiment of the values that dominated
America. The American woman was believed to share a fascination with
technology and an enthusiasm for machinery. She embraced the ideas of
efficiency, rationalization, uniformity, and discipline, and participated in
the American "body culture,"[114] with its emphasis on health, physical training, and sports. Nothing illustrated the complex links between women and
American values better than that quintessentially American form of entertainment, the all-woman precision dance team. The psychotechnician Fritz
Giese and the film critic Siegfried Kracauer, for example, both insisted that
the Tiller Girls, the most famous of these dance troupes and all the rage in
Berlin in the mid-1920s, were the consummate expression of Americanism.[115]
According to Giese, these dancing "girls" were "movement machines," who
captured America's obsession with technology, admiration for collective
discipline, and enthusiasm for rationalization. They celebrated athleticism
and neutralized eroticism in ways that were peculiarly American. The Tiller
Girls reflected the economic power and influence of American women as
well as American economic values.[116]

For many Germans the power and influence of American women were
deeply threatening; so too were the values they embodied. Technology and
efficiency, rationalization and standardization were creative, if limiting,
when valorized by men, but disturbing when embraced by women.[117]
Equality and camaraderie between male bosses and male workers promoted
productivity and profits; equality and camaraderie between women and men
subverted gender hierarchies and privileges. It was not the American
woman's economic position that most concerned Germans; greater economic
opportunity and equality were even applauded by some observers, men as
well as women. Rather, it was the American woman's influence on culture
and consumption, on home and sexuality that was troubling.

The American woman was seen as a prime promoter of mass consumption, just as she was of mass culture. Because American men devoted themselves to production and work, women were responsible for consumption
and leisure. They showed themselves particularly susceptible to the superficial, escapist and distracting features of new cultural forms.[118] Like their
German counterparts, they were the majority of movie audiences and were
assumed to view films passively and uncritically.[119] American women were
equally receptive to the worst aspects of mass consumption, according to
Adolf Halfeld, who expressed these widespread concerns in the most concise and extreme form. Women eagerly purchased the uniform and monotonous products of mass production; they fell for every fad, displaying a distinctly feminine emotional instability. Men did not serve as a counterweight
to the mediocrity and fickleness of female taste; as a result of being taught

and dominated by women, they had become feminized. "Only via the woman and her unique cultural leadership role could standardization conquer all aspects of American life," Halfeld concluded.[120]

The American woman was not only integral to the culture of consumption; she was absolutely central to *Kultur*, or what passed for it in America. "The man devoted himself to business, the woman to culture," reiterated Moritz J. Bonn in nearly every work he wrote.[121] According to Alice Salomon, there was a distinct "feminization of culture," for women were not only the principal consumers of culture, but its principal organizers, promoters, and shapers.[122] Women represented the vast majority of teachers at all levels below college. This feminization of the teaching profession, the result of abundant job opportunities for men and coeducation, was striking to Germans. Even more unusual and troubling, by European standards, was the central role that women played in promoting museums, concerts, and the theater. Men might provide the money, but women determined the cultural uses to which it was put. In so doing, women imposed their own tastes, rather than deferring to the intellectual and aesthetic judgments of men. Perhaps they had no choice, admitted some Germans, for America had no significant group of artists and intellectuals; it had no leisured aristocracy; and it had no male bourgeoisie who appreciated literature and the arts. In short, it lacked the masculine social base of *Kultur* in Europe.[123] Intellectually and organizationally, men surrendered the field of culture to women, willingly and unthinkingly.

Judgments varied on what women had created. Adolf Halfeld was predictably most upset by the feminization of all emotions, tastes, art, and thought. This was, he insisted, the American problem in its most dangerous, almost pathological form.[124] Charlotte Lütkens' assessment was more mixed. Although she admired women's independence, energy, and dedication in cultural activities, she believed that "a sphere of cultural activity so completely directed and measured by women lacks, in large measure, the tensions and subtlties . . . which enable the pure work of speculation or fantasy to come to life for society."[125] Moritz J. Bonn and Alice Salomon were more positive, arguing that although women had not created a sophisticated and introspective European culture, they had created one which emphasized the useful, the practical, and the moral. Nearly all agreed that women's cultural and social power was directly responsible for that most incomprehensible and uniquely American phenomenon: Prohibition.[126]

The culture women created was thus seen as a manifestation of values that permeated American economic life—such as practicality and concreteness—and as a complement to the one-sided, materialistic preoccupations of American economic man. It combined pragmatism and moralism, and added culture to consumption, but in ways that bourgeois Germans found to be superficial, unoriginal, and unsatisfying. Even more disturbing, American culture was judged to have "distorted the natural order of a relationship in which, so long as people can remember, woman has received the creative spark from man."[127]

Americanism turned the world upside down, not only in the public sphere of culture, but in the private sphere of domesticity. Although it is not clear whether German commentators actually observed American family life at first hand, many claimed with astonishment that the American woman was treated almost like a goddess at home. Home was not her separate sphere, in which she exerted complete control over a limited range of affairs. Rather it was a realm in which she ostensibly exercized far-reaching decision making and in which men served her needs and obeyed her wishes in a manner Germans found to be obsequious.[128] The American man not only showed verbal deference; he was even reported to wash the dishes, clean the house, and care for the children—all in order to please his demanding wife.[129] "Over there," noted Fritz Giese, "there are no separate male and female spheres of duty. Being a woman does not mean being a cook or mother."[130] As one unhappy man summarized the situation, in Europe man was the lord of the house; in America woman was the queen.[131] Women travelers, it should be noted, were more skeptical about whether such a radical redivison of domestic labor had occurred, but even they admitted with envy that American men did more around the house than their German counterparts.[132]

The home over which the American woman ruled was seen as quintessentially modern. German travelers paid no attention to the tenements and old homes in the East, focusing instead on newer single-family housing in the Midwest and West or the modern apartment buildings in places like New York. Houses were constructed in the simplest, most functional manner, they argued, and the work required to maintain them had been reduced to a minimum. Not only was there running water, electricity, and central heating; there were household appliances in dazzling abundance.[133] Even in the homes of skilled workers, one could find refrigerators, vacuum cleaners, electric cookers, and washing machines.[134] Everyone relied heavily on canned goods to simplify meals, and many families ate out frequently at the automat or soda fountain or, for special occasions, at a restaurant or club.[135] Americans had a "rational lifestyle" that was nowhere more evident than in the home.

German observers offered several explanations for such pervasive household rationalization and mechanization. First and foremost the shortage of servants and their high cost forced an alteration in the design and functioning of middle-class homes. Money could buy technology and services outside the home much more readily than it could be used to hire domestics.[136] But labor market conditions alone did not explain the radically different nature of the American home. Its far-reaching rationalization reflected the low regard in which Americans held housework. According to German observers, the American woman did not regard housework as a *Beruf*, an occupation from which to derive meaning and satisfaction. Rather, it was a boring and burdensome necessity that should be dispensed with as efficiently as possible so that more important and interesting activities could be undertaken.[137] Finally, it was believed that household technology and functional modern architecture helped the American woman overcome her inadequacies as a housewive. Many Germans shared Franz Westermann's view that "The [American] woman is a brilliant social companion and a partner for her man, assuming he earns enough money. If she wants to, she is also often a diligent business woman. But the talents of a good housewife in the German sense are usually not present."[138]

The modern American household was a prerequisite for the American woman, enabling her to pursue paid employment or cultural activities as she chose.[139] But modernity had its price. America had realized what the Bauhaus theorized, and many Germans, however much they applauded the American rationalized factory, found the American home cold and soulless. It lacked cozy nooks and superfluous spaces; it had none of the comfort and clutter and charm that ostensibly characterized its German counterpart.[140] The spacious kitchen had been reduced to a functional minimum. Such a kitchen was "the symbol of the emancipated woman," noted the trade union delegation with a deep ambivalence toward both the kitchen and the lib-eration of women it reflected.[141] And that ambivalence was widely shared. The American woman was seen as pursuing rationalization and mechaniza-tion at the expense of any proper spirit of care and nurturance. She led much of her life outside the home, as did her husband and children, so that family life and cultivated domesticity in the German bourgeois sense were miss-ing.[142] Some attributed this to the underdeveloped American need for a private sphere; others to the fact that in America "the personal life of an individualistic age can be maintained only by having recourse to drastic measures of socialization," by which was meant everything from efficiency apartments and canned goods to automats and laundry services.[143] Whether or not they viewed the American house as desirable or inevitable, most Germans shared Salomon's view that it was not a "home."[144]

The American woman was not judged more favorably when it came to love and sexuality. As sexual subject and object, she was a most puz-zling creature to German observers. Deeply involved in America's body cul-ture, she pursued physical fitness and beauty relentlessly. The result was health, strength, and performance—a rationalized body but an asexual self-presentation. She was not seen as masculine so much as neutered. "Nowhere in Europe, except in England" argued Fritz Giese, "is there this kind of accen-tuated modesty, neutralization of sexual difference, elimination of feminin-ity."[145] According to Alice Salomon, American women were "undersexed," perhaps because of their education with its stress on activity and sports, perhaps because of career demands.[146] The American woman as a new type—asexual and unerotic but distinctly modern and very powerful—both fascinated and frightened Germans who saw imitations of her at home.[147]

The American woman's behavior, like her self-presentation, diverged markedly from European norms. Some accused her of flirting continuously but setting narrow limits to that flirtation.[148] Others claimed she insisted on platonic friendships and abruptly rejected any erotic overtures.[149] All agreed that she set the rules of dating and courtship, just as she did of marriage—an "Amazon state in miniature," according to Adolf Halfeld.[150] Building on the heritage of Puritanism, she imposed a single and by European criteria, restrictive sexual standard.[151] In literature as in life, the American woman was concerned with marriage but incapable of grand passion. Love was approached in a rational, objective, rather calculating manner, and this, argued observers like Moritz J. Bonn, was the prerequisite for women's equality.[152]

For some Germans the American woman's appearance and behavior, her mixture of openness and asexuality, reflected America's own contradictory attitudes toward sexuality. For Arthur Holitscher, America was a confusing mixture of Puritanism and repression, progressive sexual attitudes and prostitution. The media flaunted sexuality, while morality condemned it.[153] To illustrate American ambivalence, Giese offered two photos. One showed a woman having her legs decorated with painted designs; the other pictured the Florida morals police measuring the length of a woman's bathing suit to be sure that she complied with the law. Flirtation, with its superficiality and allusions, epitomized American gender relations, he believed, while sexuality was silenced and suppressed.[154]

For others, the American woman was less a product of America's religious past than a preview of Europe's future. Paul Wengraf, an enthusiast of both America and Russia, praised the new woman "who adjusted to the new economic and social forms, organized her life independently, and withdrew from the egotistical rule of the man."[155] Few were as unequivocally enthusiastic. Even such admirers of the American woman and American gender relations as Bonn and Salomon, acknowledged that Germany would pay a cultural and spiritual price for imitating them. Theodor Lüddecke interrupted his extended plea for Germany to emulate America economically with a tirade about the erotic crisis he saw existing in both societies, a crisis symbolized by silk stockings and modern dances, a declining birth rate, and a new sexual morality. He admired Ford for trying to restore tradition and respectability to family and social relationships at the same time he promoted mass production and mass consumption.[156] But Lüddecke seemed unsure whether even his hero could stem the tide.

While industrialists and engineers, Social Democrats and social workers, politicians and journalists argued about the cultural consequences of Americanism and the American woman, they recognized that some form of economic restructuring would have to occur in Germany immediately. Bourgeois Germans might well believe that their past culture was superior and Social Democrats, that their economic and social projects promised a more progressive future, but both groups recognized that the American economy and economic model dominated the present.

II

MODERNIZING
GERMANY

7

The Paradoxes of Productivism

The German debate about Americanism and Fordism raged from 1924 and until the early 1930s, but Germany's intense experiment in industrial restructuring lasted only from 1925 to 1929. German industry, especially those sectors most involved in the war economy, had introduced some organizational and technological changes between 1914 and 1918 and had transformed some products and production processes during the postwar conversion to a peacetime economy.[1] But there was no sustained modernization then or in the subsequent chaotic years of inflation and hyperinflation, which erased debts, lowered rents, reduced wages, and aided exports. Inflation thereby permitted full employment and profits without industrial restructuring and encouraged a "flight into real values," regardless of how technologically backward they were. Productive efficiency and technological modernity were neither economically rewarded nor socially valued.

All that changed in 1924. The stabilization of the mark and the renegotiation of reparations made industrial restructuring not only politically possible, but also economically essential. The most precarious firms and ventures had collapsed, unemployment was soaring, and the full extent of Germany's technological and organizational backwardness was exposed. In these changed economic circumstances employers attacked state social policy as economically intolerable, while workers saw all their postwar economic and social gains threatened.[2] Labor and capital, engineers and economists, politicians and journalists all recognized that if Germany was to compete in a shrinking world market and pay reparations, and if industry was to make a profit and workers were to enjoy a higher standard of living, the economy would have to be rationalized. But the varied proponents of rationalization envisioned very different things and were unequally positioned to imple- ment those visions. As the English observer Walter Meakin dramatically expressed it:

> Just as the employers were moved to act swiftly and ruthlessly by the pressure of financial and economic circumstances after the inflation and the French occu- pation, so the destitute workers had no option in their desperate situation but to acquiesce passively in the employers' policy. Their leaders had to be content to give tacit support to the reorganization, however ruthless it might be in its first effects on unemployment, in the belief that it would be better for the work- ers in the long run.[3]

Finally, the influx of American capital from 1924 on meant that possibility and necessity could be translated into reality.[4]

The "rationalization boom," as the Austrian Socialist Otto Bauer labeled it, led to the closing of many inefficient factories and the restructuring of many others as production was concentrated, integrated, mechanized, and reorganized.[5] German industry adopted a multitude of new technologies, ranging from mechanized tools, like the pneumatic mining hammer, to sophisticated assembly lines and modern steel mills on the American model. The state, the RKW, and various engineering associations developed norms and standards while engineers, psychologists, and physiologists implemented the latest findings of psychotechnics and industrial sociology. In the eyes of the Social Democrat Otto Suhr, German rationalization represented "a *revolutionary* episode in the *evolutionary* development of technology."[6] According to Meakin, it was "a new industrial revolution."[7]

The reality of German industrial restructuring was more limited, con- tradictory, and, for all concerned, unsatisfactory than such sweeping state- ments implied.[8] Between the stabilization crisis and the world economic depression, only a few years and relatively limited capital were available to modernize Weimar's ailing economy, and actual deeds could not match the outpouring of words about rationalization.[9] The transformations within a given branch of industry as well as among different sectors were highly uneven, and many ambitious, multiyear projects for modernization slowed or stalled completely as the economic crisis began in 1929.

The achievements of the "rationalization movement" were not only lim- ited in scope but problematic in nature.[10] Proponents of rationalization had expected it to increase efficiency and productivity, lower costs and prices, raise wages and profits, and improve general welfare, although they dis- agreed about the sequence and magnitude of these changes.[11] Productivity per worker and overall productive capacity rose considerably, but neither foreign nor domestic markets expanded proportionately. Wages rose but so, too, did unemployment. Although Germans claimed to prefer Fordism to Taylorism, Taylorist techniques were introduced extensively, while neither the Fordist assembly line nor mass consumption developed on a significant scale. The technical and economic visions of industry thus came much closer to realization than did the optimistic projections of Social Democrats. Industry emerged from the years of rationalization with factories that were more modern and efficient but not fully mechanized, let alone Fordized, in terms of organization, technology, and product line. For better or worse, German rationalization bore little resemblance to economic Americanism.

The contradictory effects of rationalization on production can be seen in the activities of the RKW and in the restructuring of Ruhr mining, Ruhr iron and steel, and machine making. A subsequent chapter will assess who won and lost from rationalization by exploring costs and profits, prices and wages, skill structures, and unemployment.

The National Productivity Board

German industry began restructuring with extensive encouragement and aid from a variety of public and private institutions dedicated to promoting rationalization. The economic historian Hans Motteck estimated that in the mid- and late 1920s, there were six hundred private organizations, eighty-five state offices, and sixty-seven state research and testing institutes that worked on problems related to rationalization.[12] It took the *Handbook of Rationalization* nearly fifty pages to provide brief descriptions of the major ones. These included the National Productivity Board (RKW), the German Standards Committee (DNA), the National Committee for Conditions and Terms of Delivery, the Committee for Efficient Production, and the Committee for Efficient Management. Operating on the more narrowly technological front were such private organizations as the Association of German Engineers (VDI), the German Association for Testing of Materials, the Central Bureau for Heat Economy, and the many research institutes of the state-funded Kaiser Wilhelm Society that were devoted to chemistry, physics, and technology. Time-and-motion studies and the problems of fatigue, monotony, and joy in work were all studied by such associations as the National Committee for Time Study (Refa) and the Kaiser Wilhelm Institute for Work Physiology, while advice on vocational education was proffered by The German Committee for Technical Education (DATSCH) and the German Institute for Technical Labor Training (Dinta). Although industry was at the center of rationalization efforts, a variety of organizations devoted themselves to wholesale and retail trade, artisan work, cost accounting, and housework.[13] As Peter Hinrichs noted, many were modeled on American associations, but the degree of state involvement and the sheer number of private institutions was a product of "German thoroughness"[14]— or perhaps a caricature of it.

The state occupied a peculiar position, at once central and marginal, in the rationalization movement of the 1920s. As Robert Brady correctly argued, key government ministries were both affected by and themselves involved in rationalization efforts. These included the Ministry of Traffic, especially the railroad division, the Ministry of Labor, the Ministry of Food and Agriculture, and the Ministry of Economics. The state civil service adopted the language and to some extent the practices of administrative rationalization.[15] Yet there was no state ministry of rationalization, nor even a state committee, that was devoted to coordinating rationalization efforts in the private sector. State planning had been defeated and discredited along with socialization in the immediate postwar period, and the National Economic Council, established by the Weimar constitution, was limited and ineffectual.[16] Politicians representing virtually all political parties endorsed the idea of rationalization, but their practical role as parliamentarians was restricted to allocating state funds for private initiatives over which they had little control. The Kaiser Wilhelm Society, for example, depended on state funding, as did the engineering and industrial sociology departments of technical universities. Even more important, the RKW, the primary body for coordinating and publicizing rationalization efforts, received government subsidies.

The RKW embodied what Carl Köttgen and other industrialists so admired in America. Rationalization was to be planned and implemented by voluntary "cooperative work" among industrialists and engineers, but this work was to be state-funded on a scale unprecedented in the United States or any European country.[17] In its initial incarnation as the Reichskuratorium für Wirtschaftlichkeit in Industrie und Handwerk, the RKW was a far cry from what it became by mid-decade. Established in 1921 to further wartime efforts to standardize elements of production, the RKW enjoyed the support of the National Economics Ministry and had close ties to some engineering circles. Because the times were not conducive to rationalization, however, the RKW was poorly funded, little known, and relatively inactive.[18]

After his 1924 trip to America, Köttgen sought to remedy this situation, for, as we saw earlier, he was convinced that the combined efforts of Hoover's Commerce Department and the National Industrial Conference Board contributed significantly to high productivity in the United States. In the spring of 1925 Köttgen lobbied leading industrialists, the heads of engineering associations, and members of parliament, sending them copies of *Economic America* and inviting them to an open meeting of the RKW. There C. F. von Siemens urged the audience to learn from America without imitating it in toto. A resolution was passed to request the Reichstag to provide 1.5 million marks for an expanded RKW. Hans von Raumer, a German People's Party deputy and representative of light industry, coordinated the parliamentary end of the campaign, and the full sum, which was 10 percent of the entire budget of the Ministry of Economics, was granted.[19] The renamed Reichskuratorium für Wirtschaftlichkeit, was headed by Siemens, with Köttgen as his deputy and Herbert Hinnenthal as business manager.[20]

According to its 1926 statutes, the RKW was to promote rationalization, whose goal, in turn, was "an increase in the general welfare through less expensive, more available, and better quality products." State funding, the statutes continued, guaranteed the RKW's independence but also imposed an obligation to benefit "the entire population." The RKW was to proceed not by implementing rationalization measures itself, but by recommending appropriate action and by "encouraging and supporting cooperative work among all involved circles."[21]

In fact, the RKW never cast its net this broadly when recruiting people for its many unpaid committees. The 1921 statutes stated that the RKW was committed to "supporting individual firms" in their rationalization efforts. Although the 1926 statutes omitted this mandate, the organization's membership assured that the goal would be served. Of its 216 members in 1927, 120 represented industry, 14 were from banking, trade, and transport, 6 from large-scale agriculture, and 5 from the artisan sector. There were 34 technical and economic officials and 19 academics and scientists, among whom only Julius Hirsch represented the left. There were 11 nationalist and Catholic members of parliament, 3 from the Democratic Party (including the only 2 women), and 3 Social Democrats—Peter Grassmann from the Trade Union Confederation, August Schmidt from the Miners' Union, and Rudolf Hilferding from the SPD.[22] No wonder the left viewed the RKW so cynically.[23] Even Hinnenthal urged Köttgen to increase worker representation in order to win working-class support for rationalization.[24] The plea fell on deaf ears. According to Robert Brady, the RKW "bent its efforts almost from the start primarily to the giving of aid and advice to businessmen interested in the making of profits."[25]

The RKW established over two hundred subcommittees to study specific aspects of rationalization. Their four thousand or more voluntary members represented organizations devoted exclusively to rationalization, such as the German Standards Committee, as well as those that included rationalization among their many concerns, such as the Working Group of German Factory Engineers.[26] These committees performed the detailed research on the innumerable minute technical and organizational issues essential for successful rationalization, and they conducted the often tedious negotiations among industrialists, engineers, scientists, and economists that were necessary to achieve consensus on recommendations.

The three most active RKW committees were the Committee for Efficient Production, headed by Köttgen, which was responsible for technical problems of production, fuel efficiency, factory design, and labor processes; the Committee for Efficient Management, which focused on problems of business administration and accounting; and the National Committee for Conditions and Terms of Delivery, which sought to promulgate standards for commerce.[27] Between 1926 and 1930 these three bodies received over one million marks from the RKW.[28] An only slightly smaller amount went to the DNA, whose task was to develop and secure the adoption of efficient, scientific, and flexible norms for particular industries and the economy as a whole. The DNA, which was established in 1917 and staunchly maintained its independence in the face of the centralizing efforts of the RKW, developed over 2,200 standards during the 1920s.[29] The RKW also provided generous funding to DATSCH and to the Working Group of German Factory Engineers, as well as smaller sums to innumerable other groups with whom it cooperated, such as Refa, and special groups it established to study such topics as forestry and housework. Both the committee structure and budget of the RKW reflect its inability to centralize all rationalization organizations and efforts as it had initially hoped. They also highlight the amorphous and limitless ambitions of the rationalization movement.

To popularize the results of the work it commissioned and rally support for the rationalization project, the RKW engaged in an ambitious publication program. From 1926 to 1930 it published over eighty books and brochures on such sweeping themes as *The Rationalization Movement, Humans and Rationalization*, and *The Composition and Lowering of Costs and the Formation of Prices*, as well as on such obscure and mundane issues as *Experiences with Flow Production, Bookkeeping for Mid-sized Machine Firms*, and *Efficient Packing with Wood*.[30] The RKW *News*, a monthly newsletter, kept the interested public informed about ongoing work. Its magnum opus, the twelve-hundred page *Handbook of Rationalization*, offered a detailed discussion of standardization, vocational training, and specific measures to rationalize industrial production, administration and distribution, artisan work, and housework. Fifty pages were devoted to time-and-motion studies, for example, and nearly as many to office organization and technology. The rationalization of public administration ws covered in only fourteen pages—the same amount as welding techniques. The rationalization of artisan production was covered in nearly two hundred pages; housework in a mere twenty. This compendium of the collected wisdom of the rationalization movement contained everything that even the most passionate devotee of the subject would wish to know—and much that was probably irrelevant or boring to everyone.[31] Its publication was a testament to the belief among the RKW leadership that information would both enhance the reputation of its provider and inspire action by private business.

Neither supposition proved well founded. By decade's end criticism of the RKW mounted from within and without. The organization's business manager, Hinnenthal, repeatedly complained that both individual firms and major industrial associations paid too little attention to the recommendations of the RKW.[32] The organization itself needed better rationalization: there were too many committees, which generated friction within and among themselves as well as between the committees and the RKW leadership. Procedures for determining research topics, conducting investigations, and passing resolutions were too cumbersome and time-consuming. Of equal importance, suggestions were frequently impractical and ignored by industry because committees made recommendations for one element of production or distribution divorced from the context in which it would have to be implemented. In 1929 Hinnenthal concluded that the principal problem facing the RKW was not, as many claimed, insufficient funds but inefficient organization. If the parliament cut funds for the RKW, this might well help the RKW rethink its structure and focus its attention on the practical adoption of its many proposals.[33] Siemens and Köttgen agreed that the first phase of the organization's work, centering on drafting recommendations, was over, but they were neither clear on what the next stage should be nor sympathetic to Hinnenthal's critique. He was replaced by a businessman, Otto D. Schaefer, who had spent much of the 1920s in America.[34] The subsequent transformations in the RKW, however, came not from the initiative of its leaders but from parliamentary intervention.

In 1929 and 1930 Social Democrats, such as Rudolf Breitscheid and Otto Suhr, complained in the Reichstag and in the press that workers remained virtually unrepresented in the RKW.[35] According to Suhr, the committees to which workers belonged rarely met, and the RKW leadership had little influence on the bodies it so heavily subsidized. As a result of industrial and right-wing dominance, the RKW focused one-sidedly on economic and technical issues, ignoring the increasingly serious social consequences of rationalization. When the RKW did turn to the problems of humans, it "viewed them as a number, as a factor in cost accounting," Suhr indignantly noted.[36] Although Schaefer hoped to defeat the Social Democratic drive for greater influence by avoiding confrontation and by endlessly procrastinating, he failed. The Reichstag approved the 1930 RKW budget on the condition that the organization increase working-class representation, devote more attention to the social and health consequences of rationalization, and provide a detailed accounting of all funds spent.[37]

The story of the RKW is exemplary. Its founding had been greeted with widespread support, albeit for the most varied reasons. Industrialists viewed it as a cheap and easy way to back rationalization, for they were asked only to share information and preferences, not provide funds or implement suggestions. The organization was led by those who opposed a full-scale Americanization of production and consumption. Engineers, economists, and scientists of work viewed the RKW as essential to providing the basic technical recommendations necessary for restructuring individual firms and the economy as a whole. Social Democrats supported technical and organizational modernization unequivocally, debating only the context in which it would be implemented. But by decade's end, rationalization enthusiasts were disappointed. Industrialists had proven surprisingly unreceptive to the RKW proposals, and although Social Democrats continued to endorse the idea of such an organization, they objected to its practices. Variations on this basic scenario will be uncovered as we look at specific industries.

Ruhr Coal Mining

The Ruhr district, which stretched from Dortmund and Hagen on the south and east to Mülheim on the Ruhr and Hamborn on the north and west, had been the center of German heavy industry since the late nineteenth century. It was the major producer of iron and steel, a vital locus of machine making and metalworking, and the principal supplier of the coal that was basic to these sectors and to the industrial economy as a whole.[38] The Ruhr

mines, many of which were part of large integrated concerns that also produced iron, steel, and semifinished and finished goods, were dramatically
transformed by the rationalization movement of the 1920s. The forces pushing for rationalization were many and the methods used varied. Old mines
were closed, small and inefficient ones combined their operations above
ground and below, and work on the coal face was mechanized. Efforts were
made to introduce scientific management and improve worker training.
Finally, the extraction, processing, and utilization of coal by-products was
consolidated and steamlined.[39] The results achieved were dramatic and visible, but they were also problematic for capital and labor alike.

The problems of Ruhr mining, like the problems of so many other sectors of the German economy, began during World War I. The war economy's high demand for coal put enormous strains on the mines, where coal
was hewed largely by hand. The region's experienced and stable labor force
was drafted into military service, forcing mine owners to rely on young and
untrained miners, foreign workers, prisoners, and women. Railroad cars and
lubricants were in short supply, and machinery was overused and in dis-
repair. Management resorted to getting the easiest and best coal, paying
no attention to the long-term development of the mines. Under these circumstances workers' productivity declined and the condition of the mines
deteriorated.[40]

Many of these problems continued into the postwar period. The loss
of the Saar and Alsace-Lorraine made the Ruhr much more central to German heavy industry, and the need to pay reparations created a large demand
for coal. But the labor force remained unstable and inexperienced, and in
the immediate postwar years both food and housing were in short supply.
As productivity declined, the pressure to mechanize and reorganize grew,
further intensified by labor's postwar achievement of shorter hours and
higher wages. As the historian John Ronald Shearer has shown, mine owners responded to the conditions of the early 1920s with a mixture of old and
new techniques. Following past practice, they increased employment as demand rose. Whereas there had been 430,000 mine workers in early 1919—
roughly the same number as in 1913—there were over 560,000 by late 1922.[41]
Owners also strove to get a larger share of the coal marketing quota allocated by the powerful Rhineland-Westphalia Coal Syndicate. They introduced such innovations as pneumatic jack hammers and coal-cutting
machines. In 1913 over 97 percent of the coal was extracted using hand labor
and explosives, but by 1925 only 52 percent was.[42] Mine owners improved
aspects of the mines' infrastructure, such as winding machinery, and some
even made feeble efforts to train their expanding work force better.[43] By
1924 productivity per worker had risen, nearly approaching 1913 levels, and
employment had declined to 463,000.[44]

Demand at home and abroad fell sharply, however, and with it, the price
of coal. Mine owners initially resorted to their traditional responses to crisis:
stockpiling, short time, and layoffs, all of which left the mines unaffected,
but not the miners. In response to the rationalization movement and grow-

ing criticism of the technological backwardness of the Ruhr mines, owners embarked on a program of restructuring technology and mine organization.[45] They were aided by the Mining Association (Bergbau Verein), which established its own Committee for Industrial Economy and coordinated the work of various committees, such as the Standards Committee for Mining, to study the technical aspects of rationalization.[46]

In 1924 Ruhr mine owners began a systematic campaign of negative rationalization, closing 26 mines that produced just over 500,000 tons of coal and employed 8,000 workers, arguing that they were deemed inefficient or insufficiently profitable. These small and backward southern Ruhr mines, the "children of the inflation,"[47] were condemned to an early death once the mark was stabilized. As the stabilization crisis of 1924 gave way to the rationalization crisis in 1925, the closure campaign escalated. Thirty-two mines employing between 32,000 and 37,000 workers and producing over 5 million tons of coal were completely shut down. These were located throughout the Ruhr, not just in the old and depleted mining areas of the south, and some were large and modern operations.[48] While the Miners' Union and the SPD reiterated their principled support for negative ratio-nalization, they criticized this "closure frenzy." They asked the Reichstag to establish a committee of owners and workers to investigate the problems of production and marketing in coal mining, and urged owners to engage in positive restructuring.[49] These last requests were fulfilled, but negative rationalization continued throughout the remainder of the decade, although at a slower pace. Because the Ruhr benefited from the English miners' strike in 1926, only five mines, producing nearly 1.7 million tons, were shut; the following year—the most prosperous one in late Weimar—the same num-ber of pits, but with a miniscule productive output, were closed. In 1928, however, twelve mines with a productive capacity of nearly 4 million tons were shut. The onset of the depression merely intensified what stabiliza-tion and rationalization had begun, and from 1929 until 1934 an additional twenty-nine mines, many of them substantial, went out of production.[50]

Pit closings were promoted by the growing concentration of mine ownership in the mining industry; large companies could afford to dispose of all but their most profitable ventures. By the late 1920s the mines of the United Steel trust (Vestag), formed in 1926, produced nearly a quarter of Ruhr coal and employed nearly a quarter of mine workers. The next nine companies, which included Krupp, Gelsenkirchen Bergwerk, and Gute-hoffnungshütte, accounted for an additional 45 percent of production and employees.[51] These industrial giants led the way in technological modern-ization and reorganization.

The pneumatic jack hammer stood at the center of mechanization. Only 264 pneumatic hammers were in use in Ruhr mines in 1913; by 1925, this number had risen to 44,993, and by 1927 to 70,145. By 1929, 84 percent of coal was cut with pneumatic jack hammers and an additional 6 percent with cutting machines or a combination of machines and hammers.[52] The pneu-matic hammer proved to be easy to use and adaptable to the varied pit conditions in the Ruhr. The large coal-cutting machines used in the United States were unsuitable for the steep and changing terrain.[53] Improvements were also made in transporting coal from the coal face. In 1913 the Monopol mining company, for example, used vibrating chutes (*Schüttelrutsche*) to convey 10.6 percent of its coal from the work site. In 1927–28, 59.1 percent was transported by this method.[54] Progress was made in standardizing mining equipment and machinery, but there was no extensive electrification, and backfilling areas from which coal had been dug remained a time-consuming manual task.[55]

Once mechanization was accomplished, productivity could only be enhanced by organizational innovations.[56] Mines were sometimes combined, although this was a complex and relatively expensive process. More frequently the number of points at which coal was mined was reduced in order to improve the efficiency of the coal face being worked and service it with mechanical transportation. According to the Bergbau Verein, the number of coal faces being worked decreased from approximately 23,000 in 1926 to 15,700 in 1928.[57] According to another contemporary estimate, they diminished from 16,700 in 1927 to 12,500 in 1929 and on down to 5,290 by 1933.[58] At the Monopol mine of the Gelsenkirchen Bergwerk A.G., the number of work sites decreased from 273 in 1913 to 115 in 1927–1928. The rise in average daily production per work site from 13.2 tons to 37 tons was achieved through far-reaching mechanization.[59] Many miners continued to operate their pneumatic hammers in small and cramped areas, but the process of consolidation reached such proportions in some mines that the coal face resembled a large factory.[60]

In addition to mechanizing and concentrating work on the coal face, the major mining companies consolidated and modernized the extraction and processing of coal by-products. The myriad of small coking ovens were replaced by new, centralized ovens that had vastly expanded capacity as well as the ability to recover the by-products of coking more effectively and operate round the clock. By 1928 over 50 percent of coke was produced in such ovens. Individual firms sought to recover more gas and cooperated in transporting and marketing it through Ruhrgas A.G. They also increased their recovery of such chemicals as nitrogen and crude tar.[61]

Mine directors, managers, and engineers all argued that mining could not simply adopt, without modification, American methods of scientific management, as iron and steel producers purportedly had, yet they were eager to develop time-and-motion studies suitable to the special conditions of mining. The stopwatch and time-and-motion studies were seen as possible solutions to management's perennial problem of controlling workers. The tasks and work sites of miners and their helpers varied on an almost daily basis, group wages were common, and supervisory personnel were often far removed from the coal face. These conditions gave miners a degree of autonomy rare in factory work. Management hoped to gain greater control by conducting time studies, not only of particular tasks, but of the work day as a whole.[62]

Records of the Bergbau Verein indicate that many studies were attempted, although the results were often inconclusive or disappointing. For example, both Krupp and Gutehoffnungshütte investigated how long a miner could operate a pneumatic jackhammer without fatigue, but whereas the Krupp study reported 1–2 hours, Gutehoffnungshütte arrived at 18–23 minutes.[63] After dramatically announcing that "each work minute not utilized for winning coal results in a loss of 7–10 kg of coal," a report of the Bergbau Verein's Committee for Industrial Efficiency indicated that in one shaft fully 21,160 shift minutes, or 28 percent of the shift, were not used productively.[64] Whether individual mines conducted such studies extensively and implemented the findings is more difficult to ascertain.[65] Where they were introduced, they met with a great deal of hostility by workers, who viewed the stopwatch as a weapon to intensify work and as a cause of rising accident rates. (Owners predictably blamed rising accidents on workers' incompetence and carelessness.)[66] By 1930 some managers doubted that the benefits from time-and-motion studies were worth the opposition they aroused.[67] These efforts at control from without were supplemented by programs to transform the attitudes and behavior of miners by means of skills training, general education, and company welfare policies.[68]

In many ways mining was a textbook case of successful Weimar rationalization. Inefficient operations were eliminated, not just initially but continually. As much as possible, production was consolidated, integrated, and mechanized to achieve something approximating the Fordist idea of flow production. Mine owners and managers spoke the language of scientific management, borrowed Taylorist techniques where possible, and attempted to eliminate all waste, whether of products, time, or energy. They were committed to rationalization, not as a one-shot affair but as an ongoing process. As a result, productive capacity and productivity per worker increased markedly, as shown in Table 7-1.

Between 1925 and the peak year of 1927, production increased by 13.4 percent, and daily productivity per worker also increased dramatically. Daily production, which was 943 kg per worker in 1913, fell as low as 633 kg in 1922 to the great dismay of owners, and rose only to 946 kg in 1925. Thereafter it rose to 1,131 kg per worker per day in 1927; 1,277 kg by mid-1929;

Table 7-1. Production and Employment in Ruhr Coal

Year	Production in 1,000 tons	Employment
1913	114,530	426,033
1925	104,059	432,691
1926	112,192	385,153
1927	118,022	407,577
1928	114,577	381,975

Source: V.E., "Der Weg der Rationalisierung," Verband und Wirtschaft 8:9 (September 1929): 133.

and 1,335 kg in early 1931.[69] By 1928 a new coking oven was in use that had a capacity of 40 tons versus the 6-ton capacity of the older models, and output per worker per shift was 40 tons, as against 5 previously.[70] Such averages mask the spectacular increases in productivity in the largest and most thoroughly restructured mines. For example, between 1924–1925 and 1928–1929, output per man per shift at the Monopol Mine increased 40 percent, from 941 kg to 1,321 kg.[71] The Friedrich der Grosse Mine proudly announced that productivity for the entire work force, above and below ground, increased nearly 15 percent from mid-1925 to mid-1926. The following year it jumped another 10 percent, and in the following two years it rose a more modest 3.4 percent and 6 percent, respectively.[72]

Behind these impressive production statistics lay many economic and social problems that were integral to the triumph of productivism in Ruhr mining. The experience of the Concordia Mine is an illustrative example. In an ambitious multiyear program, the company mechanized extensively, closed inefficient shafts, reduced the number of work sites from 415 in 1926 to 51 in 1929, and modernized its coking plant. The work force was reduced from 5,839 in 1926 to 4,459 in 1928. But productivity per worker per shift fell in 1926–1927 and increased only slightly, from 998 kg in 1927 to 1,011 kg in 1928. Overall production in 1926 just surpassed the 1913 level and fell thereafter. Further restructuring measures to expand capacity and improve efficiency were undertaken, but they were not completed until late 1929. The yearly reports were filled with complaints about poor market conditions, underutilized coking capacity, and the burden of wages and state social policy. Management claimed that rationalization was disruptive and expensive, and that attempts to increase productivity and production were finally realized at a time when the coal market was weak. The Friedrich der Grosse Mine shared this pessimistic assessment of the coal market. Yet both mines instituted further rationalization, achieving even greater productive capacity and per capita productivity, in an effort to improve their situation.[73]

Coal markets were weak throughout this period, despite upswings during the English coal strike and the business boom of 1927. Ruhr coal was hurt by foreign competition at home and in world markets, and the domestic demand for coal declined. As factories, power generating plants and the railroads rationalized their operations, they consumed less fuel. Competition from such alternative energy sources as gas and oil further weakened the coal market.[74] Most important, perhaps, the rationalization movement in mining was driven by considerations of production, not marketing. Mine owners, like most German industrialists, considered supply, rather than demand, to be their industry's most pressing problem; their principal goal was to increase productive capacity and productivity per worker, not to adapt output to market prospects. By 1929 the productive capacity of Ruhr mines far exceeded demand, and coking plants were operating at 67–72 percent of capacity.[75] Nonetheless, the Bergbau Verein firmly believed that continued rationalization was essential, for only the most technologically advanced mines could prosper at home and compete in the world economy.[76] A considerably less flattering assessment appeared in the Miners' Union newspaper: "In a capitalist economic order rationalization staggers from one marketing crisis to another." Although restructuring increased productivity, markets were quickly saturated because the purchasing power of the population did not increase proportionately. Short time and lay-offs were instituted, further weakening demand. This led to "a new productivity frenzy" and the cycle began again.[77]

Capital and labor, economists and politicians, all agreed on the basic facts concerning expanded capacity, productivity increases, and inadequate markets. There was bitter disagreement, however, about their causes as well as the consequences for costs, prices, profits, and employment. While each side recognized the problems of rationalization, each accused the other of benefiting economically, despite or because of them. Before exploring these disputes in the next chapter, we will examine rationalization in the iron and steel industry, a major consumer of coal and coke and a main promoter of rationalization in mining. Iron and steel was fundamentally restructured in the 1920s, with results that were as paradoxical and problematic as those in mining.

Iron and Steel

Like Ruhr mining, the vast Ruhr iron and steel industry was central to the war effort between 1914 and 1918, but the most profound dislocations it suffered resulted not from the war economy but from the peace terms. The Versailles treaty stripped Germany of Lorraine, the Saar, and two-thirds of Upper Silesia. As a result, Germany's richest iron ore deposits and many blast furnaces and steel mills were lost. The complex networks for resource acquisition, product specialization, and marketing in which Ruhr iron and steel had been enmeshed were torn asunder. Reorganization, but not rationalization proper, of necessity began in the immediate postwar period as firms scrambled to secure new iron ore sources abroad and coal mines at home, and as they rethought their product lines and renegotiated their relationships with one another.[78] In the early 1920s new plants were built and old ones expanded, but the need for technical modernity and efficiency was not paramount under conditions of inflation. Firms attempted extensive vertical integration, linking iron and steel to coal mining and coking, on the one hand, and to machine making and the electrotechnical industry, on the other. Gutehoffnungshütte and above all Hugo Stinnes' Siemens-Rhein-Elbe-Schuckert Union were primary examples.[79]

Whatever successes were achieved—and production in 1922 did reach 88 percent of prewar levels—were wiped out by the French occupation of the Ruhr, Germany's passive resistance, and the resulting hyperinflation of 1923. By 1924 both capital and labor were suffering as production dropped and unemployment rose sharply, and the eight-hour day was eliminated in favor of twelve-hour shifts.[80] Stabilization led to the dismantling of the

Stinnes empire and required a renegotiation of the relations among firms that regulated production and marketing. A restructuring of outmoded and overexpanded plants was equally necessary.

Ruhr iron and steel embarked on a vast and intense rationalization program that continued throughout the decade. Unlike mining, iron and steel did not simply pledge allegiance to American ideas of efficiency and technical modernity while seeking out their own particular technological and organizational rationalization measures. Rather, as we saw earlier, iron and steel industrialists, their managers and engineers, traveled to America, inspecting in minute detail the factories of western Pennsylvania, analyzing technical specifications and production statistics, and scrutinizing balance sheets to determine which elements of the much-admired American blast furnaces and steel mills could be imported. Like Schmidt-Hoffmann of Gutehoffnungshütte, they were aware of significant differences in market conditions and warned against "a mechanistic adoption of American installations." Nontheless, they agreed that a far-reaching modernization and mechanization of old plants and a rethinking and reorganization of all elements of the production process were in order.[81]

The rationalization of iron and steel affected the three main components of the industry—iron production, steel works, and rolling mills.[82] Firms built new blast furnaces and Thomas and Martin steel ovens, which had larger capacities and faster operating times and were extensively mechanized to require fewer workers. By the early 1930s, 75 percent of the plants that had more than 100 workers had modernized their machinery, an achievement made easier by the fact that iron and steel ovens had to be rebuilt every few years and could be upgraded easily and relatively cheaply in the process.[83] As in mining the number of firms and work sites declined as their size increased. The number of iron producing plants in Germany decreased from 56 in 1925 to 45 in 1929. During the same period, the number of ovens was reduced from 200 to 165, of which only 115 were in operation. Both production and per capita output rose considerably. In the same period the number of steel mills declined from 119 to 89.[84] Transportation within individual mills, as well as among them, was mechanized and, where possible, different stages of production were integrated and flow production was introduced. Factory design was altered, fuel economies were realized, and research and development efforts were pooled. Time-and-motion studies were popular and their results more easily implemented than in mining. The industry also relied heavily on new forms of company social policy.

Because iron and steel mills produced semifinished goods for a great variety of finished goods industries with diverse demands, there was little effort to reduce the types of products manufactured. Individual production facilities, however, began to specialize in one or more products.[85] Finally, ownership was concentrated and production horizontally integrated.

The multiple processes of rationalization in iron and steel can best be studied by examining Vestag, the iron and steel trust. The product of large-scale consolidation, it was also a major force in further restructuring. The

negotiations among the major iron and steel producers that led to the creation of Vestag began in 1925, a year Walter Meakin characterized as "a
paradox, which puzzled most expert observers, of rising production and
increasing financial embarassments."[86] Plants that had expanded in the early
1920s now found they had vast unused capacity—frequently not of the most
technologically advanced variety—and high costs. A few, such as Stumm,
went under, and those that survived needed to rationalize thoroughly. Because capital was lacking, the formation of a trust was seen as a possible
solution to both overcapacity and capital shortages.[87]

Although nearly every major iron and steel firm participated in the negotiations about Vestag, Krupp, Mannesmann, Gutehoffnungshütte, Kloeckner,
and Hoesch refused in the end to give up their economic and technical
independence. Thyssen, Phoenix, Rheinstahl, and the Rhein-Elbe Union,
however, were willing to do so, and in May 1926 Vestag came into being,
with a capital of roughly 800 million marks. Its holdings stretched across
the Ruhr from Bochum and Gelsenkirchen through Duisburg and Hamborn
and down to Düsseldorf and Cologne. They included coal mines, coking
plants, blast furnaces, steel mills, rolling mills, and factories for specialized
semifinished iron and steel products.[88]

At its founding, Vestag employed 158,556 blue-collar workers and
14,860 white-collar workers.[89] By decade's end it mined approximately one
quarter of Ruhr coal and produced roughly 50 percent of Germany's pig
iron, 43 percent of its crude steel, and 40 percent of its rolling mill output.
Whereas Vestag produced over 6 million tons of pig iron in 1929, the next
largest firms, Krupp and Gutehoffnungshütte, manufactured just under 1.3
million tons and 923,000 tons, respectively; the figures for crude steel were
comparable.[90] Vestag's dominant position stemmed not only from its initial strength but also from its ambitious rationalization program.

Vestag faced the challenge of rationalizing not simply individual factories or a single firm—as, for example, did Krupp—but fully half of the iron
and steel industry.[91] It began with a far-reaching program of "negative"
rationalization. Between mid-1926 and 1930, Vestag closed sixteen mines, one
coking plant, five briquette factories, ten blast furnace works, eight Martin
steel plants, and eleven rolling mills.[92] Sometimes operations were shut because they were outmoded, inefficient, and costly; at other times, because
they did not fit into the new centralized and specialized production regime of
Vestag. The rolling mill division, for example, was to have only two plants
for each type of product—one to handle normal demand and one to handle
excess demand and special orders. Among universal iron rolling mills, the
Phoenix-Horde plant and the Rheinstahl-Meiderich mill were scrapped.
Dortmund Union became the principal mill and Thyssen-Mülheim was designated the subsidiary plant, but due to inadequate demand, it was closed
as well. Among tin rolling mills, Phoenix Hoerde and Thyssen-Mülheim
survived, while Phoenix Düsseldorf and Rheinstahl went under.[93] And so it
went in each special product area, with some very modern plants shut because they could only operate efficiently at near full capacity and demand

was inadequate for more than one principal producer.[94] Such a pervasive campaign of negative rationalization severely disrupted the lives of the employees and the economies of the towns where the plants were located.[95]

Negative rationalization was accompanied by an effort to maximize the remaining resources. Among iron works, for example, those producing only iron, such as the Friedrich Wilhelms Hütte, were forced to specialize in one or two types of raw iron. Large mixed works, such as Phoenix-Ruhrort and Rheinstahl-Meiderich, were to combine and modernize. Specialization was reinforced by geographic concentration, so as to improve access to resources and cut transportation costs. Iron and steel works in the western Ruhr, for example, produced primarily for export, whereas those in the eastern Ruhr supplied the domestic market. Vestag's mining operations were divided into four districts: Dortmund, Gelsenkirchen, Bochum, and Hamborn. Production focused on Hamborn in the West, and the mines Minister Stein and Hardenberg in the East.[96]

Once Vestag had concentrated production, it assessed all ongoing rationalization projects, deciding which to continue and which to terminate.[97] It then embarked on a multiyear program of new construction and modernization that both built on and disrupted earlier restructuring efforts. Sometimes the central administration dictated changes; sometimes individual factories lobbied top management for new machines or plants.[98] Between 1926 and 1928 Vestag spent 275–300 million marks for new construction and modernization. An entirely new coking operation with 894 ovens and a capacity of 5 million tons was constructed. In the steel and rolling mills, larger and more mechanized ovens were built, transportation was mechanized, and production processes were integrated. In many cases new factory buildings were required to house the new technologies and organize them efficiently. Fuel costs were cut, both by the transformation of coking and by the increased use of gas produced at various stages of production. By 1929 Vestag proudly announced that the bulk of its new construction and restructuring program was complete and that only 30 million marks would be allocated to finish the modernization of individual plants. By 1930 the economic crisis had deepened and rationalization ground to a halt.[99]

Vestag also closed administrative offices, repair shops, and research departments that were considered superfluous. Although it did not completely centralize operations in these areas, it attempted to concentrate them in a few places and promote cooperation among them.[100] Research and development efforts were reorganized along these lines and placed under the leadership of Vestag's research division, which also established such new ventures as the Committee for Time-and-Motion Studies.[101] Finally, efforts were made to standardize accounting and ordering procedures.

Measured in terms of production and output per worker, the results of rationalization were positive for both Vestag and the industry as a whole. According to the Metalworkers' Union, the rationalized iron and steel industry of the Ruhr proved that Calvin Coolidge had been right to call Germany the most Americanized land in the world.[102] The production of coke rose spectacularly, while the overall production of coal, iron, and steel by Vestag increased insignificantly or actually declined somewhat. But limiting production had, after all, been a main purpose of establishing the trust.[103]

Gains were greatest in worker productivity. In steel, for example, Albert Vögler, the head of Vestag, claimed that employment remained virtually stable at the August-Thyssen Hütte and at Dortmunder Union, while production at these plants increased in the late 1920s from 75,000 to 170,000 tons, and from 60,000 to 85,000 tons, respectively. Rheinstahl and Phoenix achieved greater production with smaller work forces, while Hörde increased employment from 4,600 to 5,700 but raised output from 40,000 to 85–90,000 tons.[104] The Thyssen works claimed that membership in Vestag enabled it to produce at capacity in 1926 and that per capita output in raw steel had risen from 420 kg/man/shift in 1914 to 810 kg/man/shift in 1927.[105] Overall employment oscillated. Although the number of white-collar employees remained stable at roughly 15,000 throughout the late 1920s, blue-collar employment rose from 158,556 in 1926 to over 180,000 in 1927 and then declined to 176,716 in 1929.[106]

For the industry as a whole, pig iron production rose from 10,088,000 tons in 1925 to 13,239,000 tons in 1929 ,while annual per capita productivity increased from 433 tons to 611 tons. During the period 1919 to 1922, blast furnaces produced 450 tons every twenty-four hours; by 1924 output reached 750 tons, and in 1927, 1,100 tons.[107] In the Martin steel works, production increased 30 percent while the work force was reduced by 20 percent. In rolling mills, which were modernized and integrated with a particular vengeance, productivity increases were especially marked. In 1927 in one part of a rolling mill, 150 workers operating on 506 twelve-hour shifts produced 20,996 tons of cast iron. Three years later, 106 workers produced 24,787 tons in 345 ten-hour shifts.[108]

Impressive as these productivity figures seem at first glance, it is not clear what they really signify. There was controversy over how accurately the available statistics measured productivity. Such experts as Robert Brady doubted that tonnage per man was an accurate measure of efficiency, given the many qualitative changes that occurred in oven size, rolling mill technology, factory transportation systems, and so on.[109] Others said it was meaningless to compare productivity per worker for shifts that were eight hours in the early 1920s, lengthened to twelve in 1924, and then reduced to ten at decade's end. Those who accepted the data as a reasonable approximation of productivity increases disagreed about what caused changes in productivity. Industry attributed the improvements to the reintroduction of the twelve-hour shift, playing down the effects of rationalization.[110] Labor condemned the twelve-hour day as exhausting and maintained that its reintroduction had not increased productivity.[111] They maintained that advanced technology and proper factory organization were central to productivity, not longer hours.[112] Such labor spokesmen as Fritz Naphtali further questioned whether workers could exert much control over productivity in highly mechanized and rationalized firms.[113]

The Committee to Investigate the Production and Marketing Conditions of the German Economy, which was set up by the Reichstag in 1926, issued a report a few years later that devoted much attention to analyzing the factors influencing productivity. The Enquete Ausschuss, as it was commonly called, was composed of technical experts, academics, and representatives of industry and the labor movement.[114] After studying the figures, visiting factories, and interviewing managers and workers, they arrived back at the position from which they had begun, that is, doubting that the complex roots of productivity increases could be neatly separated and the proportion due to wages or hours or new technology accurately assigned.[115]

While production and productivity rose, so did productive capacity—a fact that was disturbing to many. According to the Enquete Ausschuss, the iron and steel industry was overcapitalized and had excess capacity.[116] Vestag was not large enough to coordinate productive capacity and demand for the entire industry; indeed, even Vestag did not operate at more than 80 percent capacity during the best of times, and individual plants did much worse. The August-Thyssen Hütte, for example, which had operated at full capacity when Vestag was first formed, complained it was working at only 56 percent of capacity in early 1928. Yet many rationalized mills had to operate above 67 percent capacity for technical reasons; for all plants, costs rose along with unutilized capacity.[117] Social Democrats rallied behind the accusation of false investment and overcapacity, while Vestag and the industry as a whole vigorously denied all such charges.[118] Whether there was excess capacity and whether it was created by the productivist mania and misplaced market optimism of capital or by the pressure of labor's wage policy and the costs of state social welfare became a major source of controversy.

But it was far from the only one. Iron and steel industrialists relied heavily on an export strategy and kept domestic prices above those in the world market to facilitate it. This set off a predictable conflict between those who wanted rationalization to rely on low domestic prices and an expanding home market and those for whom rationalization was to be paid for, promoted, and made profitable by exports.[119] This debate became particularly intense when domestic prices were raised in 1928. Debates about whether rationalizaton created structural unemployment were not nearly as intense in iron and steel as in mining, but the experience of the industry did raise the question of whether rationalization led to significant deskilling, as the Metal Workers' Union believed, or whether it eliminated the most grueling physical labor associated with the industry, as Vestag spokesmen claimed.[120] Finally, given the inadequacies of the world market and domestic demand, as well as high prices and overcapacity, the debates on the rationality and the profitability of rationalization in iron and steel were very like those in mining. The introduction of the most modern technology and the attainment of higher productivity had altered some of the specifics in the charges capital and labor leveled at one another, but it had not altered their broader economic visions of how a rationalized economy should function.

Machine Making

The German machine industry was one of the largest, most diverse, and
most important sectors of the German economy. Unlike iron and steel,
it was a stronghold of "German quality work," and the extent to which it
was transformed reveals much about the fate of economic Americanism in
Weimar Germany.

This industrial sector produced every kind of machine tool needed for
industry and transportation, including blast furnace and rolling mill equipment, and machines for food processing, textile manufacture, and agriculture.
It also encompassed special machines and machine parts, fine optical equipment, and locomotives, cars, trucks, bicycles, and motorcycles. Some of these
were produced in large factories or by parts of large, vertically integrated
firms, such as Krupp and Gutehoffnungshütte, but most were manufactured
in the more than 17,000 small- and medium-sized firms included in the 1925
occupational census. In 1928 the machine industry employed roughly
1,112,000 workers, as against 1,031,000 in all phases of iron and steel, and
690,000 in mining. By 1926 the value of output in the industry had nearly
returned to prewar levels. The machine industry was central not only to
the domestic economy, but to the world economy as well. In 1926 a third
of the industry's production was exported, and German machinery, which
had an international reputation for high quality, accounted for a fifth of
world machine exports.[121]

Other statistics, however, suggest that the machine industry was not
immune to the ills affecting other sectors. Although Germany in 1925 produced 13.6 percent of the world's output of machinery, it had produced
20.7 percent in 1913. Production grew substantially from 1925 on, as did
excess capacity, which stood at 27 percent that year and nearly doubled in
the following one.[122] Rationalization was as needed in this sector as in coal,
iron and steel, but it was much more difficult to implement due to the diversity of products, the multiplicity of firms, and their commitment to specialized products and "quality work."

German machine firms did not refuse to rationalize; rather, they did so
in distinctive ways that bore little resemblance to Fordism. As Thomas von
Freyberg has argued in his admirable study of rationalization in this sector,
the machine industry produced machines that promoted rationalization, but
it did not fully rationalize its own production methods because its primary
goal was to maintain flexibility in the products it manufactured, in the uses
to which machines and tools were put, and in the amounts it produced.[123]
In the medium-sized and large firms in which most restructuring occurred,
the primary emphasis was on modernizing the machinery by introducing
new technologies, reorganizing workshops, and improving power sources.
In firms with over 100 workers, 426 of their divisions, or 65.2 percent, modernized machinery between 1925 and 1931. By contrast, only 77, or 11.8
percent, had introduced flow production, while 66, or 10.6 percent, had
begun serial production, and a mere 11 had built assembly lines. Generally

these encompassed only a small portion of the production process of a particular plant.[124] There was some specialization of production and decrease
in the number of models, as large firms limited what individual plants could
manufacture and small firms contractually allocated production among themselves.[125] There were also efforts to get firms to adhere to industry-wide
norms.[126] Management undertook time-and-motion studies extensively, but
their usefulness was limited by the fact that most orders were one-of-a-kind
or small-batch jobs, for which rates had to be calculated anew.[127]

To be sure, some branches were extensively restructured by the late
1920s. Among manufacturers of railroad rolling stock, for example, the number of firms and models dropped drastically, plants specialized, norms were
adopted, and flow production was introduced. But the impetus did not come
from private capital but from the state, which owned the railroads and
awarded orders only to firms that promised to rationalize.[128] Bosch, a manufacturer of spark plugs and a limited range of other auto parts, experimented
successfully with the assembly line.[129] The electrotechnical industry, which
was closely related to machine making and produced both machine tools and
consumer durables, was probably the most thoroughly concentrated and
rationalized industry in Germany.[130] By and large, however, rationalization
efforts in machine making left the workshop as the center of production for
the quality work and special order products for which the industry continued to be known.

The results of this cautious and partial rationalization were predictably
mixed. Although the type and severity of problems varied among different
sectors, some were shared by all. Machine building was very slow to adopt
norms, and it was not just the small- and medium-sized firms that were to
blame. Developing standards for such a complex sector proved arduous; getting them implemented was even more so. As late as 1930, members of the
German Standards Committee (DNA) lamented that many managers in
machine building were ignorant of or hostile to standards.[131] As in other
industries, overall production rose and productivity per worker, measured
in terms of value produced, increased from 4,230 marks in 1924 to 7,553
marks in 1929.[132] But these increases were less striking than those in coal
or iron and steel, for the degree of mechanization and reorganization was
considerably less. As in the other industries, productive capacity also
expanded. To be sure, the industry overcame the disasterous situation of
1926, when only half of capacity was utilized, but even in the most prosperous years, 1927 and 1928, over a quarter remained unused.[133]

Machine making did not face the problem of high fixed costs and technical inflexibility that rationalized iron and steel did. Thus it was able to
cut costs by cutting production, shortening hours, and firing workers.[134]
Nor were the market problems it faced as severe as those in heavy industry. Indeed, machine making as a whole was one of the few export success
stories during Weimar. If exports in 1913 are taken as 100, then exports had
reached 110.1 in 1928 and 129.6 in 1930. But the German share of world
exports of electrical and nonelectrical machines had declined from 34.8 per-

cent in 1913 to 28.2 percent in 1928.[135] Individual firms and sectors fared much worse. After World War I, for example, Krupp encountered severe problems finding substitutes for munitions production. During the inflation, the company moved into manufacturing tractors, trucks, textile machines, and locomotives, among other products, but claimed to receive few financial rewards. Despite rigorous rationalization after 1924 of all phases of its vertically integrated operations and the elimination of such unprofitable product lines as textile machines, Krupp consistently complained that markets were inadequate and machine making was unprofitable.[136]

The limitations of rationalization in the machine industry were nowhere more evident than in automobile production. In 1925 Germany produced fewer than 40,000 cars, as against 3.5 million in the United States, and it ranked eleventh in the world in terms of output per population.[137] Many factors contributed to the backwardness of the automobile industry. After World War I, car producers—of which there were nearly a hundred—were reluctant to modernize production methods. Cars were assembled individually, rather than on the assembly line; there was a proliferation of models, and parts were not standardized and interchangeable. The construction of a Daimler luxury car, for example, required a day's labor of 1,750 workers; a Ford car required that of 5.75 workers.[138] Nor had new sales methods and easier financing arrangements been introduced.

The effects of the industry's decentralized character and chronic traditionalism were exacerbated by Germany's postwar economy. Severe inflation triggered a "flight into fixed values," which led to an overexpansion of the industry and created excess productive capacity. In addition, the German state regarded cars as luxury items and taxed them heavily, thereby limiting domestic demand still further. These various negative factors interacted to create a technologically backward industry that produced expensive goods that attracted few buyers at home and could not compete abroad.[139] In the mid-1920s there was not even an enclave of American producers pointing the way forward.

Beginning in 1924 there were many plant closings and the number of German car firms was reduced from eighty-six in 1924 to thirty in 1928 and on down to seventeen in the early 1930s.[140] Nearly all phases of the production process, from the stamping plants to the final assembly, were restructured to some extent, and a variety of American techniques and tools were employed. Standardized parts were widely introduced, factories reorganized, transportation improved, and partial flow production implemented.[141] But only Opel, which came to dominate the German market, introduced American mass production methods on a large scale.[142] These piecemeal improvements increased production to over 100,000 in 1929, yet capacity was double that figure.[143]

The experience of the Daimler Motor Company provides an illustration of these processes in their most extensive and successful form. At middecade Daimler, which manufactured Mercedes cars as well as military equipment, was financially unstable and had enormous excess capacity. It first joined with the Benz Rhenish Automobile and Motor Company to form Daimler-Benz A.G. and then embarked on an extensive rationalization program. Most affected was the auto body plant at Sindelfingen, where American-style machines and the assembly line were used to produce a limited number of standardized auto bodies. More typical of the German auto industry as a whole was the restructuring of the Unterturkheim plant, where new machinery was brought in and the size and skill level of the work force was substantially reduced, but the assembly line was not installed. Rather, an improved version of the traditional group work was retained to ensure, its defenders claimed, "the pursuit of quality work." Production did improve but only 20 of Daimler-Benz's lowest-priced cars and two of its largest models were manufactured per day. It was a far cry from River Rouge and Highland Park.[144]

Despite rationalization measures, the German auto industry remained beset by problems. There was no mass demand for cars, even when prices dropped and financing improved somewhat. The problem was not that Germany did not need cars. In 1929 there was one car for every fifty-four inhabitants, placing Germany in an embarassing eighth place in this index, behind not only the United States, with a ratio of one car per five persons, but also Britain (1:23) and France (1:31) as well as Denmark, Sweden, Switzerland, and Belgium. As many observers recognized, German auto manufacturers did not produce the kinds of cars that might satisfy available demand.[145] They did not build small, efficient, and inexpensive cars for a mass market.[146] Instead, most inexpensive cars were simply scaled-down and inefficient versions of large models. Ferdinand Porsche, who was to design the Volkswagen in the 1930s, failed repeatedly to persuade German auto makers to support the development of a radically new small and cheap car.[147] The small-car market continued to be dominated by American imports and American cars assembled in Germany. Ford, for example, opened an assembly plant in Berlin in 1926; General Motors purchased the modernized and very large Opel firm in 1929; and Ford completed its Cologne production facility in 1931.[148]

Although the number of firms and variety of models had diminished considerably, the 17 largest firms still produced 50 models in 1930. While this may well have preserved the industry's reputation for quality work and enabled it to meet the discriminating tastes of middle- and upper-class consumers, it precluded the thoroughgoing rationalization that might have enabled German auto makers to expand their market at home and compete abroad. The result of this misguided market strategy was both a lack of profitability and chronic overcapacity. By one estimate, automobile companies lost 72 million marks between 1924 and mid-1930.[149] Even in the prosperous year of 1928 Daimler-Benz, which was more successful than other car manufacturers, was operating at only 70 percent capacity. Thereafter, the situation deteriorated rapidly for all companies, forcing many to go bankrupt or close parts of their operations.[150]

By the early 1930s, it was evident to numerous observers that too many companies, with too much capacity, were building the wrong kind of cars with the wrong methods and trying to sell them at uncompetitive prices to limited markets. Rationalization had increased production and productivity per worker, but it had also intensified preexisting problems of overcapacity and inadequate demand. Improving efficiency, even in this industry of limited rationalization, proved relatively easy. Marketing what was produced, cutting costs, lowering prices, and selecting product types presented more intractable problems. Some observers insisted that Germany must further rationalize the manufacture of car parts, while producing a large number of finished models, that is, combine quality work and rationalization in what came to be seen as the General Motors model. Others clung to the belief that only a Fordist strategy of mass producing one type of small, inexpensive car would save the industry.[151] No one saw a realistic way to persuade the car makers to do either.

From a purely productivist perspective, the accomplishments of the rationalization movement were not so much insignificant as contradictory.[152] Industry had succeeded in increasing production and productivity per worker without adopting those aspects of Fordist production, such as the assembly line and extensive mechanization, which it deemed too expensive or unsuitable for German market conditions. Manufacturers of finished goods continued to emphasize quality work and special orders, rather than trying to compete in mass-produced goods. Although the labor movement pushed for still further mechanization and reorganization in selected industries, such as automobiles, it applauded many of the measures industry implemented. But the shared approval of these productivist achievements did not create consensus on other issues. On the contrary, both the successes of restructuring and the excess capacity it created intensified debate on costs, prices, and profits. It heightened disputes on wages and social welfare and raised the question of whether production gains were purchased at the price of structural unemployment and an inhumane intensification of work.

In the early and mid-1920s industrial leaders, trade unionists, and engineers had often assumed that a successful productivist strategy would enable all groups to benefit—somewhat and at some point. As we will see, the rationalization of German industry created a situation in which most suffered—considerably and immediately. John Ronald Shearer's conclusion about coal mining is more broadly applicable. Industrialists, trade unionists, and engineers got what they asked for in technological and organizational terms, but did not achieve the desired economic and social results.

8

Winners and Losers

Foreign observers recognized that Germany had implemented the doctrines of rationalization more extensively than any other European country, and they lavished relatively uncritical praise on the results.[1] The Englishman Meakin even insisted that "what has been accomplished in Germany will be attempted in every country where similar industrial problems have to be faced."[2] By decade's end such positive sentiments found few echoes in Germany, for the paradoxical results of the productivist strategies pursued by industrialists, engineers, and the RKW greatly intensified the controversies surrounding rationalization.

Debate primarily centered on the closely intertwined issues of prices, costs, wages, and profits, for capital and labor had each made different assumptions about when and how much each of these variables should rise or fall. Industry anticipated that rationalization would lower costs, which would translate into somewhat lower prices and higher profits. This, in turn, would fund further rationalization and lower costs and prices yet again. At some point late in the process, wages would be raised. The trade unions wanted to start the cycle with higher wages, which were to spur rationalization that would lower costs and prices, enabling still higher wages as well as greater profits. Throughout the 1920s, capital and labor disagreed on what was actually happening to costs, prices, wages, and profits and what was possible—economically and politically. These debates also involved three related concerns: how rationalization affected working conditions; how it altered the composition of the labor force; and whether it created structural unemployment.

Industrialists and trade unionists, engineers and politicians viewed these issues as important in and of themselves and as central for assessing the efficacy of rationalization efforts. But since different groups judged rationalization by different criteria, they reached opposite conclusions about its accomplishments and irrationalities, held different policies and individuals responsible, and disagreed about who was reaping the benefits and who was paying the costs.

In retrospect, it is clear that the German labor movement and the working class in general were the principal losers in the bitter battles surrounding rationalization. The Social Democratic Party and the trade unions lacked the economic and political power to impose their vision of a fully modernized, high-wage, mass-consumption economy. Although some German workers retained their skills and enjoyed high wages, many others suffered unemployment or were threatened by layoffs, saw their skills diminished, and enjoyed neither lower prices nor greater leisure as compensation. Industry preserved its cartellized structure and its traditional export orientation. Finally, the rationalization of individual firms was not accompanied by any effort to rationalize the economy as a whole or to deal with such detrimental effects of technological modernization as structural unemployment.[3]

Although capital won, it was a Pyrrhic victory, for industrialists were unable to translate increased efficiency and productive capacity into the kind of higher profits and lower costs they sought. Industry could increase output but not demand for the goods produced; it could cut its labor force but not keep wage costs down. Thus, far from overcoming political conflicts on economic and social issues, the results of capitalist rationalization intensified them. Workers in restructured industries felt threatened both by rationalized work and the resulting unemployment. Their criticism of rationalization mounted even as their ability to act against it diminished. Trade unions and the SPD were forced to rely increasingly on the state to regulate wages and provide social welfare, while industry, especially in the Ruhr, turned ever more strongly against state interference.

Prices

The struggles to reap the benefits of rationalization were not only fought between labor and capital, but also involved consumers, a category that included the working class but was by no means identical with it. At issue were prices—ranging from the price of such raw materials as coal, to that of such finished goods as cars. All German visitors to America had commented on the American consumer, who was blessed or cursed, depending on one's viewpoint, with an abundance of goods proffered at prices that seemed astonishingly low by German standards. Analysts of the American economic miracle posited a link between extensive mechanization and reorganization on the one hand and steadily decreasing prices on the other. But whereas German technical and organizational restructuring bore some resemblance to its American counterpart, German pricing policy did not. This set off bitter disputes about whether high prices were a necessity or a choice, that is, whether they reflected high costs or resulted from regulation by cartels.

In late 1926 the Social Democratic *Gewerkschafts-Zeitung* lamented that prices had not fallen, even though productivity had increased. The liberal economist Moritz J. Bonn claimed that Germany's high and inflexible price structure was equivalent to "murder of the consumer."[4] For the remainder of the decade, similar complaints were heard from Social Democrats as well as from economic liberals, and no one contested their factual description of price movements. Between 1924 and 1929 Germany experienced significant industrial restructuring as well as severe fluctuations in the business cycle. The inflation boom was followed by the stabilization crisis of 1924; the upswing of early 1925, by the rationalization crisis of 1925–1926; and the prosperity of 1927 and 1928, by the first stage of the world depression in 1929. But wholesale prices moved within very narrow ranges, as shown in Table 8–1.

Wholesale prices for industrial raw materials, semifinished goods, and finished consumer goods decreased somewhat in the first phases of rationalization before climbing during the boom of 1927–1928, although never approaching the 1924 levels. Prices for producers' goods rose and fell but consistently remained above prerationalization levels. By any indices, prices were high. They not only exceeded prewar levels, but were above world market prices in many instances, and did not show the same tendency to fall in the late 1920s as did prices in other European countries.[5] The high and sticky prices for products at all stages of manufacturing contributed to a higher cost of living in Germany than in other European countries.[6]

As heavy industry and machine making illustrate, the experience of individual sectors varied, but the overall divergence from the American model was clear. Coal prices, for example, fell overall by 7.2 percent between 1924 and 1928 as a result of both rationalization and a glut in domestic and world coal supplies.[7] Pig iron and steel girders, on the other hand, rose. In 1925

Table 8–1. Wholesale Prices (1913 = 100)

Year	All Goods	Agriculture	Industrial Raw Materials and Semifinished Goods	Finished Producer Goods	Finished Consumer Goods
1924	137.3	119.6	142.0	128.5	177.1
1925	141.8	133.0	141.0	135.9	172.4
1926	134.4	129.3	129.7	132.5	162.2
1927	137.6	137.8	137.8	130.2	160.2
1928	140.0	134.3	134.1	137.0	174.9
1929	137.2	130.2	130.2	138.6	171.6

Source: ADGB, Allgemeiner Freier Angestellten Bund, Allgemeiner Deutscher Beamtenbund, *Wirtschaftslage, Kapitalbildung, Finanzen . . . 1925–1930* (Berlin, 1930), 17.

pig iron prices varied between 86 and 91 marks a ton, while monthly sales varied from 157,000 to 217,000 tons. The highest prices coincided with the highest sales. The following year and a half, the price stabilized at 86 marks, despite wild oscillations in monthly sales. Thereafter it dropped as low as 78 marks, only to rise again to 85 marks in 1929. Steel girders were priced at 131 marks in January 1927, when 74,000 tons were sold. A year later the price rose to 133 marks, when 91,000 tons were sold, and rose further a year later to 138 marks, despite a drop in sales to 70,000 tons. As American analysts of rationalization noted with astonishment, "prices for foundry pig iron and girders stand in no relation whatsoever to the demand for these products."[8]

The prices for pig iron and girders, like those for coal, rolling mill products, and other semifinished iron and steel goods, were regulated by cartels. Although regulated prices did not rise as sharply as free-market prices during the boom period from mid-1926 to mid-1928, they did not fall thereafter, whereas free-market prices dropped steeply.[9] Domestic iron prices, which were protected by tariffs, stood well above world market prices and above domestic iron prices in other European countries.[10] The gap between domestic and world market prices for bar iron, for example, rose from 8.60 marks in 1913 to 18.90 marks in 1925, and on to 51.80 marks in 1913.[11] Higher prices for industrial raw materials and semifinished goods drove prices up for domestic finished goods, whether machine tools or consumer durables. Manufacturers of finished goods for export, however, received rebates from iron and steel producers.[12] According to Social Democrats and economic liberals, industry's pricing policy was an attempt to purchase competitiveness in the world market at the expense of the domestic consumer.[13]

Critics blamed what they saw as an antisocial and self-defeating pricing policy primarily on the highly cartellized structure of German industry, and secondarily on tariffs. Cartels were not unique to Germany, but since the late nineteenth century they had played a more central role in economic life than in any other industrial country. These voluntary associations of industrial firms sought to regulate the market by setting prices, allocating production quotas, and often acting as sales agents as well. Virtually every industry, even those in which production was concentrated in a few firms, had at least one cartel; such complex industries as steel had several, each overseeing a select range of products. Whereas cartels were illegal in countries such as the United States, they were permitted in Germany, although the Weimar cartel law and cartel court did subject them to some weak regulation. The power of particular cartels rose and fell with the vicissitudes of a given industry as well as of the economy as a whole, but the cartel system in general prospered during the years of rationalization.[14] The existence of strong cartels did not necessarily block technical and organizational restructuring, as even the trade unions admitted, but it did distort prices.[15]

Writing in a 1927 publication of the Metalworkers' Union, A. Brandes neatly summarized the Social Democratic viewpoint: "The economic pur-

pose of rationalization, which is to lower the price of goods by sinking production costs and thereby to strengthen mass purchasing power, has been
thwarted by the cartels of German firms."[16] After all, noted factory council member Eugen Weber in a letter to the Bosch company newspaper, cartels exist to raise prices and thereby increase profits.[17] Nowhere was this
done "more crassly" than in iron and steel, argued union leader Toni Sender.
Enormous increases in productivity lowered costs, but the cartels nevertheless raised prices. Sender went on to issue a plea for "the fresh breeze of
free competition."[18] In the left's analysis, cartels were the key institutional
means of enforcing high prices at home, which, in turn, enabled industrialists "to stare as though hypnotized at markets abroad."[19] Whether lower
domestic prices would have stimulated the economy, as the Social Democrats imagined, is difficult to know. It is evident, however, that the political, institutional, and attitudinal prerequisites for attempting such a policy
were lacking.[20]

Industrialists staunchly defended their pricing and export policy, readily
admitting that it diverged sharply from the American model and from initial German expectations about rationalization. They denied that cartels
were to blame, insisting that although productivity had risen so, too, had
costs; higher prices simply reflected higher costs. The controversy on prices
can best be understood by examining the problems of cost accounting and
the self-proclaimed "cost crisis" of German industry.

Costs

Capital and labor, economists and engineers agreed that a principal aim of
rationalization should be to lower the costs of production, but there was
no consensus on whether this was achieved and no reliable body of statistics or accepted accounting procedures by which to measure it. Far from
being a straightforward and objective business tool, cost accounting in the
1920s was a rapidly shifting and highly contested set of practices. Firms
sought to modernize accounting procedures in line with industrial restructuring in order to gain accurate information on new production processes.
Academic experts sought to prescribe new categories and methods and to
decide how the high costs of rationalization were to be treated for bookkeeping purposes. In this fluid and uncertain situation, industrialists on one
side and labor leaders and academic experts on the other adopted different
methods of calculating costs, reached different conclusions about their
magnitude and movement, and held different forces responsible.

Attempts to improve and standardize cost-accounting methods, both
within firms and within industrial sectors, predated the rationalization
movement.[21] With the onset of stabilization and restructuring, this task
became more urgent; inflation no longer wiped out losses, and the technical and economic success of rationalization could only be measured if costs,
productivity, and depreciation could be accurately calculated. The Mining Association conducted surveys on the costs of running the new mining

machinery and in so doing, urged its members to calculate costs in the same way and use the same forms.[22] Throughout 1926 and 1927 Vestag complained about late and sloppy bookkeeping and insisted that its member firms must submit monthly accounts, with full and accurate statistics, divided into the appropriate categories.[23]

Efforts were made to implement these requests, and other industries followed suit, but the results were generally disappointing. In a 1930 Vestag survey, for example, some mines estimated the costs of running the pervasive pneumatic hammer 3–5 times higher than others. Understandably disturbed, Vestag concluded that standardized accounting methods were not being used.[24] A few years later the Mining Association admitted that its recommended formula for depreciating machines had proven wrong.[25] The situation was no better in iron and steel, where management complained of the particular difficulties of determining costs for semifinished and finished goods that went through several stages of production. What was to be entered as wages, what as materials, which costs were fixed, and which were proportional?[26] How did one determine which individual rationalization measures cut costs and which did not, when several were introduced simultaneously?[27] By the early 1930s the RDI was complaining that firms failed to recognize unprofitable and inefficient operations because of poor organization, inadequate oversight, and false accounting methods.[28] New methods of accounting remained in their infancy in large firms and were virtually absent in small and medium-sized ones. It had proven easier to rationalize production than administration and accounting.[29]

Despite these methodological uncertainties and statistical inadequacies—which firms occasionally acknowledged[30]—industry insisted that costs were rising because of the expense of rationalization and the attendant wage gains. This claim returns us to the controversies surrounding cost accounting.

Rationalization entailed both the closing of inefficient or redundant firms and the modernization of existing ones. The necessary capital came from self-financing and loans, in proportions that varied by firm and sector. Of interest here is not how much was spent, but how the expenses of rationalization were treated in a firm's accounts. Business included them under the costs of production, thereby raising both costs and prices. Financing rationalization through high prices, as opposed to the Fordist method of financing by expanding sales, was an attempt to recoup the cost of modernization in one year. It made economic sense for the firm but not the economy as a whole. The alternative accounting methods, preferred by academic critics of business practices, treated the expense of rationalization in part as a current cost and in part as an addition to capital value that was to be depreciated gradually. The result was to lower costs. Similar disagreements arose over how partially or fully closed firms were to be depreciated. Using the business accounting method, firms showed a loss; using the alternative procedure, they showed a profit.[31] Different calculations of costs, depreciation, and profits led to different judgments about wages.

Some contemporaries as well as several historians have attributed the cost problems of Weimar industry to the relative increase of fixed costs, that is, plant and machinery, over such variable costs as wages and raw materials. High fixed costs made it difficult to lower overall costs and prices by decreasing production if demand shrank—a problem that was exacerbated by overcapacity and overcapitalization in many industries.[32] Industrialists, however, focused only on variable costs—above all, wages and state social policy. Although historians are still debating the relative size and impact of the German wage bill in the late 1920s, Weimar industrialists had decided early on that it was both excessive and detrimental to rationalization. In 1927 the powerful VDA reiterated a common complaint among its members: "Workers have sought to obtain their share of rationalization at once instead of waiting for enterprises to be put on a firm financial basis and for that cheapening of production essential to an increase in real wages."[33] Increased wages and welfare costs ostensibly limited or nullified the reduction in costs that mechanization and reorganization brought about, thereby defeating the purpose of rationalization.[34]

Nowhere were these complaints louder than in Ruhr heavy industry.[35] Reviewing the record of its mines in 1927–1928, Vestag claimed that it could not cut costs as fast as wages were rising, despite productivity increases.[36] Iron and steel vigorously defended its price rises on the grounds of a wage-induced cost crisis. According to Fritz Springorum of the Hoesch iron and steel works, prices had not kept pace with the general price level. Of greater importance, the price rises that did occur, especially in 1928, were a result of wage increases imposed by state arbitration. He complained that the government showed no understanding of world market conditions, economic laws, or industry's need to accumulate capital. By burdening industry with wage increases and social policy costs, he said, government precipitated a cost crisis that in turn raised prices.[37]

Unmoved by industry's pleas, trade unions continued to push for higher wages and to justify them as essential for successful rationalization.

Wages

Whereas the eight-hour day had stood at the heart of conflicts between capital and labor in the early 1920s, wages did so after 1924. Wage levels, their future movement, and the means by which they were set were extremely divisive issues, serving as symbols for a host of other disagreements on the state of the economy and the power of different classes. The wage statistics collected in late Weimar are voluminous and sifting through them is tricky. Global statements about nominal wage rates in the economy as a whole, or the ratio of women's to men's wages, for example, are easier to make then those about wages as a percentage of costs in particular industries, or the real earnings of particular types of workers. Sifting through the available data is also frustrating, for it does not provide clear-cut answers to the questions which divided labor and capital—questions which were subjective and political rather than objective and economic. Were wages so high that they undermined rationalization by raising costs and prices, thereby destroying profitability and capital accumulation, as industry maintained? Or, as the labor movement argued, were they too low, thereby thwarting rationalization by undermining domestic demand and contributing to high prices, underutilization of capacity, and high costs?

By all accounts, wages improved from 1924 to 1928, before leveling off and then declining in 1930, but there are disagreements on how much. Table 8-2 presents the most optimistic assessment.

Jürgen Kuczynski attempted to calculate an average wage figure for all workers, employed and unemployed, that included losses from unemployment, short time and social insurance fees, and gains from unemployment insurance payments. His picture of nominal wages was less rosy but still positive. Taking the year 1913 as 100, nominal wages stood at 125 in 1926 and 152 in 1928, before dropping to 131 in 1930.[38] In both assessments, real wages were less impressive than nominal wages, for they did not reach 1913 levels until 1928 (and by Kuczynski's calculations, they fell below that again in 1929).[39] Both skilled and unskilled men improved their situation, but the latter did relatively better. The contractually specified hourly wage for unskilled men was 60 percent that of skilled men in 1913, 70 percent in 1924–1925, and 78 percent from 1928 to 1930.[40] Women did not fare as well: unskilled women earned only 66 percent as much as unskilled men in 1928, and the small number of skilled women earned a mere 63 percent as much as their male counterparts.[41]

During the rationalization boom the working class made gains, albeit not spectacular ones. Two disturbing features marred this picture: high unemployment, which will be analyzed later; and the practice of resolving wage disputes through state arbitration. In 1929, for example, 52 percent of the nearly 10,000 disputes about wages and hours were settled by arbitration, and in 19 percent of the cases the decision of the state mediator was bind-

Table 8-2. Gross Earnings of Workers (1928 = 100)

Year	Nominal Wages/Hour	Nominal Wages/Week	Real Wages/Week
1913–1914	53	61	93
1925	77	75	81
1926	82	78	84
1927	90	88	89
1928	100	100	100
1929	106	103	102
1930	103	95	97
1931	95	84	94
1932	80	69	86

Source: Dietmar Petzina, Werner Abelshauser, Anselm Faust, *Sozialgeschichtliches Arbeitsbuch*, vol. 3 (Munich, 1978), 98.

ing. Led by former Catholic trade union leaders, the Ministry of Labor generally handed down decisions that were considered to be more favorable to labor than to capital.[42] Thus despite the relative weakness of the trade unions after 1924 and the reserve army of the unemployed, the labor movement could defend the wages of those still working. But, as Hilferding so aptly noted in 1927, "the weekly wage is a political wage."[43] It depended as much on the balance of power in the parliament and the bureaucracy as in the economy. Moreover, it worked only as long as industrialists would reluctantly tolerate decisions they disliked.

Turning from national averages to the situation in Ruhr industry, the wage picture becomes more confused, while the dangers of labor's reliance on compulsory arbitration emerge clearly. In the labor-intensive coal mining industry, wages accounted for 50 percent of costs and were thus a constant concern of management. According to data supplied by the Mining Association, the real wages of workers in the Ruhr mines rose modestly between 1924 and 1930, but at a very uneven rate among different kinds of workers. If 1913 is taken as 100, wages stood at 87 in 1924, did not exceed 100 until 1926, and by 1930 had only reached 114. As early as 1925 those working above ground earned more than before the war, while miners on the coal face did not pass that level until 1928.[44] The wage bill per ton of coal remained relatively stable, rising to a high of 7.3 marks in 1925, then fluctuating back down to its 1924 level of 6.9 marks—one mark above the 1913 level.[45]

These uncontested statistics were interpreted in diametrically opposed ways by labor and industry. To trade unions they indicated that workers were receiving few if any benefits from rationalization, especially when high unemployment was considered along with meager wage gains. Overall buying power was not expanding, as predicted and required by the American model, and the slight decline in the wage bill per ton indicated that productivity was rising faster than wages.[46] To mine owners the insignificant drop in wages per ton meant that labor was getting more than its fair share of the benefits of rationalization.[47] Wage gains that looked modest to workers seemed exorbitant to owners. In 1928, for example, the Concordia mine claimed that a recent 8 percent wage increase forced it to speed up rationalization and fire workers.[48] Vestag lamented that mines were more burdened by wage increases, as well as by the eight-hour day and social insurance than were other industries.[49] The Mining Association summarized the owners' pessimism in its 1929 yearly report:

> At wage negotiations the employees' side continually emphasizes the strong increase in productivity per shift, from which the miner also wants to have his share. It should be noted, however, that the benefits of the increased productivity per shift, which rationalization and mechanization have achieved, have gone completely to the worker. The employer, on the contrary, has not only gone away with nothing. He has had to bear a direct loss, because the increase in productivity has lagged somewhat behind the increase in wages.[50]

Iron and steel, where wages were roughly a third of costs, had a more complex and hotly disputed wage situation than did coal mining. Iron, steel, and rolling mills hired many different kinds of workers, who were slotted into hierarchical wage structures, and wage costs varied greatly depending on the size and technological level of a given firm.[51] As both labor and capital admitted, generalizations for the industry as a whole were difficult to make and of dubious quality. According to data compiled by the Enquete Ausschuss, average weekly nominal wages rose 77 percent from their prewar level and 56 percent from their 1924 low. Although both skilled and unskilled workers benefited, improvements were considerably more substantial for the latter.[52] There was no agreement, however, on whether this translated into real wage gains. J. W. Reichert, head of the Association of German Iron and Steel Industrialists (VDESI), adamantly insisted that because wages had risen 70 percent while the cost of living had gone up only 48 percent since 1913–1914, the iron and steel worker had greater buying power. Others, including the Metalworkers' Union, were doubtful, noting that some skilled workers actually had less purchasing power than before the war. The historian Bernd Weisbrod concluded that although real wages of iron and steel workers in 1928 were 5.8 percent above their 1913 level, once taxes and social insurance payments were deducted they were only 2 percent higher—a far cry from the gains asserted by industry.[53]

The most serious controversies, however, were not about real wages but about wage costs as a proportion of total costs. Unlike in coal production, there was not even agreement about the numbers, let alone their meaning. According to the figures of the Enquete Ausschuss, wages per ton of iron and steel fell from 1926 on, and in 1929 they were only 22 and 16 percent higher, respectively, than in 1913. Although wages as a proportion of rolling mill costs were 47 percent higher than in 1913, they were just a few points higher than in 1925.[54] Neither labor nor capital agreed with these figures. Fritz Springorum, of the Hoesch mills, claimed it was impossible to separate out labor costs; one Vestag firm insinuated that the Enquete figures were not so much wrong as potentially misleading.[55] Such industry spokesmen as Ernst Poensgen, representing Vestag, and J. W. Reichert, of VDESI, cited specific amounts ranging from 30 to 40 percent, while Adam Stegerwald and Johannes Burgartz, of the Christian trade union movement, gave estimates as low as 5 percent. The truth undoubtedly lay between the two, but it is impossible to know exactly where because firms refused to reveal all their cost data fully. In addition, there was not consensus on how to calculate labor costs for semifinished goods that went through several production processes, nor on whether to include productive workers alone or all employees in a factory.[56] Since the statistics were inadequate and open to diametrically opposed interpretations, labor remained convinced that wages were too low; capital, that they were too high.

The laments of iron and steel producers sounded remarkably like those of coal mine owners, in part because they were often the same person or company. Productivity per head had more than doubled, but wage costs per ton had not fallen at all, complained director Franz Bartscherer of the August Thyssen works.[57] Workers had taken all the "fruits of rationalization," protested Reichert at the 1927 annual meeting of the VDESI.[58] Dividends were a meager 6 percent, noted Vestag apologetically in 1928, because the gains of rationalization had been eaten up by wages and state social policy. Further technical improvements were no longer desirable, it warned, and thus costs could not be cut to compensate for further wage increases.[59]

To be sure, the spokesmen for Ruhr heavy industry did not blame their troubles exclusively on wages. They admitted that the Versailles treaty and reparations, as well as interest payments, played a role.[60] Nonetheless, wage rates, wages as a proportion of costs, and German wages in comparison to lower French, Belgian, and Czech wages were the main targets of their attack—an attack that was more than rhetorical. In the fall of 1928, Ruhr heavy industry rejected both the demands of the Metalworkers' Union for higher wages and the government arbitration that subsequently granted them, choosing instead to lock out more than 220,000 workers for four weeks. Industry successfully challenged the system of binding arbitration, winning a lower wage settlement and exposing the weakness of a union movement that depended on state arbitration and industry's compliance.[61] Nevertheless industry continued to complain about the shortcomings of rationalization. In 1929 Krupp von Bohlen and Halbach insisted that

> the increased proceeds from rationalization melt away completely in increased burdens and wages, so that there is no prospect of achieving appropriate profitability. The employer cannot assert himself in this competition between rationalization and the increase of all burdens unless there is a change in attitude toward the economy [i.e., industry] in the appropriate places [i.e., the state].[62]

Ruhr industry objected not only to the size of its wage bill and the role of the state in determining it, but also to the many other social policies provided by a republic it detested. Social insurance and other social programs were not an invention of Weimar, but they expanded greatly in the 1920s. According to Harold James, who admits to providing a maximum estimate, social expenditures amounted to 57 percent of the state budget in 1925 as against 37 percent in 1913. If education and housing are omitted and only health, accident, unemployment, and old age insurance programs are considered, the figures decline to 37 percent and 19 percent, respectively.[63] The increase was substantial, and industrialists and their interest groups protested against it in the early 1920s.[64]

Those protests escalated after 1924, even though social costs as a proportion of wages in heavy industry stabilized at 8–10 percent, as opposed to 4 percent in the prewar period.[65] If 1926 is taken as 100, the rise in the cost of state social policy as a proportion of wage costs in major Ruhr firms in 1930 ranged from 101 at Mannesmann to 131 at Krupp. By contrast, the expenditures for voluntary company social policy measures ranged from 116 at Klöckner to 171 at Vestag.[66] Despite the fact that heavy industry bitterly attacked the "social burdens" imposed by the Weimar state, it was willing and able to spend freely on private programs, which, as the next chapter will show, had their own complex economic and political agendas.

Since the 1980s historians have acrimoniously debated whether German wages in the 1920s exceeded productivity gains, limited the possibilities of investment, and were at the root of a crisis that predated the depression.[67] Despite the use of sophisticated models and the marshalling of massive statistics, one participant recently concluded that no "definitive victories have been achieved."[68] Certainly this was true in the 1920s, when labor and capital argued from scantier data, incompatible economic theories, and more impassioned political convictions. Industrialists and trade unionists entered the rationalization era with opposite assumptions about how wages should move. Although each gained some ground—or so an impartial observer might well conclude—each side was bitterly disappointed in the gap between expectations and achievements, and this disappointment shaped both economic judgments and political actions.

Throughout the late 1920s Social Democrats clung to a vision of rationalization based on mass consumption. They blamed industry for depriving workers of potential benefits and for creating problems for itself. Some labor leaders, especially those within the Communist Party, insisted that real wage gains were insignificant or nonexistent; others admitted that increases were real, even if popular opinion denied it. Even the optimists protested that productivity gains outstripped wage increases and that the working class as a whole suffered the burdens of high unemployment and the increased intensity of rationalized work.[69] Inadequate wages, coupled with high prices, hurt not only the working class but industry as well. According to such Social Democrats as Fritz Tarnow, industry was blocking the expansion of mass buying power and was thereby forced to rely on a shrinking and viciously competitive world market. Labor leaders, from both the Social Democratic and Christian trade unions reiterated their conviction that consumption, not production, was the principle problem in a modern economy and that it could only be solved by adopting the American policy of high wages.[70] If German rationalization failed to produce desirable results, capital was to blame.

Profits

Given that every aspect of cost accounting was open to dispute, it is not surprising that there was great uncertainty about the degree of profitability. As many observers complained, firm balance sheets were as noteworthy for what they hid as for what they revealed.[71] Calculations of profits and losses were based on unreliable estimates of the value of fixed capital at the time of stabilization, and the depreciation rates used were viewed by many as excessive.[72] Dividends and stock prices were equally questionable indices of gains and losses.[73] Few Weimar Germans fully accepted the available data on profitability, but they were forced to use it as the basis of their arguments—as are we.

Weimar industry did not lose money, its vociferous complaints notwith-standing, but profit rates were modest, averaging 5.49 percent in 1927 for industry as a whole. In Ruhr heavy industry, which had invested in signifi-cant and expensive mechanization and reorganization, rates were lower from 1925 to 1927. They rose nearly to national averages thereafter, only to sink again with the depression. There were, however, enormous discrepancies among firms. Whereas Vestag's profits were 5.41 percent in 1926–1927 and 5.35 percent in 1928–1929, surpassed only by Mannesmann's among iron and steel producers, Krupp's profits were only 2.6 percent during 1927–1929, dropping to virtually nothing in 1929–1930.[74] In 1928 a government-appointed commission examined the profitability of coal mining, in isolation from the larger integrated firms of which mines were often a part. All members agreed on production costs, but the majority report of Professor Eugen Schmalenbach used a high depreciation figure and calculated that mines lost .27 marks per ton, whereas the minority report of Dr. Fritz Baade, based on a lower depre-ciation rate, arrived at .58 marks profit per ton.[75] A subsequent Christian trade union estimate, based on government statistics, claimed that profits per ton rose considerably in Ruhr coal in 1928 and 1929.[76]

Dividends present much the same picture. Average dividends for stock on the Berlin stock exchange stood at 5.6 percent in 1926, as against 10.2 percent in 1913. By 1928, however, they had risen to 8.2 percent; by 1929, to over 9 percent before beginning their decline.[77] On average, coal com-panies paid less than 2 percent dividends in 1925–1926, over 4 percent in 1926–1927, and again less in 1928.[78] Iron and steel did considerably better. Vestag dividends were 6 percent from 1926 to 1929 and 4 percent the fol-lowing year, but some analysts doubted that Vestag's decision to pay divi-dends indicated financial health.[79] Many Ruhr firms such as Gutehoffnungs-hütte, Mannesmann, and Klöckner paid even higher rates.[80] Profits in machine making averaged 4.5 percent in 1927–1928 and 4.8 percent the fol-lowing year.[81] Measured in terms of the value of plants, machinery, and the price of stocks, Ruhr firms were not losing ground in the late 1920s.[82]

Absolute profitability was never really the issue, except perhaps for the most precarious firms, such as Krupp. Rather, industry measured prof-itability relative to expectations and desires; it judged earnings to be wanting on both counts.[83] As Vestag succinctly argued in its 1929–1930 review of rationalization: "If the profits from this investment have not been realized to the extent anticipated, this is because the productivity increases achieved through technical improvements and rationalization measures have been greatly exceeded by the increased costs of production resulting from steadily increased wages, salaries, social payments and taxes."[84] Industry depicted itself as noble and self-sacrificing, and its efforts on behalf of its own inter-ests and those of the economy as being thwarted by selfish workers and a meddling state. Rationalization was indeed functioning irrationally and at the expense of industry, but through no fault of its own.

Against this highly politicized understanding of rationalization, the protests of labor were of no avail. For trade unions the issue was profits relative to wages and social insurance. Social Democratic trade unionists claimed
that a reading of balance sheets showed that profits, if modest, were sufficient to pay higher wages and social costs.[85] Moreover, continued investment in new plants and machinery, for whose products there was insufficient demand, indicated that firms had money to spare.[86] Finally, Social
Democrats argued, if industry wanted to secure future profitability, it had
to pay higher wages to increase domestic demand and escape dependence
on the world market. Like capital, labor viewed profits in terms of its comprehensive understanding of how a restructured economy could and should
function. But their understandings of rationalization and rationality were
as different at the end of the 1920s as they had been at mid-decade, before
the process of transformation began.

Based on these incompatible understandings, industrialists and trade
unionists each claimed to be deprived of their rightful material benefits from
rationalization. In purely monetary terms, the balance sheet was mixed. For
workers who were employed, there were modest wage gains but no significant transformation in consumption, either quantitatively or qualitatively.
Factory owners whose firms survived enjoyed modest profits, but there were
high investment expenses and persistent market problems. Industry's model
of industrial restructuring, with its high prices, cartels, and export orientation, triumphed over labor's Americanized vision of high wages and mass
domestic consumption. Both capital and labor suffered as a result. The model
did not function as expected by capital because labor costs and government
spending could not be squeezed as industry desired and because the world
market did not play its designated role. Workers, at best, held their own in
terms of wages but did not gain significant consumer benefits. Moreover
work, skill structures, and employment prospects were all adversely affected
by rationalization.

Work and Unemployment

Rationalization affected not only productivity, pay, and profits, but also
the conditions under which work was performed and the security of employment. Restructuring created work that was intense, exhausting, monotonous, and deskilled and led to mass unemployment, according to the most
prevalent charges. Although not all of these accusations were accurate and
the high rate of unemployment in late Weimar was not entirely due to industrial restructuring, there was substantial truth to labor's claims that, despite
better pay, work was more oppressive and unfulfilling and employment
much more precarious than before rationalization.

Bourgeois analysts of rationalized work across the political spectrum
have tended to emphasize its separation of planning and execution, increased
division of labor, and repetition and monotony.[87] What was probably most
apparent to the workers themselves was the feel of the shop floor, the pace

of work, and the increased risk of illness or injury. Rationalized factories were frequently more crowded, as new machines were added, mechanized transport systems introduced, and everything placed as close together as possible to eliminate wasted movement by men and materials. The resulting workplaces were frequently noisier, hotter, and more polluted as well.[88] Whether work in such mechanized and reorganized factories was physically and mentally more strenuous was difficult to determine, as even the trade unions admitted.[89] But it was widely acknowledged that the work pace was more intense. Machines, transport systems, and the occasional assembly line ran faster, supervisors pushed harder, and new wage systems presented workers with the choice of more work or less pay. Social Democratic and, above all, Communist leaders stressed the intensification of work, for that provided a way to critique the capitalist practice of rationalization without condemning rationalization per se.[90]

Although employers expressed skepticism about Taylorism, they readily undertook time-and-motion studies as the basis for setting new piece rates for wages. (Since the assembly line, which controlled the work pace regardless of wages, was not widely introduced, industrialists were reluctant to use the Fordist system of hourly wages.) They were aided by Refa, the National Committee for Time Study. Founded in 1924 by the Association of German Metal Industrialists and the Working Committee for German Factory Engineers, Refa conducted studies and published information. By 1933 it had trained over 10,000 time-study experts, who were hired by firms to clock workers on the job, recommend methods of eliminating wasted time, and set new piece rates.[91] Refa-based wage systems were especially widespread in the metal industry, where over two-thirds of the 1,100 firms surveyed by the DMV adopted them. By contrast the more complex—and, according to the trade unions, still more exploitative—Bedaux premium bonus systems existed in only 7 factories.[92]

Sickness and accident rates rose as rationalization proceeded, but the causal relationship was disputed. Workers' health insurance boards reported an increase in sick days in the late 1920s, and some doctors noted with concern a marked rise in the number of nervous ailments, which they claimed were caused by the pressures of rationalized work. Accident rates, especially in mining, climbed as well.[93] Industry insisted that rationalization made work safer and attributed the higher number of accidents to better reporting and worker carelessness. Social Democrats and Communists insisted that mechanization and reorganization, with the accompanying frenetic work pace and wage systems which encouraged overexertion and self-exploitation, made work unsafe and unhealthy.[94]

Preller's evaluation of the evidence suggests that the trade unions were correct, although the reasons rationalization increased accidents were complex. In part it was due to the increased use of machines; even more, however, to mechanized transport systems and flow production. The increased work pace played a role, as did the increased use of unskilled and semiskilled workers who were less familiar with accident prevention then their skilled co-workers.[95]

Rationalization altered not only work but also the composition of the labor force, although the transformations were less dramatic than contemporaries and historians have assumed. The image of America, coupled with the expressed fears of skilled workers, led many to believe that rationalization was displacing skilled workers on a large scale. Writing in 1933, Rudi Litzenberger claimed that factory artisans were the main victims of mechanization and that "rationalization is effecting a restructuring within the working class away from skilled workers and toward the semiskilled whose work is more or less mechanical."[96] In fact, the situation was much more complex. Rationalization did eliminate some skilled jobs, especially in those relatively rare instances when assembly line work was introduced, but it also eliminated many unskilled jobs that involved lifting and carrying.[97] The machine industry remained heavily dependent on skilled workers, who comprised 47 percent of the labor force in 1920 and over 50 percent from 1926 on.[98] Skilled workers benefited from the triumph of industry's vision of more efficient yet still specialized "quality work." Sometimes skilled workers were employed at less skilled tasks, but they retained their rank; other times, their skills and responsibilities actually increased with the introduction of rationalization.[99] Overall, German rationalization succeeded in intensifying work without significantly altering the skill structure of the working class.[100]

Many in Weimar, both inside and outside the labor movement, believed that deskilling was accompanied by a feminization of the labor force.[101] One can find evidence of factories and industries—and certainly offices—where women's work increased markedly, but men's employment rose as well, and often at a faster rate. Women did not displace men; rather they worked in newly created, monotonous, semiskilled assembly jobs and in office positions. Their rationalized jobs grew alongside of, but separate from men's jobs and, not surprisingly, they were much less well paid.[102] In other industries women remained a miniscule proportion of the labor force.[103] Mining remained an overwhelmingly male occupation, as did iron and steel and machine making, where women represented only 3 percent of the labor force throughout the late 1920s. In metalworking, office machines, electrotechnical goods, and optics, by contrast, women formed between 17 and 36 percent of the labor force in 1927.[104] Overall, women formed 31 percent of the labor force in 1925, up from 21 percent in 1907. In industrial and artisan work, however, the figure rose only slightly from 18.8 to 20 percent in the same period, and remained stable throughout the late 1920s. One in every three women was employed, as was the situation before World War I.[105] Although the number of women employed during rationalization was not substantially greater, women were more visible and closely associated with the most modern sectors of the economy.

Throughout the rationalization boom, unemployment was a reality for an unprecedented number of workers and a threat to all. During the stabilization crisis of 1924, there were 927,000 unemployed in Germany. That number fell to 682,000 the following year, then skyrocketed to over 2 million in 1926, when rationalization was in full swing, and did not fall below 1.3 million in the most prosperous years, 1927–1928. By 1929 unemployment was near 2 million again, and by 1930, over 3 million.[106] To grasp the magnitude of the problem in the most stable years of Weimar, one need only look at how trade unions were affected (see Table 8-3).

The percentage of trade union members working reduced hours was smaller, but rose and fell in a similar pattern.[107]

Analyzed by region and industry, the situation was no better. In Ruhr mining employment decreased from just over 432,000 in 1925 to between 365,000 and 375,000 in 1929. Unemployment among organized miners hovered around 2 percent, suggesting that many left the industry. Unemployment among organized metalworkers, however, oscillated between a high of roughly 19 percent in 1926 and 1929 and a low of 5.6 percent in 1928.[108] On average in 1929 there were 22 unemployed workers for every 100 who had jobs nationwide, and 17 per 100 in Westphalia. In such Ruhr towns as Dortmund, 26 out of every 1,000 inhabitants were unemployed in 1928; in Essen, where Krupp was centered, 35 out of every 1,000.[109] One could multiply such depressing statistics, but the point is clear. Unemployment had become a problem of unprecedented dimensions, as the unions and working class were painfully aware.

But what proportion of this unemployment could be attributed to structural changes rather than to the business cycle or seasonal unemployment or that "normal" or ineradicable unemployment that was estimated to hover between 1 and 2 percent?[110] Industry claimed that virtually none was due to rationalization, instead holding trade union wage policy and depressed market conditions responsible.[111] According to the well-publicized study of the economist Otto von Zweidineck-Südenhorst, rationalization and high wages, along with a shortage of capital, high prices, and weak foreign trade, were all to blame.[112] In the view of trade unionists and many later historians, however, rationalization was the principal culprit, for it caused not only the temporary displacement of workers—which even Social Democrats had anticipated—but also high levels of new, long-term unemployment as jobs were eliminated much more rapidly than new ones were created.

Calculating exact numbers was and remains impossible, but estimates based on the gap between increased production and employment provide a reasonable approximation. The Social Democrat Kurt Mendelsohn noted

Table 8-3. Unemployment as Percentage of Trade Union Membership

1907–13	1922	1923	1924	1925	1926	1927	1928	1929	1930
2.3	1.5	9.6	13.5	6.7	18.0	8.7	8.4	13.1	22.2

Source: Dietmar Petzina, Werner Abelshauser, Anselm Faust, *Sozialgeschichtliches Arbeitsbuch*, vol. 3 (Munich, 1978), 119.

that production in heavy industry increased 25 percent between 1925 and 1928, but employment levels remained even. In the consumer goods sector, which had not experienced rationalization, production and employment rose together.[113] Employment in mining, iron and steel, and machine making declined by nearly 400,000 between 1925 and 1927, calculated trade union economist Wladimir Woytinsky, because machines were pushing out men, just as they had in America, and the economy was not expanding fast enough to reabsorb them.[114] A study conducted in 1930 by the General Confederation of German Trade Unions (ADGB) estimated that 800,000 of the 5 million workers currently unemployed had lost their jobs due to rationalization, but the Metalworkers' Union considered this figure too low. The Institute for the Study of Economic Trends suggested 1 million; the government statistical office 1.5–2 million.[115]

Those industries and firms in which rationalization was greatest illustrate most clearly that economic growth and employment did not necessarily go together. Indeed, the productivism to which the trade unions were so committed was bought at the price of their members' jobs. According to the Metalworkers' Union, a third of unemployment in that sector was due directly or indirectly to rationalization. Over 91,000 jobs were lost due to specific reorganizations of production and the introduction of new technology; over 27,000 in iron and steel alone. Another 50,000 were victims of mergers, plant closings, and production restrictions.[116] For mining, John R. Shearer has calculated that between 30 and 35 percent of all mining unemployment was due to rationalization in 1926–1928 and 51 percent in 1929.[117]

Cuts in the labor force in particular firms were often dramatic, especially in 1926, a year of intense rationalization. At Phoenix, for example, employment dropped more than 5 percent in the first six months of 1925 alone, and further cuts were made when it joined Vestag the following year. At Gutehoffnungshütte, the number of blue-collar workers decreased from 8,435 in July 1925 to 6,852 in April 1926. By contrast the number of white-collar workers only dropped from 707 to 683, and their numbers actually increased elsewhere during rationalization.[118] Between the fall of 1925 and the fall of 1926, Krupp cut 6,000 workers. The following year, its total employment dropped from 65,000 to 46,000; in Essen alone, steelworkers lost 14,000 jobs.[119] The Association of German Machine Building Firms estimated that over 50 percent of the unemployment in that sector in 1925–1926 was due to rationalization.[120] In 1925 nearly 32,000 miners lost their jobs as a result of mine closings.[121]

The effects of unemployment did not fall evenly on all sectors of the working class. Ruhr towns that depended solely on heavy industry were particularly hard hit, and different age cohorts were differentially affected. Some firms singled out the oldest workers, who were thought to be least able to perform intensified work, but most cuts fell disproportionately on the young.[122] For men between the ages of 20 and 50, employment was relatively stable. When the Westphalian Steelworks fired 129 workers in late

1926, for example, 41 were younger than 20 years, while 39 were older than 40.[123] In 1914 roughly 15 percent of Krupp workers were between the ages of 14 and 20, versus less than 10 percent in 1930. The proportion of workers over 40, however, increased substantially.[124] The average age of Hoesch workers rose from 31 in 1913 and 1921 to 35 in 1926.[125] Mining tells a similar tale. In 1913, 3.7 percent of the work force was under 16, and in 1929, 1.4 percent; miners began urging their sons to look elsewhere for jobs.[126] Youth unemployment was a serious concern even before the Depression deprived most adolescents of any hope of stable employment.[127] Unemployment for women paralleled that of men but at slightly higher rates, and women were much more likely to be assigned shorttime work.[128] Unemployment among Communists was considerably higher than among Social Democrats.[129] The KPD drew more heavily from young workers than did the SPD, and management used the stabilization and rationalization crises as welcome opportunities to rid themselves of politically troublesome workers.

Rationalization and the attendant high level of unemployment thus created new divisions within the working class and compounded old ones—between the employed and the unemployed, between men and women, between skilled and semiskilled workers, between young and old, and between Communists and Social Democrats. The intensification of work and, above all, the prevalence of unemployment threatened to nullify the gains in wages and social benefits that accompanied rationalization. They further diminished the chances that the American model of mass consumption would take root in Germany.

Reactions and Responses

The effects of rationalization made a mockery of the extravagant hopes the SPD and trade unions had placed in Americanism and Fordism, but it did not shake their belief in the necessity of rationalization and the essential correctness of their endorsement. While Communists condemned the results of rationalization and held Social Democrats nearly as responsible as capitalists, Social Democrats sought to cast the contradictory character of contemporary rationalization in a more positive light and to develop practical political responses to its detrimental consequences.[130] Workers, organized and unorganized alike, expressed grave misgivings long before movement leaders had second thoughts about rationalization. But verbal protest did not translate into active and effective opposition, for rationalization had restructured work and the working class in ways that weakened organization and protest.

Social Democratic functionaries and theorists approached the ill effects of rationalization with a confidence bordering on complacency. This attitude testifies more to their economic determinism and faith in productivism than to their political astuteness or strategic sense. "Men and Machines," an article that appeared in the Miners' Union newspaper in 1928, perfectly captures the leadership's outlook. It relates the ostensibly true story of events in a factory where the work pace was intense, supervision verged on harassment, and workers' nerves were frayed. In the midst of this vola-tile situation, management called a factory meeting to announce that 14 new machines were arriving and that 75 jobs would be cut as a result. The angry workers claimed they would not passively tolerate the dismissals and called for "breaking the machines." Then "an old, bent work veteran" stood up and warned against any precipitous action. The machine was not respon-sible for the workers' plight, he argued. Machine breaking was "nonsense, a waste of power" and a strike would be "insanity." The only solution was for workers to lobby the state to pass laws to shorten hours and help the unemployed. Naturally, all the other workers in this Social Democratic morality play were persuaded by the old man's eloquence, and "the head was victorious over the heart, reason over feelings." This moral victory did not bring immediate material results, and a few days later the work vet-eran was one of seventy-five fired. "With a heavy heart he accepted his fate," but he was "enormously consoled" by the fact that he had prevented a strike and the firing of still more workers.[131] All the elements of the Social Demo-cratic response were there: an unequivocal admiration for technology, faith in the state, a refusal to sanction rank-and-file activism, and a failure to grasp the suffering and anger caused by rationalization.

In speeches and articles Social Democrats reiterated that the problem was not technology or rationalization per se, but the capitalist context within which it was occurring.[132] In the short run the solution to the detrimental consequences of rationalization was threefold: higher wages, shorter hours, and more social policy.[133] The more rationalization generated unemployment, the more ardently Social Democratic leaders preached the gospel of Ameri-canism and Fordism. Tarnow's *Why Be Poor?* was the most famous example of this.[134] When industry turned a deaf ear to their pleas, trade unionists and Social Democratic politicians argued for shorter hours, so that avail-able work could be more broadly shared and buying power thereby in-creased.[135] Finally, in 1927 the SPD worked successfully to secure the institu-tionalization of a nationwide system of unemployment insurance, which supplanted the more local, ad hoc systems existing since the early 1920s.[136]

In the long run, Social Democrats argued, the contradictory character of rationalization could be eliminated only by the transition to socialism and the planned rationalization of all elements of production and consumption.[137] Such Social Democratic theorists as Rudolf Hilferding and Fritz Naphtali were confident that rationalization was promoting just this progressive out-come. At the 1927 SPD party congress, Hilferding argued that competitive capitalism was being replaced by organized capitalism, by planned produc-tion. Cartelization, concentration, and new technology had adverse impli-cations because they led to higher prices and unemployment, but they also had revolutionary potential because they furthered the organization and socialization of the economy. The task of Social Democracy was to trans-form a capitalist economy into one controlled by the democratic state. "Economic development has posed the question of socialism," Hilferding asserted confidently. Political democracy could now be augmented by economic democracy.[138]

In 1928 Naphtali, the chief ideologue of the ADGB, elaborated the concept of economic democracy. Organized capitalism generated its own contradictions, he argued, and once workers realized the insufficiency of political democracy alone and the dangers of economic autocracy, they would seek to alter economic control and ownership. Insisting that capitalism could be and was being bent before it was broken, he cited collective bargaining and expanded state intervention as proof that the economy was coming under the control of the people, the state. (His confusion of the people and the state was all too common in Social Democratic circles.) His optimistic assessment of Weimar's efforts to rationalize the economy was summed up by the slogan "Through democratization of the economy to socialism."[139]

The concept of economic democracy was first broached in 1925 by ADGB leader Hermann Jäckel, who saw it as a possible way to involve the unions actively in rationalization.[140] It assumed much broader meaning and received greater attention in party and union debates once the Social Democrats had to grapple with the contradictions of rationalization. The optimistic assessments of Hilferding and Naphtali were ridiculed as bad politics by anarchists, dismissed as bad theory by Communists, and condemned as bad economics by industrialists.[141] But the vision and strategy they embodied had a long, although not necessarily honorable, tradition in German socialist thought. Economic democracy represented an updated version of Kautsky's deterministic Marxism and shared its strategic aversion to rank-and-file activism.[142] Both economic democracy and the Social Democrats' vision of rationalization emphasized distribution and expanded production, but not direct worker control.[143] Both held out the hope of an alternative to contemporary capitalism while promising immediate improvements within it.[144] Economic democracy encouraged Social Democrats to accept rationalization despite its short-term problems, just as the endorsement of rationalization predisposed them to accept the optimistic determinism and economism inherent in the concept of economic democracy.

This linking of economic democracy and rationalization was based on the firm conviction that capitalism inevitably must lead to socialism and that political democracy, once won, was secure. Both assumptions proved tragically wrong. Hilferding and Naphtali seriously underestimated the resilience of capitalism and the power industrialists gained through rationalization and cartels. They ignored the growing reluctance of industry in the late 1920s to make concessions to the working class and the unwillingness of key sectors to change an economic strategy built around cartels, high prices, and relatively low wages and exports. Social Democratic promises of long-term economic democratization and socialization glossed over the detrimental effects of rationalization and the fragility of workers' wage and social policy victories. The wages of those employed depended on the continued existence of the tenuous political balance of the late 1920s and on employers' reluctant toleration of binding arbitration. The success of the unemployment insurance system depended on maintaining relative economic prosperity and limiting unemployment to high but not exorbitant levels. The prerequisites for Social Democracy's defense of the working class under rationalization disappeared in the Depression, as did their optimistic assess ment of the future toward which rationalization was leading. Even before then, however, workers on the shop floor and on unemployment lines had become extremely critical of Weimar's version of industrial restructuring.

To be sure, workers did not object to all aspects of rationalized work. As the Bergbau Verein noted with relief, miners' initial hostility to mecha nization diminished when they found that it lessened their physical exer tion.[145] Similar reactions no doubt existed in other industries, especially to improved transportation within firms, which eliminated some of the heavi est lifting and carrying that the unskilled had performed. The response to the assembly line was more mixed. In 1929 the RKW *Nachrichten* glibly claimed that "the adaptation of the individual worker to chain or conveyer work is perfectly pleasant for the great majority of workers, male and female, even in undertakings in which such work does not involve an increase in wages of from 5 to 10 percent. . . ." A more sober assessment by the Metal workers' Union captures the contradictory forces that shaped workers' assessments of this most modern, most American form of work: "The magic power of the conveyer attracts the worker. The personality of the workers disappears, but they can accommodate themselves to this. They do not always do so voluntarily but under compulsion, because they would lose their daily bread if they did not follow the rhythm of the iron chain."[146]

It was less the technical and organizational aspects of rationalization that bothered workers than the conditions under which they were intro duced. Taylorist time-and-motion studies, the repeated lowering of piece rates, the constant speeding up of work, and the incessant harassment from foremen and managers obsessed with productivity—these were what work ers hated.[147] A 1927 article in the Metalworkers' Union newspaper, aptly titled "Tempo-Tempo," reflects their pervasive anger and frustration:

Technical restructuring—an excuse to lower piece rates, new machines—low ering of piece rates, increased division of labor—lowering of piece rates, improved work methods, discovered by the workers themselves—lowering of piece rates, faster work pace—lower piece rates, substitution of the unskilled and women for the skilled—an excuse to lower piece rates. . . . Everything is agitated, everything is hurried. American methods—without American wages or prices.[148]

Because these practices occurred under conditions of high unemployment, workers were fearful as well as hostile.

The stopwatch was a particularly hated symbol of what was wrong with how capitalism rationalized work. Ruhr mines did extensive time-and-motion studies and sought to replace the traditional system of group piece rates—whereby several miners worked cooperatively on the coal face and shared pay among themselves—with individual piece rates. Some workers were undisturbed and unaffected by the presence of efficiency experts; others were so fearful that they exerted themselves to the point of collapse.[149] Miners' representatives claimed that the results of time studies were mis-leadingly high, but became the norm that management demanded. At the Sälzer and Neuack mines, nearly the entire underground labor force quit as a result. Everywhere lowered and individualized piece rates encouraged safety violations, for attention to proper backfilling and timbering led to lower earn-ings. Furthermore, individualized piece rates destroyed solidarity among miners.[150] The Metalworkers' Union officially approved of time-and-motion studies, which were especially prevalent throughout the metal sector, pro-viding, of course, that they were conducted with scientific accuracy and respect for the worker and were not used to screw down piece rates.

The rank and file claimed that, in practice these conditions were rarely fulfilled.[151] In 1926, for example, a member of a Communist Party cell in a machine building factory reported that every worker was timed, preparation time was no longer added as a separate category, and all piece rates were recalculated downward. The Social Democratic factory council acquiesced to the new rate setting, and workers, fearing unemployment, did not try to sabotage the time studies, as the KPD suggested.[152] Even at the Ford assembly plant in Berlin, the work pace was incredibly high and the workers were treated no better than those in typical German firms. Although the Metalworkers' Union complained about the gap between the promises outlined in Ford's *My Life and Work* and the reality of the Berlin Ford factory, and blamed the German management, the workers themselves remained silent, unwilling to endanger their exceptionally high wages.[153]

Interviews with workers confirm their disillusionment with rational-ization. In 1930 the aristocrat Alexander Stenbock-Fermor returned to the Hamborn mine where he had worked in 1923. His former colleagues all com-plained that conditions had deteriorated markedly. "Alex, you can't imag-ine what sort of drudgery and torment there is now," lamented the miner Franz. "The firm has become incredibly arrogant. It does what it wants, what it wants. Things were almost better in [Kaiser] Wilhelm's time." The foreman Buchherr agreed. In comparison to the late 1920s, the inflation seemed almost "a golden era," he said. "Of course wages are better than then. . . . I'm speaking of working conditions. Things are steadily worse. The workday is lengthened. Overtime is common, and considerably more work is demanded of us. This frantic work pace, this system of driving workers, this constant snarling. We are no longer treated as men." For fore-men, as for workers, the fear of unemployment was paramount, as Buchherr noted with resignation: "The workers hate us, because we drive them. But we have to drive them, it is our 'duty.' And when it doesn't suit us, then it's, 'We won't keep you on. Outside thousands of unemployed are wait-ing for your job.'"[154]

The Enquete Ausschuss's interviews with miners and iron and steel workers tell a similar tale. Although the productivity subcommittee, which conducted the interviews, was unable to determine whether there was a positive correlation between higher wages and higher productivity, it did inadvertently uncover deep bitterness toward the new economic order: "Miners, especially the older ones, are fundamentally hostile to machines because they throw workers out of jobs." Miners also disliked the rigid organization of the labor process that mechanization imposed. "In general," concluded the report on mining, "since rationalization the workers' joy in work [*Arbeitsfreudigkeit*] has diminished because, as a result of mechaniza- tion, his daily quota has risen, whereas his wage has not."[155]

Steel workers acknowledged that they wanted to make more money but complained that they had little control over the pace of work and that wages were determined by the output of the blast furnaces and by the foremen. In good times wages remained at their 1924–1925 level, but the work pace was much more intense. According to one worker, productivity increased: "When the foremen comes to us in the morning and says, 'Get in there, get in there, go to it!' what can we do? If one of us raises an objection, then it's 'For you we can get ten men: If you don't like it, then you'll get thrown into the street.'"[156]

Harassment from foremen and fear of unemployment were even more pronounced among blast furnace workers. When asked if he worked harder because he had the prospect of earning more, Worker A responded, "I earned less last year and did just as well as now when I earn more. I have to eat more in order to do the work . . . more meat. If I eat plain bread, I can't do the work. In addition, I wear out my clothes." Worker B elaborated: "I have less money now and I have to work harder and eat more for that. I haven't saved anything and can't save anything." Worker F directed his complaints at supervisors: "The foreman runs through the shop more than before. He's really after everyone. . . . Before we had pauses during the shift. Now we run from one furnace to the next. If someone doesn't like it, there is some- one else to take the job." The prevalent tendency to equate rationalization with unemployment was summed up by Worker E, who noted that "as a result of high unemployment, people are forced to stay in their jobs. Fear of dismissal drives people to produce whatever they can."[157]

Workers complained not only to interviewers but to trade union lead- ers as well. Trade union congresses degenerated into stormy rhetorical battles whenever rationalization appeared on the agenda, for the radical minority was outspoken in its criticism. At the 1928 metalworkers' con- gress, for example, the Communist-dominated Essen local submitted a reso- lution attacking the majority's failure to condemn and combat rationaliza- tion and trusts. The Halle, Solingen, and Buchholz locals prefaced their pleas for greater militancy with the statement that conditions had not improved as a result of rationalization. And two Dresden locals advocated "an educa- tion campaign against the illusions of economic democracy, as well as of the League of Nations, and against the support of capitalist rationalization and the arbitration system."[158] A year later, the head of the Stuttgart local acknowledged complaints by the rank and file that rationalization was not being fought "with the necessary energy," but insisted they were unjustified: "Everyone with insight has known for a long time that we do not reject the rationalization of production, because it can mean nothing other than employing technical and organizational measures with reason."[159]

Sometimes opposition led to informal protests—absenteeism, insults to foremen, even fistfights. These were especially common in mining. In 1929–1930 the Mining Association reported 256 cases of managers being insulted and cursed out by miners. In another 68 cases, workers and fore-men came to blows.[160] Karl-Heinz Roth has argued that the new semiskilled workers created by rationalization engaged in passive resistance from 1927 on. Without support from the unions, these workers expressed their oppo-sition to new forms of work by means of absenteeism and sabotage.[161] Although there were some instances of this in the automobile and the electrotechnical industries, they were not the rule.

The prospect of job loss during a period of high unemployment made resistance extremely costly and unlikely. This was especially true in such industries as mining, where the work force was older and had families to support.[162] What economics didn't curb, politics quelled. Even though the Social Democratic union leadership could not impose its faith in rational-ization, it did effectively restrict militant and organized protest against it. Communists and left Social Democrats, who shared the Social Democrats' theoretical endorsement of technological and organizational restructuring, had no practical strategy to offer disaffected workers. The KPD came to represent the unemployed more than the employed; those party members who still held jobs reported that it was all but impossible to engage work-ers in shop floor struggles or political work.[163]

The very ways in which rationalization transformed work undermined the possibilities of both formal organization and informal protest. As Uta Stolle's pioneering study of Bayer, BASF, and Bosch shows, rationalization disrupted traditional workshops and work groups and destroyed informal networks, which had often served as a basis for more formal politics. The possibilities for communication among workers were significantly dimin-ished.[164] Reports from KPD factory cells lamented that pauses had been eliminated and supervision intensified. Workers could no longer speak dur-ing work, and "had time neither to agitate nor to listen to agitators." The contradictory effects of rationalization were neatly summarized in the asser-tion, "Flow production, which unites the operations of the worker into a complete uninterrupted process, separates the worker as a living being, as a member of a united collectivity."[165] Under these circumstances, workers' dislike of rationalization resulted only in division and demoralization, and led to their disillusionment with trade unions and the SPD.

Although the trade union and SPD leadership often seemed blind to the social consequences of economic rationalization, industry leaders and engineers were not. They acknowledged, indeed frequently overestimated, worker opposition to rationalization. But they refused to buy acceptance of it by high wages and mass consumption. Instead they developed an array of policies to create a new type of worker and working-class family.

9

Engineering
the New Worker

> A great enveloping assault by German industrialists on the soul of the German
> worker is in progress. The goal of this attack consists in nothing less than a com-
> plete restructuring of the mentality of millions of male and female workers.

With this ominous warning the Social Democratic trade unionist Fritz Fricke
began his 1927 pamphlet *They Seek the Souls*. He proceeded to deliver a
scathing attack on new forms of social rationalization in industry. His criticisms were also aimed at the German Institute for Technical Labor Training (Dinta).[1] Fricke's alarmist prose was occasioned by a proliferation of factory-based programs aimed at transforming workers' attitudes toward work
and the firm, coworkers and capitalism, family and fatherland. Dinta and
the engineers it trained ran apprenticeship programs, company newspapers,
and welfare and education services. Like several other Weimar institutions
run by scientists of work, engineers, and industrialists, Dinta claimed to
have discovered "the human being as a factor of production."[2]

Dinta was the most vocal, visible, and influential practitioner of human
rationalization in the 1920s. It shared industry's vision of a distinctly German economy that would be rationalized, efficient, and profitable yet avoid
Fordized mass production and preserve quality work. It promised to create
workers who would be committed to achievement and productivity as well
as to their *Beruf* and the firm—and all without high wages and mass consumption.[3] Although Dinta was centered in Ruhr heavy industry, it pen-
etrated many other sectors and regions. Its ideology addressed pervasive
concerns about quality work, joy in work, and the absence of a *Berufsethos*
among workers. Dinta facilitated the cooperation of academic, engineering,

179

and industrial proponents of company social policy and translated sweeping and vague statements about vocational education and work-centered identities, the factory community, and industrial leadership into very pragmatic programs for skilled and unskilled workers, employed men and their wives at home, the aged and the young. It publicized these programs with extraordinary diligence, spreading its distinctly right-wing ideology far beyond the factories in which Dinta was active.

Dinta's vision of a rationalized economy and working class was not the most modern or Americanized model developed in Germany, but neither was it the most intransigently reactionary. Dinta mixed technological modernism and social reaction with great skill and sophistication, drawing on traditions of militarism and service (*Dienst*) and combining them with cost accounting, modern psychology, and psychotechnics. It was politically flexible, functioning under Weimar even though it preferred a more authoritarian regime. Nothing illustrates the limits of Americanism and the peculiarities of German rationalization more clearly than Dinta's project for the industrial leadership of men (*industrielle Menschenführung*). And nothing illustrates the left's difficulties in dealing with rationalization as ideology and practice better than its response to Dinta. Our analysis must begin not with Dinta, but with the movement for "human rationalization," of which it was a central part.

Company Social Policy and Social Rationalization

Like so many terms in the discourse on rationalization, "company social policy" does not lend itself to succinct definition.[4] Rudolf Schwenger, an expert on company social policy in the Ruhr, insisted that company welfare was too narrow a description. Company social policy aimed at "the careful treatment of the human in the firm, his effective integration into the factory order, as well as the systematic influencing of all relations among men." It also sought "the exclusion of all influences that were foreign to or hostile to the firm," including trade unions and the state.[5] L. H. A. Geck, a leading industrial sociologist, distinguished between "company social policy," or measures benefiting workers, and "social company policy", or policies benefiting the firm economically.[6] Realizing how integrally intertwined these were, he offered a comprehensive definition that included "the totality of efforts and measures which seek the welfare of those in the firm or a regulation of their interactions in the factory itself or in the firm environment or in people's existence outside the firm."[7] The general labels for the movement of which company social policy was a central part were equally sweeping and amorphous. What scholars now term social rationalization was then called human rationalization (*menschliche Rationalisierung*), human economy (*Menschenökonomie*), human management (*Menschenbewirtschaftung*), and the virtually untranslatable *Menschenführung*, whose nearest meaning is the leadership of men.

Weimar company social policy took different forms in different firms

and sectors, and its goals were articulated in different ideological intona-
tions. Measures that promoted "the planned management of human labor
power" ranged from vocational aptitude testing and vocational advising to
apprenticeship programs, general worker education courses, company newspapers, and recreational programs.[8] Nor did company social policy stop at
the factory gate, for a variety of educational and welfare programs were
provided for working women as well as for the wives and children of male
employees. While some efforts stressed economic efficiency, others aimed
at instilling "proper" conceptions of hierarchy and obedience, and "the
optimal stimulation of joy in work."[9] Often the proponents of social rationalization espoused a factory or firm community (*Betriebsgemeinschaft* or
Werksgemeinschaft), concepts implicitly if not explicitly associated with
nationalism, antisocialism, and opposition to trade unions. Overall, human
rationalization sought to create new workers and new working-class families that would be more technically, socially, and emotionally suited to the
new rationalized work as well as more politically quiescent.

Instead of paternalism, charity, and yellow trade unions, the new company social policy stressed education, psychology, and cost accounting.
Efficiency, profitability, and human rationalization were seen as mutually
reinforcing.[10] Company social policy was premised on the acceptance of
rationalized work, even as it promised to restore joy in work, vocational
commitment, and dedication to the firm. Rather than dismissing work-
centered male identities as a phenomenon of the past, it sought to revive
them, but in a form more economically useful for capital and more politically amenable to the overtures of the right. Although company social policy
often advocated a psychotechnical restructuring of the workplace and could
be combined with wage incentives, it relied most heavily on pedagogical
and welfare measures. It sought to reshape the worker's behavior and attitudes from the inside by influencing his "work personality" or even his
whole person.[11]

Company social policy accepted, albeit reluctantly, Weimar industrial
relations, even as it sought to outmaneuver trade unions and establish a counterweight to state social policy. Proponents of company social policy insisted
that the firm was a unique social formation that must be allowed to develop
according to its own laws.[12] The firm was to be isolated from society and
serve as the basis for reforming it.

Company social policy was very much a product of war, revolution,
and the new political realities of Weimar. The massive recruitment of female
labor during World War I led to an expansion of company social policy to
serve the needs of women workers in the factory and at home.[13] The revolution of 1918–1919, the factory council movement, and the 1920 factory
council law spurred further activism on the part of industrialists. For all
their limitations, these events and achievements did politicize the factory
and increase workers' power in state and society. Yellow trade unions were
outlawed, collective bargaining was legitimated, and protective legislation
and social insurance were expanded, all of which made traditional patriar-

chal company social policy ineffective.[14] Faced with new power relationships on the shop floor as well as in national politics, industrialists, engineers, and scientists of work sought new means to counter workers' power
and preempt its expansion.[15]

Practical economic considerations also directed attention to the shop
floor and workers' attitudes. According to employers, engineers, industrial
sociologists, and psychologists human rationalization had to complement
economic and technical rationalization.[16] Productivity and profitability were
enhanced if one selected the "right" person for the "right" job by means of
aptitude tests and vocational advising. Skill training on all levels was equally
important, for the small, relatively unmechanized artisan shop—the previous training ground of most skilled male workers—could not prepare them
for the new rationalized factory, and no programs existed for the new semiskilled workers. Company social policy was also viewed as a compensation
for the physical, psychic, and social costs of rationalization. Sports programs
and daily gymnastics sessions were proposed to counteract the detrimental
effects of routinized work, and convalescent homes and workshops for the
aged and the disabled were built for those who nonetheless succumbed.
Whereas rationalization, state social policy, and collective bargaining tended
to blur the lines between skilled and semiskilled work and between male
and female jobs, company social policy sought to create hierarchical and
distinct categories by the differential awarding of material benefits and
privileges.[17]

Company social policy was influenced by the American example of the
ostensibly happy worker, who was dedicated to production, and of the
autonomous firm, which solved political and economic problems with no
outside interference.[18] But America's problems were not Germany's, and
most architects of human rationalization rejected America's specific solutions. They built company social policy on the assumption that German economic modernization would be distinct from its American counterpart, that
Germany would remain rich in men but poor in capital and domestic markets. For workers, meaning and motivation were not to come from mass consumption and mass culture.[19] Rather, it was necessary, in the words of the
industrial sociologist Peter Bäumer, "to lead the worker spiritually and intellectually into his work" so that he would "no longer confront his work
as the basis of his existence . . . with skepticism and inner rejection but
would affirm it to the best of his ability."[20]

For industrialists, company social policy was not only an aspect of
rationalization, but also a weapon against Weimar social policy. They contrasted the flexibility of factory-based programs with the rigidity of state laws,
and the differential rewarding of performance (*Leistung*) with the uniform
wage rates of collective bargaining. On a more general ideological level, they
lauded company social policy for promoting individualism, loyalty to the firm,
and a healthy particularism and denounced state social policy for undermining achievement and factory cohesion and preaching a pernicious universal-
ism.[21] Finally, the idea of a factory community was offered as an alternative

to the Social Democratic goal of economic democracy; it represented a competing vision of company and societal organization.[22]

Weimar company social policy was designed and implemented by a variety of individuals and institutions. Industrialists, academics in technical universities and research centers, and engineers in private business and the academy participated, as did such private organizations as Dinta and such quasi-public ones as the RKW. Some groups, such as the Deutsche Vereinigung were explictly political, while others claimed to be above party politics. A brief survey of this popular field will help situate Dinta.

The capitalist firm was the locus of company social policy. Many industrialists developed programs with or without the aid of organizations such as Dinta. Ruhr heavy industry was heavily involved in the new company social policy, just as it had been in earlier paternalistic forms.[23] Outside the Ruhr such metalworking firms as Bosch and the optical instrument and camera company Zeiss transformed their extensive prewar company welfare policies, while the most modern and competitive firms, such as the electrotechnical giant Siemens, embarked on vast company social policy programs.[24] Even small textile factories and construction firms pooled their resources to implement some of the new measures.

The new discipline of industrial sociology sketched the contours of and justification for a comprehensive new company social policy. Its center was the Institute for Company Sociology and Social Company Management, established after the Prussian Landtag and the Prussian Ministry of Culture concluded that engineers needed to be educated about the human side of the production process.[25] Located at the Technische Hochschule in Berlin, the institute was founded in 1928 by the economist Goetz Briefs and the engineer and enthusiast of Americanism, Paul Riebensahm. From this visible academic position, Briefs elaborated his own theory of the firm as both a source of economic and social problems and a locus for solving them. Of equal importance, he gathered around him a group of scholars, including L. H. A. Geck, Rudolf Schwenger, Peter Bäumer, and Walter Jost, who elaborated the theory of company social policy and analyzed its practice in Weimar firms.[26] The Social Science Institute at the University of Cologne had a department for industrial pedagogy. By 1932 courses on company social policy were being taught in Leipzig and in Frankfurt am Main as well. Dissertations were written on such themes as worker estrangement from the firm (*Werksfremdheit*), and human management in industry.[27]

A variety of private and semi-public institutions promoted firm-based vocational education. The German Bureau for Technical Education (DATSCH), established by the VDI in 1908, developed guidelines for courses, while the Working Committee for Vocational Training, which was a joint project of the VDI, the RDI, and the VDA, debated the broader problems of vocational training. In 1930 the Frankfurt Social Museum brought together the principal theorists and practioners of company social policy, such as Karl Arnhold, Josef Winschuh, and Ernst Horneffer, as well as their trade union critics, such as Fritz Fricke, to debate firm-based vocational education.[28] That same year the RKW, which had been reprimanded by the Reichstag for ignoring the social consequences of rationalization, began exploring aptitude testing, vocational education, workplace design, and quality work in a series of conferences and publications on "Humans and Rationalization."[29]

Engineers played a particularly prominent role in social rationalization, and their activism was not restricted to such organizations as DATSCH, or service to individual employers. They established three independent organizations to promote company social policy and train "social" engineers. The Deutsche Volkshochschule, associated with the explicitly antisocialist Deutsche Vereinigung, offered general courses for managers and engineers on right-wing economics and politics rather than teaching new leadership skills or information on company social programs.[30]

The Saarbrücken Institute for the Knowledge of Work (AFAS) was established by the Saar Employers' Association and the Saarbrücken local of the Working Group of German Factory Engineers. Run by Adolf Friedrich, who began his career as an engineer at Krupp and became a professor of social psychology at Karlsruhe, the AFAS concentrated on training engineers and foremen who would, in turn, train workers in the factories.[31] In the eyes of admirers, Friedrich's approach to *Menschenführung* combined "technology, economy, psychology, philosophy, and theology." To such critics as Willy Hellpach, it was "a mishmash of religion, psychoanalysis, and vulgar psychology."[32] Although the AFAS was important in the Saar, its influence remained purely regional.[33] The third organization of engineers was Dinta.

Engineers had many reasons to support human rationalization, for its proponents shared their basic assumptions about the place of technology in society. They addressed the persistent problems of the engineering profession, and they spoke to engineers' most far-reaching aspirations.

Weimar engineers enjoyed neither economic security nor social status. In part this was a heritage of incomplete professionalization in the pre–World War I era. Although the number of engineers had expanded greatly during Germany's rapid industrialization, the occupation remained deeply divided between those who were academically educated and those who were trained in firms. Employment situations varied greatly among engineers working in industry as well as between them and those who were state employees or free professionals. Finally, the line between engineers and technicians could not be drawn with clarity.

All this contributed to low pay and a status that was "ambivalent and contradictory."[34] The VDI failed to turn this divided and amorphous occupation into a profession. In the Imperial era it promoted technology more than technicians and recruited only one fifth of its potential members. And the VDI was only the largest of several competing organizations that claimed to represent the interests of engineers.[35] These problems persisted into Weimar and were exacerbated by a glut of engineers, especially university trained ones.[36] Of equal importance, rationalization had the ambiguous effect of making engineering central to economic modernization while decreasing the number of positions open to engineers and making many of those which continued to exist less varied and challenging.[37]

These economic problems, status anxieties and thwarted aspirations shaped the political and economic strategies of Weimar engineers. They had only the loosest ties to the Weimar party system, tolerating the republic as long as it provided prosperity, and they were susceptible to the flattery of such right-wing thinkers as Oswald Spengler and the promises of such right-wing movements as National Socialism.[38] Many abandoned their prewar stance of neutrality in the conflict between capital and labor and sought actively to neutralize class conflict.[39]

Although Weimar engineers were convinced of the centrality of technology to societal development, they realized that they were more likely to improve their status and influence by linking technology to culture or to economics or to social engineering. Numerous right-wing thinkers, some of whom were engineers, depicted technology as central to the development of *Kultur*. This reactionary modernist strand of engineering thought, which was displayed most prominently in the VDI journal *Technology and Culture*, sought to improve the status of engineers by augmenting the value of technology.[40] A more prosaic and pragmatic strategy was to tie technology ever more closely to capitalism by making the engineer a businessman with an eye for profits and an aptitude for cost accounting. The Working Group of German Factory Engineers, headed by the quintessential engineer-businessman Carl Köttgen, and the VDI journal *Technology and Economy* regarded American engineers as exemplary in this regard and sought to emulate them.[41]

Dinta subsumed arguments about culture and economics under its broader plea for the engineer to redefine himself as educator and leader.[42] The engineer's role was to modernize the German economy and prevent pernicious forms of Americanism from taking hold.

Origins and Ideology of Dinta

The proposal for an institution to promote technical education was first raised at a meeting of one of the major Ruhr heavy industry organizations, the Association of German Iron and Steel Industrialists (VDESI) in May 1925. Albert Vögler, who headed the VDESI and would become general director of Vestag in 1926, accused industry of ignoring humans as a factor of production. As a result most workers were hostile to the firm and alienated from their jobs. Vögler then introduced a series of speakers who explained the need for and the outlines of Dinta. In a talk on "Mass Psychology and Work Success," the sociologist Karl Dunkmann mixed attacks on Marxism and trade unions with pleas for "good sense in managing humans" and "humanitarianism." His final list of goals ranged from providing "intellectual enlightenment" through increasing individual effort to promoting "the family, a sense of *Heimat*, camaraderie, friendship, and the factory community." Taking a much more pragmatic approach, the psychotechnician Walther Poppelreuter elaborated the need for aptitude testing. The engineer Karl Arnhold[43] mixed pragmatism and ideology. He opened his talk with an impassioned plea "to wake the powers slumbering in our people and place them in the service of the economy," and then outlined an apprenticeship training program geared toward saving endangered adolescent boys and promoting economic prosperity.[44] A few months later Dinta, with Arnhold as its head, was established.

Arnhold was born in Elberfeld in 1884 and received his engineering training there. Prior to World War I he was employed by the G. and I. Jaeger iron works, whose director had worked in the United States and was eager to emulate American methods. There Arnhold first began organizing apprenticeship training programs. When war broke out in 1914, Arnhold immediately volunteered. As for so many of his generation, the war was a major politicizing event, and his military experience provided a model for later relationships and organizations. In 1917 he became Director of Patriotic Education and editor of the newspaper *Trench Post*, with responsibility for explaining to soldiers why they should fight. Immediately after the war Arnhold was active in various right-wing paramilitary Free Corps and then returned to Wuppertal to work in the trade school. By late 1920 he had found a new position at the Schalker Verein of the Gelsenkirchen Bergwerk A.G., where he began to set up apprenticeship training programs for boys and housework courses for girls. His career was interrupted once again by the 1923 French occupation of the Ruhr, during which he was jailed by the French.

By 1924 he was back at Schalker, where Vögler first encountered him. In *A Life for the Economy*, an anonymous biography of Arnhold that I suspect is actually an autobiography, Vögler is said to have been impressed that Schalker apprentices were working without pay during the economic and political turmoil of 1923. According to Vögler's biographer, it was the cooperation of Communists with the firm that drew Vögler's favorable attention.[45] Whether apocryphal or true, these stories reveal much about Arnhold's self-presentation and appeal. He promised to promote peace within the firm, regardless of the political turmoil beyond the factory gates, and he claimed to inspire a dedication to production that transcended political divisions. All this was to be achieved not by confronting the trade unions directly, but by creating a new type of workman.

The next recorded meeting of Vögler and Arnhold was in early 1925, when the two men journeyed—or perhaps more accurately, made a pilgrimage—to Munich to visit Oswald Spengler, prophet of Prussian socialism and reactionary modernist par excellence.[46] After listening to their plans for factory education, Spengler urged them to establish an "order of engineers," which would combine the discipline and spirit of service of the Prussian army with a "quasi-religious sense of mission" and would recreate the camaraderie of World War I front soldiers, both within its own ranks and among workers in the firm.[47] If Arnhold rejected some of Spengler's more archaic language, he nonetheless adopted his vision of a militarized pedagogy, with engineers in the central role of teacher/*Führer*. Indeed, on more than one occasion, he grandiously claimed that Dinta would take over the educational functions once performed by the Prussian army.[48]

By the mid-1920s Dinta was clearly an idea whose time had come. Within six months of its founding, the Dinta House was opened in Düsseldorf. Albert Vögler and the right-wing social philosopher Ernst Horneffer spoke at the dedication ceremonies, as did the city's mayor, Lehr, who agreed to become the official patron of the organization. In a written greeting, Spengler praised Dinta for trying to instill "a sense of honor and ambition" in German workers.[49] The Dinta House served as the training center for engineers, who then set up Dinta programs in firms, and as the editorial offices for Dinta's publishing operations. By mid-1926, 25 engineers and 12 foremen, sent by Ruhr firms, were enrolled in Dinta training programs, while other Dinta engineers had already established 24 apprenticeship-training workshops in mining and metalworking. Dinta was already publishing 18–20 company newspapers. By decade's end, Dinta ran training programs in 150–300 German and Austrian firms and published more than 50 company newspapers, which reached nearly half a million employees.[50] Dinta continued to expand until 1930 and more or less held its own thereafter, despite the Depression.

Dinta was especially strong in iron and steel, machine making, and metalworking, and to a lesser extent in mining—all sectors that had an overwhelmingly male labor force. Gutehoffnungshütte, Hoesch, Thyssen, Schalker, Friedrich-Wilhelms-Hütte, Waggonfabrik Uerdingen, and Siemens-Schuckert in Mülheim/Ruhr were among the major firms that brought in Dinta. It received active support not only from Vögler, but from such prominent Ruhr industrialists as Paul Reusch of Gutehoffnungshütte and such firms as Rheinmetall, a giant munitions and metalworking firm in Düsseldorf.[51] Dinta also ran programs in textile, rubber, cement and construction companies. Many other firms and sectors adopted Dinta ideas and policies, even though they neither sent their personnel to Dinta for training nor had a formal affiliation with Arnhold. The Ruhr was unquestionably Dinta's stronghold, but by the late 1920s it had spread into parts of central Germany and Silesia and had established a few outposts in southern Germany and in the Alpin-Montan Gesellschaft of Austria.[52] It had no influence among technologically advanced and less reactionary firms, such as those in the electrotechnical and Berlin machinery industries.

The membership of Dinta's various boards and committees suggests the range of its support. On the executive committee were Vögler, Franz Burgers, another Vestag director, and Fritz Winkhaus, general director of the Cologne-Neuessene Bergwerksverein. This solidly Ruhr heavy industry directorate was supplemented by a much broader managing committee whose twenty-four members included Anton Apold, head of Alpin-Montan Gesellschaft; Ernst von Borsig, head of Borsig; G. Lippart, director of MAN; Conrad Matchoss, professor of engineering and head of the VDI;

Rudolf Brennecke, director of the Upper Silesian Eisenbahnbedarf; as well as such prominent Ruhr industrialists as Paul Reusch, Fritz Springorum, Paul Silverberg, and Max Schlencker, head of the Langnam Verein. There was an organizational committee which included Heinrich Droste, chief editor of the *Industry Press* in Düsseldorf, August Heinrichsbauer, who ran a press service for heavy industry, and representatives of several other regional industrial interest groups. The scientific committee revealed its links to technocrats, academics, and right-wing publicists. In addition to Karl Dunkmann, Ernst Horneffer and Oswald Spengler, it had three engineering professors, including Adolf Wallichs, and a member of the Kaiser Wilhelm Institute for Iron Research.[53]

Dinta's success was due not only to Arnhold's indefatigable organizational energy or the power of his patrons, although these were undoubtedly assets. As soon as Dinta was established, Arnhold sent information about its philosophy and programs to all chambers of commerce and technical universities, to prominent industrialists who where "accessible to Dinta," and to such organizations as the Working Committee for Vocational Education.[54] Arnhold constantly asked Reusch to introduce him to his fellow industrialists, and one assumes that Vögler provided the same service.[55] Along with his assistants, Arnhold took to the lecture circuit, addressing 41 employers' associations and engineering groups in the first half of 1926 alone. This propagandistic activity continued throughout the decade, with lectures, personal meetings, glossy brochures filled with pictures of Dinta programs in various firms, and finally the publication of a regular informational magazine, *Work Schooling*.[56] Dinta also set up affiliated organizations, such as the Research Center on Heavy Work and the Society for the Friends of Dinta, and cooperated with such vocational education institutions as DATSCH, as well as with psychotechnical associations.[57]

Dinta's success was primarily due to its message: it promised to address a multitude of perceived economic and social problems with ideological clarity, pragmatic astuteness, and effective eclecticism. Although Arnhold himself did not originate most of the ideas and policies he promoted, he combined them in ways that were innovative and appealing.[58] Dinta preached the gospel of productivism and individual productivity, while flatly rejecting Fordist wage and market strategies. It celebrated modern technology but promised to obviate its detrimental effects on work and workers through education alone. It embodied a military spirit of discipline and service and elevated leadership and hierarchy in the firm to new heights. Simultaneously, it pledged to inspire individual achievement and aspiration. It vowed to depoliticize the firm without involving itself in party politics. This program perfectly reflected Arnhold's personal makeup. He was a man once described as "a former officer, now an engineer; superficially the prototypical smart American, inwardly a cadet with a dash of *Realpolitik*, always rooted in the facts."[59] Dinta's claims were sweeping and vague, yet the means it chose to achieve them were sharply defined—the new worker and the new engineer who would be instrumental in creating him. It was

precisely this promise to combine the incompatible in a sphere that employers and engineers could reasonably hope to control, namely the firm, that
made Dinta so appealing.

In Arnhold's vision of the restructured firm, engineers rather than industrialists would play the central role.[60] Engineers were to be the new
leaders of men (*Menschenführer*) and educators of the populace. They would
replace the ostensibly "rigid, mechanistic" administration of labor power
with a warm, organic leadership of workers.[61] They would put the worker
in the service of the firm and enable the firm to serve the national economy.
But the engineer as *Menschenführer* had to earn the obedience of his subordinates by his exemplary behavior, not assume it as part of his class privileges and managerial prerogatives.

The ideal new workers whom these "engineers of the feelings"[62] hoped
to create varied by sex, skill level, and employment sector. The ideal new
skilled worker would be technically well trained, but unlike his predeces-
sor, who had learned his skills from other workers in artisan shops, he would
be trained by the firm and for the firm's particular needs. He would be loyal
to the firm and adaptable (*wendig*) to the changing needs of the rationalized
production process.[63] His attitudes and character would further distinguish
him from other skilled workers. He would accord primacy to efficiency and
profitability, or to use Dinta phrasing, he would understand "economic
thinking" and be "achievement oriented." Instead of striving for mobility
into the white-collar class, he would commit himself to his job as American
workers reputedly did.[64] His relationship to his work would "allow him as
an individual, despite rationalization and mechanization in a private capitalist economy, to have a livelihood, joy in work, and satisfaction in life
within limits."[65] Of course he was to use his leisure productively and value
his family. The new skilled worker, in short, was to retain the technical
expertise and dedication to quality of the old skilled worker, while relin-
quishing the latter's control of the labor process, cultural autonomy, and
political consciousness.

The requirements demanded of the new semiskilled men were much
more modest: enhanced manual skills, an improved work ethic, a commitment to rationalization, and a minimal understanding of the production
process. Employed women were all but ignored by Dinta, while nonwaged
working women were expected to devote themselves to their roles as wives
and mothers but perform them in a rationalized manner. Dinta's model of
the new male worker was intimately related to its vision of the reformed
working-class family, in which working-class men's and women's work and
lives were clearly differentiated but at the same time restructured according to similar principles of rationalization.

Dinta ideology contained a peculiar mixture of individualism and collectivism, whose tensions were never resolved. Dinta accorded primacy to
performance (*Leistung*) and championed "the elevation of the individual from
a mass existence to a self-conscious personality." Yet it also demanded his
"bonding to the firm" (*Werksverbundenheit*)."[66] The craft tradition and craft

unions were by no means without their own tension between individual attainment and collective interests, but these interests were defined by the workers in terms of their perceived needs for material benefits, control of production, and the defense of craft culture. Arnhold had a very different vision of collective interests, in which the military provided a model for the factory community. By incorporating the individual in a hierarchical order, the military provided structure and discipline and ended isolation; it claimed to provide camaraderie among equals and an overarching sense of purpose, which was shared by superiors and subordinates. It demanded achievement, but in directions defined by others. The military also served as an exclusively male model. Yet despite Arnhold's admiration for the discipline, élan, and hierarchy of the Prussian army, he wanted neither blind obedience nor total subsumption of the individual into the whole. The new male worker was to combine individual achievement (in production but not in consumption) and militarylike "camaraderie, loyalty, and pride in his estate." In no case would he be a "child of his class."[67]

Dinta's vision of the new worker was linked to larger economic and political goals, which were presented in a rhetoric that combined the economic and the spiritual, the modern and the archaic. Dinta might wax poetic about the factory community and company leadership, but it was always adamant that the laws of capitalism were immutable and it promised to inculcate that "truth" into workers. Dinta never forgot that its first responsibility to capitalist supporters was to promote productivity and profitability. Discussions of joy in work and loyalty to the firm were invariably combined with hard-nosed cost accounting. Only programs that were "practical and economic," instead of "patriarchal or emotional," would increase productivity and promote social improvement, argued Arnhold.[68] Dinta promised that its training programs, social policies, and company newspapers would be economically profitable. At a minimum they would increase individual performance without increasing wages, and in many cases the programs might even pay for themselves. Workshops for the aged and the infirm, for example, could produce and sell brooms, thereby covering wages and eliminating the need for pensions.[69]

Dinta explicitly accepted key elements of the Taylorist and Fordist models of reorganized work, although it avoided Taylor's emphasis on maximizing individual output, preferring instead the Fordist idea of optimizing several factors of production. It did not believe, however, that economic and technical rationalization alone would solve Germany's economic problems, because workers reacted negatively to them. Dinta offered an inexpensive way to resolve this dilemma. It would neither reorganize the labor process dramatically nor endorse higher wages and mass consumption as compensation for rationalization; rather, it would restructure workers' attitudes toward work. As Ernst Horneffer trenchantly put it, the goal was "the education of people in work and for work."[70]

However difficult it might be to realize in practice, Dinta's mixture of individualism and collectivism offered a rhetorical alternative to worker soli-

darity, with its connotations of conflict and socialism, and to individualism, with its implications of mass consumption and upward mobility. It
offered a way to instill the much-admired characteristics of the American
workman—his efficiency, flexibility, individualism, and sympathetic understanding of capitalism—without his corresponding flaws—materialism, job
instability, uniformity, and egalitarianism.[71] It promised to create what so
many Germans thought they saw in America—a commitment to productivity shared by workers and employers.[72] Finally, the military model offered
workingmen an exclusively masculine and elitist self-definition, a sense of
purpose, and a work-based community that incorporated elements of the
craft tradition, yet transformed and depoliticized them.

Dinta was much more reticent about its political goals. Arnhold consistently claimed that Dinta was nonpartisan—nationalist, to be sure, but
not party political. Nor was Dinta anti-trade union, he insisted; Dinta and
the unions simply had different spheres of competence. Dinta was a vertical organization, located in and serving the needs of the firm alone, while
trade unions were horizontal organizations operating outside the enterprise.
Within the firm, factory councils had a role, but not unions.[73] Dinta frequently spoke of the need for a factory community (*Betriebsgemeinschaft*)
or company community (*Werksgemeinschaft*), but Arnhold did not envision
this as a yellow trade union of the sort advocated by the German Association of Patriotic Workers and Company Associations or by Paul Bang's
Association for a Planned Economy and Works Community.[74] Instead,
Arnhold argued, it was to be a community dedicated to production
(*Werksproduktionsgemeinschaft*), which would create a new atmosphere in
the firm, not a new organizational form.[75]

Other Dinta supporters were much more open about its anti-socialist
and anti-trade union orientation. Horneffer proclaimed as his "ideal" the
establishment of factory guilds that would include owners, engineers, managers, and workers.[76] Others couched Dinta's attack on the workers' movement in more modern terms. Max Schiefen, writing in the Dinta-operated
Phoenix Newspaper, insisted that Dinta strove for "a strong and healthy
Germany and a contented, industrious people, who valued the fatherland
and the worker more than the class struggle and the International."[77]
Arnhold's assistant, Paul Osthold, who was an economist, World War I
veteran, and activist in veterans' associations, outlined a sweeping ideological and political agenda in a pamphlet provocatively entitled *Struggle
for the Soul of the Worker*.[78] He began with the modest goal of "freeing the
worker from the loneliness of his isolated partial function in the production process," but quickly moved to the more ambitious aim of "overcoming the hostile opposition between worker and employer." His next point
went to the heart of Weimar conflicts between labor and capital: "satisfying and pacifying the worker in the current economic system with *the means
that are available to the German economy in its current situation*," that is,
without increased wages or the eight-hour day. The final goal reveals Dinta's
implicit anti-Marxism: "to bring the worker to the point that he frees his

economic striving for improvement once and for all from the poisonous conception that surplus value has been extracted from his output and with-
held from him with unscrupulous disregard."[79]

Dinta's sweeping goals drew on ideas expressed in the German debates
on Americanism, the discourse on quality work, *Beruf*, and joy in work,
and the technocratic productivism so prevalent in engineering circles. They
combined an acceptance of economic modernity with an admiration for right-
wing militarism and a conservative ideology of leadership. Dinta had very
clear ideas about how this eclectic and ambitious mix might be realized.

Constructing the New Worker

Dinta offered to perform a wide range of services for client firms, but its
primary focus was on those activities most closely connected with educating the new worker and the new working-class family for productivity, joy
in work, and political pliability. These included apprenticeship training
workshops and company schools, company newspapers, and welfare and
education programs for wives and daughters. They were to be designed and
managed by a new kind of engineer, which Dinta set about creating.

"Dinta work is engineer work," announced Arnhold on every possible
occasion. But it was not the work of just any engineers, for neither those
educated in technical universities nor the larger number trained in lower
technical schools and factories were knowledgable about the science of work
and social rationalization. Dinta set out to introduce technically trained and
experienced engineers to the theory and practice of *industrielle Menschenführung*.[80] Although the details of Dinta's training programs for engineers
changed repeatedly in the mid- and late 1920s, their general outlines remained constant. The courses, which ran from a few months to half a year,
consisted of theoretical lectures on psychotechnics, accident prevention,
youth welfare, business management, and vocational education and were
held at the Dinta House in Düsseldorf. This curriculum was followed by
practical training in established Dinta programs in the Ruhr.[81] After completing this program, Dinta engineers were encouraged to attend regular
weekend lectures in Düsseldorf given by engineers, psychotechnicians, industrial sociologists, and vocational educators on subjects ranging from labor
law, accident prevention, and cost accounting to youth recreation, workers' psychology, and kindergartens.[82] The purpose of the lectures, as well
as of the newsletter that Dinta engineers received regularly, was not only
to impart information but also to create a sense of mission, a spirit of camaraderie, and "a concept of honor like that of the old German officer corps."[83]
Beginning in 1929, other engineers as well as technical personnel, foremen,
and managers could come to the Dinta House for intensive four- or five-day
courses on such themes as psychotechnics or apprenticeship training.[84] By
1931 Dinta claimed to have taught over four hundred men in such short
programs, and as many as two hundred engineers had probably gone through
the longer, more rigorous program.[85]

Whether the Dinta-trained engineer was employed directly by the firm or was sent to it for a fixed period by Dinta itself, he was to be part of an elite that possessed more than technical competence and psychological acumen, although the importance of these qualities was certainly acknowledged. The essence of the Dinta engineer, like that of the military officer, was his leadership qualities; no mere manager, he was to be a *Führer*. In his work habits, personal interactions, and knowledge he had to be exemplary. He was always to be on the shop floor, offering practical guidance and moral support to workers. He was to have some of the openness, lack of pretense, and apparent concern for the individual worker that Germans admired in American engineers and managers. In addition, he needed to be "just," but as Arnhold emphasized, "to be just also means to be hard."[86] Such an engineer "will soon become the crystallized expression of the will of all his followers," claimed Arnhold, employing the overblown rhetoric of which he was so fond.[87] By leading men in work—their sphere of self-realization—engineers would play a central role in determining Germany's future, "in leading people to a higher stage."[88]

The first task facing the Dinta engineer was to transform apprentices into a new kind of skilled worker by establishing factory-based alternatives to artisan skill training and to state vocational schools. Vocational training was tied as closely as possible to the firm rather than to the general economic needs of the state or the broader interests of individual workers. It was to be run by Dinta-trained engineers according to Dinta principles and employing the methods that Arnhold had pioneered at the Schalker Verein.[89] Although Arnhold admired American industrialists' concern for vocational training, he did not consider their concrete programs worth imitating.[90]

Dinta first set up apprenticeship programs in such iron and steel and machine making firms as Thyssen, Gutehoffnungshütte, Krefelder Stahlwerk, and the Waggonfabrik Uerdingen. In the case of Thyssen's Friedrich Wilhelms Hütte, Dinta analyzed the chaotic state of training, prescribed a comprehensive program of reform, and promised to set it up for under 30,000 marks.[91] Many mine owners were initially hesitant to bring in Dinta, fearing that it could not teach the appropriate skills and would encroach upon management's prerogatives.[92] Others believed Dinta should be called in only if the Prussian government actually established municipally run mining apprenticeship programs.[93] Despite these qualms, roughly 20 of the 63 mines of the Bergbau Verein had established apprenticeship workshops by 1927, and between 1,000 and 2,000 of the 11,000 to 12,000 adolescent mine workers were enrolled.[94] By 1931 the number of programs had risen to 39.[95] Not all were run by Dinta or exactly according to its elaborate prescriptions, although they were in such mines as Centrum, Fröliche Morgensonne, and Minister Stein and Fürst Hardenberg. Nonetheless, according to a Bergbau Verein spokesman, the spirit of Dinta was "marching through mining."[96] Dinta also ran cooperative apprenticeship workshops, such as that for the Essen construction industry, which trained apprentices for smaller, more

dispersed firms. Estimates of the total number of Dinta apprenticeship training workshops and factory schools range from 150 to 300, and by 1930 Dinta
claimed to have trained 10,000 apprentices, virtually all of them men.[97]

Dinta's preoccupation with apprenticeships reflected the prevalent
belief that skilled workers would remain pivotal, even under rationalization.
It was also a response to pervasive fears of an impending shortage of skilled
workers and the inadequacy of existing training in *Handwerk* and factories.[98]
Since skilled workers were central to the workers' movement, control of
apprenticeship training also promised ideological and political rewards.
Finally, Dinta's emphasis on apprenticeship training addressed widespread
bourgeois anxieties about proletarian youths, who were ostensibly averse
to achievement and susceptible to the allures of mass culture, and who rejected authority at home, in the factory, and in society at large, even to the
point of criminality.[99] Arnhold's speeches were haunted by the image of
"youths who grow up on the streets, with stooped shoulders, hands in pants
pockets, hair combed in the face, cigarette dangling from the corner of the
mouth." He labeled them "a poor substitute for our 'old soldiers.'"[100] Dinta
programs deliberately segregated youths from what was considered to be
the morally and politically dangerous influence of older skilled workers.[101]
At a minimum, politics would be kept off the shop floor; perhaps the next
generation of skilled workers would even reject the unions and the SPD,
which had relied so heavily on them.

Dinta training was a comprehensive three-part program, consisting of
apprenticeship workshops, factory schools, and recreation programs. In all
phases Dinta not only worked with the apprentice but also maintained close
contact with his family, especially his mother.[102] Before embarking upon
training, an adolescent had to pass an aptitude test. In cooperation with
the psychotechnician Walther Poppelreuter, Dinta ran a testing center at
the Schalker Verein of Vestag and screened over 13,000 applicants for
skilled, semiskilled, and white collar positions; one third were being tested
for other firms.[103] If judged suitable, a youth was sent to an apprenticeship
workshop for two years. There, separated from the rest of the factory's
workers, apprentices spent five days a week learning the skills of their trade.
In iron and steel and machine making, for example, they were most often
prepared to become fitters or turners, and as even Dinta's trade union critics grudgingly admitted, they received technical training of a high quality.
In theory the training workshops would cost the firm nothing, because they
produced goods for the factories and mines to which they were attached,
but in practice they seem not to have paid for themselves.[104]

According to Peter Bäumer's sympathetic study of Dinta, the apprenticeship training workshop provided both vocational training and "moral
education, the rearing of the apprentice to manhood."[105] Youths mastered
the technology and labor processes of rationalized factories and "exercise[d]
all the bourgeois virtues," which in the eclectic list of the vocational educator Hella Schmedes included "diligence, persistence, order, responsibility, integration and subordination, camaraderie and cooperation."[106] In this

world of production divorced from politics, he would become acquainted with "economic thinking" by keeping track of his own costs and waste, producing items of use for the factory, and helping the apprenticeship training workshop to be self-supporting. He would learn the economic value of machines and the necessity of exact work as well as the power and beauty of technology. The capitalist version of productivism and technological fetishism were held up as alternatives to the socialist variants thereof.

As many outside observers noted, Dinta workshops were characterized by an almost military discipline, but obedience was not blind.[107] They stressed individual responsibility for quality and productivity, for eliminating waste and preventing accidents.[108] A spirit of competition, of "struggle" among the apprentices was encouraged, for as Arnhold insisted, "Struggle is the life of youth and should not be killed through too much protective care and leading by the hand."[109] The aim was to create a "respectable, happy, and vigorous person" who worked from desire, not external compulsion.[110]

One day a week the apprentices attended classes in the factory school. These *Werksschulen*, whose numbers expanded greatly in Weimar, were a supplement to the apprenticeship workshop and an alternative to the state vocational education schools, or *Berufschulen*.[111] In the 1920s the state made it mandatory for working adolescents to attend continuing education schools for a few hours a week. Lacking funding for vocational schools, as for so much else, the state allowed firms to privatize this part of adolescent education, while concentrating its own efforts on youths who had no access to factory schools.[112] Major firms in mining, iron and steel, and metalworking expanded their existing schools or established new ones, and by the late 1920s four-fifths of all factory schools were located in these industries.[113] Firm employees, rather than state civil servants, staffed these schools, which students could attend with little disruption to the firm's production. Of equal importance, the curriculum was geared to the specific technical needs—and political proclivities—of the firm.[114] At Vestag's August Thyssen Hütte, where Dinta was active, youths were taught some physics and chemistry and some applied math to supplement their practical training. For eight semesters they also took civics. The first courses focused on the *Beruf* of metalworking, the duties of apprentices to teachers and parents, and the history of the firm. Thereafter students were instructed about the government, the constitution, and legal questions of daily life, such as family law and contracts. During the final semesters, they were taught industrial organization, transportation and communications, and "the development of the social question in Germany".[115]

Technical training (*Ausbildung*) in the workshop and education (*Erziehung*) in the factory school were augmented by a program of sports and recreation (*Jugendpflege*).[116] According to Dinta, these programs were "the most important means of awakening and developing the personal values that slumber in the apprentice."[117] They would improve health and manual dexterity, provide needed relaxation from the rigors of rationalized work, and

increase both a competitive spirit and a sense of camaraderie among apprentices.[118] In addition they encouraged elitism, while precluding an identification with the particular culture of a craft. Apprentices were offered special recreational opportunities that isolated them from other proletarian
youths and filled all available free time. Swimming and gymnastics, hiking
and hobbies were all carefully supervised by Dinta engineers. Vestag's
Dortmunder Union claimed to have a 40-member gymnastics group, two
soccer teams, and 50-70 swimmers. In addition there was a library containing 840 books and a chess club.[119] In Merseberg and in Austria apprentices
even lived in special housing, but that was an exception.[120] At the end of
their training, Dinta apprentices were given an unheard of luxury—a week-
long trip to the German Museum in Munich, for example, or a sail on the
ship *Glückauf*, which Cardinal Schulte from Cologne had donated to
Dinta.[121] Indeed, Dinta tried to make good on its claim to shape the total
person.

In the late 1920s, Dinta developed very short training courses for the
semiskilled, in which instructors analyzed their jobs, taught Taylorist improvements, and stressed accident prevention.[122] The goal was to improve
workers' confidence, commitment, and productivity rather than transform
their skills, psyches, or politics. It is impossible to determine just how extensively Dinta implemented such programs.[123] Certainly Arnhold, with his
elitism and passion for the military, was more interested in educating what
he saw as the industrial officer corp of engineers and skilled workers than
in training the factory rank and file.

Company Newspapers and Social Programs

Dinta also attempted to reach adults, family members, and the unskilled,
but it did so outside the factory proper. Company newspapers were the
principal means. In 1926 Dinta published roughly fifty newspapers with a
circulation of 400,000; by 1934 the number of papers had doubled and
reached over 1 million employees. The largest, with circulations ranging
from 14,000 to 23,000, were published for Gutehoffnungshütte, Hoesch,
Dortmunder Union, and the Hamborn and Bochum divisions of Vestag.[124]
Throughout the late 1920s Vestag was spending nearly 400,000 marks a year
on the company papers of thirteen member firms.[125] Some company newspapers existed before Dinta; Krupp, for example, published a company
magazine in the Imperial era, while Siemens and Bosch began monthly publications after 1918. But the 1920s saw a massive proliferation of such news
organs and a transformation of their character, for which Dinta was largely
responsible.[126]

The company newspaper was to be the vehicle for inculcating
procapitalist sentiments and loyalty to the firm. Through these papers,
Arnhold promised, industrialists could teach workers the role of profits in
sustaining production and of technology in promoting progress.[127] The company newspaper "is the means of spiritually uniting all who belong to a firm.

It is the mouthpiece of the factory leadership and the mirror image of the employees," argued one Dinta publication.[128] According to another, "It places the firm constantly in the center of the consciousness of each of its workers. . . . It is suited to warm the naked, indifferent wage relation-ship."[129] These papers also covered company sports, garden clubs, and jubilees as well as company social policies for women, children, and adoles-cent girls, thereby expanding the definition of the factory community to include workers' families.[130] Their message about the primacy of the firm, the centrality of work, and the self-evident truth of capitalism was aimed not only at male employees, but also their wives—whom Arnhold believed influenced their husband's attitudes so strongly—and even their children.[131]

The Dinta company newspapers were a joint production of the indi-vidual firms and the Dinta newspaper company, Mill and Mine. They tended to have such pedestrian names as the Mine Paper, the Mill Paper, or simply the Company Paper, but the contents were more innovative than the names suggest.[132] Appearing twice a month, the papers ran from eight to twenty pages in length and were distributed free to employees. A typi-cal issue contained one or two pages of national and international economic (but not political) news, usually provided by Dinta, and a large cover photo of a new plant, product, or technological innovation that belonged to the firm in question. The inside pages, which were largely furnished by the firm, focused on technology, production processes, and accident prevention. They contained numerous articles on apprenticeship workshops and welfare poli-cies and were lavishly illustrated with first-rate industrial photography as well as portraits of long-term employees and snapshots of company recre-ation programs. They might also contain fiction, travel news, or suggestions for leisure activities.[133] The final pages had advice columns, such as "From the Realm of Women" and "Garden Tips." Initially Dinta allowed no ads, but as expenses mounted a page or two appeared to help cover costs. Like those in the socialist press, they were for such items as clothes, watches, bicycles and motor bikes, sewing machines, and furniture.[134] By contrast with many other company papers, Dinta publications seemed lively, var-ied, and modern. The Krupp Mitteilungen, for example, was a small news-letter, filled with official announcements and detailed technical news and only carried photos about safety. The Borsig paper focused on the firm at the expense of sports, women's news, and fiction. Only the Siemens Mit-teilungen was as diverse in content and as modern in layout as the Dinta papers.[135]

Dinta papers, like Dinta education programs, stressed what potentially united labor and capital. According to Arnhold, workers and managers agreed on 90 percent of all issues; the few divisive questions—which included wages, hours, trade unions, and national politics!— were to be assiduously avoided.[136] Workers were to read the papers for technological news, advice, or company gossip without encountering offensive political attacks, except perhaps on the first page, which published pro-employer social and economic analyses. Some company newspaper editors found these political editorials to be too propagandistic and controversial and seldom printed them.[137] Others, however, argued that controversial economic and political issues should be addressed head-on, but their views did not prevail.[138] Arnhold preferred to depict the world of work as a depoliticized environment, isolated from the messy conflicts of the larger society, even if this made Dinta papers rather flat and unreal.

Dinta publications were not just fascinated with technology; they romanticized it. Technology was presented as powerful, progressive, and all-encompassing; machines, as superior to the men who served them. The papers printed lavish photos of the shop floor and of the firm's finished products, although workers themselves were virtually never depicted. The Gutehoffnungshütte paper, for example, carried photos and drawings of its many factories, as well as of the bridges, machines, and ships it built. It discussed new labor processes, published some workers' memoirs about their changing occupations, and discussed safety in detail. Such portrayals drew on the images of technology that Social Democrats, trade unionists, industrialists, and engineers shared. But Dinta wanted these common images to serve quite specific purposes. It assumed that if workmen understood the entire production process and their part in it, if they saw the impressive finished products and often exotic locales to which they were sent, they would experience joy in work and identify with the firm.[139]

Dinta newspapers were less sure how to discuss leisure and consumption, for Dinta insisted that work was the realm where men defined and developed themselves, where meaning was to be found. (Correspondingly, home and motherhood were where women defined themselves, and they represented another kind of work.) Given Dinta's productivist and pro-employer orientation, this emphasis is hardly surprising. Yet neither Dinta nor the workers it hoped to reach were untouched by the mass consumption and mass culture of the 1920s. Dinta papers thus alternated between ignoring leisure and giving all sorts of advice about how to use it productively with hobbies, travel, and sports events. Some even sponsored photography contests. Consumption and more frivolous forms of recreation, such as movies, however, had no place in the Dinta vision of the new worker or his family. Dinta's women's columns displayed inconsistencies as well. Sometimes the newspapers offered advice on the concrete and mundane problems of proletarian housewives; floor mopping and diaper washing, bottle feeding and cooking were typical topics. At other times, the papers' childcare advice column was accompanied by drawings of distinctly bourgeois housewives, sitting in roomy, uncluttered, well-ventilated homes that were filled with light as well as flowers and tasteful decorations. There the mother calmly cared for her child (not children) in the proper manner.[140]

Some Dinta papers solicited articles, letters and suggestions from workers, sometimes even offering to pay.[141] The free trade unions repeatedly admonished their members not to send in contributions, but their concern seems to have been unwarranted. Audience participation did not suit the ideology of Dinta or the image of the workers it hoped to create, and efforts to encourage it were at most half-hearted. Many workers were willing to read the company newspapers, but few wrote for them.[142]

The final area in which Dinta was active involved company social policies for the relatives of men workers as well as for those who fell victim to the rigors of rationalized work. Dinta, like Weimar industy in general, did not favor company housing, for it was both unpopular with workers and costly.[143] Company stores were likewise considered outmoded and expensive.[144] Dinta talked enthusiastically about the need for workshops for the aged and infirm, which would employ older and injured workers in menial but productive work. They were supposed to be self-supporting and would ostensibly save workers from dependence and demoralization. Although the Schalker Works of the Gelsenkirchen mining company did establish a workshop for the aged, no other firm was persuaded of the economic and political value of such an endeavor.[145]

The central targets of Dinta activism outside the factory were the workmen's wives, children, and adolescent daughters. The three principal areas of outreach were home-economics education, kindergartens, and health and maternity care. None of these programs were inventions of the 1920s but their number and size increased significantly. Dinta insisted that the creation of a new skilled workingman was dependent on "the family and simultaneously on the education of the next generation of females for true German motherhood and household mangement."[146] For women at home as for skilled men in the factory, education was to play a central role, but whereas adolescent boys were taught technical skills, given a general education, and offered recreational activities, wives and daughters were trained in housework and child care. The substance of these programs will be explored in the next chapter, but here it is important to emphasize that the ideal for Dinta, unlike for such modern firms as Siemens, was to have women rationalize their housework without increased consumption, electrification, or appliances.

Company social policy and the apprenticeship training programs were two sides of the same comprehensive effort to reshape the working class, men and women, on the shop floor and in the home, in behavior and in thought. Dinta's vision of the new worker and his wife and family was rationalized but austere; it was modern but not nearly as modern as that which underlay the social policies of Siemens. Both Dinta and Siemens shared a commitment to technical training for men, but Dinta's efforts were directed at the skilled worker, whereas Siemens focused on the technical white-collar employee. Dinta wanted performance but not upward mobility and consumption, whereas Siemens validated both. For Siemens' management the model family was the "mobility-oriented small family"—an upwardly mobile white-collar worker, his nonemployed wife, and one or two children, who would be carefully educated for white-collar jobs. They would live in a modern apartment, with electricity and applicances, which the mother managed with the proper concern for efficiency and health.[147]

For Dinta the model was a reformed working-class family, characterized by efficiency without technology, improved child care without limited family size, and education without upward mobility.

Trade Union Responses

Although Dinta represented a clear threat to the Weimar workers' movements, the responses to it by Social Democrats, Communists, and Catholics were varied, ambivalent, and inadequate to the challenge. There were disputes within each movement and among them about which Dinta activities, if any, were legitimate and which were dangerous, and there was utter confusion about how to combat both Dinta's specific programs and its broad ideological message.

KPD analysts took the most unequivocally negative stance, regarding Dinta as one element in what it saw as the emerging "firm fascism" in Germany.[148] Dinta, which represented the more reactionary prong of the capitalist offensive against the working class, had achieved success, they claimed, only because the reformist equivocations of Social Democracy confused and demoralized workers. Dinta's praise of quality work masked its push for "quality exploitation"; its use of psychotechnics was hypocritical, because science could only benefit workers under socialism. They accused Dinta of seeking to divide workers by skill and pay, curb Communist influence among youth, and create a privileged elite that would pressure other workers to produce more. Its programs for reforming working-class housewifery were nothing short of ridiculous in the face of proletarian poverty.[149]

The Communist condemnation of Dinta was unambiguous but also simplistic; it recognized Dinta's political goals but neither addressed the economic problems to which Dinta spoke nor questioned its own productivism and uncritical acceptance of the principle of rationalization. The KPD lacked concrete strategies to combat Dinta and raised the spectre of Dinta primarily to condemn Social Democracy. Brief pleas for "the harshest and most bitter class struggle," were followed by detailed critiques of Social Democratic passivity and ambivalence. The Social Democrats were even accused of being willing to cooperate with Dinta programs, if only they were given a role in running them.[150]

The charge of complicity was unfounded; indeed, the temptation never existed, for Dinta was premised on excluding unions, not coopting them. Ambivalence, however, could be found in abundance among trade union functionaries and Social Democratic commentators. Such ambivalence was not about Dinta's general goals but its attitudes toward rationalization. The union movement and Dinta accepted the need for rationalized work, were committed to productivism, had faith in psychotechnics, admired the skilled worker, and desired efficient, rationalized households. Some union commentators, for example, credited Dinta with correctly diagnosing such economic problems as low productivity, dissatisfaction with work, and disaffection with the firm, but criticized it for prescribing the wrong cure. Material rewards and economic rights, not *Menschenführung*, were needed.[151] According to Fritz Fricke, America showed that higher wages and shorter hours were critical not only to solving productivity problems but to transforming company social policy from an instrument of exploitation to a system of "fair play."[152]

Others were harsher in their criticisms, rejecting Dinta's plea for an emotional identification with work and the firm. They asserted that workers should relate to their jobs and their foremen in a rational, objective manner, seek meaning in leisure and consumption and let the workers' movement, not the firm, mediate the individual's relationship to the larger economy and society.[153] But even critical trade union leaders were unsure whether Dinta was a practitioner of traditional, patriarchal social policy or a pioneer of new and dangerous methods, whether it advocated company trade unions or provided modern alternatives. Social Democrats ridiculed Dinta's claim to coexist peacefully with the labor movement, calling it a tool of right-wing capitalists—a claim that was not so much incorrect as insufficient. They did not devote much attention to Dinta's self-proclaimed unpolitical stance, perhaps because they saw it as a blatant lie, perhaps because they regarded Dinta's political views as secondary to its activities in the factory.[154]

Social Democrats condemned Dinta's efforts to transform the worker's whole personality. Or, rather, they condemned Dinta's desire to reshape the personality and life of the workingman, limit his autonomy, and redefine his loyalties. No one questioned Dinta's efforts to remold the attitudes and everyday life of the working-class housewife and her daughters. Dinta's activities outside the narrowly defined world of work were considered dangerous "encroachments" on the autonomous spheres of society and politics.[155] Yet Social Democrats were all too willing to accord Dinta legitimacy within the firm. Two quite different sets of factors pushed Social Democrats to this problematic position. By the late 1920s they had ceased contesting control of the shop floor, preferring to defend workers' rights through collective bargaining and state social policy. Moreover, Social Democrats and Dinta shared some key concerns about productivity, quality work, and skills training.[156]

The free trade unions, which had agitated for a reform and expansion of apprenticeship in the 1920s, were most open to Dinta's skills training programs.[157] Writing in *Work (Die Arbeit)*, a major trade union journal, Eduard Wietsch praised Dinta's technical education for giving workers the skills, knowledge, and flexibility rationalization demanded. Fritz Fricke was more critical of the apprenticeship training workshops, arguing that they taught not only skills but individualism, competition, and dependence on the firm. Nonetheless he, like other Social Democrats, conceded to the firm the right to control skills training; indeed, it was considered the firm's duty.[158]

Responses to company newspapers were more mixed, even though it was generally admitted that they went to great lengths to appear "harmless." As long as they focused only on the firm and sought to influence workers' attitude toward productivity, the ADGB claimed to have no objections.[159] Other observers were less sanguine, arguing that company newspapers encouraged an apolitical firm solidarity and willingness to sacrifice for capital.[160] Still others urged the trade union press to learn from the company newspapers, whose technical articles, garden tips, and reports on workers' jubilees had more appeal for the unorganized than did the dry reporting of the trade union press.[161]

Social Democrats were most critical and fearful of factory schools and youth recreation activities, even though they admitted that these Dinta programs were "damned clever."[162] The programs provided a technical and theoretical education that was narrowly tied to the needs of the firm, gave employers a disproportionate political influence on young workers, and isolated these workers from socialist youth activities and older workers. And, adding insult to injury, Dinta apprentices were not even paid for the one day each week they attended the factory school.[163]

Christian trade unionists also expressed ambivalent attitudes. Like the Socialists, they admired Dinta's skills training programs and endorsed the idea of factory-based apprenticeship workshops; many were willing to accept the factory schools, as well.[164] Dinta's appeal was not restricted to the technical and rational; its call for the development of a *Berufsethos* and a factory community resonated in a union movement that explicitly renounced class struggle and was deeply influenced by Catholic conceptions of vocation and community.[165] Moreover, leading churchmen such as Cardinal Schulte of Cologne, publicly endorsed Dinta's efforts and provided material aid.[166] Despite all this, Christian trade unions viewed Dinta with deep suspicion, for its efforts to capture the whole man conflicted with the rights and duties of parents and the church, as well as with the claims of the unions.[167] More left-wing functionaries, such as Fritz Rütten of the Christian Miners' Union, "reject[ed] Dinta because it links vocational education with one-sidedly capitalist interests."[168] Moderate trade unionists were willing to work with Dinta but attacked it for refusing such overtures.[169] Dinta was willing to coexist with trade unions, but its conception of leadership precluded cooperation with even the most moderate Christian ones.

Neither Social Democratic nor Christian trade unionists knew how seriously to take the Dinta threat.[170] Many Social Democrats dismissed Dinta as objectionable but ephemeral. Once apprentices left the protective confines of Dinta and joined their fellow workers on the factory floor, they would shed their Dinta indoctrination like caterpillars shed their cocoons and join the class struggle.[171] Echoing a popular Social Democratic theme, Hans Jahn insisted that Germany was moving inexorably from an individualistic to a collectivist age. By defining people's fate in individualistic or company terms rather than societal ones, Dinta was thus "doomed to failure."[172]

Other Social Democrats were more pessimistic. According to Erik Reger, the company newspapers regrettably were widely read and manipulated workers feelings in subtle ways.[173] Helmut Wagner argued that the influence of apprenticeship training "must not be underestimated. . . . Here is a fundamental source of the destruction of solidarity among workers, a source of indifference, against which all trade union work then struggles in vain." Unions must replace occupational identities with class consciousness and defend the economic interests of young workers, he concluded.[174] Toni Sender lamented that the fight against "these new, cunning methods of capital" was much harder than past struggles. The unions must both condemn Dinta and fight for publicly controlled vocational testing and training. But attention should not focus on economic issues alone, she concluded:

> Our community of struggle [*Kampfgemeinschaft*] must be transformed into a community of life [*Lebensgemeinschaft*]. Our understanding of the emotional and cultural needs of men caught up with machines must grow. Workers' organizations must be places toward which the young worker strives because he expects the greatest understanding for his multiform needs, inner struggles and desire for joy.[175]

Although Sender's prescription was more comprehensive, Wagner's sober, economistic recommendations and Jahn's deterministic but optimist predictions were more in tune with Social Democracy's political style and understanding of capitalist rationalization.[176] With social rationalization as with economic rationalization, the unions disputed capital's general vision but were unsuccessful at combatting particular measures that worked to the detriment of the labor movement and the working class.

The Battle for the Soul of the Worker

Dinta's accomplishments in the area of institution building are indisputable, even if exact statistics are impossible to obtain. Assessing its impact on workers is much more difficult, for sources are scarce and assessments contradictory. Moreover, Dinta was only active for three years before the Depression wreaked havoc on employment, training, and social policy, and seven years before the Nazis took power. It is evident that Dinta's attempt to rationalize the economy without Americanizing the worker had a significant influence on engineers and industrialists in the Weimar Republic and, as we will see later, on industrial relations and worker education under National Socialism. Conclusions about Dinta's impact on workers, however, must remain tentative.

Dinta had promised to preempt a shortage of skilled workers, restore joy in work, and above all increase individual productivity. The much-feared shortage of skilled workers was averted, but this was a consequence of the Depression and mass unemployment, not Dinta's educational efforts.[177] Productivity did indeed rise in the late 1920s, but technology and factory organization probably contributed more than did individual effort, and any increase in workers' efforts was more a product of the fear of unemployment than their commitment to work or to the firm. Debates on Dinta centered less around whether it enhanced productivity, than whether it influenced workers' attitudes toward work and the firm.

Dinta repeatedly proclaimed the success of its programs in speeches, articles, and glowing reports, accompanied by glossy photos of smiling apprentices at work and play.[178] (Dinta seldom let these youths speak for themselves, however.) Those who downplayed Dinta's impact on workers—and it was not only Social Democrats and Communists who did so—spoke in equally unequivocal terms. Some, like the scientists of work Alexander Hellwig and Frank Mäckbach, resorted to abstract arguments, insisting that workers valued wages, job security, and independence above all, and would not be bought off with token welfare measures.[179] Heinz Marr of the Social Musuem agreed with the Social Democratic view that Dinta was doomed, because "one should not expect from the factory more than it can give: well-ordered productive work with the best possible wages and secure work for as many as possible." Even such a factory would not be a *Heimat* or a *Gemeinschaft*.[180] Many Social Democrats and Communists all too glibly assumed that Dinta was simply providing the workers' movement with well-trained skilled workers. They felt certain that the realities of class conflict would become evident to Dinta apprentices once they were on the shop floor.[181]

When education programs were scrutinized in detail, Dinta became less sure of its efficacy; its critics, less sanguine about its irrelevance. No one felt confident to speak with certainty. The *Gewerkschafts-Archiv* expressed concern that Dinta apprentices were, in fact, developing procapitalist sentiments, narrow occupational pride, and disdain for the unskilled.[182] Later in the decade, the Communist *Ruhr Echo* complained that Dinta apprentices were controlled at work and play by engineers who were members of the Stahlhelm or fascists.[183] Occasional worker statements seemed to substantiate the left's worst fears. The Thyssen paper, for example, printed the enthusiastic report of the apprentice Goy about his trip on board the sailing ship *Glückauf*.[184] For a youth who had never been out of Hamborn, this trip to Hamburg, Kiel, and Denmark was the experience of a lifetime. Yet some of Dinta's own personnel doubted their popularity and influence. Mr. Dellweg, the instructor in the factory school at the Friedrich Wilhelms Hütte, complained repeatedly that students arrived late or skipped class, smoked, chewed gum, threw paper, and talked among themselves. He demanded more support from the firm in enforcing attendance and good behavior.[185] In 1931 the Dinta mine apprentices in Essen even participated in a miners' strike.[186]

Assessments of the influence of company newspapers were equally diverse. Dinta publicly cited circulation figures as an indication of workers' convictions, and companies considered the publications sufficiently useful to continue funding them throughout the Depression. The editors of the Dinta papers, however, were divided about their efficacy, and some mid-level managers sided with the skeptics. According to Friedrich of Vestag's Hamborn mines, it was foolish to think that the *Zechen Zeitung* could influence Ruhr miners, for it printed economic and political news in an untimely manner, refused to attack the left, and failed to offer heroic images of technology and creativity. It was, in short, an utter waste of money.[187] Some trade unionists denied that workers read such papers; others insisted that, even if they did, conditions in the firm and not Dinta's presentation of it, shaped workers' attitudes.[188]

Still other labor leaders, however, were genuinely alarmed by the spread of company newspapers. Erik Reger reported that at Schalker, the scene of Arnhold's earliest activism, workers threw out the first issues of the company paper in disgust. A few years later, however, they picked up a copy upon leaving the factory and put it in their pocket without a second thought.[189] And Schalker may not have been exceptional. If the reports of the Gutehoffnungshütte company police are to be believed, workers actually asked for the paper, especially when it contained the youth supplement.[190] The Duisburg *Volksstimme* was not alone in worrying that the company papers were especially appealing to the unorganized and less political workers. "There is a masterful psychology in these papers," it noted with regret, "that links neutral factual material and unpolitical strolls in nature and the world of the mind with *the development of a certain firm solidarity.*"[191] The DMV paper struck a more alarmist note, claiming that company papers spread "political poison."[192]

These tantalizing vignettes suggest how contradictory responses could be. The skills training that Dinta provided, the status associated with being a Dinta apprentice, and the access to special sports activities and travel all had real value and were undoubtedly appealing to many adolescents. Dinta spoke a language of quality work and respect for skills and productivity that resonated in working-class circles.[193] Yet one could enjoy the fringe benefits without endorsing the whole ideology, and quality work was as compatible with class consciousness as with the factory community. Whether most Dinta apprentices in fact stayed away from the Socialist and Communist movements after completing their training is unclear; that most faced several years of unemployment seems almost certain.[194] Such an experience may have radicalized them or may have encouraged the same kind of unpolitical passivity as their Dinta education had. When they returned to stable employment in the mid-1930s, there was no workers' movement to join, but Dinta still existed, and the Nazis were preaching its message of *Menschenführung*, the factory community, and productivity. This world may not have been entirely appealing to Dinta-trained workers, but it would have seemed familiar. Dinta's emphasis on quality work, achievement, and pride in one's job may have aided some workers in distancing themselves from the more explicitly political aspects of Nazi society. They may have helped workers understand their experiences in individualistic and unpolitical terms, even as such private retreat to work and family helped stabilize the Nazi regime.[195]

10

Housework Made Easy

Those who tirelessly preached the gospel of rationalization sought to transform not only machines, factories, and vast business enterprises, but also
the households and family lives of middle-class and, especially, working-class
Germans. Women were central to this project. Bourgeois feminists, educators, and social workers orchestrated a vast propaganda campaign to rationalize the working-class home and the proletarian housewife. Working-class
women were both the intended audience and the designated agents of the
desired changes. The anticipated benefits from household rationalization,
however, were to go first and foremost to others—husbands and children,
industry and the national economy, political parties and the state.

The impetus to rationalize housework came from diverse groups who
shared a commitment to modern technology and productivist ideologies.
There were of course Weimar Germany's famous modern architects of the
Bauhaus and the Neues Bauen movement, such as Bruno Taut and Martin
Wagner, who regarded functional modern architecture as the key to transforming working-class housing and the lives led within it.[1] Their partners
in this campaign were industrialists, Social Democrats, and bourgeois feminists. All accepted aid from the same social workers, engineers, industrial
sociologists, and vocational education teachers and coordinated their efforts
through the Home Economics Group of the RKW.[2] Each believed that
whether or not modern public housing was built, the working-class housewife could be Taylorized, the proletarian home rationalized. Each shared a
vision of a "new person" who would be "modern, clean, rational, disciplined,
as well as family oriented."[3]

Despite their shared commitments and coordinated efforts, the promoters of household rationalization pursued different, frequently contradictory political agendas. By preaching the gospel of efficiency, productivity, and austerity in the home and family, industry sought to promote that
ideology in the workplace and society at large. Whereas industry sought to
use the ideology of household rationalization to legitimate rationalization
more generally, bourgeois feminists adopted it to gain legitimacy for housework, as well as to free housewives from the most onerous burdens of
domestic drudgery. Social Democrats, or at any rate the movement's leadership, assumed that rationalization in the private sphere would promote a
progressive form of modernity, which they envisioned in terms of a healthy
and efficient home that preserved the traditional sexual division of labor,
while freeing women to be more active in the workers' movement, albeit
only in supportive roles. As a concept and as a movement, household rationalization was highly ambiguous, at once progressive and reactionary, empowering and controlling, modern and traditional.

The Weimar campaign to rationalize housework was part of an international effort to create modern, scientific homes and efficient homemakers.[4]
Despite German critiques of the American home as sterile and soulless and
of the American woman as liberated and materialistic, America was the
country that shaped both the German and European home economics movements most strongly. Yet here, as in other areas, German borrowing from
the American model was selective, eclectic, and undertaken with ambivalence. The German campaign to rationalize housework, for example, was
aimed primarily at working-class women, not middle-class ones. It envisioned
a working-class "new woman" who was not to be defined by a commitment
to waged work or career (although she might well be employed), nor by
personal independence and sexual liberation. Rather, her newness was to
derive from her scientific and rational organization of home and family, each
defined in traditional terms. She was to be as efficient, as Taylorized as her
American counterpart ostensibly was, but she was to enjoy neither new
household technology nor the standard of consumption that prevailed in
the United States. This was an austere vision of modernity in which the
new, Americanized woman was safely domesticated.

Let us turn first to the campaign to rationalize housework, reconstruct-
ing its origins, organization, and activities. We will examine the complex
images it projected, the contradictory political goals its supporters pursued,
and the ambivalent responses of working-class women and men.

The RKW and Housework

A concern with the quality of housework, mothering, and family was hardly
new to Germany in the 1920s, even if the economic, social, and cultural
effects of war, revolution, and inflation had heightened anxieties about these
issues. The German bourgeois women's movement had long stessed motherhood, housewifery, and the cultivation of women's separate sphere. The

pre–World War I Socialist women's movement, for all its critique of bourgeois feminism, also emphasized women's duties as wives and mothers, albeit
as Social Democratic ones. The state, through such educational institutions
as adolescent continuing education courses, as well as various charity organizations, sought to improve the quality of working-class homemaking by
offering cooking, sewing, and child care classes.[5] The new attention to housework did not arise from changes in the household or the practices of the
housewife. In the 1920s, as in earlier decades, housework was physically
arduous and time consuming, appliances were few, and, among the working-
class, overcrowding was common.[6] What was new in the 1920s was the tone
and substance of the campaign to reform housework, its highly organized
character, and the breadth of support for it among industrialists and engineers, conservative housewives' organizations and Social Democratic trade
unions, government officials, and educators.

The first intimations of the new concern about and conceptualization
of housework came in the wake of World War I. As several authors noted,
the war had graphically illustrated the importance of housework, not only
to the individual household, but also to the economy. In 1921, for example,
Heinz Potthof, an ardent proponent of rationalization, wrote a brochure
entitled *The Importance of the Household in the National Economy*, and this
theme featured prominently in every subsequent publication.[7] The infatuation with America also emerged early in the decade. In 1921 Irene Witte,
a champion of Taylorism, translated Christine Frederick's *The New Housekeeping*, changing the German title to *Die rationelle Haushaltführung*. Frederick, a prominent personality in the pre–World War I home economics
movement in the United States, systematically applied Taylor's principles
of scientific management to the home.[8] As Witte argued in her subsequent
book, *Home and Technology in America*, the United States was far more
advanced in household rationalization, both because industry had produced
more household equipment and because Americans adjusted to new circumstances and ideas more readily and broke with tradition more easily.[9]

In 1922 Erna Meyer added yet another new element to the emerging
discourse on household rationalization. In an article on "The Rationalization of Consumption in the Household," published in the VDI's *Technik
und Wirtschaft*, Meyer insisted that "the household, exactly like the workshop and the factory, must be understood as a manufacturing enterprise
[*Betrieb*]". Every aspect of household production, consumption, technology
and sociability needed to be systematically rethought and reformed.[10]

These early advocates of household rationalization spoke a more optimistic, a more American language than their successors were to. Household
rationalization, they argued, would not only save resources, time, money
and energy; it would also promote a new kind of consumption of household
utensils and appliances and would, by minimizing household drudgery, free
the housewife to develop her personality. Many of these claims were to be
moderated substantially later in the 1920s, but the pleas of Meyer and others
for an organization that would unite housewives and engineers, industry

and commerce behind a campaign to reform housework met with a positive response.

That organization was the Home Economics Group of the RKW, which was established in 1926 as a small advisory group of representatives of the rural and urban housewives' associations.[11] A year later both its scope and membership were significantly expanded. Housework was singled out, according to an article in a 1929 issue of RKW *Nachrichten*, because the RKW recognized the importance of the household for the national economy. In reality, the RKW was brought to that recognition by the active lobbying of Charlotte Muhsam-Werther, of the Central Office of the Housewives' Association, and by Dr. Marie-Elisabeth Lüders, a German Democratic Party member of parliament and a former social worker and educator.[12] Moreover, the mid-1920s was a time of widespread interest in housework reform, as is indicated by the fact that Erna Meyer's detailed manual for rationalizing housework, appropriately entitled *The New Household*, went through 23 printings between its publication in early 1926 and mid-1927.[13] The Home Economics Group, like the RKW generally, was as much a coordinator of the work of groups already active in rationalizing housework as an initiator of its own research and educational endeavors.

The Home Economics Group attempted to create the kind of broad-based alliance for which early advocates of household rationalization had argued. The executive committee of the Home Economics Group had one representative each from industry, trade, the artisan sector, the consumer cooperative movement, the Social Democratic trade union movement, and the National Association of German Housewives' Associations (RDH). Although men outnumbered women (forty-one and twenty-five, respectively), the Home Economics Group was the female bastion in the otherwise virtually exclusively male RKW. And the affiliations of the women members suggest the range of organizations concerned with rationalizing housework. The conservative RDH had five members, the rural housewives' association, four, and the league of home economics schools, two. The trade unions sent five women (as well as three men), while the Catholic and Protestant women's organizations had one representative each. The overwhelming majority of male members came from industry, commerce, or capitalist economic interest groups.[14]

The Home Economics Group of the RKW engaged in three main areas of activity: establishing an archive, conducting studies of methods of housework, and running an educational service. As the RKW proudly noted, these programs paralleled those of the U. S. Bureau of Home Economics, and both organizations sought to secure the cooperation of housewives, teachers, industry, universities, and research institutions in these endeavors.[15] The Home Economics Group's first accomplishment was the archive, which collected domestic and foreign literature on the rationalization of housework. By 1931 it had amassed over 44,000 brochures, newspaper articles, and books. It received 672 visitors, primarily vocational school teachers and members of housewives' organizations, and lent out over 2,000 pieces of literature.[16]

Not content to publicize the work of others, the Home Economics Group brought together "outstanding experts . . . to assess the efficiency of the labor processes involved in housework."[17] The goal was to establish "rules that were simple, practical, useful, and scientifically based."[18] With an eye for truly onerous household tasks, as well as for the culture in which they lived, the members of the Home Economics Group studied floor mopping, clothes washing, and potato peeling. The RKW justified these elaborate studies, conducted in laboratories or home economics schools, in terms of their value to both the household and the national economy. At least 10 percent of the work load of the household was taken up with floor mopping, it was noted, and another 10 percent with washing clothes and bed linen. Every year 300–500 million marks' worth of clothing and bedding were lost because they were wrongly washed.[19]

Despite the Home Economics Group's attempts at scientific accuracy and definitiveness in its studies, the results were disappointing. The laundry study found no correlation between the method of washing clothes and their durability, but it did support previous conclusions about the proper detergent to use for different materials. The search for the ideal potato peeler proved inconclusive, its authors complained, because the subjective views of the women who were polled impeded their scientific judgment of the best design.[20]

The limits of such research emerge most clearly in the floor-mopping study, which was conducted with painstaking thoroughness over a two-year period. Research determined that the mop-and-pail method was the cheapest (5.37 marks per year per 25 square meters) but required the most time (95 hours, 41 minutes, and 40 seconds per year). The least time-consuming mop-and-oil method (52 hours, 21 minutes, and 40 seconds) cost three times as much.[21] These results were widely disseminated in RKW publications, the daily press, and women's periodicals, as well as by the Home Economics Group's educational service. What lesson the housewife was to learn from them is unclear. The study failed to deal with the vital question of which method required the greatest expenditure of energy, and its authors admitted in a resigned tone that the results, arrived at under controlled laboratory conditions, could only approximate those in actual households. Moreover each floor had its peculiarities and no one method could be used continually. The floor-mopping study was more a testament to the Home Economics Group's infatuation with time-and-motion studies and to its ability to speak the then fashionable language of scientific management than a practical guide for the beleaguered housewife.

The educational service of the Home Economics Group was its most influential endeavor, for it was the means by which the RKW sought to spread the theory of rationalized housework beyond educated middle-class circles and shape the practice of working-class and lower middle-class housewives. The Home Economics Group believed that the rationalization of housework was first and foremost "an educational problem," and "a pedagogical task."[22] The group initially produced a series of teaching placards to be used in courses, lectures, and traveling exhibits. The placards, which explained the most efficient forms of knives and forks, cooking utensils, coffee pots, and water pitchers, aimed to educate women and girls about the details of the rationalized household and encourage them to buy only standardized, functional, household essentials. Such purchases were not seen as the advent of a quantitatively and qualitatively new kind of mass consumption, but they would, it was hoped, promote standardization and rationalization in industry.[23]

By the late 1920s the Home Economics Group went on to produce pamphlets that could be used as lectures to accompany slides or enlarged drawings. The pamphlet/lecture series began with *Housework Made Easy*, and continued with *Advice for Selected Cooking Utensils, Standardization in the Household*, and two studies of how to cook and heat most efficiently with a variety of stoves. The series concluded with the popularized results of the research studies discussed earlier, *Home Washing* and *Economical Floor Care*. The intended audience included adolescent girls in home economics courses, trade union women, and members of the urban and rural housewives' associations.[24] To reach these groups, the pamphlet/lectures promised to "avoid all superfluous erudition and assumed no special technical knowledge on the part of female and male listeners."[25] The text and pictures together provided a lecture that was "ready to be spoken" and thus required no time-consuming preparation.

The educational service of the Home Economics Group seems to have made progress in reaching its intended audience. In 1926 it produced and sold two thousand copies of the teaching placards and used the proceeds to repay the RKW the money it loaned for their production.[26] The placards were also widely reproduced in the daily press, women's journals, and Social Democratic trade union publications. The pamphlets, which sold for only 50 pfennig, were reprinted on a comparable scale. *Home Washing*, for example, sold out the first edition in eight weeks, and a total of twenty thousand copies were printed within a few months.[27] These pamphlets continued to be printed throughout the 1930s.[28] Because these materials were so widely disseminated, it is important to examine more closely the vision of the rationalized household and rationalized housewife they contained, a vision that was echoed in Meyer's bestseller, *The New Household*, and in Witte's *Home and Technology in America*.

The New Woman in the New Home

One of the most striking characteristics of the new discourse on the home and consumption was its wholesale adoption of the language of production. There were no sentimental discussions of the home as a separate sphere, obeying its own rules. Rather, proponents of household rationalization saw the home as an integral part of the national economy, and precisely because of this, argued that rationalization was both desirable and possible. In Witte's words,

If one looks at the work of the individual housewife in her home, if one sees with what love she carries out the individual tasks and how during her work she occasionally pauses for a minute to gaze out the window or look at herself in the mirror, the thought of applying a systematic analysis of work seems almost laugh-able. . . .

[I]f we view the housewife in her totality, or in other words, if we con-sider housework not as an individual activity but as a social function . . . we get a very different picture. Then we see that an hour of previously wasted energy saved in every household amounts to many days and years. The meaning of waste in the household becomes clear.[29]

If the household was part of the national economy, it was subject to the same kinds of analysis. Article after article insisted, "Every household must be seen as an individual enterprise. . . ." Only then, according to Erna Meyer, could "the specially constructed small enterprise of the consumer economy," namely, the home, be properly and thoroughly analyzed.[30] Cook-ing, cleaning, and washing were reduced to "labor processes" and analyzed in terms of the expenditures of money, time, material, and energy they re-quired. Witte insisted that industry had developed laws for the efficient use of energy which were equally applicable to the household. Work must be analyzed and planned, then written instructions developed (so as to follow the industrial principle of separating planning and execution) and, finally, an uninterrupted and efficient labor process executed.[31] The goals of house-hold rationalization were described in terms identical to those used for industrial rationalization: maximum output for minimum input and the elimi-nation of all waste.

The Germans were hardly alone in applying the language of produc-tion and the laws of Taylorism to the home, as the minutes of the home economics section of the International Congress of Scientific Management reveal. Yet the congress' debates suggest that they did so more rigorously than their counterparts elsewhere. The home was an enterprise that could be rationalized just like any factory; it was not a peculiar sort of workplace, whose small size and frequent poverty made total rationalization an elusive goal, as the British argued.[32] The American scientific manager Lillian Gilbreth spoke enthusiastically of applying engineering principles and time, motion, and fatigue studies to the home, but she never called the home a factory. She talked about eliminating waste from the home but also about making it a place that "satisfied individual needs . . . and created a psycho-logically healthy atmosphere for children."[33] Italian women favored ratio-nalizing the home, not merely in the interests of the national economy but, equally important, in the interests of women doing waged work.[34]

Beneath a common allegiance to household rationalization, then, lay subtle differences. The more nuanced discussions among Americans and other Europeans acknowledged that there were at best imperfect parallels between the household and the factory; the Germans asserted an identity. Whereas American, Italian, and British analysts reflected the tensions be-tween the needs and goals of the economy and the more complex ones of women and the household, the German delegates discussed the home in the abstract categories of national economy and scientific management. This unquestioning endorsement of economic efficiency as the highest goal and scientific management as the best means gave the German discourse on household rationalization a remarkable consistency and self-confidence, even though it strikes later readers as abstract, austere, and almost dehumanized.

This new language represented a reversal of the way work and home had previously been linked ideologically. In late nineteenth-century Germany, there was a widespread reluctance to endorse women's waged work outside the home, and the similarities between women's paid work—especially in textiles, the garment industry and food processing—and women's unpaid traditional tasks within the home were emphasized. Homework, which was prevalent in Imperial Germany and offered employment (especially to married women), represented an ideal in this discourse.[35] In the 1920s the linkage was reversed. Ambivalence, if not opposition, to women's waged work outside the home persisted. Nonetheless the factory—the rationalized factory—became the model for everyday life. The organized, capitalist world of production provided the criteria by which to organize and evaluate housework and mothering. Everyday life was no longer the model for women's waged work.

Many who advocated household rationalization insisted that the new home would only be successful if animated by the proper spirit (*Geist*). For some, "spirit" seems to have been shorthand for the traditional womanly virtues of moral rectitude, diligence, self-sacrifice, and nurturance. For others it represented domestic virtues plus nationalism.[36] For still others, this spirit was defined in the fashionable language of the science of work. According to Meyer, the housewife needed to develop respect for herself and her activities: "With this respect, with the consciousness of her responsibility and her own abilities, the woman will achieve joy in work for herself." Her work would become a "*Beruf.*"[37] For all, rationalization and spirit were seen to be complementary. Support for rationalization at home and in the economy became a new domestic virtue and simultaneously aided the fulfillment of old ones, as a recent study of Weimar books for home economics education reveals.[38]

No one articulated the perceived compatibility of *Geist* and rationalization better then Witte. Far from making housework "soulless, mechanical, one-dimensional, and uninteresting," rationalization, she insisted, would add new depth and meaning to housework. "In order to analyze her work in the appropriate way and reconstruct it, she [the housewife] must penetrate deep into its essence [*Wesen*]. She must observe the people with whom she comes in contact. She must learn to employ the materials, tools, and perhaps even people in the most efficient way in her enterprise [*Betrieb*]."[39] The antithesis of spirit was not rationalization but the soulless materialism that many believed had permeated the rationalized American home, family, and society at large.[40] The housewife, like the Dinta engineer, was supposed to adopt the ideology of industrial efficiency while eliminating the

inhumane aspects of modern work.[41] *Geist* helped define the German variant of rationalization and, as we will see, also helped to justify dispensing
with technology and consumption.

The ideas of duty and service accomplished the same end. Household
rationalization was not advocated in order to promote consumption, leisure,
or any ostensibly selfish version of women's emancipation. Rather, industrialists wanted the rationalized home to serve the interests of German economic recovery and development; Social Democrats hoped it would further
women's political activism and social reform; and bourgeois feminists
anticipated that it would free women to participate in higher cultural and
national tasks. Common to all was a conviction that the Taylorized housewife would be able not only to serve her own family better but also to fulfill
new economic and political duties effectively. As Meyer succinctly stated,
"Unburdening women . . . means winning time and energy for *the more
important and more difficult work on ourselves and for others*. Work thus
remains our battlecry."[42]

Although the Home Economics Group's studies of floor mopping contained much superfluous scientific jargon and relatively little useful information, the same cannot be said of the bulk of RKW publications on rationalized housework. The advice offered was simple, practical, and inexpensive
to follow. As the authors of the *Handbook of Rationalization* argued, there
was no objective way to measure energy expenditure in household tasks—
energy expenditure was a particular concern of the German science of work.
Those seeking to rationalize housework should concentrate instead on the
more modest but practical goal of exposing the worst abuses stemming from
"incorrect posture and inefficient working conditions."[43]

In pamphlets, lectures, and teaching placards, the Home Economics Group
took this admonition seriously. Numerous stick figure drawings filled such
pamphlets as *Housework Made Easy*, each illustrating incorrect and correct
postures and movements for such mundane tasks as ironing, window washing and—yes—potato peeling. If broom handles were the correct length and
wash tubs the proper height, energy could be saved and exhaustion avoided.
And sitting whenever possible was strongly recommended. After reassuring
conscientious readers that sitting was not a sign of laziness or decadence,
despite what mothers and grandmothers might say, various authors explained
how to arrange equipment so that ironing, dish washing, and vegetable peeling could be done without standing and bending.[44]

The advice on household utensils was similarly simple and practical.
Pamphlets and placards discussed only the most necessary equipment, such
as cooking pans and coffee pots, and illustrated efficient and inefficient features in simple, readily understandable drawings. Time and again home
economists argued that the standardization of basic household goods was
the key to an orderly and efficient household. Standardization would enable
the housewife to save time, money, and annoyance and get by with fewer
dishes, cooking ware and bedding. It would improve quality while decreasing prices.[45]

The tone of *Housework Made Easy* and other books and pamphlets was always encouraging and egalitarian rather than authoritarian. Readers were addressed as "Meine Damen," housework was praised by comparing it to heavy male labor, and housewives were informed that they, too, could and deserved to save energy just as factory workers did. Advice was presented in the form of suggestions, not orders. Indeed, authors repeatedly assured listeners and readers that recommendations did not amount to a "rigid and unalterable recipe for housework." Rather, individuals should pick and choose what seemed most useful or affordable.[46]

The rationalized housewife thus was one who Taylorized her work routines. The center of her home life was the kitchen, which, ideally, was small, functional, isolated from the rest of the apartment, and used by the housewife alone, rather than being the locus of all family activities as the traditional large working-class "living kitchen" had been. There she was to move with efficiency and economy, perform tasks sitting whenever possible, and use simple, functional utensils. If she mastered the simpler forms of self-rationalization, she might devise a time schedule for her day and week, organize her daily shopping into one or two efficient weekly trips, or keep accurate household accounts. Much less emphasis was placed on these more comprehensive activities than on the organized and efficient execution of individual tasks. The rationalized proletarian housewife was more a worker than a manager.

According to both household rationalizers and modern architects, the methodical life of the rationalized housewife ideally was to be led in a modern, uncluttered, well-lit and carefully arranged home. This was impossible for the vast majority of working-class women, however, as the functional apartments in the new state housing projects built during Weimar were too expensive for any but white-collar workers and a small portion of the best paid skilled workers.[47] Most working-class women were advised to rearrange existing quarters. Furniture, especially in the kitchen, was to be situated so as to eliminate superfluous motions, and as much light and air as possible were to be let in. Above all, knickknacks, excessive furniture, and nonfunctional decorations, which merely collected dust and were ugly, were to be ruthlessly purged. Only a few tasteful pictures were permitted.[48]

This was a stark image of modernity. It subjected the domestic taste of the working-class woman to ruthless critique and sought to strip the working-class home of its clutter and prized knickknacks. In their place was offered only an austere functionalism. No one who has seen pictures of impoverished working-class apartments in Berlin and other major German industrial cities can doubt that the new housing or rearranged old apartments were both more efficient and healthier. The squalor and hardship of much of early twentieth-century proletarian life should not be romanticized —but neither should the proposals for modern housing and rationalized housework. They represented an improved, albeit rather bleak, alternative rather than a utopian vision.

The discourse on rationalized housing and housework was as notable for what it excluded as for what it emphasized, for what it tacitly assumed as for what it consciously challenged. Few authors linked the need for rationalization to the growth of women's paid work or specifically addressed the double burden.[49] More broadly, no one questioned the existing sexual division of labor, which assigned all housework to women. (Women were also assumed to be responsible for childrearing, although surprisingly little attention was paid to that subject.) To be sure, Meyer mentioned that in "faraway" and "much praised" America, men were rumored to do heavy household tasks and even prepare breakfast and get children ready for school. For Germany, however, Meyer suggested briefly and in the most tentative terms that all family members should be encouraged to help at home. Even that suggestion was missing from most other works.[50]

Nor did anyone argue that certain household tasks be socialized or communalized. Each household was to be rationalized, but, unlike in industry, where jobs were specialized, each housewife would perform all tasks.[51] Neither architects, nor Social Democrats, nor feminists talked of the "one-kitchen" apartment house or debated the kinds of collective facilities and social services that the Austrian Socialists built in Vienna.[52] Marie Juchacz, a leader in the SPD, was among the few who saw the rationalization of the individual household as a step toward socialization in the private sphere; but this remained a subordinate and ill-defined theme in a discourse that stressed the short-term transformation of the individual housewife.[53] Charlotte Mühsam-Werther may have spoken for many when she told the International Congress of Scientific Management that the German rationalization movement rejected any form of collectivization because "it contradicts the true meaning of the family household."[54] Women and gender illuminate the traditionalism of the modernist vision.

Consumption and household technology played a distinctly subordinate role in the German vision of rationalization. Some historians of the American home economics movement have argued that it consciously promoted new kinds of consumption to benefit industry. Buying replaced frugality as the virtue taught in home economics courses.[55] A comparable argument cannot be made for Germany. To be sure, companies such as Siemens, the giant electotechnical concern, produced vacuum cleaners and other appliances, but a *Siemens Mitteilungen* story/ad, "How the Buschmüllers Got a Vacuum," clearly indicates the audience for whom such consumer durables were intended: a comfortable white-collar family is depicted choosing between the relative costs of a cleaning woman and a vacuum.[56]

In so far as working-class consumption was discussed, it involved household essentials. Women should purchase standardized pots, pans, silverware, and pitchers. Indeed, they were "called" (*berufen*) to promote standardization and rationalization in both production and their homes by such purchases.[57] No one was explicitly urged to throw out all existing utensils and begin anew, but the advantages of rationalized goods were continually stressed. In the judgment of the *Metallarbeiter-Zeitung*, even this modest level of consumption was unrealistic:

It is precisely the working-class woman, the overburdened housewife and mother with the smallest amount of money to whom the possibility of rationalization should be available first. But often she cannot follow the well-meaning advice. . . . If we still have good and useful cooking equipment, we must use that up first because we simply don't have the means to clean out the old radically, however much we would like to see the new in its place.[58]

Opinions varied about whether consumer durables were desirable in principle. In an article on "Rational Household Management" in the *Gewerkschaftliche Frauenzeitung,* Elfriede Behne praised the new household machines.[59] Witte, who had seen the wonders of American household technology at first hand, insisted that the efficient American home was the product of "appropriate work procedures" and not "expensive labor-saving appliances." Nonetheless, she gave lavish descriptions of mix-masters and dishwashers, vacuum cleaners and washing machines, and staunchly defended the American practice of purchasing such items on credit.[60] The RKW publications, however, did not even give a passing nod to expensive household technology. According to the *Handbook of Rationalization:*

One often encounters the view that household rationalization is identical with household mechanization, that household rationalization is only possible with the help of technical appliances. This is a fateful error. A household that is technically equipped in the most complete way is worthless if the spirit [*Geist*] that rules it fails. In addition, the great majority of low-income households would be excluded from rationalization, since mechanization is too expensive for them.[61]

The *Metallarbeiter-Zeitung* insisted that the housewife could only rationalize "without expensive appliances and upheaval" and that this might somehow "bear better fruit."[62] Meyer also made a virtue out of the necessity of limiting consumption and household technology. If women reformed their work methods and stripped their houses of knickknacks and nonfunctional furniture, machines would have little to do. To quote her most memorable claim, "The vacuum cleaner will be superfluous in the home which does not allow dust the possibility of collecting."[63]

The Ambiguities of Household Rationalization

However bleak these images of the rationalized housewife and the reformed home might appear to us, they found widespread support among diverse groups in the Weimar Republic. Industrialists, bourgeois feminists and Social Democrats alike endorsed household rationalization, and each group sought to instrumentalize the movement for its larger political and economic goals.

For such industries as furniture and electrical goods, household rationalization promised to increase demand, at least among the middle classes. For all sectors of industry it offered a means of curbing the reputedly extravagant and irresponsible spending habits of the working class and thus, presumably, limiting wage demands. "A high percentage of working-class women can neither buy correctly nor manage rationally," complained Alfred

Striemer in the *Bosch Zünder*. Working-class consumers spent far too much on funerals and frequently tried to imitate their more prosperous neighbors. Those living near subsistance were accused of wasting money on "worth-less trifles and the satisfaction of whims and impulses." The working class must be educated in rational consumption and household management, Striemer argued, for in Germany this would determine "whether we can gather the forces for a new ascent."[64]

Erich Lilienthal, writing on "The Rationalization of Private Life" in *Der Arbeitgeber*, published by the VDA, echoed these sentiments. "If much about rationalizing the economy can be taken from America," he argued, "this is certainly not the case with respect to private life." Germans had to avoid the extravagant leisure activities of the Americans, epitomized by Luna Park, the Coney Island amusement park. Germans could not aspire to the fancier cooking and kitchen technology that American housewives widely enjoyed. Rather, German working-class women needed to be edu-cated in "the reasonable use and preparation of such food as can be purchased by wages that are pegged to productivity." Similarly, the purchase of cloth-ing and household goods should be directly tied to the level of industrial efficiency. "All sides must engage in detailed educational work, whose suc-cess will be decisive for Germany's economic development."[65]

This stress on education was not idle rhetoric. During the 1920s such major industrial enterprises as Thyssen, Krupp, Gutehoffnungshütte, and Bosch established an impressive array of home economics courses. Krupp, for example, offered two year-long programs for adolescent girls who had just finished school, two 8–12 week courses for adult women, and five 2–3 month evening courses for working women. These were supplemented by a regular lecture series for wives and daughters of employees, covering such topics as "proper nutrition" and "Sundays and holidays with the family."[66] In Oberhausen, Gutehoffnungshütte established a home economics school, which approximately 30 students attended full time for half a year. There were also two so-called needlework schools, where married women and schoolgirls received instruction in sewing, cooking and cleaning on a part-time basis. The Thyssen works had a similar course plus an ambitious 12-month program in home economics and an 18-month course on child care; altogether 150–160 girls attended.[67] Some of these courses were offered under the auspices of Dinta; others, directly by the firm. Regardless of sponsor-ship, the underlying assumptions were similar. Whereas men's education programs emphasized the mastery of technology, women's education assumed that technology had not entered the home and would not do so in the foreseeable future. The ideal was to have working-class women ratio-nalize their housework without increased consumption, electrification, or appliances.

Firms also ran kindergartens and provided health and maternity care, which provided education as well as concrete services. In 1927–1928, for example, Gutehoffnungshütte ran seven nursery schools at a cost of nearly 90,000 marks, making them the single most expensive program for families.[68]

Industrial sociologists, factory social workers, and Dinta officials all agreed that nursery schools performed the important function of freeing the harried working-class housewife from the burdens of a young child or children. But she was to use her few free hours not for relaxation or self-development but rather for getting her house in order and tending to the needs of her husband and older children.[69] Nursery schools also provided the adolescent daughters of employees "training for their future vocation as mothers." Finally, they were useful for socializing boys and girls. As Miss G. Wenneker told a meeting of Dinta engineers, "It is important that one preserve the child's inborn joy in work. One should leave the child time and quiet for its activity so that the child can develop the necessary concentration in order to do faultless work later in life."[70] Peter Bäumer put it more succinctly: "education for the economy" should begin in nursery school.[71]

Firms such as Gutehoffnungshütte and Siemens also provided some pre- and postnatal care, home helpers to aid families during a mother's illness, and classes in proper childrearing. In addition, there were convalescent homes for women and vacation homes for children that gave preference to undernourished youngsters. The emphasis was on providing services and advice, or occasionally goods, but almost never money that could be spent at the discretion of the housewife. The aim was to keep the home functioning in times of crisis and improve the health and efficiency of the next generation of workers.[72]

Many industrialists and engineers were convinced that behind every happy and productive rationalized worker was a rationalized working-class housewife. In a study of factory social workers, Carola Sachse found that companies sought to create housewives who not only accomplished their work efficiently but also created a happy home environment. The companies thereby hoped to reap economic benefits from the the man's higher productivity.[73] Erna Meyer insisted that the worker who enjoyed a comfortable, well functioning, and efficient home life "will not only be more refreshed physically but also be quieter spiritually in order to accomplish his daily work and be more productive."[74]

But diminishing labor costs was not the only goal. Karl Arnhold, who designed a variety of educational programs for the wives and daughters of workers in major Ruhr firms, stressed joy in work as well as productivity. His aim was to create a new type of worker and not merely to squeeze more out of the old one. Arnhold believed that improved housekeeping was a way to create "healthy and happy families" that are "the source from which new, healthy and strong forces continually stream into our industrial enterprises."[75] For Arnhold, as for others, healthy and strong were code words for antisocialist and nationalist. The industrial sociologist Rudolf Schwenger described the emphasis Ruhr firms placed on housework education as "preventative work. . . . Economic distress, illness, demoralization, despair, and radicalism will be fought against at their source, principally in the family."[76]

Housework education, like apprenticeship training, was to be both practical and moral. Girls and women were to learn how to run the home efficiently and keep their families healthy. These skills would be useful not only in their own homes, but as a means of earning a living before marriage, or if necessary after. This was especially important in the Ruhr, where few fac-tory jobs were available for women.[77] According to Miss M. Grundels, girls were to be taught that a home required great nurturance and that "strong connections exist between the diligent performance of one's vocation [Beruf] and the growth of one's moral personality."[78] As stated in the Gutehoffnungshütte Werkszeitung, girls must be educated "so that they eventually establish an ordered home for their husband and children and thereby create for stable workers a true German Heimat in their home, whose happiness will accompany them to their workplace."[79]

Probably the least significant function served by these programs to rationalize housework was to provide concrete advice and material aid to the working-class housewife, although some women and families definitely did receive benefits. A more important purpose of the programs was to enable the worker's support network to function and aid him in properly performing his paid job. In theory these education programs would enable the working-class housewife to solve her problems on an individual basis in her own house just as the firm solved its problems on an individual basis within the factory.[80]

One suspects, however, that industry preached the gospel of household rationalization primarily for ideological reasons. It was, after all, impossible to measure or control women's unpaid domestic labor or to assess the con-crete economic effects of self-Taylorization on her own work or on indus-trial productivity. Benefits might well result, but they were not subject to the new rationalized cost-accounting measures of the 1920s. The political value of the campaign to rationalize housework was clearer. It taught the significance of efficiency, the virtues of a minute division of labor, the importance of saving time and materials. Company programs to rationalize housework attempted to legitimate an austere, productivist vision of ratio-nalization, emphasizing the individual's principal role as worker, whether in the factory or at home. They fit nicely with industry's vision of rational-ization, which stressed producers' goods and export markets, and rejected the notion that Germany could afford mass consumption of the American kind. Rather, the working class, whether occupied in the home or the fac-tory, must be encouraged or forced to increase productivity, limit its wage demands, and forego mass consumption in order to restore the German economy. No immediate rewards would be forthcoming for such sacrifices.

The rationalized factory worker would find understanding and support from the rationalized housewife; they would speak the same language and share the same values. Both would transform their work practices in a dis-tinctly modern but only partially Americanized way. His devotion to the firm would be paralleled by her devotion to the family. Both would develop a vocational ethos and experience joy in work, regardless of whether their work was genuinely meaningful. Both would be sympathetic to the prin-ciples of economic and social rationalization and restructure their lives accordingly, without seeking the benefits of mass consumption and mass culture as compensation. In short, each would combine American techniques with a German *Geist* and thereby avoid the soullessness and materialism that ostensibly permeated home, family, and society in the United States.

Women social workers, vocational education teachers and leaders of the housewives' associations eagerly endorsed household rationalization, for as ideology and practice it promised both to elevate housework and dramatically alter the life of the housewife. By speaking the pervasive language of rationalization, by showing the links between the home's economy and the nation's, by conducting time-and-motion studies and urging productivity and efficiency, these women claimed a new status for housework and denied its separateness from other economic activities. They draped housework with the mantle of science and modernity, hoping thereby to make it a profession (*Beruf*) despite its unpaid character.[81]

Rationalized housework was not only central to the economic well-being of Germany but also to women's roles as mothers and citizens. Irene Witte held up the American housewife as a model: she performed her duties as housewife, mother, and wife in a rationalized and efficient manner and thus had time to develop her own personality, interests, and knowledge.[82] Most commentators stressed the connection between rationalization and the fulfillment of women's multiple responsibilities. According to Margarethe Rudorff, women had achieved new political rights, but with them came the "duty" to promote Germany's economic recovery; one way to do so was to support rationalization and standardization in the home.[83] Marie-Elisabeth Lüders linked rationalization and politics somewhat differently in an eloquent article that appeared in both *Technik und Wirtschaft* and the *Metallarbeiter-Zeitung*:

> Women should not be freed from the scrub bucket and dust cloth because they are lazy. They should be freed from the burdens of the household in order to develop intellectual, spiritual, and cultural values and to enhance the fulfillment of their duties as mothers and citizens. We do not want to rush out of the house out of aversion to the house and home economics. Rather, we think it is a misuse of women's power for family and state if we remain within our four walls, scrubbing and polishing and with misunderstood pride think "my home, my world." Instead, we should see our home in the world. But in order to do that we must be much more emancipated from our house than we are today.

Rationalizing housework was thus "a state-political task of the greatest importance, a cultural duty."[84]

It is a long way from these exalted claims to the mundane recommendations of the RKW for ironing and potato peeling. What links them is a shared insistence on the benefits of rationalization to the nation more than for women, and an emphasis on duties rather than rights or self-fulfillment. It was traditional German bourgeois feminism in a rationalized guise.

For bourgeois feminists, household rationalization promised not only to improve the situation of the middle-class woman but also to alter dra-

matically the proletarian home. The middle-class reformers' vision of the
rationalized proletarian household conflicted with working-class realities;
bourgeois feminists, social workers, and educators promised to ease working-class women's lives, but at the expense of their culture and communities. The ideology of household rationalization enabled these reformers to
critique working-class culture in the language of "science" rather than that
of morality, politics, or class pretentions. Disorder, dirt, and inefficiency
were no longer insults to middle-class values but objectively measurable dangers to the national economy and polity. The working-class housewife's frequent trips to the corner store or co-op, which probably represented a major
form of social contact, and her love for knickknacks, cheap pictures, and deco-
rative furniture no longer symbolized merely a different lifestyle than that
of the middle classes. They were forms of behavior "scientifically" shown
to waste money, time, and energy and to endanger health.[85] For the middle-
class professional woman and housewife, just as for the industrialist and
engineer, rationalization promised to remove political and cultural conflict
with one wave of the scientific wand.

Women vocational education teachers, social workers, and activists in
the urban and rural housewives' associations taught the principles of rationalized housewifery in a variety of institutional settings. The modern housing projects of the 1920s offered lectures and films on how to live efficiently
in the new functional apartments, while in cities such as Hamburg the Office
of Housing Maintenance sponsored exhibits and lectures on how to run a
rational household in unrationalized prewar housing.[86] Courses in cooking,
sewing, cleaning, and child care, packaged in the new ideology of household rationalization, were the mainstay of continuing education for adolescent girls, whereas the curriculum for boys stressed technical knowledge
and preparation for paid work.[87] Labor Offices offered technical and general education for unemployed men but ran courses on "women's work,"
that is, child care and housework, for women.[88] The National Association
of German Housewives' Associations promoted education for rural and
urban lower-class housewives and domestic servants and advanced training for the women who would teach them.[89]

The women who taught these courses, arranged the exhibits, and
advised individual housewives were overwhelmingly middle class. Yet,
Social Democratic leaders—women and men—endorsed these efforts, for
they embraced rationalization in the home as enthusiastically as rationalization in the factory. For example, the SPD national daily, *Vorwärts*, and
its supplement for women discouraged women from seeking paid employment and sought to elevate the status of housework and mothering, which
were considered women's principal *Beruf*. The housewife must recognize
that "her work is not worthless," argued party leader Marie Juchacz.[90]
Indeed, she should analyze her work, like the engineer in the factory, and
educate herself in the new principles of rationalized housework, argued other
Social Democratic spokeswomen.[91] According to Else Loewecke-Möbus the
German working-class housewife should imitate "the modern American

woman, who feeling herself to be the director of a firm, consciously applies such scientific knowledge."[92]

The *Gewerkschaftliche Frauenzeitung* frequently exposed the detrimental effects of rationalization in the workplace but ran no comparable critical pieces on rationalization at home.[93] The *Metallarbeiter-Zeitung* stressed the importance of housework to the national economy and praised the work of the RKW. On its "Family and Home" page, it reprinted excerpts from the literature of the Home Economics Group, as well as essays by such women as Marie-Elisabeth Lüders. The ADGB yearbook argued for the importance of giving all girls formal home economics training in addition to whatever vocational education they might receive.[94]

Words were followed by deeds. Arbeiterwohlfahrt, the Social Democratic welfare and self-help organization and the main area of activism for female party members, taught its own housework courses in many towns and cities.[95] Since the SPD was prominent in many local and national governments, it was able to sponsor the construction of precisely those modern public housing projects which were considered the ideal locus of rationalized proletarian family life.

Social Democratic support for household rationalization was a feature of its support for rationalization of the economy as a whole. In the home, as on the shop floor, Social Democratic leaders and writers viewed rationalized work as scientifically determined, technologically necessary, and, despite all its possible problems, indubitably and appealingly modern. But there were additional reasons for Social Democratic leaders' endorsement of Taylorism in the home.

The rationalization of housework promised to improve the quality of home life and lessen the woman's burden without demanding any alteration in the domestic division of labor. This appealed to the traditional attitudes about women's and men's spheres that were prevalent among Social Democrats—women as well as men, members as well as leaders.[96] Eric Fromm's late 1920s survey of working-class and white-collar attitudes, for example, revealed that while 66 percent of the Social Democrats interviewed and 73 percent of the Communists thought women should work, these figures fell to 12 and 36 percent, respectively, when the question involved married women's work.[97] The left-wing *Betriebsräte-Zeitschrift* of the DMV printed articles arguing, "The well-being and spirit of the living community depends on the total personality of the housewife. . . . Homework or part-time work are a burden on her health; seasonal work creates nervousness; and a job takes reponsibility and time away from housewifely activity."[98] The idealized vision of domesticity to which the Metalworkers' Union—and, one suspects, the Social Democratic movement more broadly— aspired is suggested by the drawings that headed the "Family and Home" page of the union's paper. In one, husband and wife sit on a swing in front of a rural home, he smoking and she minding the baby. In the other, husband and wife gather around the table in a comfortable and cosy room. While he reads the paper (the *Metallarbeiter-Zeitung*, no doubt), she sews and minds the two children, who play quietly. Rationalization perhaps was seen as the modern way to attain this old fashioned ideal of home and family.

Household rationalization also was viewed positively because Social Democrats thought it would help solve the long-standing problem of low participation by women in the trade union movement and the party. According to the *Metallarbeiter-Zeitung*, the key reason why women were not active in movement affairs was that they lacked free time. Day and night the housewife cooked, sewed, cleaned, and cared for the children. Although an eight-hour day, such as men had, was inconceivable for women, rationalization could create a few free hours here and there that could be devoted to political work. This was essential, the paper stressed, because women were "the educators of youth" and "the men of today need you, the women, as comrades and co-fighters."[99] The need to rationalize housework so that women could manage a job outside the home as well was mentioned only in passing.

In promoting household rationalization, the spokesmen, and more rarely spokeswomen, for the Social Democratic movement reflected the values and life styles of the more skilled, prosperous, and respectable elements of the working class. Their endorsement of rationalization was a critique of the rougher elements of the working class and of all working-class women who failed to conform to the norms of order, discipline, organization, and productivity. In an article entitled "More Free Time for the Woman" the *Metallarbeiter-Zeitung* revealed these biases in a discussion of proper neighorhood behavior: "Certainly, one should have good relations with one's neighbors. One should be pleasant and helpful—but with moderation and purpose. When the neighbor woman asks you to watch her little ones for an hour, because she has to do something immediately, fulfill her request if you can, if you are certain that your willingness will not be misused." After further admonishing the housewife to lend food or pots and dishes sparingly, if at all, the article launched its final attack on proletarian women's culture: "Above all, dear housewife, avoid those beloved little 'chats,' on the celler stairs, in the front hall, before the apartment door, or out of the window, since they are true time robbers!"[100]

In another article on "Planned Shopping," a woman functionary of a socialist consumer cooperative complains bitterly about housewives who shop too late in the day, or several times per week, or even per day. She laments their lack of foresight, their wastefulness, their inefficiency in tones scarcely different from that of middle-class social workers and home economics teachers. Only her solution to the problem has a slightly Social Democratic twist. She organizes the other functionaries of the cooperative— but not the housewives themselves—in support of a plan to make coop members order supplies a week in advance.[101]

As we have seen, the Social Democrats emphasized the possibility and necessity of mass consumption in Germany. Again and again they argued that industry should switch from the export of producers' goods to the domestic sale of consumer products in order to initiate the happy Fordist cycle of increased rationalization, increased production, lower prices, and increased consumption. Surprisingly, this consumption-oriented vision of rationalization found no echo in the literature on the rationalization of housework. Here was an area where one could talk concretely about how a German version of mass consumption would look, for everyone admitted that Germany could not hope to become a car culture like the United States; yet there was no speculation about the mass production and consumption of household appliances, no pleas for housing and household goods to become the key sources of demand. The Social Democratic vision of consumption remained abstract; that of household rationalization austere.

This refusal to promote household appliances was due, in part, to a sober recognition of the obstacles to such consumption. According to one survey, in Berlin in 1928 only 45 percent of homes had electricity; of those homes, 44 percent only had lights, 56 percent had electric irons, but only 28 percent had vacuum cleaners.[102] In the new fully electrified housing projects, those who could afford rents often had to scimp on household furnishings and appliances.[103] But the inability to imagine the role of the home in mass consumption had other roots as well. When Social Democrats traveled to America, they visited factories, not homes; they studied automobiles, not appliances; they spoke with men, not women. And their selective vision of America reinforced their understanding of gender relations at home. The household might be important to the economy as a whole, but it was not central, just as women were politically significant but in supporting and subordinate roles. Consumption was needed, but it was tacitly assumed that men would be the principal consumers. The Social Democrats remained trapped in the dualism of the public and private spheres, even as they abstractly argued for mass consumption that blurred those lines.

And what of the working-class women at whom this propaganda barrage was aimed? Did they find the message oppressive or liberating? Information is very scanty, but it suggests divided responses. In a collection of autobiographical essays, entitled *My Workday, My Weekend,* married women textile workers used the language of efficiency experts to describe how they performed housework. Morning and evening routines were planned minutely and carried out with precision and discipline, so that the double burden of waged work and housework could be mastered. While some of these women sounded extraordinarily harried and complained about the oppressive nature of rationalized work at home as well as in the factory, others seemed to take a certain pride in having organized their time and efforts so efficiently.[104] However problematic and austere rationalizing housework was, it may have made home life somewhat easier for the working-class wife and mother, especially if she was employed outside the home. In a period when no one discussed the possibility of either consumption or the socialization of any aspects of housework or childrearing, it would have been difficult for women to imagine other solutions.

The nonemployed housewife and mother was under somewhat different pressures to reform her performance of household tasks. Adolescent girls were educated in the new theory and practices, while older women were bombarded with lectures, pamphlets, and newspaper articles, no matter which newspaper they read. Given the precariousness of proletarian life, many housewives probably read all tips on saving time, money, and materials.[105] Those whose husbands worked in firms with company social and welfare policies were offered more information and advice and subjected to more active intervention and criticism, as were inhabitants of the new housing projects. A 1920s study of working-class families in Berlin found that most housewives were diligent and orderly, although it is unclear if they practiced the precepts of rationalized housework.[106]

Since working-class homes generally lacked electricity and wages were low in comparison to American ones, the proletarian household did not benefit from technology. Working-class women nevertheless may have purchased the new standardized pots and pans and simpler dishes, especially if their husbands were skilled workers. Such industries as ceramics targeted a proletarian audience by rationalizing production and mass-producing a variety of modern styles sold at moderate prices.[107]

Many working-class women probably did rationalize their performance of household tasks, but whether they embraced the ideology of household rationalization or only adopted some of its techniques is another question. Architects complained that working-class families would not or could not transform their lifestyles to fit the new modern housing. Despite the efforts of feminists, trade unionists, and architects at "education for the new living culture," workers clung to their nonfunctional furniture, old knick-knacks, and "irrational" habits. A recent study argues that the rationalized home seemed to many workers to be rooted in "austerity, in forced asceticism, in renunciation."[108] For workingmen, there seems to have been little reason for bringing the alienated world of work into what meager private life they had.

For working-class women, whether employed or not, the situation was more complex. In her recent study of Weimar housing projects, Adelheid von Saldern argues that, despite their complaints, the inhabitants adjusted to them and adopted the new ethos.[109] In her history of working-class women in Hamburg, Karen Hagemann delivers a more mixed verdict. Many of the women she interviewed disliked functional kitchens and furniture and found most rationalization precepts too expensive to adopt. Others, however, who were part of the young, skilled elite of the working-class, regarded the new housing and the rationalization of home and family as "the embodiment of modernity and social progress."[110] For many, household rationalization may have been both alienating and appealing. It gave women a measure of control over their home and world, even if this was achieved at the price of a mechanical self-control. It provided one way to be modern, even if that meant the modern management of a traditionally defined home and family. It enabled them to be new women, even if the rationalized housewife conveyed little of the glamour usually associated with that term.

Epilogue

"Let's think about all the exaggerated hopes and illusions that the slogan of rationalization stirred up! And what remains on close inspection? Basically, precious little. . . ."[1] This pessimistic assessment, written by the doctoral student W. Löchner in 1930, was widely shared in industrial, engineering, and labor movement circles once the Depression began. From 1929 on, Social Democratic politicians and trade union leaders spoke with growing anger about false capitalist rationalization, while the rank and file equated rationalization with the unemployment from which unprecedented numbers suffered. Adopting a predictably different line, industrialists and right-wing engineers complained about over-Americanization, forced on business by labor's ostensibly exorbitant demands. But neither the formerly enthusiastic proponents of rationalization, nor the National Socialists who were to benefit from its failure, repudiated all the assumptions, expectations, and policies associated with the rationalization movement of the 1920s. Abandoning their enthusiasm for economic Americanism, they sought to cloak rationalization in new ideological guises and combine its discrete parts in new ways.

The Depression in Germany had its roots in the incomplete recovery of the mid- and late 1920s, as well as in the destabilizing effects of rationalization itself. As we saw, rationalization increased productivity without expanding markets at home or abroad. Prices held steady as did wages, due to cartelization and state arbitration, but growth was slow, profits were low, and structural and cyclical unemployment was high. Prosperity was limited, stabilization relative, and capital and labor each delivered running critiques of the inadequacies of rationalization in its current form.

227

With the American stock market crash in 1929 and the subsequent withdrawal of American loans, what stability and prosperity there were quickly evaporated. America was suddenly exacerbating Germany's problems instead of providing solutions. German production dropped gradually in 1929 and precipitously thereafter. By 1932 industry in general was operating at only 58 percent of its 1928 level, while the figure for heavy industry was a meager 47 percent. Unemployment rose from 8.5 percent in 1929 to 14 percent in 1930 and 21.9 percent in 1931. A year later 5.6 million workers, or nearly 30 percent of the employed and over 43 percent of all trade union members, were out of work. Foreign trade continued to shrink as the crisis spread and tariff barriers were raised.[2] America, so admired even by those who did not think Germany could emulate it, had proven to be as vulnerable to crisis as the weaker and more backward European countries. Its much vaunted automobile industry was operating at only one-fifth capacity in 1932, and even Ford was slashing wages and firing workers.[3] But if most Germans no longer admired Americanism, they were still convinced that some form of rationalization, suited to German conditions, should be implemented by those who had learned the appropriate lessons from the Depression.

In the mid- and late 1920s, industrialists had been critical of Fordism and hesitant about emulating Americanism. They had insisted that Germany avoid sophisticated technology, cut wages and state social programs, and invest in men rather than machines. Although they complained obsessively about disappointing profits and high state expenditures, they had not anticipated a catastrophic crisis at home or in America. Indeed, many evinced a cautious optimism about the gradual evolution of a distinctly German version of rationalization.[4]

Once the Depression hit, however, it was seen as a confirmation of their earlier critique. As a 1932 article in the Gutehoffnungshütte *Werkszeitung* argued, Germany's problems were not caused by rationalization, if one defined that as the careful planning of work. Rather, they were a result of an overinvestment in technology, a foolish imitation of America. As proof of the wrongheaded pace and character of rationalization, the author cited "one large firm, [where] assembly lines were built, but they were only operated when the board of directors was visiting."[5] Dr. Hoffman, sent to America by the Bergbau Verein in the depths of the Depression, insisted, as had earlier travelers, that Ruhr mines could learn little from American technology and organization.[6] The anger and frustration of industrialists is captured in remarks by Ernst Poensgen, an iron and steel industrialist and head of the Steel Association, who in a 1931 conversation with a colleague exclaimed in exasperation, "Don't mention science to me! We've been pumped full with science; scientific technology, scientific management, scientific market research, scientific accountancy, and so on and so on. And where has all this science brought us?"[7]

Although industrialists had rhetorically rejected demands for rapid rationalization throughout the late 1920s, they had acceded to them nonetheless. According to the Association of German Employers' Associations, wages and social costs had "forced" industry to rationalize, even though it lacked the necessary capital and such rationalization "overburdened" the economy by straining capital markets, creating excess capacity, and leading to increased unemployment and unemployment insurance payments.[8] Heavy industry did not consider itself responsible for overcapacity and misguided investment—charges which the parliamentary Enquete Ausschuss had made and which the Depression seemed to verify. After all, spokesmen for industry pointed out, no one accused American industry of overinvestment or excess rationalization just because of a cyclical crisis. It was not industrial miscalculation but union greed and the state's regulation of hours and wages that had forced inappropriately rapid modernization.[9] The technical and organizational improvements that had been implemented had not offset the burdens of reparations, wages, taxes, and social policy.[10] The result was a devastating crisis from which workers suffered, as well as capitalists.[11] In short, complained an industry analyst in 1931, "Rationalization lost its reasonable purpose of making firms competitive."[12]

Dinta echoed these arguments. The "rationalization fanaticism" and wage policies of Social Democracy had forced German industry to adopt American models, to move toward highly mechanized mass production. As the Depression made clear, this "flight into machines" had to be reversed. The "political burdens" on production, that is, taxes, wages, and state social policy, had to be lessened, and industry had to promote "quality work" and invest in training "quality workers." Dinta's program of *Menschenführung* was more essential than ever, argued Karl Arnhold.[13]

Throughout the mid- and late 1920s leading Social Democratic politicians and trade unionists had been the most enthusiastic proponents of Americanism and Fordism. They had proposed a rationalization scenario in which high wages would spur mass consumption and promote organizational and technological transformations, which would increase productivity, raise profits, and allow both further wage increases and expanded social policy. Labor and capital, producers and consumers were to benefit from such an emulation of Fordism, which would stabilize capitalism in the short run, even as it pushed the economy and society slowly but inexorably in the direction of socialism.

The reality of German rationalization diverged from the Social Democrats' vision on almost every count, and with the Depression, the American model on which it was based looked tarnished indeed. Social Democrats had painted a rosy picture of American labor, focusing only on high wages and short hours. Yet, as was noted in a 1932 article in *Die Gesellschaft* linking technical progress and unemployment, "The most astonishing part of the American economic miracle, and the one least noticed by our [German] travelers to America, was the existence of unemployment reaching into the millions in the last years of prosperity."[14] Another left-wing commentator, long critical of "the America legend," noted smugly that "anxiety about America" was over now that the United States was experiencing unemploy

ment, bankruptcies, and overproduction: "The belief that the world is entering an American era, just as there was once a Babylonian, Egyptian or Roman
one, is finished."[15]

But Social Democrats distanced themselves from Americanism without abandoning their faith in rationalization, and this was reflected clearly
in their analyses of the Depression. All Social Democrats agreed that the
fundamental cause of the Depression was the malfunctioning of the capitalist system. A 1931 SPD pamphlet on *The Spectre of Unemployment*, for
example, described Weimar rationalization as the thoroughgoing introduction of Fordism, Taylorism, and standardization, resulting in the ruthless
replacement of men by machines—a description with which industrialists
would have agreed. This disasterous outcome resulted not from labor's wage
policy, but from capital's profit mania. In response to a shortage of investment funds in the 1920s, industry modernized so that its capital could turn
over as quickly as possible. In response to foreign competition and "the
overindustrialization of the world," it cheapened goods by introducing technology and firing workers. Yet for all their criticism of capitalist rationalization, many Social Democrats probably shared Rudolf Hilferding's unfounded belief that without earlier rationalization, the German economic
crisis would have been still worse.[16]

Some Social Democrats argued that it was industry's insistence on modernizing production without assuring consumption that limited the success
of rationalization in the 1920s and led to crisis thereafter. Productive capacity could not be utilized because demand was inadequate, and demand was
inadequate because wages were too low and prices too high. Soaring unemployment reflected capital's failure to understand the form rationalization
must take in an advanced industrial economy.[17] Or as the Christian Metalworkers' Union warned, "one can only adopt Ford's assembly line without damage if one is willing to go along with his price and wage policies."[18]
Not surprisingly, men like Fritz Tarnow, who had been to America and
were most infatuated with the consumer aspects of Fordism, argued this
most strongly.

Others focused on the absence of planning.[19] According to the Austrian Socialist Otto Bauer, whose 1931 work *Rationalization/Failed Rationalization* was widely read and applauded in late Weimar, Fordism was no
longer seen as the answer to the problems of a modern economy.[20] The
rationalization movement of the late 1920s had failed because it was self-
ishly capitalist; its aim was to increase the profits of the individual firm,
not the efficiency of society. It was disasterously costly not only to workers, but to industry as well. Yet technical and organizational rationalization had to proceed, and indeed were still proceeding. Thus, concluded
Bauer and his German Social Democratic supporters, "The rationalization
of the firm demands the rationalization of the social order. The methodical
application of science to increase productivity would thereby be transformed
from a source of economic crisis and unemployment to a means of raising

the standard of living and lightening the burden of work."[21] How this was to be achieved was left unspecified.

Underlying all these arguments was the Social Democrats' unwillingness to call into question rationalization as a set of principles and assumptions about efficiency and uniformity, productivism and modern work.[22] The Depression made them pessimistic about the immediate realization of their vision of a rationalized modernity, but they remained certain that the economy and society were heading in that direction. The Social Democrats continued to endorse a process of rationalization they could not control and to rely on a state government they did not dominate, thereby displaying their ongoing inability to comprehend the reality of capitalist rationalization and the power relations behind it. They focused on what capital should do, not what the working class could do. Their criticisms of Weimar rationalization, however accurate, testified to their political powerlessness and passivity.

For Communist commentators the Depression seemed to offer irrefutable confirmation of their critique of capitalist rationalization. Even Fordist America had fallen victim to the laws of capitalist crisis, proving that Tarnow's optimistic rationalization scenario was utopian.[23] The principal new element in Communist commentaries was the assertion that Social Democratic support of capitalist rationalization was at once cause and effect of the emergence of social fascism for which both the SPD and trade unions were ostensibly responsible.[24]

The Depression thus altered neither the basic commitment of industrialists, engineers, and trade union leaders to rationalization, nor their quite different understandings of how it should proceed. Each participant in the ongoing dispute about economic modernization clung yet more tenaciously to the positions first adopted in the mid-1920s. Those initial arguments shaped their analysis of the crisis, and the facts of the crisis provided evidence to bolster the preferred rationalization scenarios.

Only the rank and file of the labor movement, who had suffered the structural and cyclical unemployment of the rationalization years and then the yet worse unemployment of the Depression, altered its views dramatically. Enthusiasm about Americanism, positive attitudes toward technology, and cautious optimism about restructuring evaporated. Movement leaders could develop elaborate explanations for why investment in production resulted in increased unemployment, but workers on the shop floor had a simple answer—rationalization.[25] The hostility with which the minority had viewed rationalization since the mid-1920s became the prevalent attitude. Anxiety about employment and skills, which had coexisted with expectations about individual and societal improvement, came to dominate all else.

If the Depression did not destroy the belief in the necessity and inevitability of rationalization, it did severely limit its ideological appeal. In the mid-1920s rationalization had been an almost magical term that encapsulated the far-reaching hopes and ill-defined but ambitious expectations of diverse classes, organizations, and individuals. After 1930 it became a sober economic concept, discussed in narrowly technical terms. Germans no longer saw rationalization as a panacea for their country's renewed economic problems, but rather, at most, as a bundle of technical and managerial measures promising modest, incremental benefits. The German infatuation with Fordism was over; Americanism did not provide an appealing model of modernity, and utopian aspirations could no longer be expressed in the language of rationalization. Solutions to society's problems would henceforth be sought in the political, not the economic sphere.

Of equal importance, the Depression severely constrained the actual process of rationalization. Operating with a drastically reduced budget, the RKW continued to establish norms and investigate the social effects of rationalization, even as it admitted that little would be implemented in the present.[26] Individual firms reduced their rationalization activities but did not cease them entirely, for some were engaged in multiyear programs that would only yield benefits if completed, while others saw further rationalization as a means to cut costs and workers and thereby survive the Depression.[27] Dinta continued the programs established in the late 1920s but could not extend them.[28]

Although rationalization slowed markedly, its detrimental effects on workers increased. Social Democrats were unable to defend wages or cushion unemployment as they had in the late 1920s, for the unemployment insurance system collapsed under the weight of millions of jobless workers. In the early 1930s the Social Democrats urged work sharing, shorter hours, and lower prices.[29] More daring trade unionists, recognizing the desperateness of the situation, went beyond such traditional reforms to advocate public works and state countercyclical measures.[30] Still others insisted that the overthrow of capitalism offered the only solution. But neither the reformist majority nor the proto-Keynesian and revolutionary minorities were able to implement their proposals.

The Nazis were the dual beneficiaries of the rationalization movement. On the one hand, they were able to come to power in part because rationalization failed to modernize and stabilize the economy and deliver on its promise of lessening, if not eliminating, class conflict through prosperity. They were aided by the paralysis and demoralization of the workers' movement, to which rationalization in no small measure contributed.[31] On the other hand, the Nazis adopted many of the ideas and policies of the rationalization movement, especially in the area of company management. Their antimodern rhetoric masked distinctly modern and rationalized forms of work organization, intensification, and wage policies.[32] If the Nazi economy as a whole, like the Nazi state, became increasingly irrational and unrationalized in the late 1930s and during World War II, individual firms nonetheless pursued aspects of the 1920s program of modernization, unconstrained by organized labor or a costly welfare state.

Hitler retained his enthusaism for Fordism. In 1934 he met with Prince Louis Ferdinand of Prussia, a grandson of the Kaiser, who was employed by Henry Ford as a "free lance roadman" in various countries. Although Hitler was offended that Ford had never tried to meet him, he praised Ford and stated his intentions to motorize Germany.[33] In 1936 Hitler visited the Ford exhibit at the Berlin automobile show, and a year later he awarded Ford the Grand Cross of the German Iron Eagle.[34]

Nazi attitudes toward Americanism were more divided. Admiration and antagonism, curiosity and condemnation coexisted uneasily. Through-out the 1930s evidence of the ongoing fascination with Americanism was evident in the prevalence of films from America, the publication of books about America, and Nazi encouragement of trips to America to study its economic accomplishments. (In 1936, for example, Ferdinand Porsche was sent to Detroit to study Ford and GM before designing the Volkswagen.) In the tradition of German reactionary modernists, Nazi ideologues criti-cized the American economic model for its materialism, advocating instead a rationalization imbued with the proper *Geist*. Technology as an abstract concept was regarded as a curse, even as individual technological accom-plishments were a source of fascination and pride to both Nazis and the population at large.[35]

Through the People's Radio and the Volkswagen, Hitler endorsed the idea of new forms of mass consumption, even though they were dissociated from Americanism and a high-wage policy; in the case of the Volkswagen, the idea never reached the production stage. Militarism, not mass consump-tion, was the Nazis' preferred solution to the problem of demand for the expanded productive capacity of industries that were rationalized during Weimar and those restructured after 1933.[36] Nonetheless, consumption did expand in the mid- and late 1930s, and the regime tolerated, even if it did not actively encourage, an escape into an ostensibly depoliticized world of work and consumption.[37] Elements of Americanism were inserted discretely but firmly into Nazi society, where they coexisted with distinctly Nazi inno-vations—consumption and concentration camps, technological rationaliza-tion and racial annihilation.

The ideology and practice of household rationalization developed in the 1920s proved entirely compatible with National Socialism. Hitler and organizations such as the Nazi Labor Front wanted the family to serve the interests of the state and the party, rather than simply those of the economy, and the idea of the rationalized household could be instrumentalized for that political end as easily as it had been for others. The Home Economics Group of the RKW continued to publish its educational literature after Hitler came to power; its bestseller in the late 1930s was *The Planned Household*, a pam-phlet "which spoke with particular forcefulness about the spiritual prepa-ration and technical management of the household enterprise."[38] The social programs of a Baden textile firm promoted the image of a housewife "who thinks and manages in a modern and rational way, but also guarantees the

traditional family ideology and *völkische Gemeinschaftsideologie.*"[39] The
housewife was to achieve this mixture of tradition and modernity, family
values and fascism, by rationalizing her work and life, with only limited aid
from new technology and mass consumption.

Dinta, which had only reluctantly come to terms with Weimar democracy and industrial relations, did particularly well under National Socialism. Dinta preferred a world of leaders and followers rather than one of
political and economic equals; a world of *Gemeinschaft* rather than *Gesellschaft*; a world of company social policy rather than state welfare. It preferred a world in which hours and wages would be set according to the needs
of individual firms and the productivity of individual workers; a world
without trade unions. This the Nazis created. Dinta rhetoric resonated with
that of the Nazis. Dinta spoke a language of separate spheres and essential
biological differences between men and women, of mothers who devoted
themselves to husbands and children, and of men who, imbued with the
elan of individual aspiration and military camaraderie, nobly and joyfully
fought the battle of production. For many, Dinta provided the bridge which
carried them effortlessly from Weimar to National Socialism.

Dinta not only preferred the world the Nazis made; it helped create it.
The 1934 Law for the Ordering of National Labor, for example, addressed
the centrality of the firm, the need for hierarchy and productivity, and the
importance of community in ways first developed by Dinta and other
Weimar proponents of social rationalization.[40] The Nazis stressed the need
for leadership in the firm and described their own activity as *Menschenführung.*[41] Throughout much of the 1930s Dinta ran the Nazi programs for
worker education. Without any significant changes in its program or personnel, Dinta joined the Labor Front in 1933 and went on to become the
Office for Vocational Education and Firm Leadership. Karl Arnhold sought
to demarcate the German science of work sharply from American rationalization and to search for "a German totality."[42] This inaugurated a new phase
of Dinta's development, he claimed, in which the firm and the engineers
were linked directly to larger national goals.[43] Dinta proudly announced this
transformation in publications in which the swastika was superimposed on
the Dinta logo. Dinta company newspapers continued to publish, dropping
their self-proclaimed political neutrality and embracing Nazi ideology.[44]

By late 1936 Dinta had vast sums of money at its disposal and was running 400 apprenticeship training workshops while another 150 were in preparation. The various Dinta training schools and programs employed 25,000
teachers and had taught 2.5 million workers.[45] And Arnhold received
an honorary doctorate. By the late 1930s, however, Dinta was eclipsed by
more sophisticated Labor Front programs, such as Beauty of Work.[46] During
World War II German workers continued to receive the dubious benefits of
rationalized management, company social policy, and the German science of
work, while the millions of foreign workers brought to Germany, many
of them as slave laborers, were subject to ruthless economic and racial exploitation that dispensed with any pretext of modernity and rationalization.[47]

After World War II company social policy retained many of the features developed in the 1920s and continued in the Third Reich—apprenticeship training workshops, company newspapers, and medical and social programs for workers' families—but Dinta's vision of the new male worker and the new working-class family, with its militaristic overtones and disapproval of consumption and mobility, became outmoded. Dinta resurfaced as the Society for Work Pedagogy, agitating on the margins of society for a conservative, distinctly German version of rationalization. In 1960 the German Federal Republic awarded Arnhold a Federal Service Cross, first class, for his service to the German economy.[48]

An investigation of how production and consumption, work and gender were debated and restructured after 1945 in East and West Germany is beyond the scope of this work. It should be noted, however, that the problems faced by Weimar proponents of rationalization were to resurface after 1945, as was the propensity to see America as a model. The story of Karl Arnhold and Dinta suggest just how complex the threads of continuity and discontinuity were from Weimar through National Socialism and on into the post–World War II era. Between the mid-1920s and the late 1950s work and the working class were fundamentally restructured, the bases of traditional workers' cultures were eroded, and the essential features of modern factory organization and technology, as well as of managerial practice and company social policy, were developed. The rationalization movement of the 1920s initiated this process of far-reaching transformation; it pioneered many specific institutions and measures and provided much of the language in which they were debated. It provided the problematic vision of modernity that was realized between the 1950s and the 1970s and is only now being called into question.

Notes

Abbreviations

ADGB	Allgemeiner deutscher Gewerkschaftsbund (General Confederation of German Trade Unions)
ASWSP	*Archiv für Sozialwissenschaft und Sozialpolitik*
BA	Bundes Archiv (National Archives)
BRZ	*Betriebsräte Zeitschrift des deutschen Metallarbeiterverbandes* (Factory Councils Journal of the German Metalworkers' Union)
BBA	Bergbau Archiv (Mining Archives)
BBV	Bergbau Verein (Mining Association)
Dinta	Deutsches Institut für Technische Arbeitsschulung (German Institute for Technical Labor Training)
DMV	Deutscher Metallarbeiter Verband (German Metalworkers' Union)
GHH	Historisches Archiv der Gutehoffnungschütte (Gutehoffnungschütte Historical Archives)
MM	Mannesmann Archiv (Mannesmann Archives)
RDI	Reichsverband der deutschen Industrie (National Association of German Industry)
RGI	*Rote Gewerkschafts Internationale* (Red Trade Union International)
RKW	Reichskuratorium für Wirtschaftlichkeit (National Productivity Board)
SAA	Siemens Archiv Akte (Siemens Archival Documents)
VDA	Vereinigung der Deutschen Arbeitgeberverbände (Association of German Employers' Organizations
VDI	Verein Deutscher Ingenieure (Association of German Engineers)
WWA	Westfalisches Wirtschaftsarchiv

1. Introduction

1. Carl Köttgen, *Das wirtschaftliche Amerika* (Berlin, 1925).

2. There is no general bibliography of the German literature on America. For a partial list, see Peter Berg, *Deutschland und Amerika, 1918–1929. Über das deutsche Amerikabild der zwanziger Jahre* (Lübeck and Hamburg, 1963).

3. *Der Arbeitgeber*, organ of the main employers' association, the Vereinigung

der Deutschen Arbeitgeberverbände, and *Technik und Wirtschaft,* the business-oriented publication of the Verein Deutscher Ingenieure, are two of the most important in this regard.

4. See for example, the *Bosch Zünder* and the *Siemens Mitteilungen.*

5. Jakob Walcher, *Ford oder Marx. Die praktische Lösung der sozialen Frage* (Berlin, 1925).

6. DMV, *Ford, seine Ideen und Arbeitsmethoden. Vortrag mit über 60 farbigen Lichtbildern* (Stuttgart, 1928).

7. *Ford und Wir,* ed. Soziales Museum Frankfurt am. Main (Berlin, 1926).

8. Beeke Sell Tower, *Envisioning America: Prints, Drawings and Photographs by George Grosz and His Contemporaries, 1915–1933* (Cambridge, Mass., 1990), 13–14. For the history of German attitudes toward America, see *America and the Germans: An Assessment of a Three-Hundred-Year History,* ed. Frank Trommler and Joseph McVeigh, 2 vols. (Philadelphia, 1985).

9. For an introduction to the vast literature on this theme, see the study by Tower. See also John Willett, *Art and Politics in the Weimar Period: The New Sobriety, 1917–1933* (New York, 1978).

10. For analyses of these, see David Abraham, *The Collapse of the Weimar Republic* (New York, 1986); Charles Maier, *Recasting Bourgeois Europe* (Princeton, N.J., 1975); and Bernd Weisbrod, *Schwerindustrie in der Weimarer Republik* (Wuppertal, 1978).

11. Probably the most widely read contemporary American assessment of the Japanese economy is Ezra F. Vogel, *Japan as Number 1: Lessons for America* (New York, 1985). For a more scholarly assessment, see Rodney Clark, *The Japanese Company* (New Haven, Conn., 1979). For a critical analysis of the Japanese automobile industry, see Knuth Dohse, Ulrich Jürgens, and Thomas Malsch, "From 'Fordism' to 'Toyotism'? The Social Organization of the Labor Process in the Japanese Automobile Industry," *Politics & Society* 14:2 (1985): 113–46.

12. Modest Rubinstein, "Die kapitalistische Rationalisierung," *Unter dem Banner des Marxismus* 3:4 (1929): 550.

13. For a discussion of Weber and rationalization, see Derek Sayer, *Capitalism and Modernity: An Excursus on Marx and Weber* (London, 1991), 92–133. Weber's own reflections on the theme appear throughout his writings on economy, authority, and bureaucracy. See Max Weber, *The Theory of Social and Economic Organization* (New York, 1964) and *From Max Weber,* ed. Hans Gerth and C. Wright Mills (New York, 1968), 196–244, 253–64.

14. For the general debate on rationalization, see Robert Brady, "The Meaning of Rationalization: An Analysis of the Literature," *Quarterly Journal of Economics* 46 (May 1932): 526–40; Robert Brady, *The Rationalization Movement in German Industry,* 2nd ed. (New York, 1974); Peter Hinrichs and Lothar Peters, *Industrielle Friede? Arbeitswissenschaft, Rationalisierung und Arbeiterbewegung in der Weimarer Republik* (Cologne, 1976); Walter Meakin, *The New Industrial Revolution* (New York, 1928); Mary Nolan, "The Infatuation with Fordism: Social Democracy and Rationalization in Weimar Germany," in *The Crisis of Social Democracy in Interwar Europe,* ed. Helmut Gruber and Walter Maderthaner (Frankfurt, 1988), 151–84; Detlev Peukert, *The Weimar Republic: The Crisis of Classical Modernity* (New York, 1992), 107–28; Gunnar Stollberg, *Die Rationalisierungsdebatte, 1908–1933. Freie Gewerkschaften Zwischen Mitwirkung und Gegenwehr* (Frankfurt, 1981).

15. Arthur Holitscher, *Wiedersehen mit Amerika. Die Verwandlung der USA* (Berlin, 1930), 11.

16. Tower, 14.

17. Henry Ford, *My Life and Work* (New York, 1922). The book was translated into German in 1923.

18. Berg, 8.

19. Alice Salomon, *Kultur im Werden, Amerikanische Reiseeindrücke* (Berlin, 1924), 7–8.

20. Jeffrey Herf, *Reactionary Modernism: Technology, Culture and Politics in Weimar and the Third Reich* (Cambridge, Eng., 1984).

21. Max Horkheimer and Theodor W. Adorno, *Dialectic of Enlightenment* (New York, 1972).

22. For a discussion of some of the forms this middle ground assumed in the Americanism debates, see Peukert, 178–90.

23. Hans A. Joachim, "Romane aus Amerika," *Die neue Rundschau* 41 (September 1930): 397–98. Cited in Anton Kaes, "Mass Culture and Modernity: Notes Toward a Social History of Early American and German Cinema," in *America and the Germans*, vol. 2, 323.

24. I am indebted to Michael Ermarth for this formulation, which he suggested in a discussion at the conference on "America/Weimar: Americanism in the Germany of the Twenties," held in Boston in March 1990.

25. For an exploration of American intentions and methods, see Emily S. Rosenberg, *Spreading the American Dream: American Economic and Cultural Expansion, 1890–1945* (New York, 1982).

26. For examples of unequivocally critical judgments, see Stollberg; Peter Hinrichs, *Um die Seele des Arbeiters. Arbeitspsychologie, Industrie- und Betriebssoziologie in Deutschland* (Cologne, 1981).

2. Journeys to America

1. Carl Legien, *Aus Amerikas Arbeiterbewegung* (Berlin, 1914).

2. Arthur Holitscher, *Amerika Heute und Morgen. Reiseerlebnisse* (Berlin, 1912).

3. Erwin Rosen, *Der deutsche Lausbub in Amerika* (Stuttgart, 1913).

4. See editor's introduction to Werner Sombart, *Why Is There No Socialism in the United States?* (London, 1976). The German original was published in 1906.

5. Hugo Münsterberg, *Die Amerikaner* (Berlin, 1904). Published in English as *The Americans* (New York, 1904).

6. Paul Riebensahm, *Der Zug nach U.S.A. Gedanken nach einer Amerika-Reise 1924* (Berlin, 1925), 3.

7. Historisches Archiv Friedrich Krupp GmbH (referred to hereafter as Krupp Archiv), FAH IV E 1186. Reusch letter to Krupp, July 23, 1926.

8. See, for example, Bernhard Goldschmidt, *Wissenswertes aus Wirtschafts- und Sozialpolitik der Vereinigten Staaten*, Schriften der Vereinigung der Deutschen Arbeitgeberverbände, 13 (1925). Goldschmidt's pamphlet was originally presented as a talk to the annual convention of the Employers' Association of the Chemical Industry. See also Valentin Litz, *Sozialpolitische Reiseeindrücke in den Vereinigten Staaten*, Schriften der VDA 11 (1925). Originally given as a talk to the Association of Berlin Metal Industrialists.

9. Fritz Tänzler, *Aus dem Arbeitsleben Amerikas. Arbeitsverhältnisse, Arbeitsmethoden und Sozialpolitik in den Vereinigten Staaten von Amerika* (Berlin, 1927).

10. Hermann Bleibtreu, "Die Entwicklung der Vereinigten Staaten," in *Technik*

und Wirtschaft 16:6 (June 1923): 121–30. This was also presented as a talk to the National Coal Council.

11. Paul Rieppel, *Ford-Betriebe und Ford-Methoden* (Munich/Berlin, 1925.)

12. Mannesmann Archiv (referred to hereafter as MM) P 4 25 49, Phoenix, Amerikaberichte; R 4 4100, deutsche Rohrenwerke, Amerikareise, letter from Röhren-Verband to Director Traut of Vereinigte Stahlwerk, December 2, 1926.

13. Historisches Archiv der Gutehoffnungshütte (referred to hereafter as GHH), 4020/7. Hüttenwerke, Reisebericht Lilge über die Besichtigung amerikanischer Berg- und Hüttenwerke im Frühjahr 1927. Many of the drawings were done from memory at night. Gutehoffnungshütte also sent Dr. Lauster, an engineer with MAN, and T. E. Suess, from the Schwäbische Hüttenwerke, both subsidiaries of Gutehoffnungshütte. GHH 4089/0 and 4089/1.

14. Otto Moog, *Drüben steht Amerika. Gedanken nach einer Ingenieurreise durch die Vereinigten Staaten* (Braunschweig/Berlin/Hamburg, 1927).

15. For an evaluation of Schlesinger's life and work, see Hans Ebert and Karin Hausen, "Georg Schlesinger und die Rationalisierungsbewegung in Deutschland," in *Wissenschaft und Gesellschaft*, Vol. 1 (Berlin, 1979), 315–34.

16. Friedrich Aereboe, *Wirtschaft und Kultur in den Vereinigten Staaten von Nord Amerika* (Berlin, 1930).

17. Julius Hirsch, *Das Amerikanische Wirtschaftswunder*, (Berlin, 1926). For information on his career, see Berg, 107.

18. Dr. G. Faldix, *Henry Ford als Wirtschaftspolitiker* (Munich, 1925).

19. Aereboe, 39; and *Bosch Zünder*, November 30, 1929, 246.

20. Moritz J. Bonn, *Wandering Scholar* (New York, 1948), 169–85, 200–300, and *Geld und Geist. Vom Wesen und Werden der amerikanischen Welt* (Berlin, 1927), 10–11.

21. Arthur Feiler, *America Seen Through German Eyes* (New York, 1928).

22. Irene Witte, *Heim und Technik in Amerika* (Berlin, 1928).

23. Anton Erkelenz, *Amerika von heute. Briefe von einer Reise* (Berlin, 1927). Landesarchiv Berlin, Nachlass Gustav Böss, Rep 200, Acc 2527, 29–30.

24. Arthur Holitscher, *Wiedersehen mit Amerika. Die Verwandlung der USA* (Berlin, 1930). Unfortunately, Holitscher's informative autobiography *Lebensgeschichte eines Rebellen*, (Berlin, 1924) covers only his prewar years in Bohemian Munich and Paris.

25. ADGB, *Amerikareise deutscher Gewerkschaftsführer* (Berlin, 1926).

26. Toni Sender, *The Autobiography of a German Rebel* (New York, 1939): 252–56.

27. BRZ 8:9 (April 30, 1927).

28. Charlotte Lütkens, *Staat und Gesellschaft in Amerika. Zur Soziologie des amerikanischen Kapitalismus* (Tübingen, 1929); "Neue Amerikabücher," *ASWSP 57* (1927): 769–802; "Europäer und Amerikaner über Amerika," *ASWSP 62* (1929): 615–30.

29. *Metallarbeiter-Zeitung*, December 20, 1924; January 3, 1925; March 29, 1926; December 25, 1926; February 5, 1927; May 14 and 28, 1927; December 3, 1927; December 12, 1928; February 16, 1929; March 23, 1929; May 24, 1930; January 24, 1931. Fritz Kummer, *Eines Arbeiters Weltreise*, 2nd ed. (Leipzig, 1986).

30. *Bergarbeiter Zeitung*, March 17 and 24, 1928; August 4, 1928.

31. *Bosch-Zünder*, July 20, 1924; August 30, 1927 and September 30, 1927; January 31, 1928.

32. Hermann Lufft, "Die geistige Krise der deutschen sozialdemokratischen Bewegung im Amerikanischen Spiegel," *Deutsche Arbeit* 11:7 (July 1926): 352–63. Lufft also wrote a biography of Samuel Gompers. See also Edmund Kleinschmitt, "Der amerikanische Geist," *Deutsche Arbeit* 10:10 (October 1925): 518–25. Kleinschmitt,

"Gegen den Wirtschaftspessimismus! Ergebnisse einer gewerkschaftlichen Studien-reise," *Der Kaufmann in Wirtschaft und Recht* 4:9 (September 1925): 405–16. Found in Siemens-Archiv-Akten (referred to hereafter as SAA), 11/Lf 395 Köttgen.

33. Alexander Friedrich, *Henry Ford. Der König der Autos und der Herrscher über die Seelen* (Berlin, 1924).

34. Friedrich von Gottl-Ottlilienfeld, *Fordismus? Paraphrasen über das Verhältnis von Wirtschaft und Technischer Vernunft bei Henry Ford und Frederick W. Taylor* (Jena, 1924), 11.

35. See Chapter 4 for a fuller discussion.

36. See Chapter 9 for a fuller discussion.

37. Lujo Brentano, "Amerika-Europa," *Die Gesellschaft* 9 (1926): 193.

38. Bergbau Archiv (referred to hereafter as BBA) 16/508. BBV, Instruk-tionsreisen ausserhalb des Ruhrbezirks, 1927–37.

39. GHH, 40420/50, Reiseberichte 1922–26; 40420/51 Reiseberichte, 1927–30.

40. Kendall Bailes, *Technology and Society under Lenin and Stalin* (Princeton, N.J., 1978), 44–53.

41. André Siegfried, *America Comes of Age: A French Analysis* (New York, 1927). The book was written at the request of the Musée Social for its series on postwar conditions in major countries.

42. Hyacinthe Dubreuil, *Robots or Men? A French Workman's Experience in American Industry* (New York and London, 1930). This is the authorized English trans-lation, sponsored by the Taylor Society.

43. Richard F. Kuisel, *Capitalism and the State in Modern France: Renovation and Economic Management in the Twentieth Century* (Cambridge, Eng., 1981), 77–92; quoted on p. 89. See also Patrick Friedenson, "Unternehmenspolitik, Rationalisierung und Arbeiterschaft. Französische Erfahrungen im internationalen Vergleich, 1900 bis 1929," in *Recht und Entwicklung der Grossunternehmen im 19. und frühen 20. Jahrhundert*, ed. Norbert Horn and Jürgen Kocka (Göttingen, 1979), 428–50.

44. Charles Maier, "Between Taylorism and Technocracy: European Ideologies and the Vision of Industrial Productivity in the 1920s," *Journal of Contemporary History* 5:2 (1970): 27–61. For the European discussion and implementation of scien-tific management in the early 1920s, see Paul Devinat, *Scientific Management in Europe*, ILO, Studies and Reports, Series B., 17. (Geneva, 1927).

45. Antonio Gramsci, "Americanism and Fordism," *Prison Notebooks* (New York, 1971), 279–318.

46. "Krise oder Abstieg?" *Magazin der Wirtschaft*," 1:20 (June 25, 1925): 707.

47. Dietmar Petzina, "Grundriss der deutschen Wirtschaftsgeschichte, 1918 bis 1945," in *Deutsche Geschichte seit dem Ersten Weltkrieg*, Vol. 2 (Stuttgart, 1973), 665–742, provides the best overview of the Weimar economy.

48. See Chapter 7 for a fuller discussion.

49. For the economics and politics of the inflation, see Charles Maier, *Recasting Bourgeois Europe* (Princeton, N.J., 1975), 233–304, 356–86, and *Die deutsche Inflation: Eine Zwischenbilanz. Beiträge zu Inflation und Wiederaufbau in Deutschland und Europa 1914–1924*, ed. Gerald Feldman (Berlin, 1982).

50. Petzina, 723–26; Gilbert Ziebura, *World Economy and World Politics, 1924–1931* (Oxford, 1990), 29–76.

51. The Dawes Plan did not set a final total sum for reparations, but Germany was to pay 1 billion marks annually from 1924 until 1927 and 1.5 billion thereafter.

52. Alfred Rühl, *Vom Wirtschaftsgeist in Amerika* (Leipzig, 1927), vii.

53. Erwin Rosen (pseudonym for Edwin Carlé), *Amerikaner* (Leipzig, 1920). This

short and inexpensive tract was aimed at a popular audience. For an account written soon after the war by a visitor who was impressed with U.S. production but not over-awed by its economic power, see the report of Bosch Director Hugo Borst in *Bosch Zünder*, October 31, 1921. For the immediate postwar reactions to Woodrow Wilson's proposals and America's political role, see Berg, 9–96.

54. Rühl, vii.

55. Siegfried Hartmann, "Amerikasucht," *Deutsche Allgemeine Zeitung*, August 13, 1925. From SAA 11/Lf 121 Köttgen.

56. Georg Freitag, "Das Haus Siemens und das RKW," *Rationalisierung* 14:1 (November 1963): 247–52. In SSA 61/Lf 109 Köttgen.

57. MM R 4 20 30 and R 4 41 03, deutsche Röhrenwerke, Paul Inden's investigation of the Fretz Moon pipe making procedure; P 4 25 49, Phoenix, 1927 Alvermann lecture on his 1925 trip.

58. Krupp Archiv, FAH IV E 1186, letter from Reusch to Krupp, July 23, 1926.

59. Köttgen, iv.

60. Karl Zwing, "Das Amerikabuch der Gewerkschaften," *Gewerkschafts-Archiv* 4:6 (June 1926): 286.

61. See ADGB, *Amerikareise* (15–22) for the clearest statement of this vision.

62. Mary Nolan and Charles F. Sabel, "Class Conflict and the Social Democratic Reform Cycle in Germany," *Political Power and Social Theory* 3 (1982): 151–56. For general histories of Weimar Social Democracy, see Richard Breitman, *German Socialism and Weimar Democracy* (Chapel Hill, N.C., 1981); Richard M. Hunt, *German Social Democracy, 1918–1933* (New Haven, Conn., 1964); Heinrich August Winkler, *Der Schein der Normalität. Arbeiter und Arbeiterbewegung in der Weimarer Republik* (Berlin/Bonn, 1985), 177–823. See also essays by Rudolf Kuda, "Das Konzept der Wirtschaftsdemokratie," and Henryk Skrzypczak, "Zur Strategie der Freien Gewerkschaften in der Weimarer Republik," in *Vom Sozialistengesetz zur Mitbestimmung*, ed. Heinz-Oskar Vetter (Cologne, 1975), 253–74, 201–28.

63. Franz Westermann, *Amerika, wie ich es sah. Reiseskizzen eines Ingenieurs* (Halberstadt, 1926).

64. Theodor Lüddecke, *Das Amerikanische Wirtschaftstempo als Bedrohung Europas* (Leipzig, 1925), 10–43.

65. Moritz Julius Bonn, *Amerika und sein Problem* (Munich, 1925), 152.

66. Holitscher, *Amerika*, 45–46.

67. Holitscher, *Wiedersehen*, 11–13.

68. Paul Wengraf, *Amerika-Europa-Russland* (Vienna/Leipzig, 1927), 39–44.

69. Feiler, 5.

70. Lütkens, *Staat*, 9, 1.

71. Adolf Halfeld, *Amerika und der Amerikanismus. Kritische Betrachtungen eines Deutscher und Europäers* (Jena, 1927).

72. Walcher, 111–58.

73. Westermann and GHH 4020/7 Lilge, trip to America.

74. ADGB, *Amerikareise*, 5–12.

75. Bonn, *Amerika*, 7–9.

76. Feiler, 12–30.

77. The phrase is from Cecelia Tichi, *Shifting Gears: Technology, Literature, and Culture in Modernist America* (Chapel Hill, N.C., 1987), xi.

78. Holitscher, *Amerika*, 303.

79. Legien, 61, 87, 90–91. He visited Detroit but not the Ford works.

80. Lütkens, "Neue Amerikabücher," 779–87.

81. Riebensahm, 3; see also Westermann, 29.
82. Editor's introductory note to Kleinschmitt, "Der amerikanische Geist," 518.
83. Litz.
84. Carl Hollweg, *Columbusfahrt. Politische, wirtschaftliche und soziale Entdecker-betrachtungen auf einer Amerikareise* (Berlin, 1925), 11.
85. Lütkens, "Neue Amerikabücher," 769–70.
86. Moritz J. Bonn, *Die Kultur der Vereinigten Staaten von Amerika* (Berlin, 1930), 13.
87. Riebensahm, 4. Even Mayor Böss, who came to see how American big cities functioned and not how the economy worked, took a day trip to inspect the Ford works. Landesarchiv Berlin, Nachlass Böss, Rep 200 Acc 2527, 29, travel itinerary.

3. The Infatuation with Fordism

1. Westermann, 99.
2. Westermann and Riebensahm were among the many who found Niagara Falls, which was described so movingly in much nineteenth-century travel literature, disappointing. For Weimar Germans, Niagara symbolized the inferiority of nature to technology. Westermann, 29; Riebensahm, 3.
3. Wilhelm Vershofen, *Die Grenzen der Rationalisierung* (Nürnberg, 1927), 61.
4. The assessment of the book's impact, which comes from Waldemar Zimmermann, "Fords Evangelium von der technisch-sozialen Dienstleistung," *Schmollers Jahrbuch* 48:2 (1924): 491, was widely shared.
5. Irene Witte, *Taylor-Gilbreth-Ford. Gegenwartsfragen der amerikanischen und europäischen Arbeitswissenschaft* (Munich/Berlin, 1924).
6. Emil Honermeier, *Die Ford Motor Company. Ihre Organisation und ihre Methoden* (Leipzig, 1925); DMV, *Ford;* Rieppel; Gottl-Ottlilienfeld; Dr. G. Faldix; Gustav Winter, *Der falsche Messias Henry Ford. Ein Alarmsignal für das gesamte deutsche Volk* (Leipzig, 1924); Peter Mennicken, *Anti-Ford oder von der Würde der Menschheit* (Aachen, 1924); *Ford und Wir.*
7. Witte, *Taylor*, 63.
8. Franz Josef Furtwängler, "Das Ford-Unternehmen und Seine Arbeiter," *Die Arbeit* 3 (1926): 184.
9. Riebensahm, 11.
10. Aeroebe, 7–11. For similar sentiments from a bitter opponent of Fordism, see Friedrich, 7–8. Observers from other countries were less likely to accord Fordism such centrality. Siegfried, for example, devotes a third of his book to the economy but mentions Ford only in passing.
11. Feiler, 57.
12. *Frankfurter Zeitung und Handelsblatt*, January 24, 1925.
13. Analysts of Fordism today regard its essence as precisely the combination of intensive accumulation, Taylorism, and mass consumption. There was no consensus among those who viewed emergent Fordism from the perspective of the 1920s. For the contemporary view, see Alain Lipietz, *Mirages and Miracles: The Crisis of Global Fordism* (London, 1987), 35–36; and Michael J. Piori and Charles F. Sabel, *The Second Industrial Divide: Possibilities for Prosperity* (New York, 1984).
14. The most comprehensive biography of Ford is Allan Nevins, *Ford: The Times, the Man, the Company* (New York, 1954); see also Allan Nevins and Frank E. Hill, *Ford, Expansion and Challenge, 1915–1933* (New York, 1957). For a more critical perspective, see Keith Sward, *The Legend of Henry Ford* (New York, 1972).

15. Ford, 64.

16. The turnover at the Ford works, which was extraordinarily high, even by the standards of mobile American labor, calls these claims of job satisfaction into question. See Stephen Meyer III, *The Five-Dollar Day: Labor Management and Social Control in the Ford Motor Company, 1908–1921* (Albany, N.Y., 1981), 80.

17. Ford, 256.

18. Nevins and Hill, 603–5; Hans Rogger, "Amerikanizm and the Economic Development of Russia," *Comparative Studies in Society and History* 23 (July 1981): 383, n. 4.

19. Helmut Lethan, *Neue Sachlichkeit 1924–1932. Studien zur Literatur des "Weissen Sozialismus"* (Stuttgart, 1970), 20.

20. Berg, 99; Fritz Neumeyer, "The Nexus of the Modern: The New Architecture in Berlin," in *Berlin 1900–1933: Architecture and Design,* ed. Tilmann Buddensieg (New York, 1987), 67.

21. Richard J. Overy, "Transportation and Rearmament in the Third Reich," *The Historical Journal* 16: 2 (1973): 400–401.

22. Riebensahm, 5. See Witte, *Taylor-Gilbreth-Ford* (64–69) for a sampling of these reviews.

23. Vershofen, 2.

24. Riebensahm, 4–5.

25. Richard Seidel, "Bücher," *Die Gesellschaft* 12 (1926): 564.

26. Hollweg, 69.

27. Witte, *Taylor,* 63–64.

28. *Frankfurter Zeitung und Handelsblatt,* January 24, 1925. Emphasis in original.

29. Fritz Tarnow, *Warum arm sein?* (Berlin, 1929), 19.

30. Zimmermann, 88.

31. Wengraf, 12–13.

32. Winter, 7.

33. Friedrich, 6–8.

34. Walcher, 10.

35. See pp. 42–50 in this volume for a fuller discussion.

36. Lee Iacocca, *Iacocca: An Autobiography* (New York, 1984).

37. Faldix, 80.

38. Furtwängler, 185; Moog, 74.

39. Nevins, 451, 466; Nevins and Hill, 279, 292–93.

40. Furtwängler, 185–86; Westermann, 106; Hirsch, 92–97.

41. Furtwängler, 185; Köttgen, 31, 142–44; Günther Wollheim, *Theorie der Technik Fords* (Munich, 1926), 20–22.

42. Vershofen, 81.

43. DMV, *Ford,* 10.

44. Friedrich von Gottl-Ottlilienfeld, "Industrie im Geiste Henry Fords," *Weltwirtschaftliches Archiv* 22:1 (1925): 23–27.

45. Walcher, 24.

46. Lüddecke, 39.

47. Köttgen, 31, 144; Rieppel, 5–10.

48. Even the engineer Westermann, who had studied Ford's methods before touring the works, was at first overwhelmed by the factory floor and admitted that the workers looked like "an ant hill stirred up with a stick." Once the tour guide had explained the logic of the organization of production, Westermann found everything

to be "so simple, so self-evident," 32–33. See Chapter 5 for a discussion of the American work pace.

49. Furtwängler, 188.

50. Lüddecke, 39. Emphasis in original.

51. Westermann, 99.

52. Reinhard Doleschal, "Zur geschichtlichen Entwicklung des Volkswagenkonzerns," in *Wohin läuft VW? Die Automobilproduktion in der Wirtschaftskrise*, ed. Reinhard Doleschal and Rainer Dombois (Reinbek bei Hamburg, 1982), 19.

53. Reichsverband der Automobilindustrie, *Tatsachen und Zahlen* (1927), 42. See Chapter 7 for a fuller discussion.

54. Elisabeth Schalldach, *Rationalisierungsmassnahmen der Nachkriegszeit im Urteil den deutschen freien Gewerkschaften* (Jena, 1930), 69, 129.

55. See Chapter 4 for a fuller discussion.

56. Köttgen, 33–34.

57. Schalldach, 17–18; Michael J. Neufield, "Taylorism, Trade Union Leadership, and Technological Change: 'Scientific Management' and the German Free Trade Unions, 1908–1923," unpublished ms, in author's possession, 34–35.

58. Eric Hobsbawm, *Industry and Empire* (Harmondsworth, 1972), 40.

59. Maier, "Between Taylorism and Technocracy," 56.

60. In addition to Westermann, see Riebensahm.

61. See Chapter 9 for a fuller discussion.

62. Heinrich Ströbel, *Schwäsische Tagwacht*, April 15, 1924. Cited in Walcher, 8.

63. Walcher, 9.

64. Schalldach, 57.

65. The phrase is from Hinrichs and Peters, 92. The literature on German Social Democracy's understanding of Marxism is vast. For an introduction to the pre-World War I period, see Günther Roth, *The Social Democrats in Imperial Germany* (Totowa, N.J., 1963); Carl Schorske, *German Social Democracy 1905–1917* (New York, 1955); Hans-Josef Steinberg, *Sozialismus und deutsche Sozialdemokratie* (Hannover, 1967). For trade union attitudes toward technology, see *Die Schwereisenindustrie im deutschen Zollgebiet*, ed. Vorstand des deutschen Metallarbeiterverbandes (Stuttgart, 1912). For an overview of the persistance of economistic Marxism in Weimar, see Nolan and Sabel.

66. Heinz Marr, "Die Moral des 'Fordismus,'" in *Ford und Wir*, 77–80; Stollberg, 131–35.

67. Preller, *Sozialistische Monatshefte* 33 (1927). Cited in Hinrichs and Peters.

68. Heinrich Ströbel advanced this argument. See Witte, *Taylor*, 68.

69. Such speculation was rare in Weimar Germany, both within the ranks of labor and without. The anarchist Rudolf Rocker argued against the separation of conception and execution; the social psychologist Willy Hellpach advocated group assembly work; and the Christian trade unionist Eugen Rosenstock favored the decentralization of production. But these dissenting voices found no echo. See Stollberg, 128–31; Joan Campbell, *Joy in Work, German Work: The National Debate, 1800–1945* (Princeton, N.J., 1989), 150–57.

70. Marr, 77–80, cited in Hinrichs and Peters, 162–63. *Women and Socialism* was the most widely read work of socialist theory in Imperial Germany. See Steinberg, 138–39.

71. Walcher provides an example of the Communist critique of Social Democratic views, as does Hilda Weiss, *Rationalisierung und Arbeiterklasse. Zur Rationalisierung*

der deutschen Industrie (Berlin, 1926), 38–43. Schalldach describes the spectrum of free trade union and SPD opinion, revealing internal debates. See also Herf, 41.

72. In addition to Walcher and Friedrich, see Eva Cornelia Schöck, *Arbeitslosigkeit und Rationalisierung. Die Lage der Arbeiter und die kommunistische Gewerkschaftspolitik, 1920–1928* (Frankfurt, 1977).

73. Weiss, 49. Emphasis in original.

74. Schalldach, 133, 137. Both the DMV and the miners' union emphasized the importance of knowing about American technology and published detailed reports from the German metalworker Fritz Kummer, who worked extensively in the United States. For one such report, reprinted from the *Metallarbeiter-Zeitung*, see *Bergarbeiter-Zeitung*, January 24, 1925.

75. Krupp Archiv, Werksarchiv 41/3–740a, sozialpolitische Abteilung, Tätigkeitsbericht, October 1, 1924–September 30, 1925.

76. Liselotte Imhof, "Technischer Fortschritt und Arbeiterschaft" (Ph.D. diss., Duisburg, 1930), 86–93. Excerpts were reprinted in *Der deutsche Metallarbeiter*, the organ of the Christian Metalworkers' Union, May 11 and 18, 1929. The editors expressed only praise for Imhof's work.

77. For an introduction to the debates on Taylorism in the United States, see Harry Braverman, *Labor and Monopoly Capital* (New York, 1974); and Judith Merkle, *Management and Ideology: The Legacy of the International Scientific Management Movement* (Berkeley, 1980).

78. Merkle, 32–42.

79. Braverman argues strongly for the prevalence of scientific management practices, but more recent works, while acknowledging the appeals of Taylorist ideas, cast doubt that they were actually implemented on the shop floor. See, for example, David M. Gordon, Richard Edwards, and Michael Reich, *Segmented Work, Divided Workers: The Historical Transformation of Labor in the United States* (New York, 1982), 146.

80. Lothar Burchardt, "Technischer Fortschritt und sozialer Wandel," in *Deutsche Technikgeschichte*, ed. Werner Treue (Göttingen, 1977), 69–70. See also Heidrun Homburg, "Anfänge des Taylorsystems in Deutschland vor dem ersten Weltkrieg," *Geschichte und Gesellschaft* 4:2 (1978): 173–74.

81. Richard Varenkamp, *Taylorismus und Massenproduktion. Historische Entwicklung und Konzeptionelle Probleme*, Primärbericht Kernforschungszentrum (Karlsruhe 1981).

82. Homburg, 173–74.

83. Peter Hinrichs, *Um die Seele des Arbeiters. Arbeitspsychologie, Industrie- und Betriebssoziologie in Deutschland 1871–1945* (Cologne, 1981), 59–68.

84. Anson Rabinbach, *The Human Motor: Energy, Fatigue, and the Origins of Modernity* (New York, 1990), 256–57.

85. Hinrichs, 58–68; Rabinbach, 256–57; Varenkamp, 6–7.

86. Rabinbach, 242–43, 256–57.

87. Hinrichs, 52–57; Homburg.

88. Stollberg, 32; Burchardt, 74; Hinrichs, 52–56.

89. Stollberg, 40, 77–78.

90. Burchardt, 76.

91. Burchardt, 75–77; Karl Hartmann, "Unternehmer, Angestellte und Arbeiter, Das Taylor-System in der Praxis," *Technik und Wirtschaft* 14:7 (July 1921): 447–49.

92. Burchardt, 81–86; Maier, "Between Taylorism and Technocracy," 45–49; Günther Neubauer, "Sozioökonomische Bedingungen der Rationalisierung und der gewerkschaftlichen Rationalisierungsschutzpolitik. Vergleichende Untersuchung der

Rationalisierungsphasen 1918 bis 1933 und 1945 bis 1968" (Ph.D. diss., Cologne, 1981), 41–51.

93. Burchardt, 88; Varenkamp, 40.

94. See Chapter 9 for a fuller discussion.

95. Friedrich Meyenberg, "Zur Kritik des Taylorsystems. Eine Betrachtung an Hand zweier Neuerscheinungen der betriebswissenschaftlichen Literatur," *Technik und Wirtschaft* 14:7 (July 1921): 402–13.

96. Campbell, 137–38.

97. Fritz Söllheim, *Taylor-System für Deutschland. Grenzen seiner Einführung in Deutsche Betriebe* (Munich and Berlin, 1922), iii–iv, 229.

98. Dietmar Petzina, Werner Abelshauser, and Anselm Faust, *Sozialgeschichtliches Arbeitsbuch*, Vol. 3 (Munich, 1978), 119.

99. Paul Devinat, *Scientific Management in Europe*, ILO, Studies and Reports, Series B, No. 17 (Geneva, 1927).

100. Hartmann, 449. The Ruhr metal-working and machine-making conglomerate Gutehoffnungshütte seconded the view that workers viewed Taylorism as intensified exploitation. Wirtschafts Archiv, Köln, Akten der Industrie und Handelskammer Duisburg. 20-500-17, Einführung des Taylor Systems 1919, April 17, 1919.

101. Schalldach, 36–37; Toni Sender, "Wissenschaftliche Betriebsorganisation und Taylorsystem," *BRZ* 7:2 (January 16, 1926): 33–34.

102. Rabinbach, 241.

103. Social Democratic and Communist publications followed developments in German industrial sociology, psychology, and physiology and debates on Taylorism, offering both critical reviews of the literature and surveys of new work in different fields.

104. Kurt Lewin, *Die Sozialisierung des Taylorsystems. Eine grundsätzliche Untersuchung zur Arbeits- und Berufspsychologie* (Berlin, 1920). The ADGB *Correspondenzblatt* made similar arguments; Neufield, 21.

105. Neufeld, 21; Theodor Meier, "Moderne Betriebsorganisation und Arbeitszeit, *BRZ* 3:5 (February 18, 1922): 165–66; G. Schubert, "Mit welchen Mitteln schönt man den menschlichen Arbeitskraft," *BRZ* 3:17 (August 5, 1922): 571–73.

106. *Protokoll der Verhandlungen des 12. Kongresses der Gewerkschaften Deutschlands, 1925,* (Berlin, 1925) 205.

107. Engelbert Graf, "Amerika als Hochburg des modernen Kapitalismus," *BRZ* 3:1 (January 3, 1922): 18.

108. Max Fiehn, "Zur Kritik des Taylorsystems," *Neue Zeit* 38:13 (December 26, 1919): 302.

109. Stollberg, 105–7; Walcher; Richard Oehring, "Rationalisierungsliteratur," *Die Internationale* 9:15 (August 1, 1926): 473–75; Maier, "Between Taylorism and Technocracy," 50–51.

110. Richard Seidel, *BRZ* 1:7 (July 15, 1920): 209–14.

111. Richard Seidel, "Bücher," *Die Gesellschaft* 11 (1925): 487–95; and "Bücher," *Die Gesellschaft* (1926): 562–64.

112. Stollberg, 106. In addition to Seidel, see the favorable reference to J. Ermanski in Toni Sender, "Wissenschaftliche Betriebsorganisation und Taylorsystem," 33–38.

113. J. Ermanski, *Wissenschaftliche Betriebsorganisation und Taylor-System* (Berlin, 1925).

114. Gottl-Ottlilienfeld, *Fordismus*, 14.

115. Friedrich von Gottl-Ottlilienfeld, "Industrie im Geiste Henry Fords," *Weltwirtschaftliches Archiv* 22:1 (1925): 22. This article was originally a lecture given to the Overseas Club in Hamburg.

116. Campbell (139) is correct to emphasize that Gottl-Ottlilienfeld significantly shaped the 1920s' debate on scientific management. But she neglects to point out that his influence was limited to the political center and right, to engineering and academic circles. The left came to a similar judgment of Fordism and Taylorism by a different route.

117. Honermeier, 122–23.

118. Campbell, 140–41; Maier, "Between Taylorism and Technocracy," 54.

119. Edmund Kleinschmitt, "Als Arbeiter bei Ford. Die innere Einheit von Mensch und Maschine," *Hamburgischer Correspondent*, December 25, 1925. Also published as "Fordismus in der Praxis," *Kölnische Volkszeitung*, December 21, 1925. SAA 11/Lf 395. Köttgen.

120. Dr.-Ing. Heidebroek, "Fliessarbeit und Arbeitsverhältnis in Deutschland," *Ford und Wir*, 47–54.

121. Waldemar Zimmermann, "Fords Evangelium von der technisch-sozialen Dienstleistung," *Schmollers Jahrbuch* 48:2 (1924): 87–119. The quote appears on p. 103.

122. Zimmermann, 95.

123. Lüddecke, 33; Witte, 57–60.

124. Honermeier (121) is one of the few to discuss wages.

125. Günther Stein, "Ford—und unsere Not," *Berliner Tageblatt* March 31, 1924.

126. Lüddecke, 32–33; and Stein.

127. Fritz Giese, "Fabrikpsychologie bei Ford und Taylor," *Betriebswirtschaftliche Rundschau* 1 (1924). Cited in Witte, *Taylor*, 66.

128. Gottl-Ottlilienfeld, *Fordismus*, 25. See also Rieppel, 33–37.

129. Moritz Julius Bonn, *Das Schicksal des deutschen Kapitalismus* (Berlin, 1926), 32.

130. Ein Fordarbeiter, "Ford und Krupp," *BRZ* 10:2 (January 26, 1929): 52.

131. Witte, *Taylor*, 6. Industrialists found this use of Ford particularly annoying. A report from the Mannesmann social policy department praised Ford for strongly attacking trade unions in his book, *Today and Tomorrow*. It concluded that Ford's views "gain significance, when one recalls that the trade union press very happily holds up Henry Ford as a great model to the German employer." MM R 140472, Sozialpolitischer Bericht, No. 14, May 3, 1927.

132. Fritz Tarnow, "Rationalisierung und Lohnpolitik," *Gewerkschafts-Zeitung*, March 20, 1926. German goods accounted for 13.2 percent of world exports in 1913 and only 9.1 percent in 1927–1929. The percentage of German national income derived from exports was 20.2 percent in 1913 and 17 percent in 1928. Peukert, *Weimar*, 118–22.

133. Wilhelm Eggert, *Rationalisierung und Arbeiterschaft* (Berlin, 1927).

134. *Metallarbeiter-Zeitung*, October 9, 1926.

135. Fritz Tarnow, "Rationalisierung und Lohnpolitik," part 2, *Gewerkschafts-Zeitung*, March 20, 1926.

136. Tarnow, *Warum arm sein?*, 58–67; Eggert, 18.

137. Petzina, Abelshauser, Faust, 119.

138. Quoted in Fritz Tarnow, "Rationalisierung und Lohnpolitik," *Gewerkschafts-Zeitung*, March 13, 1926.

139. R. von Ungern-Sternberg, "Die wirtschaftsorganisatorischen Aufgaben der deutschen Arbeiterschaft," *Die Arbeit* 2 (1925): 337.

140. Tarnow, *Warum arm sein?*, 36.

141. Ibid., 70–71.

142. Gerald Feldman, *Army, Industry, and Labor in Germany, 1914–1918*

(Princeton, 1966); Gerald Feldman, "Die Freien Gewerkschaften und die Zentralarbeits-gemeinschaft, 1918–1924," in *Vom Sozialistengesetz zur Mitbestimmung*, ed. Heinz Oskar Vetter (Cologne, 1975), 229–52.

143. Eduard Weckerle, *Gewerkschafts-Archiv* 4:5 (March 1926): 97–100.

144. Christian Schmitz, "Henry Ford und der Sozialismus," *BRZ* 6:21 (October 10, 1925): 653–56; 6:22 (October 24, 1925): 688–91.

145. Friedrich, 58, 23.

146. Walcher, 18–21.

147. Weiss, 57–58.

148. Wilhelm Vershofen, professor at the Handelshochschule in Nürnberg, shared the view that Ford cared for profit, not service, or "*verdienen statt dienen*" as he put it. *Ueber das Verhältnis von technischer Vernunft und wirtschaftlicher Wertung. Ein Beitrag zum Problem des Fordismus* (Nürnberg, 1925), 16.

149. Lüddecke, 7–8; and Lüddecke, "Der neue Wirtschaftsgeist," in *Industrieller Friede*, ed. Jerome Davis and Theodor Lüddecke (Leipzig, 1928), 9–61.

150. Berg (106) argues that National Liberals and Catholics shared a belief that Fordism stood for cooperative relationships between workers and employers, commitment to national work, and an "altruistic practical socialism of service to all." In fact, various adherents of Fordist ideology defined and weighed each tenet differently.

151. Zimmermann, 108.

152. Berger, "Wirtschaftsrationalisierung und Facharbeiterfrage," *Reichsarbeitsblatt* July 1, 1926, 127.

153. Hollweg, 69.

154. Zimmermann (88), for example, dissociated Ford from the America of Wall Street, linking him instead to Thoreau and Emerson.

155. Rieppel, 102. Heinz Marr (80) disputed this, arguing that the American idea of service was rooted in individualism and upward mobility, whereas the German idea of service was derived from the military and bureaucracy and stressed service to the community.

156. Fritz Bredow, *Bei Henry Ford. In der Schule eines Weltkindes* (Kallmünz, 1924), 8, 30.

157. Rieppel, 23.

158. Lüddecke, *Wirtschaftstempo*, 25, 7.

159. See Chapter 9 for a fuller discussion.

160. H. Benkert, "Arbeitsführung und Arbeitspädagogik im rationalisierten Betrieb," *Ford und Wir*, 25.

161. Gottl-Ottlilienfeld, *Fordismus* 40.

162. Hinrichs, 188–208.

4. American Success and German Emulation

1. Riebensahm, 16.

2. See, for example, the discussion of American engineering education and the need to introduce economics into German technical universities that was held at the annual meeting of the RKW in 1925. *Technik und Wirtschaft* 18:5 (May 1925): 143–45. This was but one of many discussions on this theme published in the VDI journal, whose title, *Technology and Economy*, reveals a preoccupation with linking these issues.

3. For information on Siemens' involvement in Weimar politics and its attitudes toward Social Democracy, see David Abraham, *The Collapse of the Weimar Republic*

2nd ed. (New York, 1986), 122–33. For Siemens' rationalization efforts and treatment of workers, see Heidrun Homburg, *Rationalisierung und Industriearbeit. Das Beispiel des Siemens-Konzern Berlin* (Berlin 1991), 343–528. For Siemens' company welfare policies, see Carola Sachse, *Siemens, der Nationalsozialismus und die moderne Familie* (Hamburg, 1990).

4. *Neue deutsche Biographie*, v. 12, ed. Historische Kommission bei der Bayerischen Akademie der Wissenschaften (Berlin, 1980), 413.

5. Herbert Hinnenthal, *Die deutsche Rationalisierungsbewegung und das RKW* (Berlin, 1927), 19.

6. SSA 11/Lh 694 Köttgen, Vortrag des Herrn Dr. Ing. e.h. Köttgen über seine Amerika-Reise in der Werks-Betriebs-Versammlung, January 8, 1925.

7. Köttgen, *Das wirtschaftliche Amerika*, iv.

8. This concern is a minor theme in the book, but a major preoccupation in Köttgen's lectures to the RKW and RDI. See his lecture, "Staatliche und privatwirtschaftliche Aufgaben der deutschen Rationalisierung," given to the April 2, 1925, meeting of the RKW and published in *Technik und Wirtschaft* 18:5 (May 1925): 133–36, and his speech to the RDI on "Amerika und Gemeinschaftsarbeit," *Veröffentlichungen des RDI* 28 (July 1925): 49–60. The business manager of the RKW, Professor A. Schiller, accompanied Köttgen on his visit and subsequently reported to the RKW on his investigation of engineering education in America.

9. Köttgen, *Das wirtschaftliche Amerika*, 70.

10. Ibid., 9–15.

11. Ibid., 23–25.

12. Ibid., 70, 136–53.

13. Ibid., 42.

14. Ibid., 3.

15. Ibid., 35–36, 44–45.

16. Ibid., 51–55.

17. Köttgen, "Arbeit," *Siemens-Mitteilungen* 54 (1923): 2–10. This piece was also published as a pamphlet (Berlin, 1923).

18. Köttgen, "Deutschlands sozialer Wiederaufbau," *Soziale Praxis und Archiv für Volkswohlfahrt* 33:12 (March 20, 1924): 235–37.

19. For a similar argument, see Ernst Poensgen, "Amerikanische und deutsche Wirtschaftsauffassungen," *Unsere Hütte* 2:8 (April 1, 1929): 3–4. *Unsere Hütte* was the Thyssen company magazine.

20. SAA, 11/Lf 694 Köttgen, list of Köttgen's speeches and articles, 1923–25; "Staatliche und privatwirtschaftliche Aufgaben der deutschen Rationalisierung," *Technik und Wirtschaft* 18:2 (May 1925): 134–36; "Das Produktionsproblem," *Weltwirtschaft* 13:6 (June 1925): 97–100; "Amerika und Gemeinschaftsarbeit," *Veröffentlichungen des RDI* 28 (July 1925): 49–60.

21. The *Siemens-Mitteilungen* published *Das wirtschaftliche Amerika* in serial form: 68 (May 1, 1925): 5–13; 69 (June 1, 1925): 2–12; 70 (July 1, 1925): 4–10. Siemens and Köttgen sent the book to several hundred industrialists and politicians in order to promote the RKW. See Chapter 7 for further discussion.

22. Ludwig Kastl, "Produktionsförderung und Absatzgestaltung nach den gegenwärtigen Wirtschaftserfordernissen," lecture delivered to the Tagung der RDI, 23–25 Juni 1925, in *Veröffentlichungen des RDI* 28 (1925): 17–18.

23. "Wirtschaftsanalyse," *Deutsche volkswirtschaftliche Correspondenz* 111 (September 23, 1925). I am indebted to Köttgen's staff for collecting, and in some cases annotating, this and subsequent reviews of *Das wirtschaftliche Amerika*.

24. Hermann Lufft, "Das wirtschaftliche Amerika," *Jahrbuch für nationalökonom-ische Statistik* 124:3 (January–February 1926): 132–40. See, in same source, Carl Köttgen, "Das wirtschaftliche Amerika. Eine Erwiderung," 599–605; Lufft, "Antwort auf die vorstehende Erwiderung," 606–10. The quote appears on p. 608. Köttgen was clearly upset by the article, viewing it as an attack on both the scientific accuracy of his book and on himself. Given his public position and prominence, he felt impelled to reply in print. SAA 11/Lf 301 letter from Köttgen to the *Jahrbuch* editor, Dr. Ludwig Elster, April 22, 1926.

25. Anton Erkelenz, "Dreissig eiserne Sklaven auf jeden Einwohner," *Vossische Zeitung*, November 22, 1925; Erkelenz repeated these arguments nearly verbatim in his book, *Amerika von Heute*, 62–70; Edmund Kleinschmitt, "Gegen den Wirtschafts-pessimismus!" *Der Kaufmann in Wirtschaft und Recht* 4:9 (September 1925): 405–16.

26. *Gewerkschafts-Zeitung*, April 25, 1925.

27. "Das Problem der Betriebsverbesserung," *Vorwärts*, November 6, 1925.

28. Kurt Heinig, "Das Wirtschaftsunternehmer," *Die Weltbühne* 21:18 (1925): 672–75 (the quote appears on p. 675); "Das fliessende Band," *Die Weltbühne* 22:3 (1926): 108–11; "Fordproblem und Arbeiterschaft," *Vorwärts*, November 18, 1925.

29. Carl Köttgen, "Erkenntnis-Gemeinschaft," *Der Arbeitgeber* 16:2 (January 15, 1926). This also appeared in the *Deutsche Allgemeine Zeitung*, December 31, 1925.

30. ADGB, *Amerikareise*, 5–12. Heinig and Furtwängler wrote the two princi-pal sections on the economy and social conditions, respectively, while Tarnow and Meyer produced the much shorter treatments of the trade union movement and work-ers' banks. It is not clear who wrote the conclusion.

31. Ibid., 16.

32. Ibid., 32–33.

33. Ibid., 37–51. See also Furtwängler's observations, 155–56.

34. Ibid., 87. See also page 51.

35. Ibid., 54–63, 66.

36. Ibid., 157–75, 175–76. Most German workers in America and bourgeois ob-servers agreed. Letter from German worker in Detroit, *Metallarbeiter-Zeitung*, January 24, 1931; Moog, 31. Lütkens admitted wages were higher but claimed they were declin-ing relative to productivity and the cost of living; see *Staat und Gesellschaft*, 74–80.

37. ADGB, *Amerikareise*, 115–17, 181.

38. Ibid., 109, 122.

39. Ibid., 254.

40. Ibid., 26–27.

41. Ibid., 17.

42. Ibid., 253.

43. Ibid., 255.

44. Ibid., 256.

45. Sender, *Autobiography*, 252.

46. Toni Sender, "Neues Ansteigen des amerikanischen Reichtums," *BRZ* 7:21 (October 9, 1926): 658.

47. Lucifer, *Die Internationale* 9:21 (November 1, 1926): 645–50.

48. Berg, 111.

49. Feiler, 147.

50. Hirsch, 15.

51. Ibid., 30–31, 40–42. The quote is from page 42.

52. "Das Geheimnis der amerikanischen Löhne," *Deutsche Allgemeine Zeitung*, February 17, 1925.

53. Moritz J. Bonn, *Das Schicksal des deutschen Kapitalismus*, 44.

54. Ibid., 45.

55. Bonn, *Geld und Geist. Vom Wesen und Werden der amerikanischen Welt* (Berlin, 1927), 81–82.

56. E. Prager, "Deutsche und Amerikanische Arbeiter," *BRZ* 6:11 (May 23, 1925): 338–39; Westermann, 129.

57. Riebensahm, 9.

58. GHH 4020/7 Reisebericht Dr. Lilge, Amerikareise 1927, 5–6.

59. GHH, 4089/0 Eindrücke der ersten Amerikareise von Dr. Ing. Lauster, MAN, 1927, 2–7.

60. MM P4 25 49 1925 Bericht über amerikanische Hochofenbetriebstechnik, 1–14.

61. Witte, *Taylor–Gilbreth–Ford*, 71.

62. Siegfried Hartmann, "Amerikasucht," *Deutsche Allgemeine Zeitung*, August 13, 1925, from SAA 11/Lf 121, Köttgen.

63. Vershofen, "Fordismus," in his *Die Grenzen der Rationalisierung*, 8.

64. Karl Arnhold, *Industrielle Menschenführung, ihre Methoden und Ziele, unter besondere Berücksichtigung der Landwirtschaft* (Breslau, 1927), 4–7.

65. Bruno Birnbaum, *Organisation der Rationalisierung Amerika-Deutschland* (Berlin, 1927), 89.

66. ADGB, *Amerikareise*, 29.

67. Bonn, *Geld und Geist*, 62.

68. Lütkens, *Staat und Gesellschaft*, 1–10.

69. Hirsch, 252–53.

70. Dr. A. Braunthal, *Gewerkschafts-Archiv* 4:5 (May 1, 1926): 214.

71. Meakin, 11. German commentators were aware of the multiple and slippery meanings of the term "rationalization." See Hinnenthal, 5–6; Vershofen, *Die Grenzen der Rationalisierung*, unnumbered first page of forward. For a survey of the many German definitions of the term in the 1920s, see Robert Brady, "The Meaning of Rationalization," 526–40.

72. Hinnenthal, 5.

73. As Alfons Steinrötter correctly noted, the German term "Rationalisierung" had an all-encompassing quality that "scientific management" or "l'organisation scientifique de travail" lacked. "Die säkulare Bedeutung der Rationalisierung" *Ruhr und Rhein* 10:29 (July 19, 1929): 948.

74. Meakin, 15.

75. RDI, *Deutsche Wirtschafts- und Finanzpolitik*, (Berlin, 1926), 21.

76. Meakin, 15; Schalldach, 20.

77. For the most comprehensive survey and detailed categorization of rationalization measures, see RKW, *Handbuch der Rationalisierung*, (Berlin, 1929). See also Hermann Mönch, "Formen der Rationalisierung," *Gewerkschafts-Archiv* 9:5 (November 1928): 261–63. In 1926 the *Frankfurter Zeitung* ran a series of articles on the meaning of rationalization in various branches of production, commerce, and finance as well as on the RKW.

78. BA, R 13 I, 122, Dr. Jakob W. Reichert, *Eisenindustrie und Wirtschaftskrise* (Berlin, 1926), 21–23; RDI, *Deutsche Wirtschafts- und Finanzpolitik*, 22; Dr. Louis Hagen, discussion session, "Tagung des RDI am 23–25. Juni 1925," *Veröffentlichungen des RDI* 28 (July 1925): 76; Dr. Paul Silverberg, "Das Deutsche Industrielle Unternehmertum in der Nachkriegszeit," "Mitglieder-Versammlung des RDI, 3–4, September 1926," in *Veröffentlichungen des RDI* 32 (Berlin, 1926): 58–59; *Magazin*

der Wirtschaft 6 (March 19, 1925): 212. For an example of free trade union acceptance of negative rationalization and concentration, see Fritz König, "Strukturveränderungen der Kapitalkonzentration," *Gewerkschafts-Archiv* 5:5 (November 1926): 227-30.

79. There is disagreement among historians about whether there was excessive and irrational investment in industry during the inflation. See Harold James, *The German Slump: Politics and Economics, 1924-1936* (Oxford, 1986), 125-27. Contemporaries seem to have believed that there was, even if they did not always agree on which particular firms should be allowed to go under.

80. *Bergarbeiter-Zeitung*, December 12, 1925. See also, October 25, 1924.

81. RDI, *Deutsche Wirtschafts- und Finanzpolitik*. This view was echoed by many other industrial organizations. See Man Schlenker, "Ausblick auf künftigen Aufgaben," *Mitteilungen des Langnam-Vereins* 1 (1925): 141-49, BBA, 15/576, Letter from Arbeitgeberverband für den Aachener Steinkohlenbergbau to Fachgruppe Bergbau/RDI, March 22, 1926. On the Verein für bergbauliche Interessen and the Zechen Verband, see *Bergarbeiter-Zeitung*, August 29, 1925. For discussions of industrialists' attitudes toward state economic and social policy, see Abraham, 106-65; James, 162-89; and Bernd Weisbrod, *Schwerindustrie in der Weimarer Republik* (Wuppertal, 1978), 299-477.

82. RDI, *Deutsche Wirtschafts-und Finanzpolitik*, 58-59.

83. VDA, *Geschäftsbericht 1925/26* (Berlin, 1927); Westermann, 127, 136; Otto Debatin, "Wirtschaftskrise," *Bosch Zünder*, November 25, 1925.

84. Köttgen, *Das wirtschaftliche Amerika*, 46-48; VDA, *Geschäftsbericht 1925/26*; BBA, 15/576 letter from Deutscher Braunkohlen Industrie Verein, Halle to Fachgruppe Bergbau/RDI, March 29, 1926.

85. Vershofen, *Die Grenzen der Rationalisierung*, 7; Karl Hartmann, "Das Taylor-System in der Praxis," *Technik und Wirtschaft* 14:7 (July 1921): 449.

86. "Bericht über die Sitzung des Reichskuratoriums für Wirtschaftlichkeit," *Technik und Wirtschaft* 18:5 (May 1925): 143.

87. For a detailed discussion of the machine tool industry's efforts to both rationalize and retain flexibility, see Thomas von Freyberg, *Industrielle Rationalisierung in der Weimarer Republik* (Frankfurt, 1989), 55-180.

88. Anonymous, *Ein Leben für die deutsche Wirtschaft. Karl Arnhold zu seinem 80. Geburtstag* (Witten, 1964), 20.

89. The phrase was used both by Carl Köttgen and the RDI. See Köttgen, "Die Ausbildung des Arbeiternachwuchses in Industrie und Handwerk," Sonderabdruck aus *Zeitschrift für Betriebswirtschaft* 4 (1924): 1; RDI, *Deutsche Wirtschafts- und Finanzpolitik*, 21.

90. Adolf Wallichs, *Die Fliessarbeit und ihre Nutzbarmachung für die deutsche Wirtschaft* (Stuttgart, 1927), 16-18. See also, *Fliessarbeit—Beiträge zu ihrer Einführung*, ed. Frank Mäckbach and Otto Kienzle, (Berlin, 1926), 1-15; Otto Schulz-Mehrin, "Rationalisierung und Kapitalbedarf," *Technik und Wirtschaft* 19:10 (October 1926): 265-68.

91. Herbert Peiser, "Fragen zur Produktionssteigerung im Lichte Ford'scher Ziffern," *Technik und Wirtschaft* 18:2 (February 1925): 58-60; GHH 4089/0, Lauster, Amerikareise, 25-26; P. Warlimont, "Die fliessende Fertigung als wirtschaftliche Frage," *Technik und Wirtschaft* 19:3 (March 1926): 79-80.

92. Köttgen, *Das wirtschaftliche Amerika*, 33-34; *Frankfurter Zeitung und Handelsblatt*, January 24, 1925; Freyberg, 155.

93. Honermeier, 124-28; Westermann, 136.

94. GHH, 4020/7 Lilge, Reisebericht 7-8, 41. See also the views of LeVrang, a

technical director of the machine tool department at Siemens-Schuckert, in Freyberg, 79–80.

95. Lüddecke, *Das amerikanische Wirtschaftstempo*, 40–41; Köttgen, *Das wirtschaftliche Amerika*, 33. He echoed this in many other articles and speeches. Robert Bosch, *Aufsätze, Reden und Gedanken*, 3rd ed. (Stuttgart, 1957), 34; Vershofen, *Die Grenzen der Rationalisierung*, 4–7.

96. Ernst Neuberg, "Bedeutung der Produktionsbeschleunigung für die Wirtschaft," *Technik und Wirtschaft* 19:4 (April 1926): 103–7.

97. See Chapter 7 for a fuller discussion.

98. C. F. von Siemens, "Eröffnungssprache," December 17, 1925, meeting of the RKW, *Technik und Wirtschaft* 19:1 (January 1926): 24–25; Hinnenthal, 11, 19; Freyberg, 302.

99. RDI, *Deutsche Wirtschafts- und Finanzpolitik*, 59.

100. The RDI was particularly incensed when Anton Erkelenz, a liberal trade unionist and DDP member of parliament, accused employers of opposing rationalization. It polled its member associations to see what progress had been made in this area. See BBA, 15/576.

101. Berg, 119; Meakin (215–18) gives a detailed summary of the ADGB's *Gegenwartsaufgaben der deutschen Wirtschaft*; Eggert.

102. DMV, *Verbandstag*, 1926, 185–215.

103. Schalldach (121–22) emphasizes the Miners' Union's opposition. A reading of their press suggests that miners' union functionaries, like their fellow trade unionists, were willing to defend technical rationalization in principle, no matter how painful the current practice. See, for example, *Bergarbeiter-Zeitung*, October 25, 1924, and August 29, 1925.

104. For one of the clearest articulations of these beliefs, see SAA 11/Lf 136 Köttgen, letter from Friedrich Olk to Ausschuss für wirtschaftliche Fertigung, 1926.

105. Richard Woldt, *Gewerkschafts-Archiv* 3:1 (1926):243. Cited in Hinrichs and Peters, 85.

106. The statement is by the Social Democrat Wilhelm Eggert, cited in Meakin, 214.

107. For a discussion of hours worked, see Ludwig Preller, *Sozialpolitik in der Weimarer Republik* (Düsseldorf, 1978), 305–9.

108. Richard Woldt, "Die heutige Krise in der Deutschen Betriebsorganisation," *Gewerkschafts-Archiv* 3:4 (October 1925), 191. Individual unions reiterated this argument. See *Bergarbeiter-Zeitung*, September 13, 1924.

109. Paul Hertz and Richard Seidel, *Arbeitszeit, Arbeitslohn und Arbeitsleistung* (Berlin, 1923). "Arbeitszeitverkürzung und Produktionsverminderung," *Gewerkschafts-Zeitung*, July 19, 1924, 249–51, July 26, 1924, 259–61.

110. Eugen Prager, "Das Arbeitszeitproblem," *BRZ* 5:16 (September 7, 1924): 466–71; Preller, *Sozialpolitik*, 271–73.

111. ADGB, *Gegenwartsaufgaben der deutschen Wirtschaft*, cited in ADGB, *Jahrbuch* (1926): 15. See also Hermberg, "Die deutsche Wirtschaft," *Protokoll der Verhandlungen des 12. Kongresses der Gewerkschaften Deutschlands* (Berlin, 1925), 187–93; DMV, *Jahr- und Handbuch* (1925): 7–9.

112. Friedrich Olk, "Wo steht die deutsche Rationalisierung?," *Die Arbeit* 1 (1926): 37.

113. Fritz König, "Zum Problem der Rationalisierungszusammenschlüsse," *Gewerkschafts-Archiv* 5:1 (July 1926): 11.

114. Joseph Jahn, "Vom Wirtschaftsgeiste der deutschen Unternehmer," *Deutsche Arbeit* 11:2 (February 1926): 79.

115. *Protokoll der Konferenz des Reichsbeirats der Betriebsräte und Vertreter grösserer Konzerne der Metallindustrie*, March 1926, 7.

116. Fritz Naphtali, "Arbeitslosigkeit und Preispolitik," *Gewerkschafts-Zeitung*, September 11, 1926, 520.

117. ADGB *Jahrbuch* (1926): 6.

118. DMV, *Jahr- und Handbuch* (1926): 53; ADGB, *Gegenwartsaufgaben der deutschen Wirtschaft*; Wladimir Woytinski, "Wirtschaftskrise und Lohnpolitik," *Die Gesellschaft* 8 (1926): 111, 118.

119. Winkler, 46–47.

120. Moog, 36.

121. See Chapter 8 for a detailed discussion of wages and the controversy surrounding them.

122. Friedrich Olk, "Rationalisierung und Arbeitsmarkt," *Die Arbeit* (1926): 561.

123. Wilhelm Fitzner, "Raubbau an der Arbeitskraft," *Gewerkschafts-Zeitung*, September 26, 1925, 563. Bourgeois observers occasionally made the same point. See the discussion on rationalizing artisans' work by the director of the Baden Commerical office, Walter Buccerins, in *Frankfurter Zeitung*, July 9, 1926.

124. For some of the many statements of this underconsumption argument, see DMV, *Jahr- und Handbuch* (1924): 17; Fritz Tarnow, "Rationalisierung und Lohnpolitik," *Gewerkschafts-Zeitung*, March 13, 1926: 145–47 and March 20, 1926: 161–63; "Unternehmertum und Arbeiterbewegung," *Gewerkschafts-Zeitung*, September 18, 1926: 531–33; "Ueber die Belebung der Wirtschaft durch Lohnerhöhung," *Gewerkschafts-Archiv* 3:5 (November 1925): 271–74; *Metallarbeiter-Zeitung*, January 9, 1926.

125. *Deutsche Arbeit* 11:12 (December 1926): 659. The German pipe manufacturer Mannesmann claimed that until 1927 the Christian trade unions were less critical of industry's approach to rationalization than their Social Democratic counterparts, in MM R 1 40 47 2, sozialpolitischer Bericht, 12, April 22, 1927. A reading of the Christian trade union press, however, suggests no such patience for deferred wages and continued high prices.

126. Eugen Prager, "Deutschlands wirtschaftliche Aussichten," *BRZ* 6:6, March 14, 1925, 168. See also Paul Hermberg, "Weltmarkt und Lohn," *Metallarbeiter-Zeitung*, May 23, 1925.

127. Edmund Kleinschmitt, "Gegen den Wirtschaftspessimismus," 415. See also, Kleinschmitt, "Nominal- und Reallöhne im Auslande und bei uns," *Deutsche Arbeit* 10:1 (January 1925): 10–25. Julius Hirsch endorsed this view of the beneficial impetus of high wages in "Wandlungen im Aufbau der deutschen Industrie," in *Strukturwandlungen der deutschen Volkswirtschaft*, ed. Bernhard Harms (Berlin, 1929), 191–226.

128. SAA 11/Lf 395 Köttgen; Heinz Richter, "Das Problem", *Nachrichten der A.G.B. Mitteilungsblatt der Arbeitsgemeinschaft Gross-Berlin im D.A.V.* 40 (September 27, 1925). In Woytinski, "Wirtschaftskrise und Lohnpolitik," 112.

129. Hirsch, "Wandlungen"; Lüddecke, *Industrielle Friede*, 25–26; Bruno Rauecker, *Rationalisierung und Sozialpolitik* (Berlin, 1926): 69–70; Tänzler, 163–65.

130. Preller, *Sozialpolitik*, 297–99, 320–21.

131. RDI, *Deutsche Wirtschafts- und Finanzpolitik*, 46. See Weisbrod, 231.

132. Kastl, "Wirtschaftspolitische Forderungen der deutschen Industrie," lecture to RDI Mitgliederversammlung, 1926, in *Veröffentlichungen der RDI*, 32 (Berlin, 1926): 24.

133. Bruno Rauecker, "Die Bedeutung der Rationalisierung," *Die Arbeit* 11 (1925): 685; "Der Kern des Rationalisierungsproblems," *Metallarbeiter-Zeitung*, July 31, 1926.

134. "Unternehmertum und Arbeiterbewegung,"*Gewerkschafts-Zeitung*, September 18, 1926: 532.

135. M. J. Bonn, "Technische oder finanzielle Rationalisierung?" *Magazin der Wirtschaft* 11:11 (March 18, 1926): 323; RDI, *Deutsche Wirtschafts- und Finanzpolitik*, 64; BA, R 13 I 101, "Denkschrift über die deutsche Eisen und Stahlindustrie," October 1926: 6.

136. DMV, *Jahr- und Handbuch* (1925): 9–10; DMV, *Protokoll der Konferenz des Reichsbeirats der Betriebsräte* (1926): 9; Olk, "Wo steht die deutsche Rationalisierung?," 38–39. For a Christian trade union critique aimed at guilds as well as cartels, see Paul Nassen, "Binnenmarkt und Ausfuhr," *Deutsche Arbeit* 11:6 (June 1926): 294.

137. See, for example, Eulenburg, 402; Hirsch, *Das amerikanische Wirtschaftswunder*, 256; Lüddecke, *Das amerikanische Wirtschaftstempo*, 60; "Wirtschaftskrise und Arbeitslosigkeit," *Gewerkschafts-Zeitung*, February 6, 1926: 74–75. For scholarly assessments that emphasize these same points, see W. A. Lewis, *Economic Survey, 1919–1939* (London, 1949); Ziebura, 62–72.

138. "Fünftägige Arbeitswoche bei Ford," *Metallarbeiter-Zeitung*, October 9, 1926.

139. Kleinschmitt, "Gegen den Wirtschaftspessimismus," 409–13. The MAN engineer Rieppel (45–46) made the same point.

140. Hirsch, *Das amerikanische Wirtschaftswunder*, 255.

141. Otto Meibes, *Die deutsche Automobil Industrie* (Berlin, 1928), 146–48.

142. Fritz Kummer, "Die Krise der deutschen Automobilindustrie," *Metallarbeiter-Zeitung*, January 2, 1926.

143. *Der Arbeitgeber* 18 (1924): 358.

144. BA R 13 I 206, VDA, Denkschrift an Reichskanzler Dr. Luther, May 12, 1925.

145. Birnbaum, 71.

146. Neuhaus, "Unsere wirtschaftliche Lage," *Mitteilung des Langnamvereins* 1 (May 26, 1925): 112–13.

147. See chapter 8 for further discussion of economic democracy and its relationship to rationaliztion. For a general discussion of the concept of economic democracy, see David Abraham, "Economic Democracy as a Labor Alternative to the Growth Strategy in Weimar Germany," in *The Political Economy of West Germany: Modell Deutschland*, ed. Andrei S. Markovits (New York, 1982), 116–40; Rudolf Kuda, "Das Konzept der Wirtschaftsdemokratie," in *Vom Sozialistengesetz zur Mitbestimmung*, ed. Heinz Oskar Vetter (Cologne, 1975), 253–74.

148. The quote appears in ADGB, *Gegenwartsaufgaben der deutschen Wirtschaft*, cited in Meakin, 219–20.

149. For a discussion of these working groups, see Gerald Feldman, "Die Freien Gewerkschaften und die Zentralarbeitsgemeinschaft, 1918–1924," in *Vom Sozialistengesetz zur Mitbestimmung*, ed. Heinz Oskar Vetter (Cologne, 1975), 229–52.

150. Weiss, 38; A. Friedrich, "Die 'Rationalisierung' der deutschen Wirtschaft," *Die Internationale* 9:6 (March 15, 1926): 169.

151. E. Pawlowsky, "Die Grundlagen der deutschen Wirtschaftskrise," *Die Internationale* 9:1 (January 1, 1926): 13; Friedrich, 165–66.

152. E. Varga, "Der marxistische Sinn der Rationalisierung," *Die Internationale* 9:14 (July 20, 1926): 433.

153. Fritz Heckert, "Grundsätzliches und Taktisches zur Erwerbslosenfrage," *Die Internationale* 9:17 (September 1, 1926): 531–35.

154. Friedrich, 169–71; and Varga, 435. For a contemporary summary of the KPD

arguments of the 1920s, see A. Enderle, H. Schreiner, J. Walcher, and E. Weckerle, *Das rote Gewerkschaftsbuch* (Berlin, 1932), 25–48. For a recent overview, see Neubauer, 122–27.

155. Eva Cornelia Schöck, *Arbeitslosigkeit und Rationalisierung. Die Lage der Arbeiter und die kommunistische Gewerkschaftspolitik 1920–1928* (Frankfurt, 1977), 56–59.

156. The KPD position was also criticized by Russians in the Red Trade Union International. Hinrichs and Peters, 100–103.

157. Lucifer, "Rationalisierung und Arbeitslohn," *Die Internationale* 9:21 (November 1, 1926): 645–50.

158. A. Enderle, "Rationalisierung, technischer Fortschritt und Gewerkschaften," *Rote Gewerkschafts Internationale* 6:5 (May 1926): 335–40.

5. Work, Workers, and the Workplace in America

1. Ford, 99.

2. Riebensahm, 19.

3. For the history of the German science of work, see Campbell, 73–107, 131–58; Hinrichs, 107–145, 208–90; and Rabinbach, 179–205, 253–64, and 271–89.

4. World War I played a crucial role in moving the theoretically oriented German science of work in an applied direction. That continued in the 1920s when attention shifted from the battlefield to the shop floor and the office. See Rabinbach, 259–62, 271–75.

5. Preller, *Sozialpolitik*, 127–28. For an overview of the debates about the human factor of production, see Gerhard P. Bunk, *Erziehung und Industriearbeit. Modelle betrieblichen Lernens und Arbeitens Erwachsener* (Weinheim and Basel, 1972), 81–292, and Campbell, 158–275. Industrialists and scientists of work were not the only ones who rhetorically reduced humans to a factor of production; trade unionists employed the same vocabulary. From the Miners' Union see, "Produktionssteigerung durch Menschenökonomie," *Verband und Wirtschaft* 1:9 (December 1922): 134–36.

6. Peter Bäumer, *Das Deutsche Institut für Technische Arbeitsschulung* (Munich and Leipzig, 1930), 12–14; RKW, *Der Mensch und die Rationalisierung*, 10–14; and Ernst Horneffer, *Der Weg zur Arbeitsfreude* (Berlin, n.d.).

7. See, for example, P. Setzermann, "Die Ausbildung des Arbeiternachwuchses. Sitzung des Reichskuratoriums für Wirtschaftlichkeit, June 21, 1924," *Technik und Wirtschaft* 17:7 (July 1924): 155.

8. Weimar Germans would have occupied a peculiar position in the debates of the 1970s and 1980s about deskilling. They would have agreed with Harry Braverman's analysis in *Labor and Monopoly Capital* that American capital was committed to far-reaching Taylorism and deskilling. But they envisioned Europe's present and future as a mixture of skill and technology, mass and specialized production along the lines argued by Michael J. Piori and Charles F. Sabel, *The Second Industrial Divide: Possibilities for Prosperity* (New York, 1984).

9. Walter Bolz, "Der Facharbeiter und die Betriebsrationalisierung," in *Menschenführung. Gedanken zur Sozialpolitik, Ehrengabe aus dem Kreise der sozialpolitischen Abteilung der Siemens-Werke für Geheimrat Dr.-Ing. Hermann Görz zum 1 Oktober 1930* (Munich, 1930), 40; Köttgen, *Das wirtschaftliche Amerika*, 33–34; *Frankfurter Zeitung und Handelsblatt*, January 24, 1925; Freyberg, 155.

10. Bolz, 39–41.

11. Setzermann, 149–51.

12. Hella Schmedes, *Das Lehrlingswesen in der deutschen Eisen und Stahlindustrie unter besonderer Berücksichtigung der Verhältnisse in Rheinland und Westfalen* (Münster, 1931), 27–8, 41–50, 58.

13. Erna Barschak, *Die Idee der Berufsbildung und ihre Einwirkung auf die Berufserziehung im Gewerbe* (Leipzig, 1929), 71.

14. Isa Strasser, "Rationalisierung und Frauenarbeit," *Rote Gewerkschafts Internationale* 6:9/10 (September–October 1926): 565. As Karen Hagemann's study of the Social Democratic milieu in Hamburg clearly shows, trade union policies reflected the fears and needs of their male members. *Frauenalltag und Männerpolitik. Alltagsleben und gesellschaftliches Handeln von Arbeiterfrauen in der Weimarer Republik* (Bonn, 1990), 481–507.

15. Lorenz Popp, "Warum bevorzugt die rationalisierte Industrie die Frauenarbeit?," *Gewerkschafts-Archiv* 1:6 (December 1928): 354.

16. Stollberg, 91–93.

17. Wladimir Woytinsky, "Arbeit und Maschine in der Deutschen Wirtschaft," *Die Gesellschaft* 2 (February 1928): 135; Strasser (648) concurred. Certainly this is the image conveyed in the 1920s film about rationalization, *Lohnbuchhalter Kremke*, in which a middle-aged male accountant loses his job to a young, woman clerical worker. See also Stephan Bajohr, *Die Hälfte der Fabrik. Geschichte der Frauenarbeit in Deutschland, 1914 bis 1945* (Marburg, 1979), 18–27.

18. Otto Richter, "Entwicklung in der Technik," *BRZ* 6:6 (March 14, 1925): 183.

19. Max Hedel, "Die Normung und ihre Bedeutung für die deutsche Industrie," *BRZ* 1:1 (April 15, 1920): 20.

20. Brady, *The Rationalization Movement*, 351.

21. Ludwig Kastl, "Wirtschaftspolitische Voraussetzungen für deutsche Qualitätsarbeit," speech to RDI Mitglieder Versammlung, 1927, *Veröffentlichungen des RDI* 37 (Berlin 1927): 22.

22. "Voraussetzungen für deutsche Qualitätsarbeit," *Gewerkschafts-Zeitung*, September 17, 1927. Leipart's 1916 article "Qualitätsarbeit und Arbeiterklasse," appeared in *Sozialistische Monatshefte* 15 (Aug, 3, 1916): 803–8. Alf Lüdtke notes these nearly identical definitions, but deemphasizes the contradictory directions in which unions and industry developed this basic definition. "'Deutsche Qualitätsarbeit,' 'Spielereien' am Arbeitsplatz und 'Fliehen' aus der Fabrik: Industrielle Arbeitsprozesse und Arbeiterverhalten in den 1920er Jahren. Aspekte eines offenen Forschungsfeldes," in *Arbeiterkulturen zwischen Alltag und Politik*, ed. Friedhelm Boll (Vienna, 1986), 82–83.

23. Sebastian Müller, *Kunst und Industrie. Ideologie und Organisation des Funktionalismus in der Architektur* (Munich, 1974), 85–96.

24. Hans Kraemer, "Wettbewerb der Völker um die Qualitätsarbeit," speech to RDI Mitglieder Versammlung, 1927, *Veröffentlichung des RDI* 37 (Berlin, 1927): 57.

25. Alf Lüdtke, "'Ehre der Arbeit': Industriearbeiter und Macht der Symbole. Zur Reichweite symbolischer Orientierungen im Nationalsozialismus," in *Arbeiter im 20. Jahrhundert*, ed. Klaus Tenfelde (Stuttgart, 1991), 370, 375–6, 378, 386. Although primarily concerned with the Nazis' use of "quality work," he expertly reconstructs the meanings the term acquired during World War I and the 1920s.

26. Kastl, "Wirtschaftspolitische Voraussetzungen für deutsche Qualitätsarbeit."

27. Toni Sender, "Brauchen wir noch Facharbeiter?" *BRZ* 7:18 (August 28, 1926): 550.

28. Karl Arnhold, "Betrieb und gewerkschaftlicher Verband als Faktoren industrieller Arbeitsschulung," in *Industrielle Arbeitsschulung als Problem*, ed. Soziales Museum Frankfurt am Main (Berlin, 1931), 34–37.

29. Many Germans believed that other European countries produced quality work, even though they emphasized the special excellence of German goods. According to the Frenchman André Siegfried, "French strength and invulnerability lie in the creative instinct and the quality and individuality of the product. The French are in fact stronger when labor is less mechanical and more personal and artistic." *America Comes of Age* (New York, 1927), 181.

30. Kastl, "Wirtschaftspolitische Voraussetzungen für deutsche Qualitäts-arbeit," 7; Kraemer, "Wettbewerb der Völker um die Qualitätsarbeit," 56–57; Vershofen, "Fordismus," 7; Karl Arnhold, "Arbeitsschulung trotz alldem," *Rheinische Westfälische Zeitung*, November 14, 1930, in GHH 400125/6.

31. Heidebroeck, "Wege zur Rationalisierung. Rationalisierung kleiner und mittlerer Betriebe," *Frankfurter Zeitung*, April 11, 1926.

32. See Lüdtke, ("'Ehre der Arbeit,'" 368) for a discussion of the respect for labor implied in the term. Kraemer ("Wettbewerb der Völker um die Qualitätsarbeit," 58) appealed explicitly to the Werkbund tradition. For the history of the Werkbund, the principal proponent of a new industrial aesthetic, see Joan Campbell, *The German Werkbund* (Princeton, 1978).

33. Kastl, "Wirtschaftspolitische Voraussetzungen für deutsche Qualitätsarbeit."

34. "Voraussetzungen für deutsche Qualitätsarbeit," *Gewerkschafts-Zeitung*, September 17, 1927, 525–27.

35. Vershofen, "Fordismus," 7; Riebensahm, 10–11. See also, Honermeier, 124–28.

36. Kraemer, "Wettbewerb der Völker um die Qualitätsarbeit," 56.

37. "Voraussetzungen für deutsche Qualitätsarbeit," *Gewerkschafts-Zeitung*, September 17, 1927, 525–27.

38. Lüdtke, "'Ehre der Arbeit'".

39. Karl Zwing, "Wirtschafts-Demokratie. Wesen, Voraussetzungen und Möglichkeiten," *Gewerkschafts-Archiv* 3:3 (September 1925): 123.

40. Setzermann, 149; *Gewerkschafts-Zeitung*, 1924, 522; Preller, *Sozialpolitik*, 289; Josef Winschuh, *Praktische Werkspolitik* (Berlin, 1923), 148–49.

41. *Reichsarbeitsblatt* 22 (October 24, 1924): 523–26; Hildegard Böhme, "Zur Entwicklung der gewerblichen Lehrlingswesen in Preussen nach dem Kriege," *Reichsarbeitsblatt* 25 (November 16, 1924): 567–71.

42. Rudolf Schindler, *Das Problem der Berufsauslese für die Industrie* (Jena, 1929), 54–55. Schindler (55) predicted that the 1932 youth cohort would be only half that of 1914.

43. Setzermann, 114.

44. *Gewerkschafts-Zeitung*, 1924, 522. "Behebung des Facharbeitermangels," *Metallarbeiter-Zeitung*, August 24, 1929.

45. Böhme, 570.

46. Barschak, 82.

47. Schmedes, 98–99.

48. Rabinbach, 264; Hinrichs, 209–24.

49. For a contemporary commentary on the new prominence of psychotechnics, see Waldemar Zimmermann, "Das Problem der rationalisierten Industriearbeit in sozialpsychologischer Betrachtung," *Schmollers Jahrbuch* 49:5 (1925): 107–8. In its 1930 yearly report, (170), the RKW estimated that between eight hundred and one thousand institutions developed and/or employed psychotechnics. These included research

institutions, private businesses, universities, vocational education organizations, such as Dinta, and state labor offices.

50. Hinrichs, 225–30; Rabinbach, 275–79; Schindler, 19–21.

51. See, for example, J. Handrick, "Berufsberatung," in *Arbeitskunde*, ed. Johannes Riedel (Leipzig and Berlin, 1925), 265–82.

52. For a discussion of both expectations and results, see RKW, *Mensch und Rationalisierung, I: Fragen der Arbeits-und Berufsauslese, der Berufsausbildung und Bestgestaltung der Arbeit*, RKW Veröffentlichungen 71, 1931.

53. Clara Mleinek, "Berufsberatung, Berufsauslese, Berufsausbildung," *Deutsche Arbeit* 10:2 (February 1925): 89.

54. Heinrich Jäcker, *Reichsarbeitsblatt* 9 (1922): 294*.

55. Walter Riemer, "Der Doppelcharakter der Berufsberatung und Eignungsprüfung als Jugendfrage und Wirtschaftsproblem," *Gewerkschafts-Archiv* 5:5 (November 1926): 231–35. Large firms usually used tests geared to the specific needs of the firm, while labor offices used more general ones. See RKW, *Mensch und Rationalisierung, III: Eignung und Qualitätsarbeit*, RKW Veröffentlichungen 87, 1933, 232–33. For a rare example of a trade union's complete rejection of aptitude testing, see, "Eignungsprüfungen. Eine kritische Betrachtung," *Metallarbeiter-Zeitung*, August 20, 1927 (written by an anonymous engineering supervisor).

56. Hinrichs, 246–54; Schindler, 41. Existing tests were criticized for failing to measure the full person in all his or her intellectual and physical complexity.

57. Vahrenkamp (*Taylorismus*, 7) emphasized that American proponents of Taylorism paid little attention to skills training. Karl Arnhold acknowledged that American firms had become more interested in apprenticeship training and that schools cooperated more readily with industry than in Germany. Germans, however, had a more modern and comprehensive system; see Arnhold, "Würdigung und Form der Lehrlingsausbildung in den Vereinigten Staaten," printed from *Der Arbeitgeber*, November 15, 1927.

58. Gerhard Adelmann estimates that two thirds of apprenticeships were served in *Handwerk* in 1907. See "Die Berufliche Ausbildung und Weiterbildung in der Deutschen Wirtschaft, 1871–1918," in *Berufliche Aus- und Weiterbildung in der deutschen Wirtschaft seit dem 19. Jahrhundert*, ed. Wilhelm Treue, and Hans Pohl, *Zeitschrift für Unternehmergeschichte*, Supplement 15, 1978.

59. Barschak, 56–67, 65–66; Fritz Fricke, *Sie Suchen die Seele* (Berlin, 1927), 27–28. For an introduction to vocational education in the 1920s, see Albin Gladen, "Berufliche Bildung in der Deutschen Wirtschaft," in *Berufliche Aus- und Weiterbildung in der deutschen Wirtschaft seit dem 19. Jahrhundert*, ed. Wilhelm Treue, and Hans Pohl, *Zeitschrift für Unternehmergeschichte*, Supplement 15, 1978, 53–73.

60. See Chapter 9 for a fuller discussion.

61. DMV, *Jahr- und Handbuch* (1927), 171. Cited in Schmedes, 141.

62. For an introduction to these debates, see Karl Mühlmann, "Lehre und berufliche Schule," in *Arbeitskunde: Bedingungen und Ziele der wirtschaftlichen Arbeit*, ed. Johannes Riedel (Berlin, 1925), 308–19. See Chapter 9 for a fuller discussion.

63. For an introduction to the debates concerning training for semiskilled and unskilled workers, see Johannes Riedel, "Die Schulung der angelernten und ungelernten Arbeitskräfte," in *Arbeitskunde*, ed. J. Riedel (Berlin, 1925), 319–26.

64. Modest Rubinstein, "Die kapitalistische Rationalisierung," *Unter dem Banner des Marxismus* 3:4 (1929): 555–58.

65. Vershofen, *Ueber das Verhältnis von technischer Vernunft*, 13. See also Vershofen, "Fordismus," 10.

66. ADGB, *Amerikareise*, 40.

67. "Von der Anspannung des Arbeiters in Amerika," *Metallarbeiter-Zeitung*, June 13, 1925.

68. Friedrich Olk, "Maschinen und Maschinengruppe," *Metallarbeiter-Zeitung* April 24, 1926.

69. Toni Sender, "Eindrücke einer Amerikareise," *BRZ* 8:6 (March 19, 1927): 163–64.

70. "Am laufenden Band bei Ford," *BRZ* 8:14 (July 9, 1927): 446 (written by an anonymous Ford worker).

71. Kleinschmitt, "Als Arbeiter bei Ford."

72. "Als Werkzeugmacher in Detroit," *Metallarbeiter-Zeitung*, December 25, 1926; (written by an anonymous machine toolmaker). "Von Menschen und Buden in Detroit," *Metallarbeiter-Zeitung*, December 3, 1927.

73. H.K. "Briefe aus Chikago," *Metallarbeiter-Zeitung*, March 23, 1929. Fritz Kummer, who reported extensively on the U.S. auto industry, also emphasized the contribution of superior machines and did not even comment on the work pace. Whether he experienced it directly is not clear from his articles. See, for example, Kummer, "Die fortschreitende Technik als Produktionsfaktor," *Bergarbeiter-Zeitung*, January 24, 1925.

74. Schalldach, 137.

75. Robert Schönhaar, "Arbeiter und Wirtschaftskrise," *Bosch Zünder* November 30, 1926, 259; Otto Fischer, "Arbeiter und Wirtschaftskrise," *Bosch Zünder*, October 30, 1926, 236.

76. "Ein Brief aus Amerika," *Bosch-Zünder*, July 20, 1924.

77. Karl Möller, "Als Arbeiter in Detroit," *Metallarbeiter-Zeitung*, May 24, 1930.

78. Bruno Rauecker, "Monotonieproblem und Sozialpolitik," *Die Arbeit* 1 (1927). For information on Rauecker, see Campbell, *Joy in Work*, 174–76.

79. For overviews of the Weimar debates about monotony, see Rauecker, "Monotonieproblem," 8–18. Adolf Wallichs, *Die Fliessarbeit und ihre Nutzbarmachung für die deutsche Wirtschaft* (Stuttgart, 1927), 50–55; Otto Streine, "Arbeitsrationalisierung und Arbeitsschutz," *Gewerkschaftszeitung*, 481–83.

80. Eduard Weckerle, "Grundsätzliches zur Maschinenfrage," *Gewerkschafts-Archiv* 8:3 (March 1928): 159–71.

81. Feiler, 140.

82. Campbell, 151–57; Hinrichs, 170–87. For the fullest statement of these widely discussed proposals, see Richard Lang and Willy Hellpach, *Gruppenfabrikation* (Berlin, 1922), and Eugen Rosenstock-Huessy, with Eugen May and Martin Grünberg, *Werkstattaussiedlung* (Berlin, 1922).

83. Rauecker, "Monotonieproblem," 12.

84. Hugo Borst, *Bosch-Zünder*, August 31, 1925, 179.

85. Moog, 76.

86. Ludwig Preller, "Fliessarbeit und Arbeiterschutz," *Die Arbeit* 2 (1927): 74. Schalldach (65–67) argued that the free trade union spokesmen were utterly confused about rationalized work and saw higher wages and mass consumption as the only solution to any problems it might raise. This ignores how positively they viewed flow production and the assembly line.

87. Preller, "Fliessarbeit," 74. Preller (66) cites the similar views of Professor Schmalenbach.

88. Westermann, 100.

89. Hellmut Hultzsch, "Ford'sche Arbeitsmethoden in der Werkstatt. River

Rouge—Erfahrungen als Fordarbeiter 42922," in *Ford und Wir*, 12–13. Emphasis in original. For similar views, see Heinrich Wirtz, "Die Werksfremdheit der Arbeiter und ihre Ueberwindung" (Ph.D. Diss., Giessen, 1929), 47–50; and Edmund Kleinschmitt, "Als Arbeiter bei Ford," *Hamburgischer Correspondent*, December 25, 1925.

90. Some ideas were borrowed from Karl Bücher's *Arbeit und Rhythmus*, which was in its sixth edition in 1924. See also Rabinbach, 174, 348, n. 150.

91. Wirtz, 23–27.

92. Ewalt Sachsenberg, "Zeitstudien und Bandarbeit," *Maschinenbau*, 3: 13 (1924): 433, cited in Freyburg, 343.

93. Schalldach (41) wrongly claims that the trade union movement ignored the issue of repetitive work. See Preller, "Fliessarbeit," 68–69; Freyberg, 342; Rauecker, *Rationalisierung und Sozialpolitik* (Berlin, 1926), 63–68; W. Vogt, "Die menschliche Arbeitskraft, das kostbarste Gut im Betrieb," *Der deutsche Metallarbeiter*, July 29, 1929, 471. Although Vogt was described as "the head of a large south German concern," the editors of this trade union journal stated that "we can completely endorse what he says." See their introduction to part 1 of the article, July 13, 1929.

94. "Am laufenden Band bei Ford," 444–45. Italics in original.

95. Ludwig Preller, "Arbeiterschutzfragen bei Fliessarbeit," *Der deutsche Metallarbeiter*, June 11, 1927; L. Heyde, "Rationalisierung und Arbeiterschaft," in *Strukturwandlungen der deutschen Wirtschaft*, ed. Bernhard Harms (Berlin, 1929) 292.

96. W. Vogt, *Der deutsche Metallarbeiter*, July 20, 1929, 452.

97. Wallichs, 54.

98. Furtwängler, "Das Ford-Unternehmen," 186–87.

99. F. Meyenberg, "Rationalisierung der technischen Betriebsorganisation," in *Strukturwandlungen der deutschen Volkswirtschaft*, ed. Bernhard Harms (Berlin, 1929), 246–47.

100. Fritz Giese, "Auswahl und Verteilung der Arbeitskräfte," in *Arbeitskunde*, ed. Johannes Riedel (Berlin: 1925), 307–8; Hollweg, 74; Rauecker, "Monotonieproblem," 12.

101. Meyer (42) suggests that the latter was true. Winter, 29–31, was one of the few dissenting voices.

102. Preller, "Arbeiterschutzfragen," 372; Vogt, 452; Köttgen, *Das wirtschaftliche Amerika*, 153.

103. Otto Ritter, "Als Feilenhauer in Amerika," *Metallarbeiter-Zeitung*, May 28, 1927; ADGB, *Amerikareise*.

104. Rieppel, 27; Freyberg, 333.

105. Otto Streine, "Arbeitsrationalisierung und Arbeitsschutz," *Gewerkschafts-Zeitung*, August 10, 1929, 498.

106. For the most thorough discussion of attitudes toward women and rationalized work, see Annemarie Tröger, "The Creation of a Female Assembly-Line Proletariat," in *When Biology Became Destiny*, ed. Renate Bridenthal, Atina Grossmann, and Marion Kaplan (New York, 1984), 250–54.

107. Renate Bridenthal and Claudia Koonz, "Beyond *Kinder, Küche, Kirche*: Weimar Women in Politics and Work," in *When Biology Became Destiny*, 44–51.

108. Freyberg, 333–34.

109. Rubinstein, 563–65.

110. E. Atzler, "Die Aufgaben der Physiologie in der Arbeitswissenschaft," *Technik und Wirtschaft* 17:8 (August 1924): 173–80; Otto Lipmann, "Praktische Wirtschaftsphychologie ('Psychotechnik')" in *Arbeitskunde*, 55–64; Rabinbach, 277–80.

111. Hugo Borst, *Bosch-Zünder*, November 25, 1925, 257–58; Vogt, 471.

112. Ludwig Preller, "Rationalisierung und Arbeitskraftverbrauch," in *Die 40-Stunden-Woche*, ed. Theodor Leipart (Berlin, 1931), cited in Lüdtke "'Deutsche Qualitätsarbeit,'" 156; Sender, "Eindrücke einer Amerikareise," 164; Brady, *Rationalization Movement*, 330–32. Leipart, head of the Trade Union Confederation, was even on the board of the Kaiser Wilhelm Institut für Arbeitsphysiologie, which Atzler headed. Brady, 330. As early as 1920, Lewin (16) insisted that psychotechnics could make work both more productive and more pleasant.

113. The DMV regarded psychotechnics as very promising but worried that unless labor had a voice in aptitude testing, firms would only eliminate the unsuitable rather than telling workers what kind of jobs they should take. DMV *Protokoll der Konferenz des Reichsbeirats des Betriebsräte*, March 1926, 13. See also, Richard Seidel, *Die Gesellschaft* 9 (September 1928): 285. Preller, "Arbeiterschutzfragen"; Hinrichs and Peters, 82–83.

114. Rauecker, "Monotonieproblem," 13; Heinrich Krieger, "Berufsauslese als Rationalisierungsmittel," *Magazin der Wirtschaft* 19 (May 13, 1926): 589.

115. Atzler; Lipmann; W. Moede, "Betriebsrationalisierung auf psychotechnischer Grundlage," *Frankfurter Zeitung*, April 22, 1926; Heinrick Krieger, "Arbeit und Ermüdung," *Frankfurter Zeitung*, December 5, 1926.

116. See Chapter 9 for a fuller discussion.

117. Schalldach, 40–41; Karl Kautsky, review of Edgar Atzler's *Handbuch der Arbeitsphysiologie*, *Die Gesellschaft* 4 (April 1928): 379–81; Richard Seidel, review of Johannes Riedel's *Arbeitskunde* and four other books on work, *Die Gesellschaft* 2:10 (1925): 488. See the series of articles on psychotechnics and human economy that appeared in a column revealingly titled "Knowledge, Vocation, Technology," *Bergarbeiter-Zeitung*, July 18 and 25, August 15, and November 14, 1925. See also Edgar Atzler, "Aufgaben und Ziele der Arbeitsphysiologie," *Die Arbeit* 10 (1926): 622–29. His talk on the same theme appeared in *Gewerkschafts-Zeitung*, July 24, 1926.

118. For a discussion of eugenics and the broad-based support for it, see Paul J. Weindling, *Health, Race and German Politics Between National Unification and Nazism, 1870–1945* (Cambridge, Eng., 1989).

119. Atzler, "Arbeitsphysiologie und Rationalisierung," *Frankfurter Zeitung*, April 28, 1926. For an example of how the science of work was seen to promote optimization, see Otto Debatin, "Wie lässt sich die Leistung des einzelnen Arbeiters steigern?" *Bosch-Zünder*, April 20, 1926, 77–80; May 31, 1926, 111–12; and June 30, 1926, 125–27.

120. Carola Sachse, *Betriebliche Sozialpolitik als Familienpolitik in der Weimarer Republik und im Nationalsozialismus mit einer Fallstudie über die Firma Siemens*, Berlin (Hamburg, 1987), 85.

121. Campbell, *Werkbund*, 159–62.

122. Schmedes, 126; RKW, *Mensch und Rationalisierung: III*, RKW Veröffentlichungen, 87, 4.

123. Schmedes, 126.

124. Heinz Potthoff, "Die sozialen Probleme des Betriebes," in *Die sozialen Probleme des Betriebes*, ed. Heinz Potthoff (Berlin, 1925), 9, 11.

125. Söllheim, 171.

126. *Die menschliche Arbeitskraft im Produktionsvorgang: Drei Vorträge gehalten auf der Gemeinschaftssitzung der Fachausschüsse des Vereins deutscher Eisenhütteleute in Bonn am 24. Mai 1925* (Düsseldorf, 1925), 2. This statement was frequently quoted. See, for example. W. Maschke, "Werksjugendpflege," *Die Arbeit* (1926): 474.

127. *Verband und Wirtschaft* 1:6 (1922): 91.

128. Christoph Schrempf, "Der Arbeiter," *Bosch-Zünder*, October 30, 1922, 249.

129. Horneffer, 8.

130. Ernst Horneffer, *Der Weg zur Arbeitsfreude* (Berlin, n.d.) was first published in *Der Arbeitgeber*, 1924. "Die Vergeistigung der wirtschaftlichen Arbeit," *Veröffentlichen des RDI* 42 (1928): 5–12.

131. "Mitgliederversammlung des RDI," *Veröffentlichungen des RDI* 32 (Berlin, 1926): 19.

132. Hugo Borst, *Bosch-Zünder*, August 31, 1925, 179.

133. Werner Conze, "Beruf," in *Geschichtliche Grundbegriffe*, ed. Otto Brunner, Werner Conze, and Reinhart Koselleck (Stuttgart, 1972), 490–507.

134. For a survey of different definitions of *Beruf*, see Barschak, 106–8.

135. W. Kalveram, "Rationalisierung der kaufmännischen Betriebsorganisation," in *Strukturwandlungen der deutschen Wirtschaft*, ed. Bernhard Harms (Berlin, 1929), 281.

136. Conze, 505.

137. Barschak, 107; Hagemann, 640.

138. Potthoff, 9.

139. Sachse, *Betriebliche Sozialpolitik*, 86–87; Wirtz, 10.

140. Potthoff, 9.

141. Lüdtke, 'Ehre der Arbeit,' 374. The obvious exception is Hendrik de Man, whose survey of workers' attitudes was revealingly entitled *Kampf um die Arbeitsfreude* (*The Struggle for Joy in Work*) (Jena, 1927). de Man, a Belgian Socialist living in Germany, was frequently mentioned in Social Democratic publications, but his book was taken no more seriously than Adolf Levenstein's *Die Arbeiterfrage* (Munich, 1912), a more extensive but methodologically weak prewar survey. Social Democrats, who prided themselves on their sober and scientific outlook, seem to have had little interest in investigations of workers' subjective feelings.

142. For the pessimistic view, see *Metallarbeiter-Zeitung*, February 3, 1923, and Campbell, *Joy in Work*, 160–61. For the optimistic view, see Georg Schubert, "Die sozial-psychologischen Wirkungen der Lohnarbeit," *BRZ* 6:19 (September 12, 1925), 600–602; and Richard Woldt, "Arbeitsfreude," in *Probleme der sozialen Betriebspolitik*, ed. Goetz Briefs (Berlin, 1930), 141–42.

143. Erik Nölting, "Das Problem der Arbeitsfreude," *Bergarbeiter-Zeitung*, November 12, 1929.

144. Franz Laufkötter, "Wissenschaftliche Betriebsführung, aber nicht auf Kosten des arbeitenden Menschen," *Metallarbeiter-Zeitung*, January 17, 1925.

145. Nölking, "Das Problem der Arbeitsfreude," *Bergarbeiter-Zeitung*, November 12, 1927; Willett, 95–168.

146. Richard Seidel, for example, criticized any effort to find meaning in work or retain ideas of *Beruf*. Increased productivity led to increased *Entseelung* (soullessness), and that simply had to be accepted. See "Die Rationalisierung des Arbeitsverhältnisses," *Die Gesellschaft* 7 (1926): 13–35.

147. Westermann, 34. According to Moog (57), "Everything seems to be a sport." See also GHH *Werkszeitung*, October 16, 1926.

148. Moog, 77. Westermann (34) makes the same argument.

149. Lüddecke, *Das amerikanische Wirtschaftstempo*, 16. Rosen, 42, 51. (Reprinted in the *Bosch-Zünder*, May 30, 1921).

150. Söllheim, 179.

151. Litz, 14. Hollweg (80–87) claimed to have asked a Ford worker what he would do if he had family problems and wanted to put down his tools and think about them

for a minute. "There's time for that afterwards," replied the worker. Siegfried (158–59) also noted that American workers "enter wholeheartedly into the task of production."

152. Lüddecke, *Das amerikanische Wirtschaftstempo*, 76.

153. GHH *Werkszeitung*, May 29, 1926.

154. Walcher, 28.

155. Josef Winschuh, "Die soziale Doppelgesicht der Rationalisierung," *Magazin der Wirtschaft* 11 (March 14, 1929): 396. Bonn used almost the same words: "Work is a means to earn money, to rise up, not a *Beruf* to which one is spiritually bound;" *Kultur*, 146.

156. Brentano, 196. Lufft (358) made the same point, emphasizing that Americans placed no value on remaining in a particular trade.

157. Winschuh, "Das soziale Doppelgesicht der Rationalisierung," 396; Halfeld, 25; Martin Wagner, "Das ist Amerika," *Gewerkschafts-Zeitung*, December 6, 1924; Winter, 19.

158. Schalldach, 48.

159. Oswald Bamberger, "Als Metallarbeiter in Amerika," *Metallarbeiter-Zeitung*, December 12, 1929.

160. Josef Voigtländer, "Vom Sinn der Arbeit," *Metallarbeiter-Zeitung*, December 8, 1928.

161. Bonn, *Geld und Geist*, 74.

162. Richard Woldt, "Die deutschen Gewerkschaften in der Nachkriegszeit," in *Strukturwandlungen der deutschen Volkswirtschaft*, ed. Bernhard Harms (Berlin, 1929), 504.

163. Martin Walser, "Die Arbeit am Band," *Gewerkschafts-Zeitung*, July 18, 1925. Cited in Berg, 116.

164. "Betriebswirtschaft und Betriebsräte, *Metallarbeiter-Zeitung*, December 6, 1924; Schalldach, 90–92.

165. Nölting; Johann Gröttrup, "Die Maschine vor dem Weltgericht," *Bergarbeiter-Zeitung*, January 9, 1926.

166. Fritz Tarnow, "Das Berufsethos des Arbeitnehmers," *Die Arbeit* 6 (1929): 382; Nölting; Preller, *Sozialpolitik*, 130; Rauecker, "Monotonieproblem," 15–18; Schalldach, 95–96. Socialists were not the only ones to argue for the emerging central-ity of free time over work, but they did so much more enthusiastically than others. See L. Heyde, "Rationalisierung und Arbeiterschaft," in *Strukturwandlungen der deutschen Volkswirtschaft*, 293.

167. Günter Dehn, *Proletarische Jugend* (Berlin: 1929), 39. Cited in Peukert, 178.

168. Barschak, 126–27; Otto Debatin, "Arbeitsfreude," *Bosch-Zünder*, March 28, 1923, 52; Riedel, in *Arbeitskunde*, ed. Johannes Riedel (Leipzig and Berlin, 1925) 326; Schindler, 12–13.

169. The German terms *betriebliche Sozialpolitik* and *soziale Betriebspolitik* were used more or less interchangeably for a variety of measures that in the United States are referred to as welfare capitalism.

170. Goetz Briefs, forward to Rudolf Schwenger, *Die betriebliche Sozialpolitik im Ruhrkohlenbergbau* (Munich and Leipzig, 1932). For a similar view, see Eugen Rosenstock, "Sozialpolitik und Arbeitsrecht," in *Arbeitskunde*, 81–84.

171. Josef Winschuh, *Praktische Werkspolitik: Darstellung einer planmässigen Arbeitspolitik im modernen Fabrikbetriebe* (Berlin, 1923). Campbell (*Joy in Work*, 165) provided the only biographical information on Winschuh that I have found. Two of Winschuh's contemporaries, Adolf Geck and Ernst Michel, singled out the innova-tive character of his thought. See Geck, "Das Werden der betrieblichen Sozialpolitik

als Wissenschaft in Deutschland," *Schmollers Jahrbuch* 58:1 (1934): 59–60; and *Grundfragen der betrieblichen Sozialpolitik* (Munich and Leipzig, 1935), 22; Ernst Michel, *Sozialgeschichte der industriellen Arbeitswelt* (Frankfurt, 1960), 196.

172. Winschuh, *Praktische Werkspolitik*, 35–65, 167–93.

173. Ibid., 63.

174. Winschuh, "Die psychologischen Grundlagen der Werksarbeitsgemeinschaft," in *Die sozialen Probleme des Betriebes*, ed. Heinz Potthoff (Berlin, 1925) 268. Italics in original.

175. Robert Bosch, "Zum sozialen Frieden," *Bosch-Zünder*, January 30, 1926, 2; Georg Schlesinger, quoted by Otto Debatin, "Betriebsmenschen untereinander," *Bosch-Zünder*, June 30, 1925; Wichard von Moellendorff, *Volkswirtschaftliche Elementar-vergleiche zwischen Vereinigten Staaten von Amerika, Deutschland, Grossbritannien, Frankreich, Italian* (Berlin, 1930), 4; cited in Volker R. Berghahn, *The Americanisation of West German Industry, 1945–1973* (Cambridge, Eng., 1986), 29; GHH, 4001219/4, C. Canaris, lecture to Deutsche Normenausschuss, December 11, 1927.

176. Max Muss, "Arbeiterseele und Wirtschaftsgesetzlichkeit," *Zeitschrift für die gesammte Staatswissenschaft* 82:2 (1927): 317; GHH 4089/0 Lauster, 11. Halfeld, 148.

177. Westermann, 123.

178. Moog, 97–98.

179. Lüddecke, *Das amerikanische Wirtschaftstempo*, 68. For a confirmation of Lüddecke's grim view of German factories, see Wirtz, 51.

180. GHH 4089/0, Lauster, 10.

181. For a less harmonious picture of shop floor relations, see Lizabeth Cohen, *Making a New Deal* (Cambridge, Eng., 1990), 188–89.

182. Lüddecke (*Das amerikanische Wirtschaftstempo*, 17) recognized the impor-tance of language in creating informality but not its rather deceptive character.

183. Halfeld, 148.

184. For a Christian trade union view, see Hermann Lufft, "Aus meinen amerikanischen Erfahrungen," *Deutsche Arbeit* 11:1 (January 1926): 24–28; Lufft worked as an accountant. Dubreuil (28–53), head of the French General Confederation of Labor, also praised American managers for treating workers well. Unlike German trade unionists, however, he did complain that American workers were not especially friendly to one another and ate in hasty silence.

185. Paul Otto, "Bilder aus amerikanischen Betrieben," *BRZ* 10:16 (August 10, 1929): 501.

186. Ibid., 522; "Die 'gesunde' Auffassung des amerikanischen Arbeiters," *Metallarbeiter-Zeitung*, May 14, 1927. ADGB, *Amerikareise*, 137.

187. ADGB, *Amerikareise*, 137.

188. Otto, 521.

189. "Die 'gesunde' Auffassung des amerikanischen Arbeiters."

190. Siemens in Freyberg, 239; Aereboe, 36; Robert Bosch, "Wie kommen wir zum wirtschaftlichen Frieden?" in *Industrielle Friede*, ed. Jerome Davis and Theodore Lüddecke (Leipzig, 1928), 70. See Chapter 9 for a fuller discussion.

191. Stuart D. Brandes, *American Welfare Capitalism, 1880–1940* (Chicago, 1984), 28. For a history of Ford's welfare programs, which were run by the Ford Soci-ology Department until 1921, see Meyer, 96–145, 197–99, and Nevins and Hill, 332–51.

192. Brandes describes various programs but does not distinguish the substance and aims of 1920s programs from earlier ones. For a very nuanced analysis of welfare capitalism in Chicago firms, see Cohen, 159–83.

193. David Montgomery, "Thinking about American Workers in the 1920s," *International Labor and Working-Class History* 32 (Fall 1987): 5.

194. Hollweg, 77; Robert Holthöfer, "Sozialismus und Betriebsverfassung. Neue Gesichtspunkte der Unternehmerpolitik," *Ruhr und Rhein* 10:40 (October 4, 1929): 1,290. Holthöfer also praised American welfare capitalism for being pragmatic and nonideological.

195. W. Starcke, "Wirtschafts- oder Sozialpolitik," in *Industrielle Friede*, ed. Jerome Davis and Theodore Lüddecke (Leipzig, 1928), 80–88. Montgomery (4) suggests that this perception was correct: "The autonomy of the entreprise was the *sanctum sanctorum* of interwar management [in the United States]."

196. Rosen, 53; Westermann, 36; review of Köttgen's book, *Industrie und Handels Zeitung*, April 5, 1925, found in SAA 11/Lf 395.

197. Rieppel (32) noted that Ford was especially concerned that programs pay for themselves. Geck, *Grundfragen der betrieblichen Sozialpolitik*, 10–15; Ludwig Schmidt-Kehl, *Die deutsche Fabrikpflegerin* (Berlin, 1926), 29; Bonn, *Kultur*, 187.

198. Karl Dunkmann, "Sinn und Bedeutung der industriellen Wohlfahrtspflege," *Der Arbeitgeber* 2 (January 15, 1928): 32.

199. Feiler, 157.

200. Alfred Rühl, *Vom Wirtschaftsgeist in Amerika* (Leipzig, 1927), 104–6.

201. Christian and liberal trade unionists had even less to say than their Social Democratic counterparts and most of that was purely descriptive. See Erkelenz, 104–8; Theodor Brauer, "Amerika und Wir: Der Sozialkampf," *Deutsche Arbeit* 12:4 (April 1927): 196.

202. ADGB, *Amerikareise*, 132–33; Toni Sender, "Die Kehrseite des amerikanischen Wirtschaftswunder, II," *BRZ* 7:14 (July 3, 1926): 432–37; Lütkens, *ASWSP* 59 (1927): 772; Sachse, *Betriebliche Sozialpolitik*, 97–102.

203. Muss, 315–20; ADGB, *Amerikareise*, 95–206, 237–40; Holitscher, *Wiedersehen*, 104; Feiler, 162, 166–67, 187.

204. Bonn, *Kultur*, 184–85.

205. Lütkens, *Staat und Gesellschaft*, 27–32; Sender, "Die Kehrseite des amerikanische Wirtschaftswunders, I," *BRZ* 7:13 (June 19, 1926): 404–8.

6. The Cultural Consequences of Americanism

1. Lüddecke (*Das amerikanische Wirtschaftstempo*, 7) argued that "Americanism is first and foremost an intellectual attitude [*Geisteshaltung*]." Wengraf (30) described it as "a world view" and "a way of leading one's life."

2. Lütkens, "Europäer und Amerikaner über Amerika," 624.

3. Adolf Halfeld, *Amerika und der Amerikanismus. Kritische Betrachtungen eines Deutschen und Europäers* (Jena, 1927), xiii. For information on Halfeld, who was very widely read, see Tower, 15, fn. 7.

4. While American mass culture, especially American movies, were extensively analyzed in Weimar Germany, mass culture did not feature directly in the debates about economic Americanism. Mass consumption did. Debates about women and gender that were central to discussions of mass culture, however, did inform German discussions of the American economy. For discussions of mass culture and Americanism, see Kaes. For the association of mass culture and women, see Andreas Huyssen, "Mass Culture as Woman, Modernism's Other," in *Studies in Entertainment: Critical Approaches to Mass Culture*, ed. Tania Modleski (Bloomington, Ind., 1986) 188–207; Patrice Petro,

Joyless Streets: Women and Melodramatic Representation in Weimar Germany (Princeton, 1989).

5. Bonn, *Kultur,* 286; *Prosperity: Wunderglaube und Wirklichkeit im amerikanischen Wirtschaftsleben* (Berlin, 1931), 46.

6. For an introduction to the history of American consumer culture, see *The Culture of Consumption: Critical Essays in American History, 1880–1980,* ed. Richard Wightman Fox and T. J. Jackson Lears (New York, 1983).

7. Tichi (17–26) emphasizes how pervasive the new technology and its products were in everyday life, education, and mass culture.

8. Peukert, *Weimar,* 174.

9. Paul Rohrbach, *Amerika und Wir. Reisebetrachtungen* (Berlin, 1926), 176–79; Vershofen, *Ueber das Verhältnis von technischer Vernunft* , 13–14. In the view of more than one German, the effects of the automobile were revolutionary. See, for example, Bonn, *Kultur,* 156.

10. The discrepancy between the number of radios and telephones per capita in America and those in Germany was smaller than that for cars, but still significant. For radios it was 131 versus 66 per 1,000; for telephones, 165 versus 52. Peukert, *Weimar,* 174.

11. Witte, *Heim und Technik in Amerika.* For Bonn, see especially *The Crisis of American Capitalism* (New York, 1932).

12. Brentano, 200–201.

13. Feiler, 122.

14. Alfred Rühl, *Vom Wirtschaftsgeist in Amerika* (Leipzig, 1927), 2. Holitscher (*Wiedersehen mit Amerika,* 92) made the same point in almost the same words. While Americans now associate this kind of architecture with the Bauhaus, many Weimar Germans saw America as the embodiment of modern functionalism.

15. M. J. Bonn, *Amerika und sein Problem* (Munich, 1925), 88.

16. Hirsch, 219.

17. Halfeld, 137.

18. Bonn, *Kultur,* 6. Bonn cites this as one of the two dominant views of America, the other being uncritical praise. He shared neither.

19. Bonn, *Geld und Geist,* 78–79. Lütkens, *Staat und Gesellschaft,* 169.

20. Rosen, 50.

21. Halfeld, 17–20.

22. Bonn, *Amerika,* 78.

23. Wengraf, 41–42.

24. Holitscher, *Wiedersehen mit Amerika,* 92–93.

25. ADGB, *Amerikareise,* 56–64.

26. Wengraf, 42.

27. Rohrbach, 187–88.

28. Feiler, 123.

29. Salomon, *Kultur im Werden,* 73.

30. Hirsch, 119–220.

31. Berg, 141; Herf; Lethan, 25–27; C. W. E. Bigsby, "Europe, America and the Cultural Debate," in *Superculture: American Popular Culture and Europe,* ed. C. W. E. Bigsby (London, 1975), 6–10. As both Berg and Bigsby emphasize, Oswald Spengler was particularly influential in articulating this critique.

32. John Czaplicka, "Amerikabilder and the German Discourse on Modern Civilization, 1890–1925," in Tower, *Envisioning America* (Cambridge, Mass., 1990), 39–44.

33. Bonn, *Kultur*, 155. Rohrbach, 174–75; Rühl, 111–16.

34. Hirsch, 223–24.

35. There were, of course, many who did analyze mass culture, especially the movies. The Social Democrats, who had a vast network of cultural organizations, were especially concerned with the new forms of commercial mass culture. For discussions of movies, see Kaes and Petro. For a discussion of Social Democracy and mass culture, see W. L. Guttsman, *Workers' Culture in Weimar Germany* (New York, 1990), and Adelheid von Saldern, "Arbeiterkulturbewegung in Deutschland in der Zwischen-kriegszeit," in *Arbeiterkulturen zwischen Alltag und Politik*, ed. Friedhelm Boll (Vienna, 1986), 29–70.

36. Bonn, *Amerika*, 126; Feiler, 262–67; Halfeld; Lütkens, *Staat und Gesell-schaft*, 186–196; Rühl, 30–31.

37. Rohrbach, 175.

38. BBA, 16/472, letter from Dr. Bergassessor Matthiass to Prof. Dr. Herbst, June 1, 1922.

39. Lüddecke, *Das amerikanische Wirtschaftstempo*, 79–80.

40. Feiler, 68,

41. Wengraf, 29.

42. Witte, 10.

43. Rühl, 22–26.

44. Karl Schacht, "Amerikanische Wirtschaftsmentalität," *Ruhr und Rhein* 9:49 (December 6, 1928): 49.

45. Salomon, 17–22.

46. Westermann, 120.

47. Critics included Halfeld, 5, and Feiler, 260–61.

48. Rosen, 15.

49. Ibid., 19.

50. Westermann, 18–19.

51. Rosen, 20.

52. Erkelenz, *Amerika von Heute*, 79–80. See also Westermann, 121.

53. Halfeld, 5.

54. Mennicken, 11, 15–20, 30–31, 42, 50.

55. Ibid., 38–40.

56. Köttgen, *Das wirtschaftliche Amerika*, 56; Lüddecke, *Das amerikanische Wirtschaftstempo*, 15–19; Rosen, 16.

57. Schacht.

58. Wengraf, 36–37; Westermann, 121–23.

59. Rosen, 37.

60. Wengraf, 36 and 45. Moog (11–13, 23–24) made a very similar argument.

61. Halfeld, xvi; Hirsch, 224; Wengraf, 42.

62. Holitscher, *Wiedersehen mit Amerika*, 173.

63. Rühl, 45; Martin Wagner, "Das ist Amerika," *Gewerkschafts-Zeitung*, December 6, 1924, 483–85; Bonn, *Kultur*, 291; Holitscher, *Wiedersehen mit Amerika*, 177–78.

64. See, for example, Otto Hommer, *Die Entwicklung und Tätigkeit der deutschen Metallarbeiterverbandes* (Berlin, 1912), 118, fn. 1.

65. Birnbaum, 12; A. Schilling, "Erziehung zur Wirtschaftlichkeit an den technischen Hochschulen in Amerika und Deutschland," *Technik und Wirtschaft* 18:5 (May 1925): 139.

66. Vershofen, *Ueber das Verhältnis von technischer Vernunft*, 13–116.

67. Lüddecke, *Das amerikanische Wirtschaftstempo*, 23–24.

68. Bonn, *Kultur*, 152. See also *Geld und Geist*, 78–79.

69. At times Bonn (*Kultur*, 71) came close to arguing that mass production created uniform consumption which in turn created standardized needs.

70. Lütkens, "Neue Amerikabücher," 774; Bonn, *Prosperity*, 54–55; Riebensahm, 12–13; ADGB, *Amerikareise*, 68. Roughly two-thirds of American furniture and gas stoves and three-forths of other consumer durables were purchased on installment credit in the mid-1920s. See Nancy Cott, *The Grounding of Modern Feminism* (New Haven, 1987), 146.

71. Bonn, *Amerika und sein Problem*, 89; Brentano, 200–201.

72. Marr, 75–76.

73. For that ethos, see T. J. Jackson Lears, "From Salvation to Self-Realization: Advertising and the Theraputic Roots of the Consumer Culture, 1880–1930," in *The Culture of Consumption*, ed. Fox and Lears (New York, 1983), 1–38.

74. Bonn, *Amerika und sein Problem*, 75.

75. Rühl, 4.

76. ADGB, *Amerikareise*, 28, 59–60.

77. Halfeld, 25; Rühl, 5; Rieppel, 27; Salomon, 73.

78. Halfeld, xiv, 122–23.

79. F. Warlimont, "Die fliessende Fertigung als wirtschaftliche Frage," *Technik und Wirtschaft* 19:8 (March 1926): 79–81. For an opposing view, see L. Zeitlin, "Wege zur Rationalisierung. Rationalisierung im Grosshandel," *Frankfurter Zeitung*, June 17, 1926.

80. Wengraf, 57.

81. *Metallarbeiter-Zeitung*, May 29, 1926; May 28, 1927; February 16, 1929.

82. Friedrich Olk regretted that there was no "economic instrument" comparable to the Prussian army to educate Germans about the value of mass-produced goods. See Olk, "Fliessarbeit," *Gewerkschafts-Zeitung*, April 3, 1926; Schalldach, 72. See Chapter 10 for further discussion of Socialist and bourgeois efforts to educate consumers.

83. On America, see Stuart Ewen, *Captains of Consciousness: Advertising and the Social Roots of Consumer Culture* (New York, 1976). For the Social Democratic view, see ADGB, *Amerikareise*, 68–69.

84. For a particularly clear statement of this qualified embrace of mass consumption, see Bruno Rauecker, "Wege und Möglichkeiten der Rationalisierung," *Die Arbeit* 12 (1925): 743–45. For a view from the Christian trade union camp, see Theodor Brauer, "Amerika und wir. Der Wirtschaftskampf," *Deutsche Arbeit* 12:3 (March 1927): 140; and Kleinschmitt, 410–11.

85. Kurt Heinig, "Autoismus," *Weltbuhne* 22:1 (1926): 72–74.

86. Lütkens, "Neue Amerikabücher," 774–75.

87. Tarnow, *Warum arm sein?*, 42.

88. Winkler, 80, 89–90.

89. Adelheid von Saldern, "Die Neubausiedlungen der Zwanziger Jahre," in *Neubausiedlungen der 20er und 60er Jahre*, ed. Ulfert Herlyn, A. Saldern, and Wulf Tessin (Frankfurt, 1987), 59–67; and "The Workers' Movement and Cultural Patterns on Urban Housing Estates and in Rural Settlements in Germany and Austria during the 1920s," *Social History* 15:3 (October 1990): 333–54. For an illuminating discussion of Austrian Socialist efforts to create the "new person," see Helmut Gruber, *Red Vienna: Experiment in Working-Class Culture, 1919–1934* (New York, 1991).

90. Otto Richter, "Die Entwicklung der Technik," *BRZ* 6:4 (May 23, 1925): 348–49; Schalldach, 179–80.

91. For an illuminating discussion of why the auto industry had an overwhelmingly male workforce while the electrotechnical industry employed a significant proportion of women, see Ruth Milkman, *Gender at Work: The Dynamics of Job Segregation by Sex During World War II* (Urbana, 1982).

92. For discussions of women in Weimar, see *When Biology Became Destiny: Women in Weimar and Nazi Germany*, ed. Renate Bridenthal, Atina Grossmann, and Marion Kaplan (New York, 1984); Ute Frevert, *Women in German History: From Bourgeois Emancipation to Sexual Liberation* (Oxford, 1986), 149–204; Atina Grossmann, *Reforming Sex: The German Movement for Birth Control and Abortion, 1920–1950* (New York, forthcoming); Hagemann.

93. Petro, 40. Atina Grossmann emphasizes that women were at the cutting edge of modernity and tradition. See "'Girlkultur,' or Thoroughly Rationalized Female: A New Woman in Weimar Germany?" in *A Century of Change: Women in Culture and Politics*, ed. Judith Friedlander, Blanche Cook, Alice Kessler-Harris, and Carroll Smith-Rosenberg (Bloomington, Ind., 1985), 62–80; and "German Women Doctors from Berlin to New York: Maternity and Modernity in Weimar and in Exile," *Feminist Studies* 19:1 (Spring 1993): 65–88.

94. The exceptions were Lütkens, *Staat und Gesellschaft*, and the Communist journalist, Maria Leitner, *Elisabeth, ein Hitlermädchen. Erzählende Prosa, Reportagen und Berichte* (Berlin/Weimar, 1985), 112–20.

95. F. Langenberg, "Zum Problem der Frauenarbeit in der Metallindustrie," *BRZ* 10:25 (December 14, 1929) 767; Martin Wagner, "Das ist Amerika," *Gewerkschafts-Zeitung* December 6, 1924, 485.

96. For an excellent discussion of images of the New Woman and proletarian women in the Communist press, see Petro, 90–110, 127–39. For a comparison of the Communist and Social Democratic press, see Uta Veneman, "Representations of Women in the Leftist Press During the Mid- to Late 1920s," unpublished master's thesis, New York University, 1992. For Communist attitudes toward proletarian women and reproduction, see Atina Grossmann, "'Satisfaction Is Domestic Happiness': Mass Working-Class Sex Reform Organizations in the Weimar Republic," in *Towards the Holocaust: The Social and Economic Collapse of the Weimar Republic*, ed. Michael N. Dobkowski and Isidor Wallimann (Westport, Conn., 1983), 265–93; and "The New Woman and the Rationalization of Sexuality in Weimar Germany," in *Powers of Desire: the Politics of Sexuality*, ed. Ann Snitow, Christine Stansell, and Sharon Thompson (New York, 1983), 153–71. For one variant of the Social Democratic New Woman, see Chapter 10 in the present study.

97. It is not clear if Weimar analysts of America had read Münsterberg's book, which was published first in German and then immediately translated into English, but they described the American woman in almost exactly the same terms as he used. Münsterberg, *The Americans*, 558–89.

98. Bonn, *Kultur*, 267; *Geld und Geist*, 147; Holitscher, *Wiedersehen von Amerika*, 159.

99. Halfeld, 218.

100. Fritz Giese, *Girlkultur: Vergleiche zwischen amerikanischen und europäischen Rhythmus und Lebensgefuhl* (Munich, 1925), 107–8; Salomon, *Kultur im Werden*, 25–26.

101. Giese (97) labeled the American girl and the American woman as *Berufsmenschen*. Salomon (26) claimed American women took their careers more seriously than did European women.

102. Employment statistics are both unreliable and difficult to compare across countries, but roughly one quarter of American women were in the labor force as op-

posed to roughly one third of German women. For American women and work in the 1920s, see, Cott, 129–54, and Alice Kessler-Harris, *Out to Work: A History of Wage-Earning Women in the United States* (New York, 1982), 217–49.

103. Holitscher, *Amerika*, 387.

104. Bonn, *Geld und Geist*, 146–47. American women did marry at higher rates, and may have had somewhat better job opportunities, due in part to greater prosperity during the 1920s.

105. Holitscher (*Amerika*, 386) emphasized how active American women were in social reform and philanthropy.

106. Salomon, 27.

107. Lüddecke, *Das amerikanische Wirtschaftstempo*, 87. This view existed before World War I as well. See Fritz Voechting, *Ueber den amerikanischen Frauenkult* (Jena, 1913), 21–33.

108. Salomon, *Kultur im Werden*, 24. For her 1930s experiences, see her autobiography, *Charakter ist Schicksal* (Weinheim and Basel, 1983), 307, and the afterword by Joachim Wieler, 325–29, 335–37.

109. Aereboe, 27.

110. Feiler, 249.

111. Giese, 105. See also, Aereboe, 27.

112. See, for example, Voechting, 1–20.

113. Halfeld, 218–19.

114. The term is Giese's (96).

115. Giese; Siegfried Kracauer, "The Mass Ornament," *New German Critique*, 5 (Spring 1975): 67–70; Lethan, 43–44; Peter Jelavic, "Revues in Berlin," paper presented at a conference on "America-Weimar," Cambridge, Mass., March, 1990.

116. Giese, 82–95, 119–22.

117. Germans judged the German new woman in the same way. See Grossmann, "'Girlkultur.'"

118. Huyssen.

119. Petro, 66.

120. Halfeld, 220–23.

121. Bonn, *Geld und Geist*, 153.

122. Salomon, *Kultur im Werden*, 69–70.

123. This had troubled prewar observers as well. See Voechting, 108–9.

124. Halfeld, 209.

125. Lütkens, *Staat und Gesellschaft*, 196.

126. Hirsch, 232–33. Prohibition was seen as promoting both production and consumption, for it ostensibly prevented people from wasting money, time, and energy on drink.

127. Halfeld, 209.

128. Westermann, 27.

129. Giese, 106; Halfeld, 214.

130. Giese, 106.

131. Voechling, 34.

132. Erna Meyer, *Das neue Haushalt. Ein Wegweiser zur wissenschaftlichen Haushaltsführung* (Stuttgart, 1927), 181–83.

133. Bonn, *Geld und Geist*, 148–49; Witte, *Heim und Technik*, 21–48. In 1910 one in ten American households had electricity. By the late 1920s, the vast majority of urban homes did. David E. Nye, *Electrifying America: Social Meanings of a New Technology* (Cambridge, Mass., 1990), 239.

134. ADGB, *Amerikareise*, 126.

135. Bonn, *The Crisis of American Capitalism* (New York, 1932), 59–60. Salomon (*Kultur im Werden*, 45–6) complained that women would always invite her to their clubs or to a restaurant but never home for a meal. Cott (146) confirms the prevalence of prepared foods.

136. Bonn, *Crisis of American Capitalism*, 52–64; Salomon, *Kultur*, 44.

137. Giese, 105–107.

138. Westermann, 27–28.

139. ADGB, *Amerikareise*, 162–68; Bonn, *Kultur*, 272–73; Salomon, 44.

140. Bonn, *Crisis of American Capitalism*, 52–64; Halfeld, 34, 103.

141. ADGB, *Amerikareise*, 128.

142. Salomon, *Kultur im Werden*, 49–50.

143. Ibid., 42; Bonn, *Crisis of American Capitalism*, 52–53.

144. Salomon, *Kultur im Werden*, 41.

145. Giese, 122.

146. Salomon used "undersexed" in English in her text, perhaps because she found the concept to be distinctly American. *Kultur im Werden*, 27.

147. Petro (110) notes that the German discussion of the German New Woman often portrayed her as de-eroticized, while the working-class woman was "tragically maternal." See also Grossmann, "The New Woman," 156–62.

148. Giese, 120–21.

149. Holitscher, *Wiedersehen mit Amerika*, 160–1; Westermann, 27.

150. Giese, 120–21; Halfeld, 214.

151. Bonn, *Kultur*, 282; *Geld und Geist*, 170; Hirsch, 237.

152. Bonn, *Geld und Geist*, 156–57; Bonn, *Kultur*, 284. After her trip to America, the writer Marta Karlweis produced a series of biographical sketches of American women, all of whom led exotic, bizarre, or tragic lives. But her book deliberately sought out the exceptional rather than the typical. *Eine Frau reist durch Amerika* (Berlin, 1928).

153. Holitscher, *Wiedersehen mit Amerika*, 160–64.

154. Giese, photos opposite 103.

155. Wengraf, 37.

156. Lüddecke, introduction to *Industrielle Friede*, 54–56.

7. The Paradoxes of Productivism

1. For the wartime economy, see Gerald Feldman, *Army, Industry and Labor*; Jürgen Kocka, *Facing Total War: German Society, 1914–1918* (Cambridge, Mass., 1984).

2. For a contemporary statement of how all these factors interacted to spark the rationalization movement, see Kurt Mendelsohn, "Kaufkraftsteigerung und Kapitalbildung im Wachstumsprozess der deutschen Wirtschaft," *Gewerkschafts-Zeitung*, September 1, 1928, 551.

3. Meakin, 249.

4. Vahrenkamp, *Durchsetzung*, 10.

5. Otto Bauer, *Rationalisierung-Fehlrationalisierung*, (Vienna, 1931), 158. It is all but impossible to separate the plant closings due to stabilization from those due to rationalization, i.e., to a planned modernization of a firm or trust. This is especially true of closings in late 1924 and early 1925. Such closings continued into late 1925 and early 1926, however, and the latter were generally part of a systematic reorganization

of firms and sectors. According to Rocker, 910 firms went out of business in April 1925; by October the number had risen to 1,797. In January 1926, the number of bankrupcies totaled 3,645, but thereafter the number per month decreased, until October 1926, when the number reached 632. Rudolf Rocker, *Die Rationalisierung der Wirtschaft und die Arbeiterklasse* (Berlin, 1927), 6.

6. T. Thomas, E. Lederer and O. Suhr, *Angestellte und Arbeiter* (Berlin, 1928), 30. Cited in Bauer, 9.

7. This was the title of Meakin's study of rationalization.

8. While most contemporary observers emphasized how extensive restructuring was, some insisted that, in fact, very little rationalization occurred. See, for example, D. Warriner, *Combines and Rationalization in Germany, 1924–1928* (London, 1931), 29–32.

9. In his early studies of rationalization, Vahrenkamp suggested that it might be misleading to conflate rhetoric and reality, and subsequent studies of rationalization have borne this out. Vahrenkamp, *Taylorismus* 13–14, and *Durchsetzung*, 17. James (148–49) shares this view of the limited nature of rationalization in the 1920s. Freyberg (23–35) summarizes the current debate on the extent of rationalization.

10. The term "rationalization movement" was coined by the first business manager of the RKW, Herbert Hinnenthal, and the contemporary American scholar Robert Brady used it as the title of his book. The term captures not only the comprehensiveness of the efforts undertaken but also the ideological and emotional commitment of so many to the theory and practice of rationalization.

11. This point was made by R. Brady, "The Meaning of Rationalization," 539, and by Franz Petzold, "Wesen, Möglichkeiten und Grenzen der Rationalisierung" (Ph.D. diss., Hamburg, 1931), 6.

12. Hinrichs, 125.

13. For the most complete listing of these many associations, institutes, and organizations, see RKW, *Handbuch der Rationalisierung* (Berlin, 1930), 6–53; and Brady, *The Rationalization Movement*, 422–26.

14. Hinrichs, 125.

15. Jane Caplan, *Government Without Administration: State and Civil Service in Weimar and Nazi Germany* (Oxford, 1988), 51, 61, 81, and 84.

16. Brady, *The Rationalization Movement*, 374–82.

17. This point was made very strongly by the RKW's business manager, H. Hinnenthal. SAA 11/Lf 120 Köttgen, "Anregungen für die Umstellung des RKW," from Hinnenthal to Köttgen, July 26, 1929.

18. Birnbaum, 77; Brady, *The Rationalization Movement*, 49; RKW, *Handbuch der Rationalisierung*, 8. The state gave the RKW funds in 1921 but not in the ensuing three years. Hinnenthal, 19.

19. For Köttgen's and Raumer's lobbying activities in the spring of 1925, see the letters and memos in SAA 11/Lf 114 and 115, Köttgen; and GHH 4001210/4, letter from RKW to GHH Büro Woltmann, undated. For the text of Siemens' speech at the April 2, 1925, RKW meeting, see SAA 11/Lf 114 Köttgen; Birnbaum, 78.

20. RKW, *Handbuch der Rationalisierung*, 8. C. F. von Siemens had been involved in the RKW since its founding in 1921. See SAA 4/Lf 668, C. F. von Siemens, Bericht der Grundungs Versammlung der RKW, June 10, 1921.

21. Hinnenthal, 33.

22. *Metallarbeiter-Zeitung*, April 2, 1927. Hinnenthal, who broke down the 1926 figures slightly differently, came up with much the same result: 54 percent industrialists, 20 percent civil servants, 7 percent academics and scientists, 5 percent parliamen-

tarians; trade unionists, the press, artisans, agriculture, and banking each had 2 percent representation; housewives and wholesale and retail trade each had one percent.
SAA 11/Lf 112 Köttgen, letter from Hinnenthal to Köttgen, October 12, 1926.

23. *Metallarbeiter-Zeitung*, April 2, 1927; *Bergarbeiter-Zeitung*, May 16, 1925.

24. SAA 11/Lf 112, Köttgen, letter from Hinnenthal to Köttgen, October 12,
1926. Raumer, who had steered the RKW bill through the Reichstag, proudly wrote
Siemens that he had kept the trade union representation to a minimum. SAA 11/Lf
115, Köttgen, letter from Raumer to Siemens, April 20, 1925.

25. Brady, *The Rationalization Movement*, 387.

26. BA ZSg 1, 185/1 (2), "Jahresbericht des RKW 1928," 3. SAA 11/Lf 112
Köttgen, Köttgen speech, delivered December 17, 1925, at RKW meeting.

27. Brady, *The Rationalization Movement*, 422–23; RKW, *Handbuch der
Rationalisierung*, 19–21, 23–24, and 39–40.

28. BA ZSg 1, 188/1 (4) "Jahresbericht des RKW, 1930," 29.

29. Brady, *The Rationalization Movement*, 422; RKW, *Handbuch der Rationalisierung*, 14; Hinnenthal, 13. For more information on the strained relationship between the RKW and the DNA, see SAA 11/Lf 105 Köttgen, letter from C. Canaris
to Köttgen, October 17, 1925; SAA 11/Lf 113, letters from Köttgen to W. Hellmich,
September 15, and October 27, 1925; letter from Köttgen to Canaris, September 18,
1925; letter from Hellmich to Canaris, September 21, 1925; letter from Canaris to
Hellmich, September 24, 1925; letters from Hellmich to Köttgen, October 9 and 24,
1925; letter from Siemens to G. Klingenberg, October 29, 1925.

30. *Die deutsche Rationalisierungsbewegung und das RKW*, RKW Veröffentlichungen 4 (1927); *Der Mensch und die Rationalisierung*, part 1, RKW Veröffentlichungen 71 (1931); part 2, 83 (1933); part 3, 87 (1933); *Kostenaufbau, Kostensenkung,
Preisgestaltung*, RKW Veröffentlichungen 80 (1933); *Erfahrungen mit Fliessarbeit*, part
1, RKW Veröffentlichungen 22 (1928); part 2, 69 (1931); *Zweckmässige Verpackung aus
Holz*, RKW Veröffentlichungen 5 (1927); *Einheitsbuchführung*, RKW Veröffentlichungen 9 (1927).

31. The *Handbook* went into its second edition within six months of publication, but it is unclear who purchased the book or how it was used. The RKW emphasized that it aimed at a wide, popular audience and not specialists. BA, ZSg 1 185/
1 (3), "Jahresbericht des RKW, 1929," 4.

32. SAA 11/Lf 106 Köttgen, report from Hinnenthal to Köttgen, on his first
year as RKW business manager, January 18, 1927; Hinnenthal to Köttgen, "Denkschrift
der Geschäftsführenden Vorstandsmitglieder der RKW," October 27, 1927.

33. SAA 11/Lf 120 Köttgen, report from Hinnenthal to Köttgen, "Anregungen
für die Umstellung des RKW," July 26, 1929.

34. SAA 11/Lf 120 Köttgen, unsigned memo with Köttgen's name penciled at
the top, December 16, 1929; an unsigned and undated report, entitled "Reichskuratorium," was included with the December 16 memo.

35. SAA 11/Lf 107 Köttgen, report on a December 19, 1929 discussion between
Peter Grassmann, a member of parliament and of the RKW finance committee, and
Rudolf Breitscheid of the SPD; report on a December 21, 1929 discussion in Reichstag
among Grassmann, Breitscheid, and Otto Schaefer.

36. Otto Suhr, "Das Reichskuratorium," *Die Arbeit* 7 (1930): 455–64, quote
appears on p. 459.

37. SAA 11/Lf 107 Köttgen, letter from Schaefer to Köttgen, December 30, 1929;
SAA 4/Lf 668 C. F. von Siemens, letter from Schaefer to executive and finance committees of RKW, May 22, 1930.

38. For the history of Ruhr mining and miners in the nineteenth and early twentieth centuries, see John R. Shearer, *The Politics of Industrial Efficiency in the Weimar Republic: Technological Innovation, Economic Efficiency, and Their Social Consequences in the Ruhr Coal Mining Industry, 1918–1929* (Ph.D. diss., University of Pennsylvania, 1989), 21–103; and Klaus Tenfelde, *Sozialgeschichte der Bergarbeiterschaft an der Ruhr im 19. Jahrhundert* (Bonn, 1977).

39. For a discussion of rationalization in all German mines in the 1920s, see Brady, *The Rationalization Movement*, 67–102.

40. Shearer, 104–23.

41. Ibid., 131, 138.

42. Peukert, 116; Shearer, 161.

43. Shearer, 137–251.

44. Meakin, 36, 59.

45. Ibid., 36–37; Shearer, 300–304, 322.

46. Brady, *The Rationalization Movement*, 75; Shearer, 367–68. BBA, 16/48, "Jahresbericht, Verein für Bergbauliche Interesse, 1925."

47. Theodor Wagner, "Krise und Zechenlegen," *Gewerkschafts-Archiv* 3:6 (December 1925): 306.

48. Brady, *The Rationalization Movement*, 73; Meakin, 40; Fritz Neuhaus, *Die Zechenstillegungen im Südrandbezirk des Ruhrgebietes* (Ph.d. diss., Cologne, 1939), 73–78.

49. *Bergarbeiter-Zeitung*, May 15, 1926; "Voraussetzungen und Grenzen der bergbaulichen Umstellung," *Verband und Wirtschaft* 4:8 (August 1925); *Gewerkschafts-Zeitung*, August 29, 1925.

50. Brady, *The Rationalization Movement*, 73; Neuhaus, 83.

51. Brady, *The Rationalization Movement*, 73–74.

52. BBA 16/52, "Jahresbericht, Bergbau Verein, 1929."

53. BBA 16/50, "Jahresbericht, Bergbau Verein, 1927"; BBA 10/571, Circular distributed by Bergbau Verein to mine directors, March 28, 1928.

54. Shearer, 363.

55. Brady, *The Rationalization Movement*, 76; BBA 16/ 49, "Jahresbericht, Bergbau Verein 1926," 81; and 16/50 "Jahresbericht, Bergbau Verein 1927," 56. The Bergbau Verein maintained that electrification would be too expensive because the machinery used in the Ruhr was small and used little energy; BBA 10/571, circular from Bergbau Verein to mine directors, March 28, 1928.

56. BBA, 15/575, lecture by Bergassessor Dr. Haack to Bergbau Verein, Ausschuss für Betriebswirtschaft, February 1927; F. W. Wedding, "Die Rationalisierung im rheinisch-westfälischen Steinkohlenbergbau untertage," *Ruhr und Rhein* 9(22): 770–71.

57. BBA, 16/50, "Jahresbericht, Bergbau Verein, 1927," 53; BBA 16/51, "Jahresbericht, Bergbau Verein, 1928," 52.

58. Neuhaus, 70.

59. Shearer, 363.

60. BBA 15/575, article by G. Ludwig, "Die neuste Entwicklung der Grossbetriebe in flachgelagerten Flözen des Ruhrbezirks," *Glückauf* 46 (1930): 1053–57, and 47 (1930): 1080–87.

61. Brady, *The Rationalization Movement*, 82–93.

62. BBA 16/472, Bergrat von Rossum, "Bericht zur Tagung der Bergschulfachleute in Dresden," June 10, 1927; BBA, 16/49, "Jahresbericht, Bergbau Verein, 1926," 78; BBA 15/476, Mining engineer Jaschke, "Angewandte Zeitstudien im Braunkohlenbergbau," *Zeitschrift für Gewinnung und Bewertung der Braunkohle* 22

(1926); BBA 15/575, Bergassessor Mühlefeld, "Die wissenschaftliche Betriebsführung im Bergbau," *Bergbauliche Rundschau* 1:8 (November 26, 1927).

63. BBA, 16/474, March 9, 1926.

64. BBA, 16/474, Bergbau Verein, Ausschuss für Betriebswirtschaft, Bericht 7, "Die Zeitstudie im Untertagebetriebe," October 1927.

65. In 1928 a resolution was submitted to the Prussian Landtag, probably by the KPD, asking the government to regulate the use of stopwatches in mines. Employers' associations were incensed and the Landtag refused to comply, but no one provided statistics on the extent of the problem. BBA, 15/233, circular issued by the Prussian Ministry for Trade and Commerce to the mining directors, March 2, 1928; Memo from Arbeitgeberverband der Kaliindustrie (Employers' Association of the Potash Industry), April 3, 1929; circular issued by the Employers' Association of the Obersilesian Mining Industry, April 17, 1928; BBA, 15/575, "Mitteilungen der Fachgruppe Bergbau," 5, February 25, 1928, and March 9, 1928.

66. *Bergarbeiter-Zeitung*, March 10, 1928; BBA, 16/50, "Jahresbericht, Bergbau Verein," 1927," 72–73.

67. BBA, 16/471, "Niederschrift der Sitzung des Ausschusses für Betriebswirtschaft," January 16, 1930.

68. See Chapter 9 for a fuller discussion.

69. BBA, 15/1083, Bergbau Verein, "Stimmungsbericht," April 1, 1932; Bauer (39) and Rocker (8) use the same statistics to show that both capital and labor agreed on the facts about productivity.

70. Brady, *The Rationalization Movement*, 84.

71. Ibid., 78.

72. BBA, 10/53, Friedrich der Grosse, "Geschäftsberichte," 1927–28, 1928–29.

73. BBA 8/160, Concordia A.G., "Geschäftsberichte," 1926–1929, 1931–32; BBA 10/53, Friedrich der Grosse, "Geschäftsbericht," 1927–1928.

74. Brady, *The Rationalization Movement*, 95–100; Shearer, 278–82.

75. Brady, *The Rationalization Movement*, 101.

76. BBA 16/50, "Jahresbericht, Bergbau Verein, 1927," 61.

77. *Bergarbeiter-Zeitung*, May 17, 1930.

78. Brady, *The Rationalization Movement*, 104–5; Meakin, 90–92.

79. For a thorough discussion of the economics and organization of the industry throughout the inflation see Gerald D. Feldman, *Iron and Steel in the German Inflation, 1916–1923* (Princeton, N.J., 1977).

80. Ibid., 443–45.

81. GHH 4089/1, Schmidt-Hoffmann's reaction to the Suess report on "Amerika und Nutzheranwendung hieraus für deutsche Betriebe," March 14, 1928.

82. For overviews of the rationalization of iron and steel, see Brady, *The Rationalization Movement*, 109–13, 136–37 and DMV, *Die Rationalisierung in der Metallindustrie* (Berlin, 1933), 31–48.

83. DMV, *Die Rationalisierung*, 48.

84. Ibid., 32–38.

85. Brady, *The Rationalization Movement*, 112.

86. Meakin, 97.

87. Warriner, 40.

88. Brady, *The Rationalization Movement*, 108; Meakin, 102–3; "Zwei bedeutsame Geschäftsabschlüsse aus der westdeutschen Montanindustrie, *Verband und Wirtschaft* 7:4 (April 1928) 54.

89. Bernhard Dietrich, *Vereinigte Stahlwerk* (Berlin 1930), 115.

90. Brady, *The Rationalization Movement*, 108–9.

91. For Krupp, see Wolfgang Zollitsch, *Arbeiter zwischen Weltwirtschaftskrise und Nationalsozialismus. Ein Beitrag zur Sozialgeschichte der Jahre 1928–1936* (Göttingen, 1990), 25–30.

92. Diedrich, 112.

93. MM R 1 4110, Karl Wallmann, "Bericht über der Auswirkung des Zusammenschlusses auf die Betriebe," undated, probably late 1926.

94. MM R 4 4150, letter from Director Wallmann to Director Essen, of Düsseldorf, and Director G. Klinkenberg, of Dortmund.

95. Mülheim, for example, lost both machine building and the Thyssen central administration offices after Thyssen joined Vestag. See Otto Berger, *Mülheim an der Ruhr als Industriestadt* (Ph.D. diss., Cologne, 1932), 111–12.

96. MM R 1 40 351 Vestag, "Geschäftsbericht," January–September 1926; Meakin, 106–7; Diedrich, 107–110.

97. MM P 4 25 26, "Bericht über die Prüfung des Bauzustandes der bei den Hüttenwerke des Vestag in Angriff genommener Neubauten," March 18, 1926.

98. Diedrich, 113; MM R 4 4110, Vestag, "Neubauprogramm der Röhrenwerke," memo dated July 25, 1927; Stahl- und Walzwerke, Thyssen-Mülheim, "Neubauprogramm," April 1929.

99. Diedrichs, 113; MM R 1 40 35 1, Vestag, "Geschäftsberichte," October 1, 1927–September 30, 1928; October 1, 1928–September 30, 1929; and October 1, 1930–September 30, 1931.

100. DMV, *Die Rationalisierung*, 37.

101. MM R 4 4158 circular issued by Vestag, Research Division, to all works, dated January 1, 1928.

102. *Metallarbeiter-Zeitung*, March 19, 1927.

103. The increase in coking capacity resulted from an effort by Vestag to become self-sufficient in that area.

104. Brady, *The Rationalization Movement*, 122.

105. Archiv Thyssen, A 5401, "Vortrag beim Besuch der Pressevertreter zu Hamborn-Bruckhausen," November 11, 1926; and "Vortrag gelegentlich des Besuches des Vereins deutscher Eisen und Stahlindustrieller," March 18, 1927.

106. Diedrich, 115; Brady, *The Rationalization Movement*, 124.

107. *Metallarbeiter-Zeitung*, March 19, 1927.

108. DMV, *Die Rationalisierung*, 44.

109. Brady, *The Rationalization Movement*, 122–24. See also, Weisbrod, 55–58.

110. Krupp Archiv, WA 59/20, Responses of the Hoesch firm to a questionnaire distributed by the Enquete Ausschuss subcommittee on productivity December 14, 1926. WA 59/4, notes on a meeting of industrialists from Hoesch, Dortmunder Union, and Rheinstahl to prepare for a subsequent meeting with the subcommittee.

111. Krupp Archiv WA 59/21, response to the Enquete Ausschuss questionnaire by the factory council of Dortmunder Union, undated, but questionnaries were circulated in late 1926 and early 1927.

112. The Metalworkers' Union had argued this point since the early 1920s because industrialists repeatedly blamed lowered productivity on the eight-hour day. See, for example, BRZ, May 27, 1922, and November 11, 1922.

113. Krupp Archiv W59/21, Fritz Naphtali, "Vorläufiges Gutachten über die Material der Dortmunder Union," November 11, 1927.

114. For details on the founding and composition of the Enquete Ausschuss, see W. Grävell, "Organisation und Aufgaben des Enquete Ausschusses," *Technik und*

Wirtschaft 19:12 (December 1926): 321-25; *Jahrbuch des ADGB*, 1926, 28-35. Of the five subcommittees that carried on the investigation, one was exclusively devoted to analyzing the effects of wages and hours on productivity.

115. Krupp Archiv, WA 59/2, Enquete Ausschuss, 4; Sitzung des IV. Unterausschuss für Arbeitsleistung (meeting of the subcommittee on productivity), June 26, 1926, and W 59/4, meeting of industrialists to prepare for a subsequent meeting with the productivity committee, November 5, 1926. While some industrialists applauded the Enquete Ausschuss and urged honesty, others favored a strategy of overwhelming the committee with numbers to manipulate and confuse it; see Krupp Archiv WA 59/4, for the industrialists' discussion on Enquete Ausschuss productivity committee, October 26, 1926. For the final report of the Enquete Ausschuss, see, Ausschuss zur Untersuchung der Erzeugungs- und Absatzbedingungen der deutschen Wirtschaft, Vol. 4, *Arbeitszeit, Arbeitslohn und Arbeitsleistung im Hochofenbetrieb* (Berlin, 1929); and vol. 7, *Arbeitsleistung in Stahl- und Walzwerken und ihre Abhängigkeit von Arbeitszeit, Arbeitslohn und anderen Faktoren* (Berlin, 1930).

116. K. Mendelsohn, "Wirtschaft und Politik der Enquete-Bericht über die eisenschaffende Industrie," *BRZ* 12:2 (January 24, 1931): 25.

117. Alfred Sohn-Rethel, *Economy and Class Structure of German Fascism* (London, 1978), 29; Archiv Thyssen A 5401, Lichtbildervortrag aus Anlass des Besuches der Marine, February 27, 1928.

118. Brady, *The Rationalization Movement*, 125; BA R 13 I 336, letter from Jakob W. Reichert to Ernst von Borsig, March 16, 1931.

119. See, for example, "Erhöhung der Eisenpreise," *Magazin der Wirtschaft* 4:3 (January 19, 1928): 77-80; and F. Springorum, "Selbstkostenkrise der deutschen Eisenindustrie," *Wirtschaftsdienst* 13:3 (January 20, 1928): 1-4.

120. DMV, *Die Rationalisierung*, 32-48; Archiv Thyssen, *Das Werk* 7:11 (November 1927), excerpt from a speech by Dr. Helmut Poensgen on "Die Rationalisierung in der Wirtschaft."

121. Brady, *The Rationalization Movement*, 140-42.

122. Ibid., 139-40.

123. Freyberg, 112-13.

124. DMV, *Die Rationalisierung*, 86.

125. GHH 40813/0, Bericht über l. Konzernsitzung der Werkzeug-Ingenieure, May 26, 1926; GHH 400 1012011/ob, Reusch Nachlass, Maschinenfabrik Esslingen to Reusch, December 22, 1926; 400 1012011/1, Agreement between MAN and Maschinenfabrik Esslingen about what each would produce, February 19, 1927; Brady, *The Rationalization Movement*, 145-46.

126. Brady, *The Rationalization Movement*, 150-52; Freyberg, 217-18.

127. Freyberg, 125-37.

128. Brady, *The Rationalization Movement*, 157-60; *RKW Handbuch der Rationalisierung*, 1093-1109; Warriner, 201.

129. Freyberg, 155-56.

130. The electrotechnical industry has been thoroughly studied by Freyberg, 181-258, and Heidrun Homburg, *Rationalisierung und Industriearbeit. Das Beispiel des Siemens-Konzerns Berlin, 1900-1939* (Berlin, 1991). For an overview in English, see Brady, *The Rationalization Movement*, 169-195.

131. Brady, *The Rationalization Movement*, 150-54; Freyberg, 125.

132. DMV, *Protokoll des elften Konferenz des Reichsbeirats der Betriebsräte und Konzernvertreter der Metallindustrie*, December 1931, 36.

133. Brady, *The Rationalization Movement*, 150; Freyberg, 41. These statistics

were compiled by the major interest group serving the industry, the Verein deutscher Maschinenbau Anstalten.

134. Freyberg, 174–80.

135. Ziebura, 69–70.

136. Krupp Archiv, FAH IV E 10a, Berdrow study of restructuring at Krupp, from 1919 to 1926. The material was collected during these years but not written up until 1934–1936; Krupp, "Jahresberichte, 1918–1930."

137. Doleschal, 19; Meibes, 25.

138. Bernard P. Bellon, *Mercedes in Peace and War: German Automobile Workers, 1903–1945* (New York, 1930), 14.

139. Meibes, 79–109; Doleschal, 19; Schmitt Arnau, *Tagebuch* 183.

140. Brady, *The Rationalization Movement*, 147. As late as 1928, there were still 30 or more firms. "Der Entscheidungskampf um den deutschen Automobilmarkt," *Ruhr-Rhein Wirtschaftszeitung*, March 8, 1928.

141. DMV, *Die Rationalisierung*, 111–115; DMV, *Jahr- und Handbuch* (1927), 118–20; (1928), 40–42.

142. Arthur Pound, *The Turning Wheel: The Story of General Motors Through Twenty-Five Years, 1908–1933* (Garden City, N.Y., 1934), 250–51.

143. Doleschal, 19; DMV, *Jahr-und Handbuch* (1929), 47.

144. Bellon, 209–11; Brady, *The Rationalization Movement*, 147.

145. Paul Friedmann, "Der Weg der Deutschen Automobilindustrie," *Magazin der Wirtschaft* 8 (February 21, 1930): 379–81.

146. Meibes, 118–20.

147. Walter H. Nelson, *Small Wonder: The Amazing Story of the Volkswagen* (Boston, 1965), 21–39; Herbert A. Quint, *Porsche: Der Weg eines Zeitalters* (Stuttgart, 1951), 95–105.

148. Simon Reich, *The Fruits of Fascism: Postwar Prosperity in Historical Perspective* (Ithaca, N.Y., 1990), 107–9; Nevins and Hill, 372–73.

149. DMV, *Jahr- und Handbuch* (1930), 99. The figures came from the *Vossische Zeitung*.

150. Bellon, 215. DMV, *Jahr- und Handbuch* (1929), 47.

151. Wilhelm Vershofen, "Das Rationalisierungsproblem in der deutschen Automobilindustrie," *Magazin der Wirtschaft* 45 (November 8, 1928) was an example of the former, whereas Friedmann argued the latter, as did M. Hahn, "Die Schicksalsstunde der deutschen Automobilindustrie," *Ruhr und Rhein*, February 22, 1929, 237–41.

152. James (148–49) is wrong to dismiss the extent of rationalization.

8. Winners and Losers

1. James W. Angell, *The Recovery of Germany* (New Haven, Conn., 1929), 189; National Industrial Conference Board, *Rationalization in German Industry* (New York, 1931), v.

2. Meakin, 8.

3. This is the central argument of Bauer's book. See Rudi Litzenberger, *Die volkswirtschaftlichen Auswirkungen der deutschen technischen Rationalisierung auf die Produktionsfaktoren Arbeit und Kapital in der Nachkriegszeit* (Ph.D. diss., Cologne, 1933), 70. See also Sohn-Rethel, 28–30.

4. "Zur Lage der deutschen Wirtschaft, 3: Die Rationalisierung," *Gewerkschafts-Zeitung*, September 18, 1926, 535.

5. AD6B, *Wirtschaftsloge, Kapitalbildung, Finanzen* (Berlin, 1930), 17. James (157–61) deemphasizes high prices and cartels.

6. According to a contemporary calculation, published in the VDI journal, *Technik und Wirtschaft*, the German cost of living rose from 135 on January 1, 1925, to 153 on January 1, 1929. For France, the figures were 104 and 108, respectively; for Austria, 105 to 106. There is no explanation of how the calculations were arrived at. Ernst Neuberg, "Der Einheitspreisladen als Anreiz zur Massenfertigung," *Technik und Wirtschaft* 22:11 (November 1928): 294. A more recent index, calculated for a working-class family of five and using the year 1928 as 100, shows a rise from 93 in 1925 to 101 in 1929. Petzina, et al., 107.

7. National Industrial Conference Board, 69.

8. Ibid., 101. Figures are from the same study, Appendix Tables 23 and 24, 176–77.

9. Ibid., 110–11. Warriner, 50–51.

10. "Erhöhung der Eisenpreise," *Magazin der Wirtschaft* 4:3 (January 19, 1928): 78.

11. K. Mendelsohn, "Wirtschaft und Politik. Der Enquete-Bericht über die eisenschaffende Industrie," *BRZ* 12:2, (January 24, 1931): 28.

12. For a discussion of the AVI agreements between the Association of Manufacturing Industries and Ruhr heavy industry, see Maier, *Recasting Bourgeois Europe*, 526–27.

13. M. J. Bonn, "Rationalisierung und Handelspolitik," *Magazin der Wirtschaft* 20 (May 17, 1928): 771. "Rationalisierung für das Volk," *Bergarbeiter-Zeitung*, March 5, 1927.

14. For overviews of the cartel system in Weimar, see National Industrial Conference Board, 10–11, 30–59; and Warriner, 125–45. Brady provides details on the cartels of each industrial sector he surveys.

15. DMV, *Protokoll des elften Konferenz des Reichsbeirats der Betriebsräte in der Metallindustrie*, December 1931, 86. Cartels did not necessarily promote rationalization, as Warriner points out, 44.

16. *BRZ* 1:8 (January 8, 1927): 2.

17. *Bosch-Zünder* 8:9 (September 30, 1926): 210.

18. Toni Sender, "Preiserhöhung trotz Rationalisierung," *BRZ* 8:5 (March 5, 1927): 134, 136.

19. "Zur Lage der deutschen Wirtschaft, 2: Weltmarkt und Inlandmarkt," *Gewerkschafts-Zeitung*, September 11, 1926, 518.

20. Dietmar Petzina, "Was There a Crisis Before the Crisis? The State of the German Economy in the 1920s," in *Economic Crisis and Political Collapse: The Weimar Republic, 1924–1933*, ed. Jürgen Baron von Kruedener (Oxford, 1990), 17.

21. O. Schulz-Mehrin, "Gemeinschaftsarbeit auf dem Gebiete der Selbstkost-enrechnung im In-und Auslande," *Technik und Wirtschaft* 14:12 (December 1921): 735–47. BBA 10/122, Verwaltungsrundschreiben of the Friedrich der Grosse mine, 1921–1922. These deal with efforts to standardize procedures for ordering and accounting and to obtain detailed information on each department and operation.

22. BBA 16/625, Circular from F. W. Wedding of Bergbau Verein to all member mines, April 26, 1926; and 15/575, Bergbau Verein, Ergebnis der zweiten Rundfrage über Mechanisierungskosten der Kohlengewinnung im Ruhrbezirk, July 1927.

23. MM R 4 5304, Circular from Vestag to member firms, May 27 and October 20, 1926; R 4 4007, Circular from Vestag to member firms, December 3, 1926; January 17, 1927.

24. BBA 16/471, letter from Vestag to Wedding of Bergbau Verein, April 15, 1930.

25. BBA 16/471, minutes of meeting of Ausschuss für Betriebswirtschaft of Bergbau Verein, April 16, 1934.

26. H. Kreis, "Aufbau und Gliederung der Kosten im Bergbau- und Hütten-wesen," in RKW, *Kostenaufbau*, 27.

27. BA, R 13 I/102, report on meeting of Group 3, iron economy, Enquete-Ausschuss, January 18-21, 1928; Freyberg, 199.

28. BBA 16/469, circular from RDI to all member associations, April 29, 1932.

29. Hellwig and Mäckbach, 107, 119-20.

30. BA R 13 I/102, report on meeting of Group 3, iron economy, Enquete-Ausschuss, January 18-21, 1928. See also, Krupp WA 59/8, Hoesch's answer to IV sub-committee, Enquete Ausschuss.

31. W. Prion, "Bilanz und Kalkulation bei der Rationalisierung," *Technik und Wirtschaft* 20:5 (August 1927): 201-5; Hellwig and Mächbach, 136-42; Hans Hirsch-stein, "Technischer Fortschritt und Preisrückgang," *Magazin der Wirtschaft* 33 (August 15, 1930): 1532. For a KPD critique of business accounting methods, see G. Rei-mann, "Bürgerliche Betriebswirtschaft und Marxismus," *Die Internationale* 11:14 (July 15, 1928): 504-9, and 1:15 (August 1, 1928): 522-26.

32. Sohn-Rethel, 28-30. He relied on the well-publicized contemporary study of E. Schmalenbach; James, 158-59; Weisbrod, 89-90. Industrialists noted this problem on occasion. See the comments of C. F. von Siemens, *Magazin der Wirtschaft* 11 (March 17, 1927): 408.

33. Frieda Wunderlich, *Labor Under German Democracy* (New York, 1940), 32–33. See also, BA R 13I 215, VDA, "Denkschrift zur Lohnbewegung," February 1928.

34. For the statements of several businessmen on this issue, see *Ruhr und Rhein* 9:10 (March 8, 1928). Academic observers, such as Litzenberger (67), saw wages and social policy costs as a key element in this process but did not single them out exclu-sively as industry did.

35. Weisbrod, 70, 77-78.

36. BBA 55/38002 (1), confidential report, "Lage und Entwicklung der Abteilung Bergbau der Vereinigte Stahlwerk A-G, 1927-28," August 1928.

37. BA R 13I 215, Fritz Springorum, "Selbstkostenkrise der deutschen Eisen-industrie," *Wirtschaftsdienst* 13:3 (January 20, 1928).

38. Preller, *Sozialpolitik*, 156.

39. Ibid., 158.

40. Petzina, et al., Table b, 99.

41. Ibid., Table c, 99.

42. Preller, *Sozialpolitik*, 358-63; Wunderlich, 43-48, 77-86.

43. SPD, *Protokoll über die Verhandlungen des Parteitages der Sozialdemokratischen Partei Deutschlands* 1927, 170.

44. BBA 16/53, "Jahresbericht des Bergbau Vereins, 1930," 81.

45. Franz Vogt, "Rationalisierungserfolge im deutschen Bergbau," *BRZ* 11:10 (May 17, 1930): 304; Weisbrod, 64-65.

46. Herbert Cunz, "Der Reallohn im Ruhrbergbau," *Deutsche Arbeit* 12:10 (October 1927): 536-39; *Verband und Wirtschaft* 8:6 (June 1929): 90.

47. Weisbrod, 64. According to one industry estimate, if wages had remained stable, wage costs per ton would have dropped by 25 percent.

48. WWA F 26, Nr. 4, Concordia, Geschäftsbericht, 1928.

49. BBA 55/38002 (1) Vestag report on mining, 1928.

50. BBA 16/52, "Jahresbericht des Bergbau Vereins 1929," 63.

51. See, for example, the figures compiled by Gutehoffnungshütte, which showed wages ranging from 7.46 marks to 8.9 marks among basic iron and steel workers in different firms, and between 6.82 marks and 8.3 marks for rolling mill and semifinished goods workers. GHH, 4000149/2, September 1925.

52. BA R 13I 336, Vestag report on Enquete-Bericht über die deutsche eisenerzeugende Industrie, April 14, 1931; Weisbrod, 132–33.

53. BA R 13I 372, J. W. Reichert, "Die Löhne in der deutschen Eisenschaffenden Industrie," offprint from *Stahl und Eisen* 7 (1929): 4. *Metallarbeiter-Zeitung*, February 8, 1930; F. Lackmann, *Die Arbeitsverhältnisse der Schwerindustrie, untersucht am Beispiel der Arbeiterschaft von Gelsenkirchen im Vergleich zu anderen Städten und Gewerben* (Ph.D. diss., Cologne: 1930), 104–9. Preller, *Sozialpolitik*, 157; the calculation was Kuczynski's; Weisbrod, 136.

54. Weisbrod, 66.

55. BA R 13I 336, Vestag report on the Enquete Bericht, April 14, 1931, 24; Weisbrod, 67.

56. Weisbrod, 67; Reichert, "Die Löhne," 1; BA R 13I 372, Johannes Burgartz, "Der Lohnanteil in der eisenerzeugenden Industrie," *Deutsche Arbeit* (1929), 347–63. This article, which used confidential industry figures for one unnamed firm, was very upsetting to industry, but no reply was published because that would have required a detailed discussion of costs that "would create more damage than good, since the other side won't be convinced in any case." BA R 13I 372, letter from Karl Raabe of Klöckner to Reichert, July 29, 1929.

57. Weisbrod, 62.

58. BA R 13I 124, "Bericht über die Mitgliederversammlung des VDESI," June 15, 1927, 54–55.

59. MM R 1 40 35 1, Vestag, 3, "Geschäftsbericht," October 1, 1927–September 30, 1928.

60. BA R 13I 218 Rundschreiben des VDESI, February 1929.

61. See Weisbrod (415–57) for a detailed discussion of the complex negotiations surrounding this lockout.

62. Krupp Archiv, *Kruppsche Mitteilungen* 20:2 (January 25, 1929): 9.

63. James, 48. The insurance figure was to rise to 51 percent in 1932 due to unemployment. For the finances of specific programs, see Preller, 462–63.

64. See Chapter 4 for a fuller discussion.

65. Reichert, 6; Weisbrod, 71.

66. Weisbrod, 71.

67. For an overview of this debate, see, Winkler, 46–47. For the English translations of the principal argument in favor of an excessive wage bill, see Knut Borchardt, *Perspectives on Modern German Economic History and Policy*, (Cambridge, Eng., 1991), 143–203. For the principal supporters and critics of the Brochardt thesis, see *Economic Crisis and Political Collapse*. James (192–96) agrees with Borchardt.

68. Jürgen Baron von Kreudener, introduction to *Economic Crisis and Political Collapse*, xxix.

69. "Das Wirtschaftsjahr 1927," *Gewerkschafts-Zeitung*, Janaury 21, 1928, 33–35; "Die Lohnentwicklung in Deutschland während der Rationalisierungsperiode," *Rote Gewerkschafts-Internationale* 8:6 (June 1928): 351–52; *Bergarbeiter-Zeitung*, March 15, 1930; *Metallarbeiter-Zeitung*, December 21, 1929; DMV, *Protokoll des 11 Konferenz des Reichsbeirates der Betriebsräte der Metallindustrie*, 1931, 58–60. *Rationalisierung und Wirtschaftskrise* (Berlin, 1930), 16–21.

70. For a sampling of these views, see Friedrich Olk, "Erfolg und Krise der Rationalisierung in Deutschland," *Gewerkschafts-Zeitung*, July 30, 1927; "Die Kaufkraft unseres Binnenmarktes," *Deutsche Metallarbeiter* 30 (July 23, 1927): 429–31; *Bergarbeiter-Zeitung*, December 31, 1927; Kurt Mendelsohn, "Kaufkraftsteigerung und Kapitalbildung im Wachstumsprozess der deutschen Wirtschaft," *Gewerkschafts-Zeitung*, September 1928, 551–54; and "Preissenkung oder Lohnerhöhung? *Gewerkschafts-Zeitung*, March 2, 1929.

71. "Jahresbericht des Vereinigten Stahlwerke," *Magazin der Wirtschaft* 12 (March 22, 1929): 453–55.

72. Weisbrod, 82–85.

73. Brady, *The Rationalization Movement*, 342.

74. Weisbrod, 84. These are the figures from the Enquete Ausschuss.

75. Meakin, 75–82; Warriner, 196.

76. Herbert Cunz, "Die Rentabilität des Ruhrbergbaues," *Deutsche Arbeit* 14:10 (October 1929): 541–46.

77. Litzenberger, 56.

78. National Industrial Conference Board, 70.

79. "Bilanzen," *Magazin der Wirtschaft* 8 (February 21, 1929): 284; Warriner, 119.

80. Weisbrod, 85.

81. DMV, *Jahr- und Handbuch* (1929): 58.

82. Weisbrod, 78; *Metallarbeiter-Zeitung*, March 19, 1927.

83. While some analysts emphasized how low German profit rates were in comparison to those in America, industry spokesmen did not. See Hellwig and Mäckbach, 131.

84. MM R 140 35 1, Vestag, "Geschäftsbericht," October 1, 1929–September 30, 1930.

85. "Zwei bedeutsame Geschäftsabschlüsse aus der westdeutschen Montanindustrie," *Verband und Wirtschaft* 7:4 (April 1928): 53–58; "Die Jahresabschlüsse," *Metallarbeiter-Zeitung*, March 31, 1929.

86. Brady, *The Rationalization Movement*, 342.

87. See, Bauer, 102–5, and Chapter 5 for a fuller discussion.

88. Lüdtke, "'Deutsche Qualitätsarbeit,'" 175–6; Uta Stolle, *Arbeiterpolitik im Betrieb. Frauen und Männer, Reformisten und Radikale, Fach- und Massenarbeiter bei Bayer, BASF, Bosch und in Solingen (1900-1933)* (Frankfurt, 1980), 203.

89. Theodor Leipart, *Die 40 Stunden Woche: Untersuchungen über Arbeitsmarkt, Arbeitsertrag und Arbeitszeit* (Berlin, 1931), 85–103.

90. For the KPD argument, see Isa Strasser, "Aus der Werkstatt der Rationalisierung in Deutschland," *RGI* 7: 8–9 (August/September 1927): 485–91.

91. Hinrichs, 132–6; Stollberg, 52–3.

92. DMV, *Rationalisierung*, 192–93; Paul Gliese, "Aenderungen der Arbeitsmethoden und ihre Wirkung für die Arbeiterschaft," *BRZ* 11:14 (July 12, 1930).

93. Gustav Sobottka, "Die kapitalistische Rationalisierung und ihre Folgen für die Arbeiterschaft," *RGI* 8:10 (October 1928): 566–67; Leipart, 111–12.

94. Preller, *Sozialpolitik*, 139–41; H. Mattutat, "Rationalisierung und Arbeiterschutz," *BRZ* 9:16 (August 2, 1928): 493–96; Wilhelm Swienty, "Der Einfluss der Rationalisierung auf Betriebsunfälle und Gesundheitszustand der deutschen Arbeiterschaft," *Die Internationale* 10:4 (February 15, 1927): 107–14, and "Die Folgen der kapitalistischen Rationalisierung," *Die Internationale* 11:15 (August 1, 1928): 516–22.

95. Preller, *Sozialpolitik*, 478.

96. Litzenberger, 57.

97. See Stolle's discussion of these developments in Bosch, 197; Zollitsch, 41–42; 67–71.

98. Freyberg, 230.

99. Preller, *Sozialpolitik*, 118–20; *Deutsche Metallarbeiter*, October 8, 1927.

100. Mooser, 63.

101. Litzenberger, 10.

102. Renate Bridenthal, "Beyond *Kinder, Küche, Kirche*: Weimar Women at Work," *Central European History* 6 (June 1973): 148–66; Hagemann, 370–73, 639–40.

103. For a survey of women's work in Weimar, see Bajohr, 168–218.

104. DMV, *Die Rationalisierung*, 12. For a detailed breakdown of these figures, as well as an indication of the union's growing interest in the problem of women's work, see DMV, *Die Frauenarbeit in der Metallindustrie* (Stuttgart, 1930).

105. Mooser, 32; DMV, *Die Frauenarbeit*, 8.

106. Petzina, et al., 119.

107. Preller, 166–67.

108. Schöck, 77–80; Weisbrod, 134–35.

109. Petzina, et al., 121.

110. ADGB, *Jahrbuch*, 1930, 27; Briefs in Harms, 67.

111. See, for example, BBA 15/1083, Stimmungsbericht, July 1, 1931; 15/235 Stimmungsbericht, October 1, 1932. This argument, popular in the 1920s, was used again by German employers in the 1980s: "Das ist der Weg zurück ins 19. Jahrhundert," *Der Spiegel* (April 15, 1985): 15–20.

112. Goetz Briefs, "Eine Analyse der strukturellen Arbeitslosigkeit," *Magazin der Wirtschaft* 38 (September 22, 1927): 1447–49.

113. Kurt Mendelsohn, "Funf Jahre Rationalisierung," *Die Arbeit* 2 (1930): 124.

114. Wladimir Woytinsky, "Die deutsche Industriestatistik," *Die Gesellschaft* 11 (November 1918): 428–30.

115. ADGB, *Jahrbuch*, 1930, 28–29; DMV, *Protokoll des elften Konferenz des Reichsbeirats der Betriebsräte der Metallindustrie*, 1931, 53; Litzenberger, 20; D. Petzina, "The Extent and Causes of Unemployment in the Weimar Republic," in *Unemployment and the Great Depression in Weimar Germany*, ed. Peter D. Stachura (New York, 1986), 29–48.

116. DMV, *Die Rationalisierung*, 25–26.

117. Shearer, 392.

118. MM R 2 1002, August 6, 1925; R 1 35 28, article from *Rheinisch-Westfälische Zeitung* March 18, 1926; GHH 400149/2, April 28, 1926; Brady, *The Rationalization Movement*, 339. See MM P 2 25 49 for the anguished debate among Phoenix managers about expanding white-collar employment in the mid-1920s.

119. Krupp Archiv, FAH IV E 10a, Berdrow report 1935–37.

120. Schöck, 150.

121. Neuhaus, 109.

122. The authors who emphasize how adversely older workers were affected by rationalization do not cite statistics. Litzenberger, 9; Eric D. Weitz, *Conflict in the Ruhr: Workers and Socialist Politics in Essen, 1910–1925* (Ph.D. diss., Boston University, 1982), 259. The Ruhr statistics I have gathered suggest youth were the real victims.

123. MM P 1 25 76 Westfälische Stahlwerk, Belegschaft, November 1, 1926.

124. Krupp Archiv, WA 41/3 740a, sozialpolitische Abteilung, Tätigkeitsbericht, 1928–1929, 1929–1930.

125. Krupp Archiv, WA 54/8 Hoesch answer to the questionnaire circulated by Enquete Ausschuss Subcommittee IV, n.d.

126. BBA, 16/53, Bergbau Verein, "Jahresbericht 1930," 78; Vossen, 34–35.

127. ADGB, Jahrbuch, 1930, 30–33. Archiv Thyssen, Das Werk 6:7 (October 1926); Detlev Peukert, "The Lost Generation: Youth Unemployment in the End of the Weimar Republic," in The German Unemployed, ed. Richard J. Evans and Dick Geary (New York, 1987), 172–93.

128. Wladimir Woytinsky, Der deutsche Arbeitsmarkt (Berlin, 1930), 73–75.

129. Schöck, 57–58.

130. Lucien Revo, "Zur Frage der Rationalisierung," RGI 7:4 (April 1927): 241–47.

131. "Menschen und Maschinen, (Nach einer wahren Begebenheit)," Bergarbeiter-Zeitung, October 13, 1928.

132. For some of the many examples, see K. Schäfer, "Die Rationalisierung," Gewerkschafts-Archiv 8:1 (January 1928): 6–12; and Edwin Grützner, "Vom Wesen kapitalistischer Rationalisierung," Gewerkschafts-Archiv 11:1 (July 1929): 28–32.

133. "Rationalisierung und Arbeiter im Steinkohlenbergbau," BRZ 10:3 (February 9, 1929): 70; Rogier, 37.

134. Diessmann's speech at DMV, Verbandstag, 1926, 122–24; Toni Sender, "Tendenzarbeit des Instituts für Konjunkturforschung," BRZ 8:18 (September 3, 1927): 545–49; Kurt Heinig, "Konjunktur und Arbeitslosigkeit," Gewerkschafts-Zeitung, February 19, 1927, 105–7.

135. A. Braunthal, "Die Lage der arbeitenden Klasse in Deutschland," Gewerkschafts-Archiv 7:4 (March 1927): 100–101; Tarnow, "Wandlungen des Arbeitszeitproblems," Die Arbeit 4(1928): 201–12; Lüdtke, "Deutsche Qualitätsarbeit," 162.

136. Preller, Sozialpolitik, 363–76.

137. Johann Kretzen, "Schlagwort 'Rationalisierung'," BRZ 11:19 (September 27, 1930): 598–602; T. Sender, "Rationalisierung und Arbeitslosigkeit," BRZ 12:4 (1931): 76.

138. SPD Protokoll über die Verhandlungen des Parteitages des Sozialdemokratischen Partei Deutschlands, 1927, 165–91.

139. Fritz Naphtali, Wirtschaftsdemokratie. Ihr Wesen, Weg und Ziel (Frankfurt, 1977), 35–200.

140. Winkler, 468–69.

141. Rocker, 45–48; L. Leontiew, "Der 'organisierte Kapitalismus' und die 'Wirtschaftsdemokratie'," Unter dem Banner dens Marxismus 3:5 (October 1929): 660–87; BBA 16/478, letter from Bergbau Verein to Mann, containing excerpts from Bergbau Verein "Geschäftsbericht," April 23, 1928.

142. Vahrenkamp, Taylorismus, 17.

143. David Abraham, "Economic Democracy as a Labor Alternative to the Growth Strategy in Weimar Germany," in The Political Economy of West Germany: Modell Deutschland, ed. Andrei S. Markovits (New York, 1982), 132. For a general discussion of economic democracy, see Abraham, 118–40, and Rudolf Kuda, "Das Konzept der Wirtschaftsdemokratie," in Vom Sozialistengesetz zur Mitbestimmung, ed. Heinz Oskar Vetter (Cologne, 1975), 253–74.

144. Tarnow made this point about economic democracy; Winkler, 470–1.

145. BBA, 37/6, Versuch und Verbesserung auf der Rheinstahlzechen im Jahre 1924.

146. This quote is from the Metallarbeiter-Zeitung. Both it and the RKW quote are taken from International Labor Office, The Social Aspects of Rationalization, Studies and Reports. Series B, 18: 320, fn. 2.

147. Zollitsch, 38.

148. Metallarbeiter-Zeitung, July 2, 1927.

149. BBA, 16/473, *Bergarbeiter-Zeitung*, March 10 and 22, 1928.

150. BBA, 16/473, letter from Arbeiter- und Angestelltengruppe der Arbeits-kammer für den Kohlenbergbau to Zechen Verband, October 10, 1928.

151. DMV, *Die Rationalisierung*, 300–303; *Metallarbeiter-Zeitung*, December 1, 22, 1928.

152. (anonymous), " Die Hölle der Rationalisierung," *Die Internationale* 9:20 (October 15, 1926): 626–29.

153. "Ford in Deutschland," *Metallarbeiter-Zeitung*, February 5, 1927.

154. Graf Alexander Stenbock-Fermor, *Deutschland von Unten. Reisen durch die proletarische Provinz, 1930–1931* (Frankfurt, 1980), 105 and 103.

155. Ausschuss zur Untersuchung der Erzeugungs- und Absatzbedingungen der deutschen Wirtschaft, Unterausschuss 4, Vol. 2, *Die Arbeitsverhältnisse im Steinkohlen-bergbau in den Jahren 1912–1928* (Berlin, 1928), 260–74; according to Zollitsch (40–41), older miners disliked the pneumatic jack hammers, but young miners preferred them as long as they earned good money.

156. Ausschuss zur Untersuchung der Erzeugungs- und Absatzbedingungen der deutschen Wirtschaft, Unterausschuss 4, Vol. 7, *Die Arbeitsleistung in Stahl- und Walzwerken und ihre Abhängigkeit von Arbeitszeit, Arbeitslohn und anderen Faktoren* (Berlin, 1930), 79–80, 93.

157. Ausschuss zur Untersuchung, Vol. 4, 48–53.

158. *Metallarbeiter-Zeitung*, March 2, 1928.

159. DMV, *Protokoll der Konferenz des Reichsbeirats der Betreibsräte der Metall-industrie*, 1929, 40.

160. BBA, 15/1083. Bergbau Verein Stimmungsbericht, July 11, 1930.

161. Karl-Heinz Roth, *Die "andere" Arbeiterbewegung* (Munich, 1976), 97.

162. Shearer, 383.

163. V. Demar, "Die Rationalisierung der Produktion und die politische Arbeit im Betrieb," *Die Kommunistische Internationale* 20 (1927): 976–82; reprinted in Hinrichs and Peters, 269–75.

164. Stolle, 251–52. See also, James Wickham, "Social Fascism and the Divison of the Working-Class Movement in the Frankfurt Area, 1929–1930," *Capital and Class* 7 (Spring 1979): 1–34.

165. Demar, 271–72.

9. Engineering the New Worker

1. Fricke, 3.

2. Arvand Dach, *Menschenbehandlung in der Industrie. Eine betriebssozio-logische Studie* (Ph.D. diss., Technische Hochschule Carola-Wilhelmina zu Braun-schweig, 1931), 23. For a contemporary assessment of these new efforts, see RKW, *Der Mensch und die Rationalisierung. Bericht über die Tagung am 27. u. 28. Februar 1931* (Berlin, 1931); also published as RKW, *Mensch und Rationalisierung, I: Berufsauslese, Berufsausbildung und Bestgestaltung der Arbeit* Veröffentlichungen 71 (Berlin, 1931). For overviews of the Weimar debates about the human factor of production, see Bunk, 81–292; Campbell, *Joy in Work*, 158–275; Hinrichs, 208–90.

3. Karl Arnhold, "Betrieb und gewerkschaftlicher Verband als Faktoren industrieller Arbeitsschulung," in *Industrielle Arbeitsschulung als Problem*, ed. Soziales Museum, Frankfurt am Main (Berlin, 1931), 34–38, and "Industrielle Menschen-führung, ihre Methoden und Ziele unter besondere Berücksichtigung der Landwirt-

schaft," lecture given to the Betriebswirtschaftliche Tagung, Breslau, May 31, 1927 (Breslau, 1927), 4–7.

4. Sachse, *Betriebliche Sozialpolitik als Familienpolitik*, 5.

5. Rudolf Schwenger, *Die betriebliche Sozialpolitik im Ruhrkohlenbergbau* (Munich and Leipzig, 1932), 4–5.

6. L. H. Adolf Geck, *Grundfragen der betrieblichen Sozialpolitik* (Munich and Leipzig, 1935), 29, 61.

7. Geck, 55–56.

8. Bäumer, 1. The most comprehensive survey of rationalization measures is contained in the RKW, *Handbuch der Rationalisierung*. The best contemporary introductions to the range of new company social policies are by Dach and Geck, and in *Probleme der sozialen Betriebspolitik*, ed. Goetz Briefs (Berlin, 1930).

9. Bäumer, 1.

10. See, for example, RKW, *Mensch und Rationalisierung, I*, Veröffentlichungen 71: 297–98; and Karl Kurnehm, "Die sozialpolitische Stellung des modernen Unternehmers," *Menschenführung. Gedanken zur Sozialpolitik. Ehrengabe aus dem Kreise der sozialpolitischen Abteilung der Siemens-Werke für Dr.-Ing. Hermann Görz zum 1. Oktober 1930* (Berlin, 1930), 7.

11. E. Bramesfeld, "Memorandum," *Memoires*, International Congress of Scientific Management (Amsterdam, 1932), 78–82.

12. Schwenger, 5.

13. Tim W. Mason, "Zur Entstehung des Gesetzes zur Ordnung der nationalen Arbeit, vom 20. January 1934: Ein Versuch über das Verhältnis 'archaischer' und 'moderner' Momente in der neuesten deutschen Geschichte," in *Industrielles System und Politische Entwicklung in der Weimarer Republik*, ed. Hans Mommsen, Dietmar Petzina, and Bernd Weisbrod (Düsseldorf, 1974), 338. For a history of women factory social workers and factory social policy toward women workers, see Carola Sachse, *Industrial Housewives: Women's Social Work in the Factories of Nazi Germany* (New York, 1987).

14. Briefs, "Probleme der sozialen Betriebspolitik," 5–7.

15. See Chapter 5, for a fuller discussion. See also Dach, 17. Dr. Ulrich Trortzsch rightly insists that without postwar economic and political conflicts, company social policy would have been much more limited. See his intervention in the roundtable discussion in Pohl, ed., *Betriebliche Sozialpolitik*, 77.

16. Sachse, *Betriebliche Sozialpolitik als Familienpolitik*, 72–73. According to Sachse (342) company social policy came to be primarily concerned with issues of "production politics" rather than "party politics." While this may have been true for some academics and for companies like Siemens, for Dinta, the two concerns were more balanced.

17. Mooser, 91–92.

18. R. Kaufmann, "Um die Seele des Arbeiters," *Vossische Zeitung*, January 13, 1927, cited in *Arbeitsschulung* 1:1 (October 1, 1929).

19. Stolle, 253.

20. Bäumer, 21–22.

21. For one of the most scathing and reactionary attacks on state social policy, see Ernst Horneffer, *Frevel am Volk. Gedanken zur deutschen Sozialpolitik*, 2nd ed. (Leipzig, 1930).

22. Paul Osthold, a Dinta collaborator, argued that Weimar social legislation was using the firm as a base from which to move toward the goal of economic democracy. *Das Werk* (Thyssen) 5:10 (January 1926): 490. See also, "Um die Seele des Arbeiters," *Gewerkschafts-Archiv* 5:6 (December 1926): 300.

23. The most comprehensive survey come from Schwenger, *Sozialpolitik im Ruhrkohlenbergbau*, and *Die betriebliche Sozialpolitik in der westdeutschen Grosseisenindustrie* (Munich and Leipzig, 1934).

24. For an uncritical overview of company social policy at Bosch, see *Sozialpolitik bei Bosch*, ed. Robert Bosch (Stuttgart, 1951). For Zeiss, which under Ernst Abbe pioneered prewar company social policy, see Dr. Frl. Schomerus, "Die soziale Betriebspolitik der Zeisswerke mit besonderer Berücksichtigung der Carl-Zeiss-Stiftung," in *Probleme der sozialen Betriebspolitik*, ed. Goetz Briefs (Berlin, 1930), 27–36. Two works by Sachse, *Siemens* and *Betriebliche Sozialpolitik als Familienpolitik*, detail Weimar innovations as background to the investigation of Siemens company social policy under National Socialism. For Siemens' view of its own social policy, see *Menschenführung. Gedanken zur Sozialpolitik*.

25. Geck, 27.

26. Preller, 221; Sachse, *Betriebliche Sozialpolitik als Familienpolitik*, 91–93. There is some confusion about whether the institute was established in 1927, as Preller and Geck maintain, or 1928 as reported in RKW *Nachrichten*, 3:5 (May 1929): 130, and Sachse, 91.

27. RKW-*Nachrichten* 3:5 (May 1929): 130; Geck, 35; Wirtz did his study of *Werksfremdheit* at Giessen, while Dach wrote his analysis of human management at Braunschweig with Theodor Geiger and F. Meyenberg.

28. *Industrielle Arbeitsschulung als Problem*, ed. Soziales Museum Frankfurt am Main (Berlin, 1931).

29. Sachse, *Betriebliche Sozialpolitik als Familienpolitik*, 452, fn. 4; RKW, *Mensch und Rationalisierung I*, Veröffentlichungen 71. See also *Der Mensch und die Rationalisirung, II: Mensch und Arbeitsgerät*, Veröffentlichungen 83, and *Der Mensch und die Rationalisierung, III: Eignung und Qualitätsarbiet*, Veröffentlichungen, 87, both 1933.

30. GHH, 4001020/7, Deutsche Volkshochschule Berlin 1924–1930. This file contains the correspondence between Gutehoffnungshütte and the Deutsche Volkshochschule about the courses which the latter offered and the reactions of GHH managers who participated in them. The exact relationship between the Volkshochschule and the Deutsche Vereinigung is unclear, but by 1929 announcements about deutsche Volkshochschule courses were being sent out by the Deutsche Vereinigung. For information on the Deutsche Vereinigung before World War I, see Elaine Glovka Spencer, *Management and Labor in Imperial Germany: Ruhr Industrialists as Employers, 1896–1914* (New Brunswick, 1984), 55–56.

31. RKW, *Mensch und Rationalisierung I*, 186; Sachse, *Betriebliche Sozialpolitik als Familienpolitik*, 69.

32. Bunk, 131–132; for a detailed picture of the activities of the AFAS, see Bunk, 82–128.

33. Dach (74–80) emphasizes the similarities between Dinta and the AFAS, while Bunk stresses their differences (292), but they agree on the localized influence of the AFAS.

34. Konrad Jarausch, *The Unfree Professions: German Lawyers, Teachers and Engineers, 1900–1950* (New York, 1990), 17–18. See also, Kees Gispen, "Engineers in Wilhelmian Germany: Professionalization, Deprofessionalization, and the Development of Nonacademic Technical Education," in *The German Professions, 1800–1950*, ed. Geoffrey Cocks and Konrad H. Jarausch (New York, 1990), 104–22.

35. Jarausch, 20–22, 65; Gert Hortleder, *Das Gesellschaftsbild des Ingenieurs. Zum Politischen Verhalten der Technischen Intelligenz in Deutschland* (Frankfurt, 1970),

19–20. The Verein deutscher Diplom Ingenieure recruited only the academically trained, while the Bund technisch-industrieller Beamter functioned as a trade union.

36. Although enrollment in technical universities declined after 1923, over-crowding continued throughout the decade. In 1926, for example, over 8 percent of technical employees were unemployed; Jarausch, 40, 56, 60.

37. Preller, *Sozialpolitik*, 135–36; Karl-Heinz Ludwig, *Technik und Ingenieure im Dritten Reich* (Düsseldorf, 1979), 35–39.

38. Jarausch, 48, 72.

39. Ludwig, 27.

40. Freyberg, 321–23; Herf, 152–88; Jarausch, 64.

41. Hortleder, 59–61. For some of the many articles on this theme in *Technik und Wirtschaft*, see A. Schilling, "Die Bewirtschaftung der technischen Wissenschaften," 17:2 (February 1924): 33–37; A. Schilling, "Erziehung zur Wirtschaftlichkeit an den technischen Hochschulen in Amerika und Deutschland," 18:5 (May 1925): 136–42; G. Leipart, "Ingenieur und wirtschaftliches Denken," 19:1 (January 1926): 1–11; and F. zur Needen, "Ingenieur, Chemiker und Kaufman Hand in Hand," 21:2 (February 1928): 29–36.

42. Bäumer, 127.

43. Arnhold, a man whose politics and company social policy programs were very consistent, was most inconsistent about the spelling of his first name, using Carl and Karl indiscriminately. Following the lead of two recent works in English by Campbell and Rabinbach, I have used Karl in the text. In bibliographic citations, however, I have given whichever spelling occurred.

44. *Die menschliche Arbeitskraft im Produktionsvorgang*, 1, 8–9, 15.

45. For details of Arnhold's early life, see *Ein Leben für die Wirtschaft*, 1–12; Gert von Klass, *Albert Vögler: Einer der Grossen des Ruhrreviers* (Tübingen, 1957), 289.

46. For a discussion of Spengler and other reactionary modernists, see Herf, 49–69; Vögler had been in contact with Spengler at least since the early 1920s and had met with him prior to the 1925 meeting; Oswald Spengler, *Briefe 1913–1936* (Munich, 1963), 181, 193, 211, 264.

47. Bunk, 193–198.

48. C. Arnhold, "Industrielle Führerschaft im Sinne des Deutschen Instituts für technische Arbeitsschulung," in *Probleme der sozialen Betriebspoldik*, ed. Briefs, 11–17; Arnhold, in *Die menschliche Arbeitskraft im Produktionsvorgang*, 15 and 22; Arnhold, speech given to the Reichsorganisation für persönliche Berufsvermittlung (RANO) in Berlin, March 3, 1927, and printed by RANO; and Arnhold, "Industrielle Menschenführung, ihre Methoden und Ziele unter besondere Berücksichtigung der Landwirtschaft," 7.

49. *Reden aus Anlass der Indienstnahme des Dintahauses zu Düsseldorf am 30. Mai 1926 mit einem Geleitwort von Oswald Spengler* (no further bibliographical information available).

50. Dinta statistics are notoriously slippery. Different Dinta publications offer partial and often conflicting numbers. Dinta "Tätigkeitsberichte," 1926–1933. Dinta, *Unsere Werkzeitungen*, n.d., 1–2; *Wesen, Wollen und Wirken der DINTA-Werkzeitungen* (Düsseldorf, 1933), 3–4. Hinrichs (287) cites the figure of 300, which seems inflated. The most complete list I have found is in the RKW, *Mensch und Rationalisierung*, I (156–79), which for 1930 lists 58 individual firms that had Dinta-operated insitutions and 96 other factories which participated in Dinta-operated cooperative teaching institutions.

51. GHH, 400101226/11 A, Dinta "Tätigkeitsbericht," October 6, 1925–Janu-

ary 15, 1926; GHH 400101226/11 A, letters from Reusch to Arnhold, December 19, 1925, and January 25 and 29, 1926; GHH 4020/1, Dinta list of board of directors, 1926. Before the Dinta house opened, Rheinmetall gave Dinta rooms in which to run courses; see *Reden aus Anlass*, 3.

52. Dinta (Gelsenkirchen, n.d.), 5; The Dinta "Tätigkeitsberichte," which appeared twice a year, reveal the organization's progress; RKW *Mensch und Rationalisierung*, I, 159–179.

53. GHH 4020/1, Dinta printed list of members of committees, 1926.

54. GHH 400101226/11, Dinta "Tätigkeitsbericht," October 6, 1925–January 15, 1926; Dinta *Arbeitsgebiet und Organisationsplan*, n.d. It is not clear whether "accessible to Dinta (*dem Dinta erreichbaren*) referred to location or politics.

55. GHH 400101226/11, Arnhold letters to Reusch, February 4, May 15, and October 11, 1926, February 7, 1927; and Reusch to Arnhold, January 29, May 12, June 17, September 18, and October 13, 1926. There is no Vögler Nachlass.

56. GHH 4020/1 Dinta "Tätigkeitsbericht," January 16–March 15, 1926, and March 16–August 15, 1926; *Aus der Arbeit des Dinta. Eine Bilderschau*, ed. Hauptschriftleitung der Vereinigten Werkszeitung des Dinta (Gelsenkirchen, n.d.); BBA, 55/25000, *Arbeitsschulung* 1:1 (October 1929).

57. BBA 55/25000, *Arbeitsschulung*, 1:1 (October 1929); Bunk, 205–7; Campbell, 254–55; the Society of Friends of Dinta claimed to have 90 institutional and 400 individual members when it was established in 1929; BBA, 37/ 90, Arnhold lecture, Protokoll der I Mitgliederversammlung, Gesellschaft der Freunde des Dinta, 1929.

58. Campbell (*Joy in Work*, 259) emphasizes Dinta's lack of originality because she looks primarily at the organization's ideas and not at its concrete practices.

59. Erik Reger, "Die wirkliche Arbeiterpresse," *Die Weltbühne* 25:10 (1929): 367.

60. This insistence on the centrality of the engineer created some tension between Dinta and employers about who would have final control over both programs and personnel.

61. Karl Arnhold, "Werkszeitungen in der Idee," *Der Arbeitgeber* 20 (October 15, 1928): 507.

62. The phrase was used by Bertolt Brecht in an interview about *Mann ist Mann*, cited in Willett, 153.

63. Karl Arnhold, "Die menschliche Arbeitskraft im Produktionsprozess, ihre Schulung und Erhaltung," lecture given to the Verein technischer Grubenbeamter (Oberhausen, n.d.), 3.

64. Ibid., 5.

65. Dach, 57.

66. Ibid., 48.

67. Ibid., 55 and 57.

68. Arnhold, "Betrieb und gewerkschaftlicher Verband als Faktoren industrieller Arbeitsschulung," 49. See also, Carl Arnhold, "Richtige Begriffe, richtige Taten," *Gelsenkirchener Allgemeine Zeitung*, March 10, 1927.

69. Karl Arnhold, "Betriebsingenieur als Menschenführer," lecture given to the Berliner Bezirksverein deutscher Ingenieure, March 2, 1927 (Dinta, n.d.); Karl Arnhold, "Arbeitsschulung im Rahmen des Betriebes, gemäss den Grundsätzen des Dinta," in *Industrielle Arbeitsschulung als Problem*, ed. Soziales Museum Frankfurt am Main (Berlin, 1931), 33–49; DINTA (Gelsenkirchen, n.a.), 2; anonymous, *Ein Leben für die Wirtschaft*, 39–40; Paul Osthold, *Das Alters- und Invalidenwerk der Gelsenkirchener Bergwerks A. G., Abt. Schalker* (Düsseldorf, n.d.); and Archiv Thyssen, A 5049, Ausbildung August Thyssen Hütte Hamborn nach Vorschlagen DINTA, n.d.

70. Ernst Horneffer, *Der Ingenieur als Erzieher* (Essen, 1926), 12.

71. Paul Osthold, *Der Kampf um die Seele unseres Arbeiters* (Düsseldorf, n.d.), 26–27.

72. Dach, 47.

73. GHH 4020/1, Dinta "Tätigkeitsbericht," January 16–March 15, 1926, 6; Karl Arnhold, "Das DINTA zwischen Werks-und Arbeitsgemeinschaft," *Wirtschaftliche Nachrichten für Rhein und Ruhr*, Sonderdruck 29 (July 21, 1926); *Das DINTA und die Gewerkschaften*, a pamphlet published under Osthold's name as part of the book *Der Kampf um die Seele unseres Arbeiters*, and also published under Arnhold's name, *Wirtschaftliche Nachrichten für Rhein und Ruhr* (offprint) 6 (February 10, 1927); Bäumer, 122.

74. Wirtz, 83–96, 116.

75. Arnhold, "Das DINTA zwischen Werks- und Arbeitsgemeinschaft," 3; *Arbeitsschulung* 1:1 (October 1929): 1. Other advocates of the new company social policy, such as H. Landmann, the director of social policy at Borsig, made similar arguments. See Landmann, "Die betriebspolitischen Bestrebungen der Borsig-Werke," in Briefs, *Probleme der sozialen Betriebspolitik* (Berlin, 1930), 40–41.

76. Horneffer, *Der Weg zur Arbeitsfreude*, 11. Arnhold never commented on this idea publicly. In a correspondence with Holz of Gutehoffnungshütte, Arnhold wrote, "If we hesitate a little to try to test the feasibility of Horneffer's idea, that is less because of reservations on principle than because of lack of money." GHH 4020/1, Dinta, 1925–1928, letter from Arnhold to Holz, June 22, 1926. See also, letter from Holz to Arnhold, June 9, 1926.

77. Max Schiefen, "Dinta: Die neue kommende Facharbeiterbildung," *Phoenix-Zeitung*, January 2, 1926.

78. For information on Osthold, who went on to edit the *Deutsche Bergwerkszeitung* in 1928, see Campbell, 252, and Sachse, *Betriebliche Sozialpolitik als Familienpolitik*, 448, fn. 8.

79. Osthold, 7.

80. GHH, 400101226/11A, Reusch Nachlass, Horneffer speech, April 24, 1926. Dach (23), a student and advocate of Dinta, argued that training mid-level leaders was "the great and very thorny task which the future has to solve."

81. Bunk, 229–31; GHH 4020/1, Dinta. "Die Stellung der Bereitschaftsingenieure I u. II und der Einsatzingenieure," n.d., *Dinta* (Gelsenkirchen, n.d.), 2–3; RKW, *Mensch und Rationalisierung I*, 153–54.

82. GHH 4020/1, has a list of all the lecture topics from 1926 to 1928; BBA, 55/25000, Dinta "Tätigkeitsbericht," 1925–1928, report on lectures for those years. Neither source gives attendance figures.

83. GHH, 4020/1, "Die Stellung der Bereitschaftsingenieure I und II. und der Einsatzingenieure," 3; Bunk, 231; GHH 4020/1, and 400101226/11 A, have copies of the *Mitteilungen für aus dem Dinta hervorgegangene Männer*. They contained enthusiastic reports on Dinta activities, provided practical tips, and listed job openings.

84. GHH 400101226/11 A, program for psychotechnical training course, September 22–26, 1929; BBA, 37/90, program for vacation course on "Die Arbeitsstudie im Dienste der Lehrwerkstatt," Oktober 19–24, 1931.

85. GHH 400101226/11b, letter from Arnhold to Reusch, July 13, 1931, and a 1931 list of 101 participants in the short courses from October 1930 through March 1931. Three-quarters were from mining, but since this is the only list by industry, it is impossible to know how representative it is. Hinrichs (285) says that as of March 1928, 91 engineers had taken the long course.

86. Carl Arnhold, "Industrielle Führerschaft im Sinne des Deutschen Institutes für technische Arbeitsschulung," 13; Arnhold, "Die Arbeitskraft im Produktions-prozess," 2.

87. Anonymous, *Ein Leben für die Wirtschaft*, 35–36.

88. Karl Arnhold, "Der Betriebsingenieur als Menschenführer," lecture at VDI monthly meeting, Berlin, March 2, 1927, 9.

89. Many individual firms, such as Bosch and Siemens, also consolidated voca-tional training under their control, but they did not use Dinta engineers or adopt the Dinta ideology; Preller, 455–56; anonymous, "Vierzig Jahre Bosch-Lehrling," in *Der Lehrling im Hause Bosch*, ed. Robert Bosch GMBH (Stuttgart, 1953), 38–50.

90. Carl Arnhold, "Würdigung und Form der Lehrlingsausbildung in den Vereinigten Staaten," *Der Arbeitgeber* (special issue) 22 (November 15, 1927). Although Henry Ford ran an apprenticeship school in his own factory, there is no indication that Arnhold knew about it or imitated it; Ford, 211–13.

91. Archiv Thyssen, FWH 250/00, Dinta Vorschläge für die Neugestaltung der Lehrlings Ausbildung bei FWH, December 23, 1927; Helmut Uebbing, *Berufliche Bildung bei der Thyssen AG* (Duisburg, 1979), 42–50.

92. Schwenger, *Die betriebliche Sozialpolitik im Ruhrkohlenbergbau*, 70; BBA, 10/69, notes of April 12, 1927, meeting with Generaldirector Klein and Gruben-vorstand.

93. BBA, 15/913, letter from RDI Fachgruppe Bergbau to Heinrich, Verein für bergbauliche Interesse, February 28, 1928. For more on mine owners' reactions to the government's plan, see BBA 15/911, allgemeine Erhebungen über den Stand der Ausbildung.

94. BBA, 15/914, allgemeine Erhebungen über den Stand der Ausbildung, and lecture by Heinrich of the Verein für bergbauliche Interesse, "Der gegenwärtige Stand der Ausbildung der bergmännischen Nachwuches im rheinish-westfäslichen Kohlen-gebiet," given to the Kohlensyndikat, March 21, 1927, 1–4; BBA, Bestand 16/50, "Jahresbericht des Vereins für bergbaulichen Interessen, 1927," 81–87.

95. RKW, *Mensch und Rationalisierung I*, 182–83.

96. BBA, 15/914, Heinrichs lecture; *Aus dem Arbeit des Dinta*, 6–8.

97. Dach, 51, fn 4. There were no girls in apprenticeship programs in mining, iron and steel, and metalworking. Of the 14 textile firms in which Dinta was active, six trained only boys for skilled jobs, one trained boys and girls, and one only girls. The remaining five offered some semiskilled training to girls; RKW, *Mensch und Rationalisierung* I, 156–79. It is impossible to estimate how many firms imitated Dinta methods without employing Dinta engineers.

98. Josef Wilden, "Werklehrling-Werkgehilfe-Werkmeister," *Der Arbeitgeber*, 18 (September 15, 1928): 454–55; Rheinishe-Westfälisches Wirtschafts-Archiv, 20-1-12-5, "Bericht der Industrie und Handelskammer Essen, Mühlheim-Ruhr und Oberhausen betr. Lehrlingsausbildung," September 30, 1925.

99. Peukert, *The Weimar Republic*, 89–95. For an introduction to the major Weimar survey of young workers and their discontents, see Campbell, *Joy in Work*, 185–200.

100. Karl Arnhold, "Industrielle Menschenführung, ihre Methoden und Ziele," 7. See also Archiv Thyssen A/5049, "Das Ausbildungswesen auf der Aug. Thyssen Hütte Hamborn nach Vorschlägen des Dinta," 1926.

101. *DINTA*, 2; anonymous, *Ein Leben für die Wirtschaft*, 23, 27–30.

102. W. Dill, "Die zweijährige Ausbildung von Berglehrlingen übertage," *Berg-und Hüttenmännischen Zeitschrift Glückauf* (offprint) 3, 1927.

103. RKW, *Mensch und Rationalisierung*, III, 41–43; Schwenger, *Die betriebliche Sozialpolitik in der westdeutschen Grosseisenindustrie*, 41–45; Schindler, 41. Dinta employed the methods of others and did not seek to innovate in this area.

104. Dinta promised that apprenticeship training workshops would be self-supporting in half a year. Thyssen's management underlined this promise in red and added an exclamation point that probably expressed doubt. See Archiv Thyssen A/5049, "Das Ausbildungswesen August Thyssen Hütte Hamborn nach Vorschalgen Dinta," 1926, 22–23; Archiv Thyssen A/5048, letter from engineer Brau to director Bartscherer of Thyssen, dated August 16, 1928, informing him that the apprenticeship training workshop was running a deficit and would likely do so for a few years.

105. Bäumer, 54–55.

106. Schmedes, 152; Archiv Thyssen A/5049, "Das Ausbildungswesen August Thyssen Hütte Hamborn nach Vorschlagen Dinta, 7.

107. Schmedes, 152–53.

108. Bäumer, 55–61; Schmedes, 152–53.

109. Anonymous, *Ein Leben für die Wirtschaft*, 27.

110. Bäumer, 62.

111. According to P. Dehen, who wrote the major study of factory schools, 62 of the 125 that existed in 1927 were established after 1918. See Peter Dehen, *Die deutschen Industriewerksschulen in wirtschafts-, wohlfahrts- und bildungsgeschichtlicher Beleuchtung* (Munich, 1928), 264–70.

112. Barschak, 152–53. In fact, roughly 25 percent of adolescents, most of whom were girls and/or unskilled, did not attend vocational schools or factory schools. See Mooser, 55; Gladen, 56–57.

113. Dehen, 7, 264–70.

114. Barschack, 149–53; Dehen, 164–70, 261.

115. Archiv Thyssen, A/5048, Werksschule der Vestag, August-Thyssen-Hütte. Dehen (202–3) published a similar curriculum from a large machine tool factory in Berlin. It is not clear if the firm was influenced by Dinta.

116. Dinta firms were hardly the only ones concerned with sport in the 1920s. Siemens had extensive programs. See SAA 14/Lg 992, "Jahresbericht der Werkschule," 1926–1927; *Siemensmitteilungen* 98 (February 1, 1927): 30–32; and SAA 11/16/Lb 371, Nachlass Haller, article from *Deutsche Allgemeine Zeitung*, May 16, 1930; Sachse, *Betriebliche Sozialpolitik als Familienpolitik*, 82–83, 346–49. Sports programs were not restricted to youths. Vestag had 16 company sports associations in which seven thousand workers participated. See Schwenger, *Betriebliche Sozialpolitik in der westdeutschen Grosseisenindustrie*, 160.

117. Osthold, "Das Dinta und die Gewerkschaften," 48; also published under Arnhold's name, *Wirtschaftliche Nachrichten für Rhein und Ruhr* (special issue) 6 (February 10, 1927).

118. Bäumer, 63–64; Fr. Fröhlich, "Bewirtschaftung der menschlichen Arbeitskraft," *Technik und Wirtschaft* 18:9 (September 1925): 261; RKW *Mensch und Rationalisierung*, III, 39–40; Schwenger, *Die betriebliche Sozialpolitik im Ruhrkohlenbergbau*, 102–5. Schwenger, *Die betriebliche Sozialpolitik in der westdeutschen Grosseisenindustrie*, 63–70; Uebbing, 52–53. Various Dinta publications printed articles praising the benefits of sports programs. See, for example, GHH, *Werkszeitung*, October 16, 1927; *Arbeitsschulung* 1:1, October 1929.

119. Archiv Thyssen, VSt/276, "Bericht über den Stand der Werkschule des Vestag, Dortmunder Union," February 15, 1928.

120. *Aus der Arbeit des Dinta* has pictures of recreational activities for nearly all the firms whose programs it covers.

121. *Ein Leben für die Wirtschaft*, 64.

122. Bäumer, 34–38; Dinta's Forschungsstelle für industrielle Schwerarbeit provided the technical job analyses and recommendations for such courses and increased Dinta control of them.

123. Barschak, 88, fn 60.

124. "Die Werkszeitschrift von ihren Anfängen bis zur Gegenwart," *Informationen für die Mitglieder des Vereins für soziale Betriebspraxis* 36 (Sept. 1, 1954): 1–3.

125. Archiv Thyssen, VSt/233, 1932 report on costs and circulation of company newspapers.

126. Anne Winkelmann, *Die bergmännische Werkszeitschrift von 1945 bis zur Gegenwart* (Ph.D. diss., Berlin, 1964), 43–55.

127. Karl Arnhold, "Werkszeitungen in der Idee," *Der Arbeitgeber*, 20 (October 15, 1928).

128. *DINTA*, 3. See also Dinta, *Unsere Werkzeitungen*, n.d., 10.

129. Dinta, *Unsere Werkzeitungen*, 1–2.

130. The Thyssen paper, *Das Werk*, prided itself on being a "company paper and simultaneously a family magazine"; Archiv Thyssen, *Das Werk* 1(1): 1.

131. Archiv Thyssen, VSt/233, "Bericht über der Reichs-Jahrestagung 1928 der Vereinigten Werkszeitungen am 28. September 1928, Cologne," 8. At the same meeting, Dr. Schmidt of GHH advocated starting a children's supplement to compete with Social Democratic ones, but this was never done, "Bericht," 38–39.

132. My analysis of these papers is based on reading the full run of the Gutehoffnungshütte *Werkszeitung* and selected issues of the Thyssen publication, *Unsere Hütte*, and the *Phoenix Zeitung*. Besides papers produced by Dinta, I also read the company papers published by Siemens, Krupp and Bosch, as well as the Thyssen magazine, *Das Werk*, aimed at a distinctly middle-class audience.

133. The Gutehoffnungshütte paper had a great deal of this, while the Phoenix one focused more exclusively on technology and the firm.

134. Archiv Thyssen, VSt/233, "Bericht über der Reichs-Jahrestagung 1928 der Vereinigten Werkszeitung," 31–33. See, for example, the Thyssen paper, *Unsere Hütte*, February 16, 1929, and August 3, 1929.

135. *Kruppsche Mitteilungen*, 1920–1930; Alfred Striemer, "Werkszeitungen," *Technik und Wirtschaft* 19:11 (November 1926): 306–8.

136. Archiv Thyssen, VSt 233, "Bericht über der Reichs-Jahrestagung 1928," 27.

137. GHH 400 1921/13, report of Schmidt (December 7, 1925, p. 3) on RDI meeting of company newspaper editors, held December 3, 1925.

138. Archiv Thyssen, VSt 233, "Bericht über der Reichs-Jahrestagung 1928." See also Archiv Thyssen, VSt 233, April 4, 1931, "Bericht über eine Besprechung von Werkszeitungsbearbeiter," March 31, 1931.

139. Archiv Thyssen, *Phoenix-Zeitung*, July 4, 1925, opening editorial; Schwenger, *Betriebliche Sozialpolitik im Ruhrkohlenbergbau*, 189; Alf Lüdtke, "Images of Industry, Silences of Work: Domination, Re-Appropriation and 'Eigensinn' in German Factories," unpublished ms. in author's possession, 9–12.

140. Archiv Thyssen, *Phoenix Zeitung*, 1925 and 1926 contained numerous examples of both of these columns for women.

141. GHH 400 0921/13, letter from Schmidt to Dr. Hilbert, March 2, 1928; letter from Kellermann and Schüring to Schmidt, April 5, 1928.

142. There was only one letter to the editor in the entire 1925 run of the *Phoenix Zeitung*, but in 1928 the editor of the Rheinische Stahlwerk paper claimed 43 blue- and white-collar workers had sent in contributions in 1927. This paper had no letters-to-the-editor column, however, because it feared opponents of the company paper would use it; Archiv Thyssen, VSt/233, results of questionnaires sent to all editors of company newspapers in Vestag firms, September 28, 1928, 34–35. *Bosch-Zünder* (not published by Dinta) did solicit contributions eagerly, but its editor, Otto Debatin, defined acceptable material so narrowly and criticized dissenting views so harshly that by the late 1920s no workers participated; *Bosch-Zünder*, December 20, 1928.

143. Schwenger, *Betriebliche Sozialpolitik im Ruhrkohlenbergbau*, 204–5.

144. MM P 22536, letter from central administration of Phoenix to Phoenix in Hamm, November 12, 1924. Archiv Thyssen, A 596/4, memo from Feldmann, November 1926; Niederschrift der Besprechung, April 29, 1926, Bochum; letter from Hauptrevision to Vestag, Abt. Bergbau, Essen, November 17, 1926.

145. Paul Osthold, *Das Alters- und Invalidenwerk der Gelsenkirchener Bergwerks-AG.*

146. Karl Dunckmann, in *Die menschliche Arbeitskraft im Produktionsvorgang*, 9.

147. Sachse, *Siemens*, 214–17, 256.

148. Hinrichs and Peters, 86.

149. "Der Kampf um die Seele der Arbeiterschaft," *Die Internationale* 10:9 (May 1, 1927): 276–79; Alex Eggener, "Aus der Praxis der 'wissenschaftlichen Betriebsorganisation,'" *Die Internationale* 11:1 (January 1, 1928): 18–22; E. Ostermann, "Auf der Jagd nach der 'Seele des Arbeiters,'" *Rote Gewerkschafts-Internationale* 8:9 (September 1928): 504–5.

150. "Der Kampf um die Seele der Arbeiterschaft," 279. See also, "Das Leben eines Dintaschülers im Bergbau," *Ruhr Echo*, June 5, 1929.

151. SAA 11/Lf 395 Köttgen, Paul Ufermann, "Technische Arbeiterschulung durch die Industrie," *Deutsche Werkmeister-Zeitung*, January 1926, 28–29; Josef Voigtländer, "Vom Sinn der Arbeit, *BRZ*" 9:25 (December 8, 1928): 779; Hedwig Wachenheim, review of Wunderlich, *Fabrikpflege*, *Gewerkschaftliche Frauen-Zeitung*, May 15, 1926, 35–36; "Gewerkschaft oder Werksgemeinschaft," *Bergarbeiter Zeitung*, August 7 and 14, 1926.

152. Fritz Fricke, "Grundlagen und Methoden der neuen psychologischen Arbeitspolitik der Unternehmer," *Gewerkschafts-Zeitung*, May 21, 1927, 286.

153. Ludwig Preller, "Beruf und Freizeit in ihren kulturellen Zusammenhängen," in *Arbeitskunde*, ed. Johannes Riedel (Berlin, 1925), 244–50; Richard Seidel, "Die Rationalisierung des Arbeitsverhältnisses," *Die Gesellschaft* 7 (1926): 29; Richard Woldt, "Betriebsingenieur und Betriebspolitik," in *Probleme der betrieblichen Sozialpolitik*, ed. Goetz Briefs (Berlin, 1930), 142–43.

154. Fritz Fricke, "Die Rechtfertigung des Dinta," *Die Arbeit* 5 (1928): 291–99; Karl Zwing, "Sozialmensch oder Betriebsmensch," *Gewerkschafts-Archiv* 8:1 (January 1928): 40–41; "Die Menschenbewirtschaftungsanstalt oder die 'kalte' Werksgemeinschaft," *Metallarbeiter-Zeitung*, June 18, 1928; "Blütenlese aus Werkszeitungen," *Gewerkschafts-Zeitung* July 30, 1927.

155. Preller, *Sozialpolitik in der Weimarer Republik*, 456; Fritz Fricke, "Gewerkschaften und soziale Betriebspolitik," *Die Arbeit* 9 (1930): 611; Bäumer, 141; *Bergarbeiter-Zeitung* 13, March 26, 1927.

156. Sachse, *Betriebliche Sozialpolitik als Familienpolitik*, 102–3; Anna Geyer, "Die Berufsausbildung der Arbeiterin," *Gewerkschafts-Archiv* 2:2 (February 1923), 97; Karl Naskrensky, "Mensch und Maschine im Produktionsprozess," *Gewerkschafts-Archiv*

2:2 (February 1925): 112–16; Theodor Wagner, "Menschenorganisation im Bergbau," *Bergarbeiter-Zeitung*, June 13, 1925. Dinta frequently reminded the unions of these shared concerns. See, for example, *Dinta und die Gewerkschaften*, 43–47.

157. ADGB, *Entwurf eines Berufsausbildungsgesetzes* (Berlin, 1929), 3–6; RKW, *Mensch und Rationalisierung*, I, 198–204.

158. Eduard Weitsch, "Das Dinta als gemeinsames Problem der Gewerkschaften und der freien Volksbildung," *Die Arbeit* 10 (1927): 686; Fricke, *Sie Suchen die Seele*, 23–24, 28–29; Fricke's reply to Arnhold, in *Industrielle Arbeitsschulung als Problem*, ed. Soziales Museum, Frankfurt am Main (Berlin, 1931), 135; Wirtz, 73–74. For positive Christian trade union views, see G. Wieber, *Der deutsche Metallarbeiter*, May 5, 1928.

159. Karl Zwing, "Das Problem der Werkszeitungen," *Gewerkschafts-Archiv* 7:1 (January 1927): 38.

160. Fricke, *Sie Suchen die Seele*, 29; Duisburg *Volksstimme*, July 22, 1929, cited in *Arbeitsschulung* 1:1 (October 1, 1929): 19.

161. Alexander Knoll, "Werkszeitungen und Gewerkschaftspresse," *Gewerkschafts-Zeitung*, February 19, 1927, 107–8.

162. Anna Siemsen, "Zum Problem der Berufsschule und der Berufsausbildung," *Gewerkschafts-Archiv* 5:5 (November 1926): 220–26; Dehen, 172.

163. *Jahrbuch des ADGB*, 1927, 224–29; H. Schliestedt, "Erziehung und Ausbildung der Jung-Metallarbeiter," *BRZ* 8:23 (November 12, 1927): 710–14.

164. See, for example, Theodor Brauer, "Berufsausbildung in der Industrie und das 'Dinta,'" *Der deutsche Metallarbeiter*, May 21, 1927, 323–24; Dach, 99; Dehen, 174–75.

165. See, for example, Clara Mleinek, "Berufsberatung, Berufsauslese, Berufsausbildung," *Deutsche Arbeit* 10:2 (February 1925): 89–91.

166. *Ein Leben für die Wirtschaft*, 64. Dinta had actively cultivated the church's support. GHH 4020/1 Dinta, cover letter to copy of an article by Schulte on "The Christian Conception of Vocation and Modern Economic Life," that Dinta sent to its supporters. The article appeared in the *Kirchlicher Anzeiger für die Erzdiözese Köln*, March 1, 1927.

167. *Deutsche Arbeit* 12:8 (August 1927): 440, and 12:9 (September 1927): 495; Karl Arnhold, "Betrieb- und gewerkschaftlicher Verband als Faktoren industrieller Arbeitsschulung"; and Fritz Rütten, comment in *Industrielle Arbeitsschulung als Problem*, ed. Soziales Museum, Frankfurt am Main (Berlin, 1931), 57, 74–75.

168. Fritz Rütten," comment in *Industrielle Arbeitsschulung*, 58.

169. MM R 140 47.2, sozialpolitischer Bericht 33, May 12, 1928; *Deutsche Arbeit* 8 (August 1927): 441.

170. The Metalworkers' Union newspaper, for example, seemed consistently more worried by Dinta than was the Miners' Union paper, even thought Dinta was extremely active in both industries.

171. "Ausbildung von Bergjungleute durch das Dinta," *Bergarbeiter-Zeitung*, September 1, 1928, 278–80. For a Christian trade union version of the same optimistic assessment, see *Der deutsche Metallarbeiter*, April 2, 1927.

172. Hans Jahn, "Um die Seele der Arbeitenden!" *Gewerkschafts-Archiv* 7:4 (April 1927): 171. For a similarly deterministic and teleological statement, see J. Luserke, "Was haben wir von der 'rationellen Betriebsführung' zu erwarten?" *BRZ*, 10:6 (March 23, 1929): 177–78. Communists made similar arguments. See Walter Fleiss, *Internationaler Sozialistischer Kampfbund* 10 (October 1, 1927), cited in *Arbeitsschulung* 1:1, (October 1, 1929).

173. Erik Reger, *Die Weltbühne* 10 (March 5, 1929): 18. See also, Duisburg *Volksstimme*, July 22, 1929, cited in *Arbeitsschulung* 1:1 (October 1, 1929); *Metall-arbeiter-Zeitung*, May 21, 1932.

174. Helmut Wagner, "Rationalisierung und Berufsausbildung," *Gewerkschafts-Archiv* 5:4, (October 1926): 199.

175. Toni Sender, "Das 'Dinta' im Kampf um die Arbeiterseele," *BRZ* 8:9 (April 30, 1927): 261–62.

176. See Schalldach (96–97) for a general critique of positions like those of Wagner and Jahn.

177. *Metallarbeiter-Zeitung*, September 14, 1929.

178. See, for example, *Aus der Arbeit des Dinta. Eine Bilderschau* (Gelsenkirchen, n.d.).

179. Alexander Hellwig and Frank Mäckbach, *Neue Wege Wirtschaftlicher Betriebs-führung* (Berlin, 1928), 37.

180. Heinz Marr, comment, *Industrielle Arbeitsschulung als Problem* (Berlin, 1931), 65.

181. Some bourgeois observers also feared Dinta apprentices would become class conscious as soon as they finished their training. See *Frankfurter Zeitung*, February 22, 1927, cited in MM R 1 40 47.2, sozialpolitischer Bericht, 13, April 22, 1927.

182. Helmut Wagner, "Rationalisierung und Berufsausbildung," *Gewerkschafts-Archiv* 5:4 (October 1926): 199.

183. "Die Dinta auf der GBAG, Gelsenkirchen," *Ruhr Echo*, February 7, 1929; and "Tod Dem Dinta-Faschismus," *Ruhr Echo*, March 8, 1929.

184. Archiv Thyssen, *Unsere Hütte*, 1929.

185. Archiv Thyssen, FWH 250/00, memo from Dellweg to Arnhold, July 7, 1928.

186. Bunk, 255.

187. Archiv Thyssen, VSt/233, Auszug aus der Ausführungen der Gruben-steigers Friedrich, Hamborn, 1929.

188. DMV, *Protokoll der Betriebs-Räte Konferenz*, January 1928, 14; *Metall-arbeiter-Zeitung*, March 3, 1928; Bunk (237) surmises that most workers probably did not read company papers, or at least not the economic articles in them.

189. Reger, 366.

190. GHH 400 150/4, reports from company police to Frl. Dr. Schmidt, January 25, 1926; February 22, 1927, August 19, 1929.

191. Duisburg *Volksstimme*, July 22, 1929; cited in *Arbeitsschulung* 1:1 (October 1929). Emphasis in original.

192. *Metallarbeiter-Zeitung*, July 9, 1927.

193. Lüdtke argues that Nazi rhetoric praising work found approval among work-ers. "'Ehre der Arbeit'," 374, 381.

194. For the experiences of Ruhr workers, see Ulrich Herbert, "'Die guten und die schlechten Zeiten,'": Ueberlegungen zur diachronen Analyse lebensgeschichtlicher Interviews," in *'Die Jahre weiss man nicht, wo man die heute hinsetzen soll': Faschismus-Erfahrungen im Ruhrgebiet* (Berlin, 1983). For a more general survey, see Zollitsch.

195. Herbert; Detlev Peukert, *Inside Nazi Germany* (New Haven, 1982), 101–25; Zollitsch, 70–71.

10. Housework Made Easy

1. For an introduction to the work of these architects and the vast literature on them, see *Architectural Association Quarterly* 11: 1 (1979), which is entirely devoted

to social housing in Weimar; *Berlin 1900–1933, Architecture and Design*, ed. Tilmann Buddensieg (New York and Berlin, 1987); and Gisela Stahl, "Von der Hauswirtschaft zum Haushalt, oder wie man vom Haus zur Wohnung kommt," in *Wem gehört die Welt. Kunst und Gesellschaft der Weimarer Republik*, ed. die neue Gesellschaft für bildende Kunst (Berlin, 1977), 87–109.

2. Until recently, scholars have ignored these groups. An exception is Barbara Orland, "Effizienz im Heim. Die Rationalisierungsdebatte zur Reform der Hausarbeit in der Weimarer Republik," in *Kultur und Technik* 4 (1983): 221–227.

3. Saldern, "Die Neubausiedlungen der Zwanziger Jahre," 63.

4. For an overview of the international dimensions of the household rationalization movement (which, however, concentrates on household technology), see Siegfried Giedion, *Mechanization Takes Command* (New York, 1948), 512–627. For the American movement, see Ruth Schwartz Cowan, *More Work for Mother* (New York, 1983), 151–192; and Giesela Bock and Barbara Duden, "Arbeit aus Liebe–Liebe als Arbeit: Zur Entstehung der Hausarbeit im Kapitalismus," in *Frauen und Wissenschaft*, ed. Gruppe Berliner Dozentinnen (Berlin, 1977), 118–199. For the contemporary discussions, see *International Congress of Scientific Management*, Memoires, Rome, 1927; Paris, 1929; Amsterdam, 1932.

5. For the bourgeois women's movement, see Richard Evans, *The Feminist Movement in Germany, 1894–1933* (Beverly Hills, 1976); Ute Frevert, *Women in German History: From Bourgeois Emancipation to Sexual Liberation* (Oxford, 1988) 107–30; Irene Stoehr, "'Organisierte Mütterlichkeit' Zur Politik der deutschen Frauenbewegung um 1900," in *Frauen suchen ihre Geschichte*, ed. Karin Hausen (Munich, 1983), 221–49. For Social Democratic women, see Jean H. Quataert, *Reluctant Feminists in German Social Democracy, 1885–1917* (Princeton, 1979). For education programs see Gerda Tornieporth, *Studien zur Frauenbildung* (Weinheim/Basel, 1979).

6. Hagemann, 90.

7. Heinz Potthoff, *Die Bedeutung des Haushaltes in der Volkswirtschaft* (Berlin, 1921).

8. Christine Frederick, *Die rationelle Haushaltführung: betriebswissenschaftliche Studien*, translated by Irene Witte (Berlin, 1921). For information on Frederick and the American home economics movement, I am indebted to the unpublished paper of Marilynn Johnson, "The Cult of Domestic Efficiency, 1910–1935" (1983). See also, Bock and Duden, and Cowan.

9. Irene Witte, *Heim und Technik in Amerika* (Berlin, 1928), v–vii.

10. Erna Meyer, "Rationalisierung der Verbrauchswirtschaft im Haushalt," *Technik und Wirtschaft* 15:2 (February 1922): 116.

11. BA, NL Lüders 69, letter from Herbert Hinnenthal to Lüders, June 28, 1927.

12. *RKW-Nachrichten* 3:1 (January 1929): 1–2, and 3:4 (April 1929): 1. Both Mühsam-Werther, who was close to conservative industrial political circles, and Lüders, a liberal, claimed major credit for the founding of the Home Economics Group and remained bitter enemies throughout the 1920s. BA NL Lüders 69, letters from Mühsam-Werther to Lüders, August 26, 1926, and December 14, 1926. Reply from Lüders, Dec. 16, 1926.

13. *Das neue Haushalt. Ein Wegweiser zur wissenschaftlichen Hausführung* (Stuttgart, 1927). For information on the Housewives Associations, see Renate Bridenthal, "Class Struggle Around the Hearth: Women and Domestic Service in the Weimar Republic," in *Towards the Holocaust: Anti-Semitism and Fascism in Weimar Germany*, ed. Michael Dobowski and Isidor Walliman (Westport, Conn., 1983); and "'Professional' Housewives: Stepsisters of the Women's Movement," in *When Biology Became*

Destiny: Women in Weimar and Nazi Germany, ed. Bridenthal et al. (New York, 1984), 153-73.

14. SAA 11/Lf 107 Köttgen, Verzeichnis der Mitglieder der Gruppe Hauswirt-schaft beim RKW.

15. BA Z Sg 1 185/1 (3) "Jahresbericht des RKW, 1929," 194-95. Authors such as Witte (59-89) provided detailed descriptions of not only the national Bureau of Home Economics, but also of organizations and activities on the state and local level in the United States.

16. BA, Z Sg 1 185/1 (3) "Jahresbericht des RKW, 1929," 191.

17. *RKW-Nachrichten* 3:1 (January 1929): 1-2.

18. BA, Z Sg 1 185/1 (3) "Jahresbericht des RKW, 1929" 191.

19. *RKW-Nachrichten* 6:8 (August 1932): 109. The Home Economics Group's publications are filled with such statistics, whose origins are never explained and whose accuracy is impossible to ascertain.

20. BA, Z Sg 185/1(4), "Jahresbericht des RKW, 1930," 141.

21. *RKW-Nachrichten* 3:8 (August 1929): 219-20. The research results also appeared in other publications. The *Handbuch der Rationalisierung* (1050) admitted the tentative nature of these results.

22. BA Z Sg 1 185/1 (3) "Jahresbericht des RKW, 1929," 189.

23. SAA, 11/Lf Köttgen, Nov. 19, 1928. *RKW-Nachrichten* 3:7 (July 1929): 187-88.

24. *RKW-Nachrichten* 4:11 (November 1930); BA Z Sg 1 185/1 (4) "Jahresbericht des RKW, 1930," 146-47.

25. *RKW-Nachrichten* 4:11 (November 1930): 341-42.

26. SAA 11/Lf Köttgen, December 24 and 28, 1926.

27. BA Z Sg 1 185/1 (6), "Jahresbericht des RKW, 1932-1933," 81.

28. BA Z Sg 1 185/2 (1), RKW Schriftenverzeichnis, 1939, 3-4.

29. Witte, 48-49.

30. Meyer, "Rationalisierung der Verbrauchswirtschaft," 116.

31. Irene Witte, "Rationelle Haushaltsführung. Praktische Ergebnisse einer ameri-kanischen Studienreise," *International Congress of Scientific Management, Memoires*, Part 2, Vol. 1, Rome 1927, 313.

32. *International Congress of Scientific Management, Memoires*, Vol. 2 (Amster-dam, 1932), 8-31.

33. Ibid., Vol. 1, Part 1 (Rome, 1927), 142; and Vol. 1, Part 2, 29-34.

34. Ibid., Vol. 1, Part 1 (Rome, 1927), 146.

35. For a thorough discussion of homework see Barbara Franzoi, *At the Very Least She Pays the Rent: Women and German Industrialization, 1871-1914*, (Westport, Conn., 1985).

36. See, for example, Bäumer, 90; Gutehoffnungshütte, *Werkszeitung*, July 19, 1930, 8-9.

37. Meyer, *Das neue Haushalt*, 3-4.

38. Tornieporth, 311-15.

39. Witte, *Heim und Technik*, 51-52.

40. See Chapter 6 for a fuller discussion.

41. Orland (227) argued that the rationalized home was to remain the antithesis of the world of work. For many advocates of rationalization, both home and work were redefined in similar ways.

42. Meyer, *Das neue Haushalt*, 2; emphasis in original.

43. RKW, *Handbuch der Rationalisierung*, 1044.

44. G. Villwock, *Hausarbeit leicht gemacht* (Berlin, n.d.); *RKW-Nachrichten* 4:11 (November 1930). Even before the RKW began circulating its pamphlets on a large scale, the *Metallarbeiter-Zeitung* (May 28 and October 29, 1927) repeated the same message.

45. See, for example, *RKW-Nachrichten* 5:1 (January 1931): 14–15; Margarethe Rudorff, *Die Normung in der Hauswirtschaft* (Berlin, 1927). The most comprehensive vision of the effectively arranged and standardized working-class household was presented by Marie-Elisabeth Lüders, "Normung und Haushalt," *Technik und Wirtschaft* 20:1 (January 1927). A shortened version appeared in the *Metallarbeiter-Zeitung*, April 30, 1927.

46. Villwock. See also Meyer, *Das neue Haushalt*, 4.

47. Von Saldern, 53–62; Hagemann (79) noted that 95 percent of Hamburg workers lived in prewar housing.

48. Among household rationalizers, Lüders articulated the new rationalized aesthetic most clearly. Interestingly her views were reprinted in the Social Democratic press. See, for example. *Gewerkschaftliche Frauenzeitung*, August 15, 1927. Among architects, Bruno Taut was the most passionate publicist of this view, arguing that housewives had to change their tastes now in order to be ready for the new housing at a later date. See Bruno Taut, *Die neue Wohnung. Die Frau als Schöpferin*, (Leipzig, 1924).

49. An exception was Elsa Herrmann, *So ist die neue Frau*. See the excerpt in Helgard Kramer, "'Rationelle Haushaltsführung' und die 'neue Frau' der zwanziger Jahre," *Feministische Studien* 1 (1982): 123–26.

50. Meyer, *Das neue Haushalt*, 181–83.

51. Stahl, 104.

52. Günther Uhlig, *Kollektivmodell 'Einküchenhaus.' Wohnreform und Architekturdebatte zwischen Frauenbewegung und Funktionalismus, 1900–1933* (Giessen, 1981), 75–88, 97–106. For a critical assessment of Viennese Socialist housing, see Gruber, 46–65.

53. Hagemann, 106–14.

54. *International Congress of Scientific Management, Memories*, Part 2, Vol. 1 (Rome, 1927), 349.

55. Ewen; Johnson, 2–4; Rapp and Ross, 100; Cowan argues that poorer households did gain access to some household technology, though not as fully or as securely as the middle classes. 172–91.

56. *Siemens-Mitteilungen* 75 (December 1, 1925): 11–13. For an analysis of the values that the newly rationalized lower middle-class family was to embody, see Carola Sachse, "Von 'Güterströmen' und 'Menschenströmen.' Betriebliche Familienpolitik bei Siemens, 1918–1945," in *Unter allen Umständen: Frauengeschichte(n) in Berlin*, ed. Christiane Eifert and Susanne Rouette (Berlin, 1986), 221–24.

57. *RKW-Nachrichten* 5:1 (January 1931): 14–15.

58. *Metallarbeiter-Zeitung*, February 14, 1931.

59. Elfriede Behne, "Rationelle Haushaltführung," *Gewerkschaftliche Frauenzeitung*, March 15, 1928, 23–24, and May 15, 1928, 39–40.

60. Witte, *Heim und Technik*, 21–48.

61. RKW, *Handbuch der Rationalisierung*, 1038–39.

62. *Metallarbeiter-Zeitung*, August 20, 1927.

63. Meyer, *Das neue Haushalt*, 6.

64. *Bosch Zünder* 6:5 (May 31, 1924): 118.

65. Erich Lilienthal, "Rationalisierung des Privatlebens," *Der Arbeitgeber* 9 (May 1, 1928): 212.

66. Schwenger, *Die betriebliche Sozialpolitik in der westdeutschen Grosseisenindustrie*, 131.

67. GHH 40018/2, Wohlfahrtseinrichtungen, April 22, 1927. Schwenger, *Die betriebliche Sozialpolitik in der westdeutschen Grosseisenindustrie*, 131. It is not clear who taught these courses. Most were probably vocational education teachers or women trained in the burgeoning field of factory social work for women. Although Dinta sponsored such programs, it did not train the teachers.

68. GHH 40018/11 Werksfürsorge, Abt. Schulen, "Jahresbericht 1927/8," 2.

69. GHH 4020/1, Arnhold's introduction to lectures on company social policy, April 21, 1928; GHH *Werkszeitung*, July 19, 1930, 8–9.

70. GHH 4020/1, lecture by Frl. G. Wennecke, April 21, 1928.

71. Bäumer, 88. He also argued that children could learn proper family roles there.

72. Schwenger, *Die betriebliche Sozialpolitik im Ruhrkohlenbergbau*, 170–74; *Die betriebliche Sozialpolitik in der westdeutschen Grosseisenindustrie*, 132–35.

73. Carola Sachse, *Industrial Housewives: Women's Social Work in the Factories of Nazi Germany* (New York, 1987).

74. Meyer, "Rationalisierung der Verbrauchswirtschaft," 119.

75. GHH 4020/1, Dinta, April 21, 1928.

76. Schwenger, *Die betriebliche Sozialpolitik im Ruhrkohlenbergbau*, 162.

77. Sachse, *Betriebliche Sozialpolitik*, 219; GHH 40018/11 brochure on *Handarbeitsschulen*, April 1925; Schwenger, *Die betriebliche Sozialpolitik im Ruhrkohlenbergbau*, 181.

78. GHH 4020/1, lecture by Frl. M. Grundies, April 21, 1928.

79. GHH *Werkszeitung*, July 19, 1930, 8–9; Bäumer argued the same point, 90.

80. Otto Schenz, "Meine betriebspolitischen Versuche und Erfahrungen," in *Probleme der sozialen Betriebspolitik*, ed. Goetz Briefs (Berlin, 1930), 66.

81. Meyer, *Das neue Haushalt*, 3–6; Stahl, 105.

82. Irene Witte, introduction to her translation of Friedrich's *Die rationelle Haushaltführung*, vii.

83. Rudorff, 23.

84. Lüders, "Normung," *Metallarbeiter-Zeitung*, April 30, 1927.

85. Middle-class clutter was also criticized by these same reformers, but that represented a disagreement within a class that shared much else.

86. Saldern, 62; Hagemann, 116–17.

87. Barschak, 140–41; Hagemann, 124–29.

88. *Jahresbericht der Preussischen Gewerbeaufsichtsbeamten und Bergbehörden*, 1927, Regierungsbezirk Münster, 392, 404; Regierungsbezirk Koblenz, 505; Karin Hausen, "Unemployment Also Hits Women: The New and the Old Woman on the Dark Side of the Golden Twenties in Germany," in *Unemployment and the Great Depression in Weimar Germany*, ed. Peter D. Stachura (New York, 1986), 100.

89. Renate Bridenthal, "'Professional' Housewives," 162; Margarete Blasche, *Käte Delius, Wegbereiterin für eine neue Epoche des ländlich-hauswirtschaftlichen Bildungswesens* (Hannover, n.d.), 5–6.

90. *Frauenwelt*, January 10, 1924, 1; cited in Uta Veneman, "Representations of Women in the Leftist Press During the Mid to Late 1920s" (unpublished ms. in author's possession). I am endebted to Veneman for letting me quote from her master's thesis.

91. Else Loewecke-Möbus, "Hausfrau und Wirtschaft," *Frauenstimme*, August 18, 1927, and Anna Geyer, "Die Berlinerin in Wirtschaft und Politik," *Frauenstimme*, August 2, 1928, cited in Veneman.

92. Loewecke-Möbus, cited in Veneman.

93. *Gewerkschaftliche Frauenzeitung*, November 15, 1927, and March 15, 1929.

94. ADGB, *Jahrbuch*, 1925, 142–43.

95. *Jahresbericht der Preussischen Gewerbeaufsichtsbeamten und Bergbehörden*, 1928, Regierungsbezirk Düsseldorf, 560.

96. Veneman strongly argues this point.

97. Erich Fromm, *Arbeiter und Angestellte am Vorabend des Dritten Reiches* (Stuttgart, 1980), 185–86. See also, Adelheid von Saldern, "Arbeiterkulturbewegung in Deutschland in der Zwischenkriegszeit," in *Arbeiterkulturen zwischen Alltag und Politik*, ed. Friedhelm Boll (Vienna, 1986), 57–58.

98. Bernhard Faust, "Arbeitserleben und Freizeit," *BRZ* 6:13 (June 20, 1925): 410.

99. *Metallarbeiter-Zeitung*, January 1 and April 16, 1927.

100. Ibid., January 1, 1927.

101. Ibid., July 7, 1928.

102. Brady, *The Rationalization Movement*, 199.

103. Saldern, "Neubausiedlungen," 58.

104. Grossmann, "*Girlkultur*, or Thoroughly Rationalized Female," 72–75.

105. Hagemann, 45. Company newspapers sometimes offered tips and recipes suitable only for white-collar families and thus ignored; H. Reinirkens, "Werkszeitungen," *BRZ* 7:7 (March 27, 1926):222. At other times, their advice was identical to that in the Social Democratic and bourgeois press.

106. *Familienleben in der Gegenwart*, ed. Alice Salomon and Maria Baum (Berlin, 1930), 149.

107. *Keramik in der Weimarer Republik, 1919–1933*, ed. Tilmann Buddensieg (Nuremberg, 1985).

108. Stahl, 99–100.

109. Saldern, "Neubausiedlungen," 67–70. She admits her sample of interviews with inhabitants of such projects is somewhat biased, because the most discontented residents would have moved and were thus not surveyed.

110. Hagemann, 82–84, 101–2, 111–13.

Epilogue

1. W. Löchner, *Grundsätzliches zur Rationalisierung* (Ph.D. diss., Tübingen, 1930), 36, cited in Freyberg, 328.

2. Petzina, et al., 61, 73, 119.

3. Nevins and Hill, 586–88.

4. Rudi Litzenberger, "Die volkswirtschaftlichen Auswirkungen der deutschen technischen Rationalisierung auf die Produktionsfaktoren Arbeit und Kapital in der Nachkriegszeit" (Ph.D. diss., Cologne, 1933), 50.

5. "Ist Rationalisierung im Betrieb Unsinn?" *GHH Werkszeitung*, May 21, 1932.

6. BBA, 16 /515, travel report of Dr. Hoffmann to BBV, February 2, 1931.

7. Sohn-Rethel, 28.

8. VDA, *Geschäftsbericht* (Berlin, 1930), xiii, 314–17. BBA 16/478 Mitteilungen der Arbeitgeberverbände Unterelbe und Hamburg-Altona, 3 (February 1, 1930): 1–3.

9. BA, R 13 I 230, Ernst Poensgen, "Falsche Massnahmen der Schwerindustrie?" *Deutsche Allgemeine Zeitung*, August 2, 1931; BA R 13 I 336, discussion of J. W. Reichert's report on Enquete-Ausschuss report on iron industry, March 1931; BBA, 16/478, E. Jüngst, "Die Rationalisierung im Ruhrbergbau," *Zeitschrift des oberschlesischen Berg- und Hüttenmannischen Verein zu Kattowitz* 2 (1931):78.

10. Krupp Archiv, "Jahresbericht," October 1, 1929–September 30, 1930.

11. BA R 13 I 233, Langnam Verein, "Bebel hat recht: Ohne Profit raucht kein Schornstein," 1932.

12. BBA 15/576, unsigned typescript, "Fehlleitung des Kapitals? Wer trägt die Verantwortung?," September 11, 1931.

13. Paul Osthold, *Die Schuld der Sozialdemokratie. Die Zerstörung von Staat und Wirtschaft durch den Marxismus* (Berlin, 1932), 166-86; Karl Arnhold, "Wo liegen Deutschlands Möglichkeiten?," *GHH Werkszeitung*, January 14, 1933; GHH 400125/6, Arnhold, "Arbeitsschulung trotz alldem," *Rheinisch-Westfälische Zeitung*, November 14, 1930; GHH 400101226/11b, letter from Arnhold to Reusch, May 12, 1932.

14. Mark Mitnitzky, "Technischer Fortschritt und Arbeitslosigkeit," *Die Gesellschaft* 4 (1932): 355.

15. Felix Strössinger, "Zur Amerikalegende," *Die Weltbühne* 27 (1931): 721-22.

16. *Gewerkschafts-Zeitung*, 48, 1930, cited in Hinrichs and Peters, 97.

17. Fritz Tarnow, *Kapitalistische Wirtschaftsanarchie und Arbeiterklasse. Referat, gehalten auf dem Leipziger Parteitag der S.P.D. am 1. Juni 1931* (Berlin, 1931); Friedrich Olk, "Vor dem zweiten Abschnitt der deutschen Rationalisierung," *Die Arbeit* 3 (1930): 156-60, and "Zu teuer rationalisiert!" *Die Arbeit* 11 (1930), 733-37.

18. "Ist die Rationalisierung eine wirtschaftliche Notwendigkeit?" *Der deutsche Metallarbeiter* 31:4 (January 25, 1930): 54.

19. A. Dünnebacke, "Der strukturelle Charakter der Krise und die Arbeitslosigkeit," *BRZ* 11:25 (December 20, 1930): 779-81.

20. Bauer, 202; Stollberg, 102-4.

21. Bauer, 164-65, 226. For one of the clearest German statements of this argument, see Adolf Dünnebacke, "Technische Entwicklung, ihre soziale Auswirkung und sozialpolitischen Konsequenzen," in DMV, *Protokoll der elften Konferenz des Reichsbeirats der Betriebsräte und Konzernvertreter der Metallindustrie*, 27, 67.

22. *Das Gespenst der Arbeitslosigkeit und die Vorschläge der S.P.D. zu ihrer Ueberwindung* (Berlin, 1931). See also Otto Suhr, "Das Reichskuratorium für Wirtschaftlichkeit (RKW)," *Die Arbeit* 7 (1930): 454-55.

23. August Enderle, Heinrich Schreiner, Jakob Walcher, and Eduard Weckerle, *Das rote Gewerkschaftsbuch* (Berlin, 1932), 29-67.

24. *Rationalisierung und Wirtschaftskrise* (Berlin, 1930), 34.

25. *Metallarbeiter-Zeitung*, September 12, 1931.

26. SAA 11/Lf 407, letters from Schaefer to Reichskanzler, October 6, 1930, and from Schaefer and Köttgen to Reichswirtschaftsminister, November 5, 1932; BA Z Sg 1 185/5(10), Schaefer, *Das Reichskuratorium für Wirtschaftlichkeit 1933*, RKW Sonderdruck, January 1933.

27. BBA 8/160, Concordia Geschäftsberichte 1931 and 1932; MM R 1 40 35 1, Vestag, Geschäftsbericht, 1929-1930; Ausserordentliche Generalversammlung des Vestag, November 29, 1933; Erik Reger, "Die Schuldfrage der Rationalisierung," *Die Weltbühne* 28 (1932): 407-10; *Metallarbeiter-Zeitung*, September 12, 1931. In general, rationalization continued more strongly in mining than in basic iron and steel; Zollitsch, 28-35.

28. GHH 400101226/11b Dinta, *Mitteilungen für den Betriebsbeamten*, May 1, 1931.

29. *Das Gespenst der Arbeitslosigkeit*, 31-32.

30. Tarnow, "Kapitalistische Wirtschaftsanarchie," 24; Robert A. Gates, "Von der Sozialpolitik zur Wirtschaftspolitik? Das Dilemma der deutschen Sozialdemokratie in der Krise, 1929-1933," in *Industrielles System und Politische Entwicklung in der Weimarer Republik*, ed. Hans Mommsen, Dietmar Petzina, and Bernd Weisbrod (Düsseldorf, 1977), 206-25.

31. Freyberg, 370.

32. Tim W. Mason, "Zur Entstehung des Gesetzes zur Ordnung der nationalen Arbeit," and Tilla Siegel, "Lohnpolitik im nationalsozialistischen Deutschland," *Angst, Belohnung, Zucht und Ordnung,* ed. Carola Sachse et al, (Opladen, 1982), 54–199; a shorter English version of Siegel's article, "Wage Policy in Nazi Germany," appeared in *Politics & Society* 14:1 (1985): 1–52. See also Albrecht Ritschl, "Die NS-Wirtschafts-ideologie: Modernisierungsprogramm oder Reaktionäre Utopie?" in *Nationalsozialismus und Modernisierung,* ed. Michael Prinz and Rainer Zitelmann (Darmstadt, 1991), 48–70.

33. Nevins and Hill, 561.

34. Simon Reich, *The Fruits of Fascism. Postwar Prosperity in Historical Perspective* (Ithaca, N.Y., 1990), 116.

35. Hans Dieter Schäfer, "Americanism im Dritten Reich," in *Nationalsozialismus und Modernisierung,* 199–215; and Schäfer, *Das gespaltene Bewusstsein. Deutsche Kultur und Lebenswirklichkeit, 1933–1945* (Munich, 1981), 128, 147.

36. For overviews of the Nazi economy, see Sohn-Rethel; B. H. Klein, *Germany's Economic Preparations for War* (Cambridge, Mass., 1959); and Alan Milward, *The German Economy at War* (London, 1965).

37. Schäfer, *Das gespaltene Bewusstsein,* 117–22.

38. BA Z Sg 1 185/2 (1) RKW Schriftenverzeichnis, 1939, 3–4.

39. Ulrike Ludwig-Buehler, "Frauen zwischen Familie und Fabrik. Frauenerwerbs-tätigkeit in der badischen Textilindustrie am Beispiel der Firma Schiesser AG zwischen der Weimarer Zeit und 1945" (Staatsexamensarbeit), 33–34.

40. Mason. For a contemporary discussion of the same point, see Adolf Geck, "Das Werden der betrieblichen Sozialpolitik als Wissenschaft in Deutschland," *Schmollers Jahrbuch* 58 (1934): 569.

41. Jeremy Noakes, *Government, Party and People in Nazi Germany* (Exeter, 1980), 22.

42. BBA 37/92, Arnhold's speech to Jahrestagung der Vereinigten Dinta Werk-zeitungen, October 26, 1934.

43. Bunk, 264-65, fn 60.

44. *Wesen, Wollen und Wirken der Dinta-Werkzeitungen* (Düsseldorf, 1933), 2–3; Campbell, *Joy in Work,* 325.

45. Ronald Smelser, *Robert Ley: Hitler's Labor Front Leader* (Oxford, 1988), 191–92. See also, John Gillingham, "The 'Deproletarianization' of German Society: Vocational Training in the Third Reich," *Journal of Social History* 19 (Spring 1986): 423–32. Dinta reports read remarkably alike before and after 1933. See BBA 37/92, Mitteilungen 20, November 1, 1934.

46. Rabinbach, 287.

47. For the most comprehensive study of foreign labor in Nazi Germany, see Ulrich Herbert, *Fremdarbeiter. Politik und Praxis der 'Ausländer Einsatzes' in der Kriegswirt-schaft des Dritten Reiches* (Berlin, 1989).

48. *Ein Leben für die Wirtschaft,* 75–76.

Bibliographic Essay

The 1920s literature on rationalization and Americanism in Weimer Germany is voluminous, and aspects of both broad themes have been extensively analyzed by scholars in recent decades. I will not present an exhaustive list of the available primary and secondary materials; scholars desiring such a list can consult the bibliographies in such recent works as Heidrun Homburg, *Rationalisierung und Industriearbeit* (Berlin: Haude and Spener, 1991), and Carola Sachse, *Siemens, der Nationalsozialismus und die moderne Familie* (Hamburg: Rasch und Röhring, 1990). Rather, I will indicate the types of archival sources and primary materials that were central to my arguments and the secondary works in English and German that I found most useful.

General Overviews

Although rationalization is mentioned in nearly all economic and social histories of Weimar, the only general surveys remain those done in the 1920s and 1930s. The most useful works in English are Robert Brady, *The Rationalization Movement in German Industry* (Berkeley: University of California, 1933), and Walter Meakin, *The New Industrial Revolution* (New York: Brentano's, 1928). Valuable works in German include *Die Bedeutung der Rationalisierung für das deutsche Wirtschaftsleben*, ed. Industrie- und Handelskammer zu Berlin (Berlin: Georg Stilke, 1928), and *Strukturwandlungen der deutschen Volkswirtschaft*, ed. Bernhard Harms (Berlin: Reimar Hobbing, 1929). The principal assessments of the accomplishments and shortcomings of the rationalization movement are the Reichskuratorium für Wirtschaftlichkeit, *Handbuch der Rationalisierung* (Berlin: RKW, 1929), and the many volumes of the *Gesamtbericht des Enquete Ausschusses zur Untersuchung der Erzeugungs- und Absatzbedingungen der deutschen Wirtschaft* that were published between 1928 and 1931.

The theme of Americanism has been treated more extensively by cultural historians than by social and economic ones. See, for example, John Willett, *Art and Politics in the Weimar Period: The New Sobriety, 1917–1933* (New York: Pantheon, 1978); Beeke Sell Tower, ed., *Envisioning America: Prints, Drawings, and Photographs by Georg Grosz and his Contemporar-*

ies, 1915-1933 (Cambridge: Harvard, 1990); and Frank Trommler and Joseph McVeigh, eds., *America and the Germans* (Philadelphia: University of Pennsylvania Press, 1985). The important exception is Detlev J. K. Peukert, *The Weimar Republic: Crisis of Classical Modernity* (New York: Hill and Wang, 1992). For German publications, see the rather unanalytical but informative work by Peter Berg, *Deutschland und Amerika, 1918-1929. Ueber das deutsche Amerikabild der zwanziger Jahre* (Lübeck and Hamburg: Matthiesen, 1963).

Economic Americanism

Fordism in particular and the American economic model in general were debated extensively in economic travel literature, articles, and book reviews in the daily and monthly press and in technical publications. For an introduction to the debates, see *Ford und Wir*, ed. Soziales Museum Frankfurt am Main (Berlin: Industrieverlag Spaeth and Linde, 1926), and Peter Berg.

For the views of industrialists, the most useful works are Carl Köttgen, *Das wirtschaftliche Amerika* (Berlin: VDI, 1925), and the meetings and publications of the Reichverband der deutschen Industrie. The Köttgen Nachlass in the Siemens Archiv has a valuable collection of reviews of Henry Ford's autobiography from the business press. For the views of engineers, I relied heavily on the Verein deutscher Ingenieure publication *Technik und Wirtschaft*. The travel reports of engineers such as Valentine Litz, *Sozialpolitische Reiseeindrücke in den Vereinigten Staaten* (Berlin: VDA, 1925); Otto Moog, *Drüben steht Amerika . . . Gedanken nach einer Ingenieurreise durch die Vereinigten Staaten* (Braunschweig, 1927); Paul Riebensahm, *Der Zug nach U.S.A. Gedanken nach einer Amerikareise* (Berlin: Julius Springer 1924); and Franz Westermann, *Amerika, wie ich es sah. Reise Skizzen eines Ingenieurs* (Halbestadt: H. Meyers, 1926) offered both the technical perspective of engineers and the economic outlook of industry.

Social Democratic views on Fordism, mass consumption, and the secrets of American economic success were surveyed insightfully in the late 1920s by Elisabeth Schalldach, *Rationalisierungsmassnahmen der Nachkriegszeit im Urteil der deutschen freien Gewerkschaften* (Jena: Gustav Fischer, 1930), and more superficially and simplistically in the 1980s by Gunnar Stollberg, *Die Rationalisierungsdebatte, 1908-1933. Freie Gewerkschaften zwischen Mitwirkung und Gegenwehr* (Frankfurt: Campus, 1981). My analysis relies on innumerable articles in Social Democratic trade union publications, such as *Die Arbeit, Die Gesellschaft, Gewerkschafts-Archiv, Gewerkschafts-Zeitung, Betriebsräte-Zeitschrift des Deutschen Metallarbeiter Verbandes,* and the *Metallarbeiter-Zeitung*. The free trade union delegation report, *Amerikareise deutscher Gewerkschaftsführer* (Berlin: ADGB Verlag, 1926), the DMV, *Ford, seine Ideen und Arbeitsmethoden* (Stuttgart: DMV, 1928), and the protocols of the yearly congresses of the Deutscher Metallarbeiterverband and the Allgemeiner deutscher Gewerkschaftsbund illuminate the appeals of Americanism and the debates about it. For the most enthusiastic endorsement, see Fritz Tarnow, *Warum arm sein?* (Berlin: ADGB Verlag, 1929), as well as his numerous newspaper articles.

Communist attitudes toward rationalization and Americanism have been studied by Eva Cornelia Schöck, *Arbeitslosigkeit und Rationalisierung. Die Lage der Arbeiter und die kommunistische Gewerkschaftspolitik, 1920–1928* (Frankfurt: Campus, 1977). The most complex analysis is offered by Jakob Walcher, *Ford oder Marx. Die praktische Lösung der sozialen Frage* (Berlin: Neuer Deutscher Verlag, 1925). More typical and critical, are Alexander Friedrich, *Henry Ford, der König der Autos und der Herrscher über die Seelen* (Berlin: Neuer Deutscher Verlag, 1924), and Hilda Weiss, *Rationalisierung und Arbeiterklasse* (Berlin, Führer Verlag, 1926). The two journals I consistently consulted were *Die Rote Gewerkschaftsinternationale* and *Unter dem Banner des Marxismus*.

Information on Christian trade union views is scantier but can be found in the publications *Deutsche Arbeit* and *Der deutsche Metallarbeiter*. The Christian trade union functionary Edmund Kleinschmitt wrote an interesting analysis of the American economy entitled, "Gegen den Wirtschaftspessimismus! Ergebnisse einer Gewerkschaftlichen Studienreise," *Der Kaufmann in Wirtschaft und Recht* 4:9 (September 1925), 405–16.

Some of the most interesting assessments of economic Americanism come from authors who were not directly tied to industrial interests or to the labor movement. Among those with a more or less leftist perspective are Julius Hirsch, *Das amerikanische Wirtschaftswunder* (Berlin: S. Fischer, 1926), and Charlotte Lütkens, *Staat und Gesellschaft in Amerika. Zur Soziologie des amerikanischen Kapitalismus* (Tübingen: J. C. B. Mohr, 1929). For a more right-wing perspective, but one which evinces much more enthusiasm for Fordism than did big business, see Friedrich Gottl-Ottlilienfeld, *Fordismus* (Jena: Gustav Fischer, 1926), and Theodor Lüddecke, *Das Amerikanische Wirtschaftstempo als Bedrohung Europas.* (Leipzig: Paul List, 1925). Moritz J. Bonn represents the classical free-market liberal assessment of America and Germany. Of his many works, the most insightful are *Amerika und sein Problem* (Munich: Meyer and Jessen, 1925); *Das Schicksal des deutschen Kapitalismus* (Berlin: S. Fischer, 1926); and *The American Adventure: A Study in Bourgeois Civilization*, (New York: John Day, 1933), a translation of his *Kultur der Vereinigten Staaten von Amerika* (Berlin: Wegweiser, 1930). Finally, two rather idiosyncratic but insightful accounts are by the editor of the *Frankfurter Zeitung*, Arthur Feiler, *Amerika-Europa* (Frankfurt: Societäts Druckerei, 1926), translated as *America Seen Through German Eyes* (New York: New Republic, 1928); and Alice Salomon, *Kultur im Werden: Amerikanische Reiseeindrücke* (Berlin: Ullstein, 1924).

Work

Industrial sociology was a growth industry in Weimar, and its founding fathers wrote prolifically. For an introduction to the debates on joy in work,

"German quality work," vocational education, and company social policy, see Goetz Briefs, "Betriebssoziologie," *Handwörterbuch der Soziologie*, ed. Alfred Vierkandt (Stuttgart: Ferdinand Enke, 1931); L. H. Adolf Geck, *Grundfragen der betrieblichen Sozialpolitik* (Munich and Leipzig: Duncker and Humblot, 1935); *Die sozialen Probleme des Betriebes*, ed. Heinz Potthoff (Berlin: Industrieverlag Spaeth und Linde, 1925); Josef Winschuh, *Praktische Werkspolitik* (Berlin: Industrieverlag Spaeth und Linde, 1923). The RKW published three volumes on *Mensch und Rationalisierung*. See RKW, *Veröffentlichungen*, 71 (1931); 83 (1933); and 87 (1933).

Contemporary works on issues concerning vocational education include Erna Barschak, *Die Idee der Berufsbildung und ihre Einwirkung auf die Berufserziehung im Gewerbe* (Leipzig: Quelle und Meyer, 1929); *Industrielle Arbeitsschulung als Problem*, ed. Soziales Museum Frankfurt am Main (Berlin: Industrieverlag Spaeth und Linde, 1931); Rudolf Schindler, *Das Problem der Berufsauslese für die Industrie* (Jena: Gustav Fischer, 1929); and Hella Schmedes, *Das Lehrlingswesen in der deutschen Eisen und Stahlindustrie* (Münster: August Baader, 1931).

The debate about meaningful work, monotony, and industrial relations was also treated in articles in the major trade union publications cited above as well as at meetings of the Reichsverband der deutschen Industrie and in company newspapers, such as the *Bosch Zünder*.

Several more recent works help contextualize these debates. Most interesting is Anson Rabinbach, *The Human Motor: Energy, Fatigue and the Origins of Modernity* (New York: Basic, 1990). Joan Campbell, *Joy in Work, German Work: the National Debate* (Princeton, N.J.: Princeton University Press, 1989) is encyclopedic but unanalytical. For German works, see Gerhard P. Bunk, *Erziehung und Industriearbeit* (Weinheim and Basel: Beltz, 1972); Peter Hinrichs, *Um die Seele des Arbeiters: Arbeitspsychologie, Industrie und Betriebssoziologie in Deutschland* (Cologne: Pahl Rugenstein, 1981); and Ernst Michel, *Sozialgeschichte der industriellen Arbeitswelt* (Frankfurt: Josef Knecht, 1960). On the complex meanings and wide appeal of the concept of *deutsche Qualitätsarbeit*, see Alf Lüdtke, "'Ehre der Arbeit': Industriearbeiter und Macht der Symbole. Zur Reichweite symbolischer Orientierungen im Nationalsozialismus," in *Arbeiter im 20. Jahrhundert*, ed. Klaus Tenfelde (Stuttgart: Klett-Cotta, 1991).

Mass Consumption and the American Woman

Nearly all the works cited on economic Americanism and Fordism consider to some degree the desirability and possibility of mass consumption as well as the cultural and gender consequences of the American economic model. Additional works of particular interest are Arthur Holitscher, *Wiedersehen mit Amerika. Die Verwandlung der USA* (Berlin: S. Fischer, 1930), and Paul Wengraf, *Amerika–Europa–Russland* (Vienna and Leipzig: Verlagsanstalt Dr. Zahn und Dr. Diamant, 1927). Both works are cautiously enthusiastic about the culture of consumption. For a critical and pessimistic view, see

Adolf Halfeld, *Amerika und der Amerikanismus: Kritische Betrachtungen eines Deutschen und Europäers* (Jena: Eugen Diedrichs, 1927). Irene Witte, *Heim und Technik in Amerika* (Berlin: VDI Verlag, 1928), was most insight- ful on the implication of mass consumption for the home.

The American woman, the American home, and American middle-class marriages were discussed in individual chapters or passing comments in most works by middle-class travelers to America, whether they were industrial- ists, engineers, journalists, or politicians. Social Democratic and Commu- nist travelers rarely commented. There is no Weimar analysis as compre- hensive as Hugo Münsterberg's discussion in his prewar study, *Die Amerikaner* (Berlin: E. S. Mittler, 1904), but most commentators followed his line of argument. The most original and provocative analysis is Fritz Giese, *Girlkultur: Vergleiche zwischen amerikanischen und europäischen Rhythmus und Lebensgefuhl* (Munich: Delphin, 1925), while the most admiring is Alice Salomon, *Kultur im Werden.*

The most useful recent works on culture, gender, and Americanism in Weimar are Atina Grossmann, "Girlkultur or Thoroughly Rationalized Female: A New Woman in Weimar Germany?" in *Women in Culture and Politics,* ed. Judith Friedlander et al. (Bloomington: Indiana University Press, 1986), 62–80; Andreas Huyssen, "Mass Culture as Woman: Modernism's Other," in *Studies in Entertainment: Critical Approaches to Mass Culture,* ed. Tania Modleski (Bloomington: Indiana University Press, 1986), 188–207; and Patrice Petro, *Joyless Streets: Women and Melodramatic Representa- tion in Weimar Germany* (Princeton, N.J.: Princeton University Press, 1989). For a critical understanding of Social Democratic attitudes toward mass consumption and new lifestyles, see Adelheid von Saldern, "Die Neubausiedlungen der Zwanziger Jahre," in *Neubausiedlungen der 20er und 60er Jahre,* ed. Ulfert Herlyn, Adelheid von Saldern, and Wulf Tessin (Frankfurt: Campus, 1987).

Rationalization in Selected Industries

My case studies of the effects of rationalization in coal, iron and steel, and machine making were drawn from primary research in the Bergbau Archiv and the company archives of Gutehoffnungshütte, Mannesmann, Krupp, and Thyssen. The *Gesamtbericht des Enquete Ausschuss* was invaluable, as were the materials gathered for it and the debates surrounding it that were found in the company archives. The *Metallarbeiter-Zeitung,* and to a lesser extent the *Bergarbeiter-Zeitung,* reported regularly on the progress of rationalization in their industries, and the DMV produced a major study, *Die Rationalisierung in der Metallindustrie* (Berlin: DMV, 1933). The effects of rationalization on wages and profits were debated in the trade union press as well as in industrial publications and economic journals, such as *Magazin der Wirtschaft.* Dissertations written by engineering and economics students in the 1920s provided information on aspects of rationalization in selected factories or towns.

Four secondary works were especially helpful. In addition to Robert Brady, these include Thomas von Freyberg, *Industrielle Rationalisierung in der Weimarer Republik* (Frankfurt: Campus, 1989); Uta Stolle, *Arbeiterpolitik im Betrieb: Frauen und Männer, Reformisten und Radikale, Fach- und Massenarbeiter bei Bayer, BASF, Bosch und in Solingen, 1900-1933* (Frankfurt: Campus, 1980); and John Ronald Shearer, *The Politics of Industrial Efficiency in the Weimar Republic: Technological Innovation, Economic Efficiency, and their Social Consequences in the Ruhr Coal Mining Industry, 1918-1929* (Ph.D. diss., University of Pennsylvania, 1989). Two English works on the German automobile industry contain useful sections on rationalization or the lack thereof: Bernard P. Bellon, *Mercedes in Peace and War: German Automobile Workers, 1903-1945* (New York: Columbia University Press, 1930), and Simon Reich, *The Fruits of Fascism: Postwar Prosperity in Historical Perspective* (Ithaca: Cornell University Press, 1990). A full-scale study of the Weimar automobile industry remains to be done.

My analysis of the activities of the Reichskuratorium für Wirtschaftlichkeit is based on the voluminous publications of that organization, especially the *Handbuch der Rationalisierung*, the *RKW-Nachrichten*, and the periodic *Veröffentlichungen* on diverse subjects. The Bundes Archiv has the yearly reports, as well as a sampling of memos, correspondence, and meetings. The Köttgen Nachlass at the Siemens Archiv has reports and papers relating to his involvement in the RKW. The only history of the RKW is Hans Wolfgang Büttner, *Das Rationalisierungs-Kuratorium der Deutschen Wirtschaft* (Düsseldorf: Droste, 1973).

Dinta

There is no one repository for material on Dinta, but material exists in abundance. Reports on Dinta activities in firms and copies of Dinta publications and company newspapers were found in company archives, above all the Thyssen Archiv and the Historisches Archiv Gutehoffnungshütte. Copies of the writings of Karl Arnhold, the anonymous biography, *Ein Leben für die Wirtschaft* (Witten: Märkische Druckerei, 1964), the polemics of Ernst Horneffer, such as *Der Weg zur Arbeitsfreude* (Berlin: Reimar Hobbing, n.d.), and those of Paul Osthold, such as *Der Kampf um die Seele unseres Arbeiters* (Düsseldorf: Industrieverlag, n.d.), are readily available in libraries.

Although the full history of Dinta, spanning Weimar, the Nazi era, and the early Federal Republic, remains to be written, there are short overviews in Campbell, Hinrichs, and Rabinbach. More informative but uncritical is the Weimar study by Peter Bäumer, *Das Deutsche Institut für Technische Arbeitsschulung* (Munich and Leipzig: Schriften des Vereins für Sozialpolitik, 181/I, 1930). Also useful are Arvand Dach, *Menschenbehandlung in der Industrie: Eine betriebssoziologische Studie* (Ph.D. diss., Technische Hochschule Braunschweig, 1931), and Rudolf Schwenger, *Die betriebliche Sozialpolitik im Ruhrkohlenbergbau* (Munich and Leipzig: Duncker und Humblot, 1932), as well as his work *Die betriebliche Sozialpolitik in der westdeutschen Grosseisenindustrie* (Munich and Leipzig: Duncker und Humblot, 1934). Carola Sachse's study of *Siemens, der Nationalsozialismus und die moderne Familie* offers both the best recent analysis of company social policy and a study of the alternative Weimar model to Dinta.

For an understanding of the engineers whom Dinta recruited, I relied on Konrad Jarausch, *The Unfree Professions: German Lawyers, Teachers and Engineers, 1900-1950* (New York: Oxford, 1990); Gert Hortleder, *Das Gesellschaftsbild des Ingenieurs* (Frankfurt: Suhrkamp, 1970); and Karl-Heinz Ludwig, *Technik und Ingenieure im Dritten Reich* (Düsseldorf: Athenäum, 1979). For insight into engineers and other reactionary modernists, see Jeffrey Herf, *Reactionary Modernism: Technology, Culture and Politics in Weimar and the Third Reich* (New York: Cambridge University Press, 1984).

Housework

My analysis of the rationalization of housework is based on three types of sources: the educational material published by the RKW Housework Group; analytical and prescriptive works on home economics in America and Germany; and archival material on the company social programs of heavy-industry firms for married women and the vision of home and family they embodied. Among the most important analytical and prescriptive works are Erna Meyer, *Das Neue Haushalt. Ein Wegweiser zur wissenschaftlichen Hausführung* (Stuttgart: Frank'sche Verlagshandlung, 1927), as well as her numerous articles published in trade union, engineering, and women's publications; and Irene Witte, *Heim und Technik in Amerika.* Sachse's works, *Siemens* and *Industrial Housewives: Women's Social Work in Factories in Nazi Germany* (New York: Haworth, 1987), are the major recent studies on this theme.

Index